GALE GORDON

FROM MAYOR OF WISTFUL VISTA TO BORREGO SPRINGS

BY JIM MANAGO

GALE GORDON: FROM MAYOR OF
WISTFUL VISTA TO BORREGO SPRINGS
©2016 JIM MANAGO

ALL RIGHTS RESERVED.

No part of this book may be reproduced in any form or by any means, electronic, mechanical, digital, photocopying, or recording, except for in the inclusion of a review, without permission in writing from the publisher.

Published in the USA by:

BEARMANOR MEDIA
P.O. BOX 71426
ALBANY, GEORGIA 31708
www.BearManorMedia.com

ISBN-10: 1-59393-912-4 (alk. paper)
ISBN-13: 978-1-59393-912-0 (alk. paper)

FRONT COVER: GALE GORDON. FROM THE COLLECTION OF STEPHEN COX.

DESIGN AND LAYOUT: VALERIE THOMPSON

TABLE OF CONTENTS

ACKNOWLEDGMENTS . . . 1

INTRODUCTION . . . 3

PART ONE: GALE GORDON'S LIFE AND CAREER . . . 9

    CHAPTER ONE: THE BRITISH CONNECTION . . . 11

    CHAPTER TWO: A DRAMATIC START . . . 17

    CHAPTER THREE: A COMEDIC TURN . . . 35

    CHAPTER FOUR: BUSY ON THE AIR! . . . 41

    CHAPTER FIVE: "OH YOU DO-O-O-O!" . . . 69

    CHAPTER SIX: FINALLY, A TELEVISION CO-STAR? . . . 85

    CHAPTER SEVEN: A NEW WAY OF LIFE . . . 93

    CHAPTER EIGHT: LUCY'S FOIL . . . 107

    CHAPTER NINE: "A WONDERFUL PERSON" . . . 129

PHOTO GALLERY . . . 141

PART TWO: GALE GORDON'S COMEDY MOMENTS ON RADIO . . . 171

    CHAPTER TEN: FIRST SEASON AS MAYOR LATRIVIA (1941–1942) . . . 173

    CHAPTER ELEVEN: SECOND SEASON AS MAYOR LATRIVIA (1942–1943) . . . 209

    CHAPTER TWELVE: SELECTED MOMENTS AS RUMSON BULLARD (1947–1952) . . . 241

APPENDIX . . . 265

    SELECTED BIBLIOGRAPHY . . . 267

    RECIPE . . . 269

    FILM, RADIO AND TELEVISION CREDITS . . . 271

    EMMY AWARD NOMINATIONS . . . 371

    AUTHORSHIP . . . 373

    INDEX . . . 375

DEDICATION

I dedicate this to Ben Ohmart,
Who twice asked me to write this book
&
To the memory of Don Quinn,
Writer of the Fibber McGee and Molly *radio show*

Acknowledgments

My thanks for information and interview material from Gale Gordon's co-stars, including Gloria McMillan, the late Shirley Mitchell, and Jeanne Russell. In addition, I thank Dina-Marie Kulzer, Fred Jee (Chamber of Commerce, Borrego Springs), Howard Rayfiel, Chuck Schaden, Clair Schulz, Mel Simons, Tom Watson, and Brock Weir. Also thanks to Lucie Arnaz Luckinbill who kindly put me in touch with Wanda Clark (Lucille Ball's secretary), and her late Uncle Cecil Smith.

My appreciation goes to Randy Bonneville for again helping me compile the credits, despite the difficulty of verifying much of the circulating information. As he noted, a definitive list of Gordon's credits is something that we, as fellow researchers, together all work toward achieving one day. In short, we should not consider each other competitors. For that reason, I would appreciate any additions or corrections. Please contact me via my blog devoted to Gale Gordon (http://galegordonstory.blogspot.com/).

In addition, there are unnamed individuals who helped in some way, including librarians responsible for providing much needed support. Thanks to all the newspapers; including *Chicago Daily Tribune, Los Angeles Times, New York Times,* and *Washington Post* for the use of quotes. Posthumous thanks to those individuals that made the Copley Productions' *A New Way of Life*, which superbly captured Gordon's narration of life in the desert.

Most importantly, I offer a very special thanks to my partner Donna Manago for summarizing and transcribing Gordon's radio shows. I would have been lost without her diligent research assistance.

Finally, thanks to my publisher, BearManor Media, who made this endeavor a reality.

INTRODUCTION

The Chicago radio host and interviewer Chuck Schaden once observed that Gale Gordon had a "flair for performing comedy." In his long career primarily on stage, radio and television, Gordon never seemed to stop generating laughs no matter how predictable or repetitive his various characters were. *The New York Times* said critics praised him for "his nifty slow-burn turns," and for being "always amusing in a state of high dudgeon."

In 1968, at the age of 8 years old, I first discovered his impressive ability to make me laugh. I seemed to be literally glued to my portable black and white television set and virtually a prisoner to my bedroom every Monday night loving Gordon's Harrison Carter getting upset as he reacts to the ludicrous antics of Lucille Ball's Lucy Carter in *Here's Lucy*. For the next six years, I do not think I ever missed a single episode of that quirky comedy show. I studied, absorbed, and enjoyed every intonation or utterance of this mustached, often mean but likeable character. Nowadays, my opinion of the show featuring an obsessive control freak and the story limitations make Gordon's role seem tiresomely repetitive and too predictable at times. Nevertheless, he had a knack for making you laugh no matter how often he did the same thing over again.

Much later on, I learned that Gordon got his start way back in the early 1930s on radio. In fact, he became the highest paid person in that medium then, as he kept busy by appearing in countless dramatic shows, many playing recurring characters. His talent for making people laugh began at the start of the 1940s, when he turned his concentration to comedy and perfected his blowhard characterization.

His first regular comedic role came with his Mayor LaTrivia role on radio's *Fibber McGee and Molly*. Eventually he would reach his pinnacle in this format. The role that set Gordon in top form on radio and that still holds up well today is when he played the high school Principal Osgood T. Conklin in *Our Miss Brooks*. Listening to Gordon build an icy slow burn to an outrageous outburst is a delight. His calmness gradually disappears and his frustration grows until it finds an ultimate release. Gordon's skill here at expressing his explosive temper is unmatched by anyone else. At times, it seems that his radio work is even better than his later but similar characterizations done on television.

More important than that, he could excel in other roles, besides merely being the angry, grouchy, hotheaded boss, Principal, or other authority figures that we associate him with. Though most no longer remember him for proving his versatility as a great character actor in all genres, we remember him even less for being a fine lead actor. However, the truth is that the vast array of surviving radio shows proves he could do practically every part, both character and lead, so very well.

Gordon's experience on radio for more than 20 years had tremendous influence on developing his later talent. Even as early as 1948, the press, perhaps exaggerating a bit, reported that Gordon had reached his 5,000th radio show appearance. As a result of his enormous productivity, Gordon had thoroughly practiced and honed his perfect diction and timing by the time he became a regular on *Here's Lucy*. By 1968, it seemed to be so effortless and so easy for him to dazzle an audience.

After completing my first biography of actress Shirley Booth back in the summer of 2007, I eagerly sought another project. My publisher, Ben Ohmart, suggested Gale Gordon since he was one superb talent who never had a book written about him, but he definitely deserved to have one. I agreed, especially as Gordon had interested me greatly as well.

Though Ben anxiously wanted to be the publisher of this first biography for about six years by then, he was quite reluctant to assign this task, and wisely, he would not ask just anyone to tackle it. He knew that the immensely productive actor made this project tedious and difficult. He also knew that Gordon, as with Booth, had no children or relatives to help provide personal information. In addition, Ben knew instinctively that it must be a monumental task, given Gordon's amazingly large number of radio credits. Only when I insisted on this labor of love, then Ben responded saying, "Go for it!"

A few months later, after conducting several interviews and writing about fifty pages, I agreed to terminate my connection to this project. Of course, Ben had another author in mind that expressed interest in researching and writing Gordon's story, and Ben had confidence that he was better equipped to do the project justice. The author in question was Gale's agent at one time, and Ben thought he could add the personal touch. Time went on. Six years later and that author, from what I believe was a health problem and/or disinterest, did not deliver a manuscript.

In August of 2014, I heard from Ben that the project was open again, and again he wanted to find the right person to research and write Gordon's story. I immediately wanted to revisit this project with the intent to complete it, and so I signed onto the project once again.

In studying Gordon more closely in the last year, I reconsidered my perception that Gordon's acting range was limited to the perfection of the blowhard character. Listening to a wide variety of his radio shows has made me more fully appreciate his masterful character acting, but also to sample his lead acting.

Yes, we know Gordon best for portraying the type of person that is pompous, cranky, prissy, stuffy, and at times mean. However, the real man behind the mask was so much the opposite. His colleagues and friends often spoke of him as a humorous, sweet, and pleasant man. Many who met him expected him to be like his characters—a real pain in the ass!

My goal in returning to this biography and seeing it through to completion is to inform the public of what they did not know about him. I tried to dig as deep as I could to find whatever personal life I could discover about a very private man. The project has been daunting, since few of those who knew him well are still living. Nevertheless, one non-negotiable part of this project has always been that I wanted to be as fair and accurate as humanly possible in chronicling the details of Gordon's life.

During his lifetime, Gordon did see an entire chapter of a book dedicated to him. After reading Dina-Marie Kulzer's *Television Series Regulars of the Fifties and Sixties in Interview*, an impressed Gordon observed: "You sometimes fantasize about what a person could write about you . . . Let me put it this way, it could not have been better. For me, it's always been 'Co-starring Gale Gordon.' Your book made me feel like a star. I've had mentions in other books, of course. . . but this is the first time anyone has devoted a chapter to me."

Kulzer rightly noted that Gordon deserved more than a mere chapter in a book. At the start of learning about my endeavor, she declared, "I know Gale Gordon would have been thrilled to have a biography written just about his life."

However, I do admit many have deemed his personal life so plain and lacking in excitement and scandal. When my publisher approached Gordon's publicist Michael B. Druxman some years back, the latter responded: "There's really no book there . . . aside from the filmography, what would you write? He did his job, made no scandalous headlines, and lived a quiet life with his wife in the desert town of Borrego Springs."

He added quite appropriately, "Gale's approach to acting was much like that of Arthur Treacher, Hollywood's quintessential English butler, who once described his job as: 'You say the words. You take the money. You go home.'"

In a sense, Druxman ultimately seems to have hit upon the essence of Gordon's life. Indeed, to tell Gordon's story one must accept that, unlike other actors and Hollywood personalities living in the fast lane most of the time, much (if not all) of his private life may seem rather dull as it connects to some mundane activities on his ranch property in the desert.

Nevertheless, I intended that this book would be a good read that would enlighten and entertain. As a special personality of a bygone era, my hope is that in the first part of this book you will come to some understanding of Gordon the man, via the limited biographical information that exists; as well as Gordon the actor, via his overwhelming career credits.

In addition, I wanted to share with you some of Gordon's hilarious comedy personas in the second part of this book. For that, I offer the comedy moments of his Mayor LaTrivia as developed in the *Fibber McGee and Molly* radio series written by Don Quinn. The verbal brawls that LaTrivia has with the McGees are priceless, and they are certainly some of the best comedic moments ever heard on radio. I have provided a selection of relevant dialogue spoken by Gordon in the first three years that he played the Mayor. In addition, I have included some excerpts of another one of Gordon's characters: namely, Rumson Bullard from *The Great Gildersleeve*.

Finally, I am confident that no one reading this book will overlook this man's superb contribution to radio and television history anymore. I hope that the man himself would have been pleased with my passionate efforts. My years of study have helped me enjoy many more of his characters. Indeed, I am thankful for the memorable characters played by Gale Gordon, which has kept me, and now I hope that it will keep you, laughing!

JIM MANAGO
MARCH 2016

PART ONE:
GALE GORDON'S LIFE AND CAREER

Chapter One: The British Connection

"The last thing in the world I should have done was go into the theater because [I] was inordinately shy as a young man. I couldn't open my mouth. At a party, I was the one stuck up against the wall. I was embarrassed about talking. I felt that I couldn't talk well."

—Gale Gordon

He stood five feet, eight inches, weighed around 170 pounds, had a natty moustache, and a booming voice. We all knew him as Gale Gordon. However, his real name was Charles Thomas Aldrich, Jr. Some of his best-known characters that he played throughout his life on radio, television and films were irritable, temperamental, and volatile. We knew what to expect when we heard his voice on radio, particularly as Mayor LaTrivia on *Fibber McGee and Molly* or as high school Principal Osgood T. Conklin on *Our Miss Brooks*, or saw his frustrated face on television alongside Ball, playing Mr. Mooney or Harrison Carter.

Although he was capable of much more, it is as comedic supporting actor that we have come to know him best. It is primarily for several blowhard characters. With his extraordinary talent for convincing us that he was whatever part he played, few would imagine that the man behind the mask was so very different.

Charles Thomas Aldrich, Jr. was born in New York City on February 20, 1906. Often we read that he got his start on the Canadian stage in *The Dancers*, appearing with his mother under the tutelage of actor Richard Bennett in 1923.

Gordon told Schaden: "Well, I was in a play in New York on Broadway with Richard Bennett who was the father of Joan,

Constance and Barbara Bennett. And that was the start of my career. I was 17 years old and I've been working in the theater, television, or radio ever since."

However, there are no records of Gordon in the cast list of this Broadway production starring Bennett, which ran for 133 performances starting on October 17, 1923. Perhaps he was not the regular performer, but a substitute or stand-in, but he himself claimed that his professional career started with Bennett.

Whether he started on a Broadway or a Canadian stage, it does not really matter. More important is the fact that Bennett noticed Gordon's speech problems and offered assistance in ameliorating the problem.

In his final years, he yearly returned to Canada to perform in dinner theater productions. However, between the start and end of his career, Gordon consistently and unceasingly performed his craft primarily in the United States. Interestingly, his distinct vocalizations gave fans the impression that he was born in Great Britain.

Gordon's British connection stemmed from his living in England for his first eight years of life due to his parents' professional responsibilities. His father, Charles Thomas Aldrich, had been an Ohio-born vaudevillian. His mother named Bertha S. Leger (or St. Leger), and known on stage as actress Gloria Gordon, was born in West Darby, Lancashire, England.

A 1911 Census of England and Wales, signed by Gordon's father, listed ages with his father being 41, his mother Bertha was 35, and Gordon (Charles Jr.) was 5. They lived at 57 Woodside Park Road, North Finchley, London, England in a 12-room dwelling. His parents listed their occupation as music hall artists working on their own account.

Living in the Aldrich household were Gordon's sister, Jewel S. or Jewel St. Leger, 3; who was born in Liscord, Cheshire, England on January 14, 1908, though she was an American national. In addition, there was Christopher Wilson, a retired insurance official, and his wife Elizabeth L. Wilson, both 65 and born in Liverpool, Lancashire, England, both described as the applicant's father and mother-in-law; the married Marion Josephine Lacey, 28, described as cousin-in-law; and a single nurse named Eva Hughes, 20.

Gordon's sister Jewel would later adopt the name of Judy and go on to marry an award-winning writer, Richard E. Wormser.

The story often told is that his mother believed that her son was destined to become wealthy someday. Because of her strong interest in numerology, she wanted him called Gale as the name adds up to eight; that is, the sign of money.

One informative document indicating his timeline is Gordon's application for permission to go to England in 1922. First, Gordon was born in 1906 at 103 West 80th Street in New York City. According to this record, he resided in England from sometime in 1906 until August 4, 1914. Gordon certainly knew the latter date as he noted on the application, "day war declared by England."

It indicates that Gordon departed on a ship named *Philadelphia* from Southampton, England and arrived in the New York, New York port of the United States on August 13, 1914. Then the account gets confusing. He supposedly returned to England when he was 17 to attend Woodbridge School in Suffolk. Then when he returned from the United States, he got an opportunity for the first time to appear on stage in Canada.

Another application later in 1922 indicated he was a student, and then he resided at 126 30th Street in Woodcliff-on-Hudson, New Jersey. His reason for going to England is that he intended to visit his mother and grandmother. In addition, he listed going to France as well, but the reason is illegible.

Whatever the case, he started touring in stock companies early on. He returned to the United States after the Canadian production of *The Dancers* ran its course. In 1925 or 1926, Gordon's mother had an engagement in California to do a skit there. From that point on, the Gordons stayed in the United States.

Gordon got his first chance to be on a local radio station, KFWB-Hollywood, California, in 1926 when he reportedly played his ukulele and sang a tune, "It Ain't Gonna Rain No More," but it did not go over well.

As regards his first ambition, Gordon told Kulzer: "Actually, I wanted to be a toe dancer. My mother did an act in London. She had two girls who did a little ballet number while she changed gowns between the songs and she was performing. And when the ballet slippers wore out, she brought them home to me. I put them on and could walk all over the house on my toes, up and down stairs and everything else. The toe dancer phase lasted only for a short time, as long as my mother was doing the act with the ballet dancers."

What is most interesting about Gordon's youth is that a physical defect is responsible for his unique voice. It had an unusual start. Gordon explained to Kulzer: "My voice, I have to say, is kind of miraculous because I was born with a cleft palate. As a matter of fact, my first trip to England was when I was 18 months old. My mother knew of a doctor in London who specialized in repairing cleft palates to a great extent in children. It was a very, very serious thing in those days.

"So my mother, being English, took me back to England for the operation to repair the split roof of my mouth which almost developed into a hair lip but was prevented by this operation. The fact that I can talk at all is a miracle. I don't have anything in the back of my throat, there's no uvula. The doctor's look at it and they get dizzy. It's a hole. It's only by the grace of God that I can talk at all."

The throat surgeon from Hartley Street in London, a Dr. May, operated to correct Gordon's defect. In time, Gordon would perfect his quite distinctive voice, and it would become his prime asset. Whether on stage, radio, television, or film, Gordon's voice, combined with superb dramatic and comedic timing made his usual condescending characters seem natural and effortless."

Gordon similarly told Schaden: ". . . I was born with a cleft palate and it was only by the grace of God that and a very wonderful operation that was performed when I was eighteen months old in England that I could talk at all because from the time I was born till the time that [I] was nearly two years old I could only make strange sounds because the roof of my mouth split open at birth.

"And so I never had any therapy [to] speak of, except that my grandmother, bless her heart, was very insistent that as a young man at 5, [or] 6 years of age that I speak very clearly and distinctly which she would have insisted on anyway. And that's the only really training, real training that I had. So my voice just may be to the grace of God and as I say so very wonderful care. (Uh, uh,) otherwise, I never took any singing lessons or anything like that. It just happens the my voice is I guess very distinctive and I'm very grateful for it. . . . It was rather an unusual thing . . . very, very lucky indeed."

On another occasion, Gordon noted, "My father was a vaudevillian, and my mother was principal boy in pantomime among other things, such as light musical comedy. She was also in television years ago with Marie Wilson in *My Friend Irma*. My mother played the landlady 'Mrs. O'Reilly.'

"I started out at the bottom, by the way. I didn't have a speaking part and made just $15 a week in a play off-Broadway. And then as I got into it, and began to learn lines and get parts, I found that when I knew what I had to say, I had absolute confidence. Everybody I knew as a young man used to say, 'This man has no nerves!' Well, I was as nervous as anyone else, but I had the confidence of knowing what I was going to say. That confidence helped me through a great many trials and tribulations, and finally made my nervousness worthwhile."

Chapter Two: A Dramatic Start

"I'm not a compulsive actor. To me it's just a job to do. I turn it off as soon as I leave the studio, I couldn't give you a single line of dialogue the next day. I can't stand these actors who are always 'on.'"
— Gale Gordon

It did not take long for Gordon to distinguish himself as the busiest radio actor in the 1930s and 1940s. However, his start as an actor happened in the mid-1920s.

The first mention of Gordon in the press is as part of the cast in a Potboiler Art Theater production of *The Little Clay Cart*. That production, based on a 6th century Sanskrit story by King Shudraka, played for a week under the direction of Ole M. Ness. On December 5, 1926, the *Los Angeles Times* (hereinafter referred to simply as *LAT*) mentioned him first in the credit list of eight players.

Later on, Gordon remembered the leaner days early in his career when he started working in radio in 1927, receiving $2.50 for each half hour show and his agent getting 10 percent of that.

A play featuring the 22-year old Gordon and his mother caused some consternation. On July 5, 1927, *LAT* described the current Majestic fare, *Her Unborn Child* as "a problem play for modern youth and modern parents. . . . This drama written by Howard McKent Barnes "is said to be creating a sensation in Chicago where it is now in its twentieth week. The story written around a boy and a girl, innocent of life, and blind to the tragic consequences of youthful folly, and the working out of their problem.

"Though daringly written, the play is said to carry a simple, forceful message, a message that has significance for every modern girl and modern mother. Five of the cast are still part of the 'younger generation.' Ruth Hill, Belle Green, True Boardman, Gale Gordon and Doris Mortlock all play various types of modern youth."

Another clip quoted Barnes as saying: "Not sensationalism, but merely frankness, and honesty in dealing with a vital sociological problem have motivated this drama."

The July 5, 1927 edition of the paper followed-up with an article, "Speaker Will Discuss Birth Control Today." Estelle Lawton Lindsey, journalist and Los Angeles' first female City Council member had spoken on the topic of birth control as Barnes' sociological drama "had been causing, it is said, a stir in club circles since its premiere at the Majestic a week ago."

In "Pilgrimage Play Cast Announced," *LAT*, July 16, 1929; and "Holy Story to Be Told Again," *LAT*, July 21, 1929, Gordon is credited with playing one of the most despised men in history; namely, Judas Iscariot. The production's very large cast had 135 actors with 84 having speaking parts. The play had Ian Maclaren portraying Christ, and had staging in the hills surrounding the Hollywood Bowl as envisioned by Christine Wetherill Stevenson. It first premiered there nearly ten years earlier in 1920. It differed from the typical Passion Plays limited to portraying Christ's last week, as this play presented important events in Christ's entire life.

Four months later on November 25, 1929, *LAT* reported that Guy Bates Post and the Henry Duffy Players at the Hollywood Playhouse presented a play called *The Climax*. "Gale Gordon, who was last seen in *Skidding*, will play the role of John Raymond, the doctor."

In the many theatre productions featuring the young Gordon, the press often pictured him with other actors, including Bernice Elliot in *Skidding*, which played at the President Theatre (dates unknown).

A few days later, on November 30, 1929, *LAT* plugged the play again, saying Gordon has the part of the young doctor in *The Climax*, a comedy drama by actor-playwright Edward Locke.

Apparently, Gordon got some more attention when he decided to continue working through the holiday season. The December 14, 1929 article in *LAT* entitled "Gordon Decides to Work during Holiday Season" makes it known just by the title that he had already become a known actor. The piece noted, that "Out of nine Christmas days, Gale Gordon has been idle only one. That was a holiday. 'I never want a vacation period at that time again,' says Gordon, who has the role of the young doctor in *The Climax*, which Guy Bates Post and the Henry Duffy Players are presenting at the Hollywood Playhouse.

"Gordon decided to spend his Christmas vacation at Pensacola, Florida. He hung around the naval aviation station very anxious to go up in a flying boat. Finally, he got a chance to go up one morning in a pursuit plane. The airboat went up 3000 feet, then climbed another 3000 feet and then went into a nosedive, tailspin or something. The pilot just managed to avoid crashing to earth, but the airplane was badly disabled and drifted around for an hour or so before being rescued by another plane.

"'No more vacations for me,' says the young actor."

Gordon continued to receive mentions in the cast for plays performed at the Hollywood Playhouse. On November 24, 1930, *LAT* reported, "Gay Seabrook, popular ingénue, has been engaged by Henry Duffy for a role opposite Leo Carrillo in *The Bad Man*, which Duffy is presenting for two weeks at the Hollywood Palace beginning Sunday. Others in cast: Charlotte Treadway, Gale Gordon . . ."

The 1930 U.S. Federal Census listed Gordon's address as 81 Laurel Pass, Los Angeles. The 24-year-old reported that he worked in the stage industry, and that he owned a home with a declared value of $3,000. The document noted that he could read, write and speak English. However, most notably from that record is that Gordon did not own a radio set. Ironically, in a short time, he would become one of the busiest radio actors ever.

Gordon always said that he got his real start on radio from Kay Van Riper who wrote and starred in dramatizations of Queen Elizabeth; Mary, Queen of Scots; etc. He played her leading man. He told Mel Simons in a June 15, 1975 phone interview the details of exactly how he got his start in radio. Gordon: ". . . radio was a sort of a novelty in those days, and particularly out here in California. We were very behind the times as far as initiating radio programs."

He explained: ". . . and I was out of work and somebody said we'll call up radio stations and you might do that. It's easy work, you read from a piece of paper. You don't have to memorize lines or anything or put on makeup or get dressed up in costumes and so forth."

When asked if he began his career as leading man for Mary Pickford on *The Mary Pickford Show*, Gordon responded: "Oh, no, no, no. No, I started in 1931 or 1932. In Hollywood, there was a woman named Kay Van Riper who wrote a great many different series for radio and I got on that show calling up the studio one day.

"I'd been on the road, and someone said, 'Why don't you try radio,' you know, as more or less of a sort of a joke, but for a couple or three dollars, you know, this is what they paid in those days, so I figured it would help out.

"So I called up the studio at Warner Bros., and a woman answered and I said, 'I'm interested in doing radio,' and I gave her my credits up to that point and so forth, and she said, 'Come down tomorrow at ten o'clock to the studio,' and I did, and went in and waited around for a long time, and I saw this young woman, who I met with who was in charge of the office.

"She wrote the scripts and answered the phone and so forth, and finally she saw me, and I'd been sitting there for so long, and she said, 'What do you want?' and I said, 'Well, I want to see Miss Van Riper,' and she said, 'Well, I'm Miss Van Riper,' so I said, 'Well, I talked to you yesterday and you told me to come down,' and she looked at me as if I was a fool.

"She said, 'When you were on the phone I thought you were a middle-aged Englishman,' and I said. 'Oh,' and so she said she had a part, a character part in a script that she'd written, and I said, 'Yes,' and so I'd wind up getting two dollars to two and a half dollars, and then she had another idea. She said, 'Well, I'll need you in something else.'

"She did mostly historical things, and I did two or three series with her, and then she said there was a series called *English Coronets*, and I'd play Charles II (inaudible) Elizabeth and so forth, and those became very, very, very popular. They were only local shows in Hollywood and they were sponsored by Barker Brothers Furniture.

"I started out as playing the lead in those at five dollars a show, and the second season I asked for $7.50 and reluctantly I was paid that, and then the third season I asked for $10.00, and they wouldn't pay $10.00 for a radio actor. It was way just out of line, so they let me out of one, and it wasn't as successful as the others had been, and so they finally the fourth year called me back and I got $10.00 a show, and I was the highest paid radio actor in Hollywood at that time."

Gordon reminded Schaden that all the agents for the actors took 10% out of the two dollars and fifty cents they paid. When the unions came in, Gordon said, "then it became it was against the law actually for an employer to hire you and then take ten percent because that isn't Kosher (laughing as he said it) no matter how you look at it. And the studios did it for years and years and years. Finally, of course, it was outlawed, and we got more than two dollars and fifty cents. Finally, out here we got five dollars. I wasn't allowed to work at one station because I asked for three dollars for a show, and they thought I was too stuck up and much too expensive they wouldn't hire me.

". . . I played everything juveniles, heavies in particular. And well, of course, in radio we had to do dialects or we couldn't work, because in those days if you were employed to do a part on a show, it was assumed that you will be able to double or do two parts so that the employer could have a show with ten people in it and get five actors and the five actors would do the ten parts."

Schaden asked, "You didn't take double commission on those ten parts?"

Gordon responded, "Oh no, no, no" (both laugh).

Gordon added, "Well I did French, German, Irish, English of course, having gone to school in England. I did that a great deal. Played a great many Englishmen. And everybody in radio had to do at least two or three dialects. There was a dialect we called the International dialect of which is a little mish mash of everything and (we) used that if we had to be (from) some obscure country we don't quite know what it was, but it satisfied the listeners so that was all that was necessary."

As often was the case, Gordon did not receive on-air credit in a large number of radio programs during the 1930s. Oftentimes the cast has an unidentified voice that sounds like him.

Carrillo was one of the regular leads in some of the plays Gordon did; including, *Lombardi Limited* and *The Bad Man*, at the Hollywood Palace, and Gypsy Jim at El Capitan Theater. Though Carrillo never mentioned Gordon in early press reports, Carrillo was not easy to work with. However, he did provide good learning experience for actors.

On March 7, 1932, in "Carrillo Cast Learning to Juggle Lines," *LAT* reported that the cast has "to keep apace of the star's (Carrillo) ad-libbing, adding words and lines which do not appear in the script, and which he changes at every performance. He has been known, just by way of variety, to change entire speeches around about, and if the actors are not always on the alert, lines are apt to be lost and cues fumbled. Any actor who has appeared with Carrillo will agree that it is an unusual experience, for it tends to keep them strictly on their toes every minute they are on the stage."

One of the earliest radio shows that credits Gordon is the 1932 syndicated *Adventures in Strange Lands*. The episode entitled "Continental Express" included Hanley Stafford in the cast. Gordon found regular radio work in the syndicated serial *Tarzan of the Apes*, which started on September 12, 1932. The 286-episode show ran three times a week with the first WOR New York broadcast listed as January 23, 1933. The show, based on the novel by Edgar Rice Burroughs, had Gordon as Cecil Clayton, and Stafford as Count Raoul de Conde and James Pierce as Tarzan.

Gordon continued doing stage work while doing radio shows. On March 20, 1933, the press reported that Riper appeared on Paramount Theater's stage dressed as Mary, Queen of Scots in royal robes. It took two weeks to find a replica of the Queen's evening dress. *LAT*: "With Gale Gordon, radio actor, Miss Van Riper will re-enact a scene from her current radio series dealing with the remains of Mary, Queen of Scots. Gordon will portray the role of the Earl of Bothwell who, in the sketch, kidnaps the monarch and marries her. Miss Van Riper last appeared at the Paramount interpreting the Queen Elizabeth role."

Another early press clip from this period (date unknown) said that Gordon "is doing a nice job as a supporting actor for film stars on NBC's *Hall of Fame* broadcasts."

However, Gordon did not always do things right. For instance, in a 1933 radio show named *The Seal of the Don*, True Boardman played the dagger-wielding crusader hero Don Hancock (pronounced Doane Hancock), and heavily-accented Gordon played the villainous and oppressive Mexican Governor Manuel Mitchell Turena. Radio actress Mary Jean Higby told of an experience one time making a wax recording of the fifth and final episode done at 4 a.m. after a series of mishaps in this modern Robin Hood story.

Higby: "The last scene had the heroine (Barbara Luddy) trapped by the villain (Gordon) and, although she did not know it, about to be rescued by Don Hancock (Boardman).

"'If only Doane Hancock knew,' she was saying. 'He would save me.'

"An ugly laugh from Gale. 'You'll never see him again,' he gloated.

"A clatter of hooves . . . a shout . . . a door bust open . . .

"'At last!' Barbara cried.

"'So it's you,' snarled Gale. 'You again, Dan Hoe-cake!'

"He threw down the script, stretched out on the floor, and wept. The powers that be decided to make the last recording on another night, and the cast staggered out into the dawn to try to find an open restaurant and have breakfast."

Other shows from this time with Gordon included *The Goldbergs, Mutiny on the High Seas, Sweethearts of the Circus,* and *Death Valley Days.*

Gordon often played the dispatcher, the host and/or the narrator over the next few years in *Calling All Cars*, the police drama series of the day, starting with the broadcast on December 20, 1933.

While adding to his radio roles, he continued to develop his stage skills as his name gradually ascended importance in show casts. In "Talented Group Cast in Drama," *LAT*, December 19, 1933, Gordon was reported as one of the three actors receiving support from others: "Augustin J. Glassmire, directing *Love Chiselers*, which will open Christmas night at the Belasco Theater, had assembled a talented group of youngsters for roles in support of Marian Lord, Charlotte Treadway and Gale Gordon. They are Velma Gresham, Mabel Marden, Dave O'Brian, Michael Whalen and Richmond Lynch."

In the 15-minute syndicated series, *Tarzan and the Diamond of Asher*, it seems that Gordon joined Stafford with episode #31. He began turning up in episodes of *Mama Bloom's Brood*. In the 37th show in 1934, he played a character named Mr. Grenville.

On January 8, 1934, *LAT* names Gordon as being part of the cast in the farce comedy *Love Chiselers*, which played for a third week at the Belasco Theater.

Another early reference to Gordon's radio work is from *LAT* on March 6, 1934. The paper reported, "Continuing the atmosphere of desert romance, adventure and mystery, *The Song of Araby* comes on the air with its third episode over KFL at 9:30 p.m. Charles Carroll, who bears a striking resemblance of Buddy Rogers, plays the leading role and a new member of the cast will be introduced in the person of Gale Gordon, portraying the storyteller."

On September 2, 1934, *LAT* reported, "Kay Van Riper's *American Caravan* is presented tonight at 9 p.m. through KFWB, with Gale Gordon, perennial Van Riper principal, again playing a leading role. The actress-author is en route to California from New York, so the show will go on without her. Van Riper is one of the outstanding dramatic stars of the air on the west coast, and although she has had many offers to go east for sponsors, she prefers to remain in California."

Another undated news clip noted that Van Riper appeared at the Paramount Theater with Gordon, "presenting a scene from the current series of historical dramas which she creates for KFWB. Station officials and entertainers will turn out to give both of them a send-off."

The press coverage picked up when Gordon joined up with Mary Pickford. When the premiere show of *Mary Pickford and Company*, entitled "The Church Mouse," hit the airwaves on NBC network on October 3, 1934, Mary's billing is, "The best known woman in the world."

LAT's Carroll Nye noted, "Miss Pickford makes her debut at the head of radio's first stock company over NBC and KFI at 5 p.m. in *The Church Mouse*, a romantic comedy by Ladislas Fodor, which provided her with a vehicle for a recent personal appearance tour. The series will be produced in the Hollywood NBC studios and members of the company are Jeanette Nolan, Ted Osborn, Crawford Kent, Gale Gordon and James Eagles."

In the episode, Gordon plays Skylar Thompson, President of an International Banking firm, who decides that he will have no more women working in his office. The narrator sets up the premise of the story as follows, saying, "Although he has a genius for finance, Skylar is also human and has human weaknesses. In fact, he is so human that this morning he had to dismiss his pretty secretary, Dolly Frye, because she distracted him from his work. Girls like you are for the evening. . . ." Dolly gets six months of salary, and Skylar gets Dolly's phone number, and so he settles down to his work.

Complexities arise when the frightened and hungry Suzie Wade (Pickford) enters Skylar's office. She eases into his office like a frightened mouse. Suzie is literally without food and as poor as a church mouse. As in Gordon's later character of banker Mr. Mooney, he asks her in a serious-minded tone, "How did you get in here?"

Suzie is not interested in romantic involvement as she just asks for a job to help herself and her family. The skeptical Skylar initially turns her down, but then offers her a trial job. Although he feels for her plight, he explains to her that he just fired his secretary. Then he relents. Interestingly, she turns out to be a very efficient worker who puts him on task at times. Skylar calls her a "human dynamo."

Dolly tries to make Suzie feel uncomfortable, saying that she is too business-like and that Skylar is not interested in her as a woman. Nevertheless, Skylar plans a party for Suzie because she works so hard and he wants to make amends for hurting her feelings. At the party, he is surprised at how stunning she looks ("Why Suzie!")

When he gets close to her and tries to kiss her, Suzie wants to get closer as well. It is a difficult moment for Suzie as a jealous Dolly made Suzie feels like Skylar sees her as an office machine. Nevertheless, Suzie really wants Skylar to ache for her. Then an interruption comes at the decisive moment. Skylar is astonished when Suzie seizes the opportunity to escape the tension when she suddenly goes off to Paris with her two male escorts.

Listeners are surprised when Skylar exclaims, "I'll be damned!" What one may find most memorable in retrospect regarding this episode is not that Gordon teamed with the prolific and well-known silent actress, but that he said that line.

Indeed this episode gives Gordon moments for us to hear his fine talent. He even gets a chance to express anger at the escorts and offer us that explosive temper that we became familiar with on television many years later. Skylar's anger is over the fact that he found out the escorts left Suzie in Paris by herself.

A spoiler alert is called for with the show ending when Skylar explains: "You're finally awake Suzie, you see ahead of you a new world. A world full of unexpected joy and it needs only one word." He steps in for a kiss. She obliges. He comments about her lovely feet and ankles, and "wonderful eyes so deep that a man can drown in. Ah! What a mouth." He clears his throat. He gets serious again and wants her to take dictation. He recites about loving her and not being able to tell her. He has her spell out the word mouse. The episode ends as she squeals with delight!

Simply put, Gordon's Skylar played the suitor won over by the honest and sweet Pickford's Suzie, and she finally admits she loves him.

Two weeks later, on October 17, 1934, *LAT* reported: "Mary Pickford and her radio stock company swing into production of Barry Connors's comedy, *The Patsy*, on KFI at 5 p.m. in which the diminutive first lady of cinemaland will play the role of the frustrate Patricia Harrington, a lass who, anxious to become popular, buys a book on personality and learns the art of clever repartee.

"Gale Gordon, who plays the leading role opposite Miss Pickford, also heads the cast in *Jewels and a Sword*, a drama dealing with a situation in the life of Charles II of England, which serves as the first presentation in the revival of *Tapestries of Life* on KHJ at 9:15 p.m. . . ." The newspaper pictured Mary Forbes and the Roman Soldier played by Gale Gordon.

Of course, one could credit Gordon with helping other stage actors break into radio, even though the time line from these accounts sometimes seems contradictory. One such person is Barbara Luddy, a tiny four foot eleven actress, who played in other stage productions as Gordon did for Henry Duffy's group at the El Capitan.

Higby explained how Gordon helped Luddy find work on radio. Higby: "She had been on a tour of Australia in a play starring Leo Carrillo. On its return to Hollywood, the company was to open at Henry Duffy's El Capitan Theater. It arrived to a great flurry of publicity, a triumphal opening, and rave reviews in the papers. The next night Barbara trotted jubilantly down to the theater to find it plastered with bankruptcy notices.

"The padlocked door at the El Capitan was Barbara's introduction to the Depression. She got on intimate terms with it immediately. When her savings had dwindled to the vanishing point, Gale Gordon, an old friend from previous and more lasting Duffy productions, suggested she turn her attention to radio. There was an opportunity for a young couple on a local station. The show went on at 8 a.m. with rehearsal at 6:30. There were no salaries attached to the enterprise, but Gale was sure that it was the open door to the entertainment world of the future. He convinced Barbara and they started their early-morning vigil. It was six months before they landed their first paying radio jobs—*English Coronets.*"

Unfortunately, Higby may have gotten the title wrong as Gordon's first paying job for he had stated that Van Riper did several other series with him before *English Coronets.* Elsewhere Higby explains: "[Hanley Stafford] left this $7 *Coronets* bonanza at the end of three weeks; however, to take a job with a stock company in Arizona and was replaced by Gale Gordon."

In *LAT*, October 29, 1934: "Gale Gordon has accepted an offer to appear in Kay Van Riper's forthcoming New York production of *Coronets.*"

Higby added that when she did a broadcast of an unnamed adaptation of a yet-to-be released Warners' picture, "I was glad to see Gale Gordon in the cast. We had known one another long before either of us had heard of radio."

In *LAT*, November 7, 1934: "Mary Pickford's radio play originates in New York today and comes through KFI at 5 p.m. She is presenting A. A. Milne's comedy-drama, *Michael and Mary*, which tells the story of two English lovers who go blithely through life, ever shadowed by a spirit of danger which continuously threatens their romance. Gale Gordon, who did himself proud in the Hollywood productions, again appears as Mary Pickford's leading man."

On December 16, 1934, George M. Adams, Jr. of the *Washington Post* reported: "Kay Van Riper's colorful *English Coronets* series, featuring the crowded life of Henry VIII. . . Today's episode shows Henry wedded to Catherine of Aragon whom he finds dull. A son is born to them, and with its death six weeks later, relations between Catherine and the King are strained into the break, which had such a far-reaching effect on English history and that of the church.

"Henry is played by Gale Gordon, who was Mary Pickford's leading man on the air. Helen Choate is heard in the part of Catherine. Miss Van Riper writes and directs *English Coronets* and will later appear in the part of Anne Boleyn when that lady enters the action of the play."

Many of the shows from this period were of 15-minute duration. For example, in 1935, Gordon appeared in several episodes of a 15-minute radio show entitled *That Was the Year*, which dramatized real events of different years narrated by Gerald Mohr. The shows with Gordon included retelling the events of 1897, 1901, 1916, and 1918.

Gordon played in the Hearst syndicated 15-minute radio series *Front Page Drama* sponsored by *The American Weekly*. In the episode entitled "Night Work," broadcast on March 1, Gordon played a public prosecutor who capitalizes on his knowledge of a crime. The following week he played a very different role, this time as a paranormal expert who helps a ghost find peace in "The Ghost Doctor."

Before it became the memorable film serial with Olympic swimming champion Larry "Buster" Crabbe, Gordon played the lead character in *The Amazing Interplanetary Adventures of Flash Gordon*. That radio serial, based on the Alex Raymond comic strip, began its radio run on April 27, 1935 with Himan Brown producing. With the second episode, the show's title changed to *The Amazing Interplanetary Adventures of Flash Gordon and Dale Arden*.

Gordon told Schaden: ". . . I was in New York and auditioned along with everybody else in those days you didn't do any part at all without auditioning with ten or twenty, thirty, forty people without auditioning. I got the part merely on my voice. The fact that my name was Gordon didn't mean a thing. I was just cast as the part. I did it for eight or ten episodes I think then I came back to California, but I did, I was the original Flash Gordon on radio."

In the same year, Gordon offered his voice on episodes of *The March of Time*. The 15-minute program had Harry Von Zell as the announcer.

He returned to *Front Page Drama* on May 17 with episode #108 called "Love Forever," playing a man who was murdered because he changed his mind regarding a proposal of marriage. He continued to appear in the anthology series, some of the episodes included #119: "Grand Passion," #120: "Stowaway," and #128: "Black Gold."

The Amazing Interplanetary Adventures of Flash Gordon again changed its name with the 24th show on October 13, 1935 to *Flash*

Gordon and Jungle Jim. The show continued under that title for the 25th and 26th episode. Then the following week's show is simply *The Adventures of Jungle Jim*. Gordon erred when he said that he did only a few episodes.

In 1936, Gordon appeared in another rendition of *Tarzan*. This radio show, produced by Frederick Shields, starred Carlton KaDell as Tarzan, with Gordon playing a character named O'Rourke.

To celebrate Washington's Birthday in 1936, the Red and Blue networks offered a tribute, including mobile unit broadcasts from Mount Vernon, from McConker's Ferry of the Delaware River (famed for Washington's Crossing of the Delaware), Valley Forge, and Independence Hall. Gordon portrayed Washington in a dramatized portion of the hour-long show.

In what may be his only other Broadway theatre credit (besides Gordon's oft mentioned, but undocumented role in *The Dancers* from 1923), Gordon played Agamemnon in the short-lived original Greek tragedy, *Daughters of Atreus*.

On October 11, 1936, the *New York Times* reported simply, "*Daughters of Atreus*—Wednesday evening at Forty-fourth Street Theatre. Variations on a Grecian theme, with Eleonora Mendelssohn (American debut), Maria Ouspenskaya, Joanna Roos, Edward Trevor, Olive Deeing, Eric Wollencott, Harry Irvine, Thomas Coffin Cooke, Hal Conklin, Edgar Stehli and Gale Gordon."

In an undated clipping, entitled "Gordon Paged," we are told, "Gale Gordon is being paged for William Saroyan's stage production *Jim Dandy*." Another clipping said he was in a theatrical production of *Gypsy Jim*, which stated that this romantic comedy had the supporting cast of Gordon, as well as Gavin Gordon, Marion Clayton, Mitchell Harris, and others.

Although he never got detailed coverage, Gordon often got just his name dropped among others in connection with various theatrical productions, mostly in Los Angeles. As an example, from *LAT*: "The humorous trials of a son who tries to run his father's broom factory for a year make up the plot of *New Brooms*, the Frank Craven comedy now in its eighth week at El Capitan. Robert McWade is seen in his original role of the father, which he created in the Broadway production, and Jason Robards is the son. Others in the cast are Helen Ferguson as the housekeeper and Alice Buchanan,

Marie Knox, Bernice Elliott, Frank Dawson, William Macauley, Willie Marks, William Eugene, Gale Gordon, William Robyns and David Campbell."

In *LAT*, May 25, 1937: "An early-California 'fiesta' is to highlight the first episode of the new (*Cassandra*) series, with the announcement of the betrothal of Elena to Don Felipe. Bill Hatch will handle the musical assignment of the new *Cassandra* series, and Gale Gordon yesterday signed for a role in the presentation . . .

"*Cassandra*, the story of California's romantic, yet turbulent days, which has been over KHI as a tri-weekly presentation shifts to KNX and the western Columbia network today, to become a weekly half-hour show at 5 p.m."

Sometimes he played a leading part as with the adult role of Milton Hershey in a 15-minute radio episode entitled "The Chocolate King" from the show #25 of *Captains of Industry*, broadcast July 1, 1937. Sometimes he played minor characters; for example, the captain of the boat owned by the father of the famed Republican Mark Hanna in episode #32 of this show, heard on August 19th.

LAT, October 17, 1937 reported, "Kay Van Riper's *English Coronets* (KHJ–8:30 p.m.) concludes today with Queen Elizabeth's death. A group of well-known radio actors return to their original roles for this episode. They are Duane Thompson, Ted Osborne, Johnny Gibson, Fred MacKaye, Fred Harrington, Gale Gordon, and Charles Carroll."

By this point, Gordon had the experience of a seasoned professional. Higby noted, "The old timers could weather any mishap. Barbara Luddy and Gale Gordon went on talking when the lights went out during *Coronets*. Afterward, Barbara said, 'We never could understand why, if there was a power failure, the mikes stayed on and only the lights went out.' Having been the victim of more than one irresistible impulse, I think I can guess. But whatever the cause, Barbara and Gale saw to it that there was no dead air."

Gordon showed some involvement in current concerns of the time as he appeared as a speaker at the Hollywood Women's Club on October 27, 1937 (*LAT*), along with John Gibson, Forrest Bonn and Gloria Gordon, according to an article entitled "Sterilization Selected as Club Topic Today." At the event, Dr. Rose Bowers discussed "Sterilization, Breeding from Culls or Survival of the

Unfittest." There is no report of what Gordon had to say, as no coverage of the discussion exists. The fact that Gordon never had children may have had some connection to why he would be a speaker with his mother at a conference on sterilization.

Gordon even played the villain in a popular radio serial, *Speed Gibson of the International Secret Police* beginning on September 20, 1937 with "The Case of the World Against the Octopus." Speed is the 15-year-old orphaned nephew of Clint Barlow, of the International Secret Police. Barney Dunlap is his dopey sidekick who helps Speed in tracking "The Octopus" gang. Here Gordon had steady work showing his nefarious skill playing "The Octopus."

The show ran several times a week, with a total of one hundred and seventy-eight episodes. Gordon first shows up in the fifth show as the villain with an Asian-sounding heavy accent. He appears alongside some regulars that were in many other shows with Gordon at this time. The first one hundred chapters focus on fighting "The Octopus" throughout the Orient. The next 78 chapters, "The Atlantian Expedition" has "The Octopus" pursued in Africa. The cast included Stafford, John Gibson (as "Barney Dunlap"), Ed Gardner, Elliot Lewis, Sam Edwards, and Howard McNear.

Gordon played a pharmacist in the radio series *Doctor Christian*, beginning with the first episode broadcast on November 7, 1937. In that episode, the Doctor (Jean Hersholt) has no choice but to do an operation in a shack.

More memorable today is the syndicated Christmas-themed story *The Cinnamon Bear*, even though Gordon's parts as Weary Willie the Stork and the Ostrich were miniscule. The daily serial ran for 26 days from November 29 until December 24, 1937. The story told of the Cinnamon Bear named "Paddy O' Cinnamon," and how he pursued the Crazy Quilt Dragon who stole the silver Christmas Star. Two youngsters, Judy and Jimmy, assist Paddy. Among the many radio talents heard were Stafford, McNear, Elvia Allman, Joseph Kearns, Elliott Lewis, Lou Merrill, Frank Nelson, etc.

In 1938, Gordon doubled (played two parts) in episode #10 called "The City Beautiful" of the Mormon historical series named *The Fullness of Times* syndicated by The Church of Latter Day Saints. Gordon played a congregate that objected to Elder Woodruff leaving the church. Later when Woodruff spreads the gospel, Gordon plays a neighbor who assists Woodruff with a place to stay, and then joins the church.

"The Story of John Wanamaker," the 50th episode of *Captains of Industry* from January 2, presaged the character type that he would repeat most of his adult life. Yes, it is as early as 1938 that we get a sample of Gordon's knack for playing the blustery boss whose employee asks for a raise and a share of the business. This is one of the earliest examples of Gordon playing the screaming hard-nosed authoritarian. It is a role that we often identify him with much later on. Indeed, it is counter-productive for the boss to behave in this way as his employee (here John Wanamaker) vows to open up his own department store in competition to his boss.

Although Gordon's character type that he hit upon here, and later elsewhere, is quite funny, the reality is that having to deal with this type of controlling person is certainly not so tolerable or funny in real life. However, Gordon knew how to make audiences laugh nonetheless.

Gordon even showed his fine talent at delivering advertising copy in *Log Cabin Jamboree*, a radio show featuring Jack Haley, Warren Hull (as announcer), Wendy Barrie, Virginia Verrill, Ted Fio Rito and his orchestra. In the broadcast from January 15, 1938, Gordon and Stafford do the dramatized commercial encouraging listeners to eat pancakes with Log Cabin Syrup (copper griddle premium).

One hears Gordon's perfect-sounding diction and fine comedic skill coming through as he played the strong-tongued boss of Baby Snooks' father in the Fanny Brice/Hanley Stafford segments of the *Good News of 1938* radio programs.

In the radio series *Big Town*, Gordon played District Attorney Miller. The May 2 rehearsal of the broadcast entitled "The Case of the Missing Milk," had crusader Steve Wilson (Edward G. Robinson) going after a milk protection racket. Claire Trevor and Stafford co-starred, with KaDell as the announcer. Gordon made additional appearances on the series, including a show in which Wilson went after a poultry racket.

Gordon continued to be a regular cast member in 1938 on a number of dramatic radio shows, including *Calling All Cars* and *Front Page Drama*. On the *Lux Radio Theatre*, Gordon often doubled, as with the Jack Benny comedy, "Seven Keys to Baldpate," broadcast on September 26.

Gordon did the announcing for *The Wonder Show* beginning on October 14. The show featured Jack Haley, and like many shows of the time, named for its sponsor, Wonder Bread (and Hostess Cupcakes). The show's promotion said it had the novelty of featuring an "intellectual discussion" without scripts, "for the first time on any comedy show."

As the actor making more than one appearance in a series, Gordon often made numerous appearances from time to time on the popular radio shows of the day. He returned to *Doctor Christian* on October 18 with "Baby on the Doorstep," on December 13 with "Sweet Genevieve," and the following year on March 21, 1939 with "Mr. Meeks."

In 1939, Gordon appeared on the *Joe E. Brown Show* broadcast on March 25, playing Mr. Bullhammer, the company proprietor, and Brown playing his employee. When he is sickened, Gordon's character asks Brown to take over the office. Various antics, including sales people trying to sell via limericks, occur with Brown in charge. Even when Bullhammer returns, the wackiness continues.

A recurring role in the 15-minute serial *The Shadow of Fu Manchu* began on May 8. It told the story of the murderous Dr. Fu (Ted Osborne) who vowed to kill Sir Nayland Smith (Stafford). Gordon played Dr. James Petrie, who is under threat as well while living near Baker Street's famous detective, Sherlock Holmes. Edmond O'Brien played Inspector Rymer. The show ran thru November 3 (episode #155), and it is based on the Sax Rohmer story, "The Insidious Dr. Fu Manchu," published in 1913.

Nearly a week after his first appearance on *The Shadow of Fu Manchu*, Gordon continued on another serial, #185 of *The Adventures of Jungle Jim* on May 14.

Gordon continued almost unceasingly as it now seems, offering his voice for various radio shows, including the commercials, such as for *Good News of 1939*. Gordon appeared along with his mother Gloria, doing doubles on *Lux Radio Theatre* on September 11 in *The Awful Truth*. On November 13, he doubled again on Lux's version of *The Champ*.

The following year, *Chicago Daily Tribune* on January 8, 1939 reported: "*Cinderella in Reverse*, a radio drama starring Irene Rich, will be heard during the weekly broadcast from Hollywood over WENR-NBC at 8:45 p.m. Gale Gordon will play opposite Miss Rich."

Gordon's credit list quickly grew as he played a number of supporting roles in many radio shows. Some of the many other seemingly countless shows he did are mentioned here, with a complete list in the credits section of this book. The radio programs ran the gamut from juvenile to dramatic to soap opera and everything else imaginable.

A breakthrough moment was about to occur. At the end of 1939, Gordon would be part of a show that would forever change the emphasis in his radio roles. It would evolve into one of his most important early regular roles, and it would make him the comedy character actor we have all come to love. The show would give him the role of Mayor LaTrivia written with Gordon in mind by the one-man talent Don Quinn. The show was NBC's popular *Fibber McGee and Molly*.

In Gordon's first appearance on the series, broadcast on December 26, 1939, he plays Molly's now wealthy ex-boyfriend, Otis Cadwalader. Since he has assumed that the McGees are wealthy too, they go out of their way to impress him with hilarious results, even including having the character of pompous Gildersleeve (Hal Peary) serve as their butler.

Gordon's watershed moment as far as radio is when he played Mayor LaTrivia nearly two years later, but his first appearance at this point is the start of his long association with the comedy radio show. Eventually Gordon would excel as radio's best-known and most-loved supporting comedy actor.

Gordon told Simons: "Radio was very, very kind to me, and I was very, very lucky to do so many things with so many great people, but all the big movie stars. You know, for me it was great thrills ... It was a delight."

Chapter Three: A Comedic Turn

"I just have an ear and I have an instinct for knowing how long I can wait before giving the punch line."

—Gale Gordon,
Mel Simons interview, June 15, 1975

The plethora of radio work that kept Gordon extremely busy during the 1930s through the 1950s also helped him find his life-long mate. Gordon met his wife Virginia B. Curley, AKA Bernice Curley (born January 8, 1911 in Missouri) while appearing on a radio show called *Death Valley Days*. They married in Kingsman, Arizona on December 27, 1937. Supposedly, the couple would continue to celebrate their anniversary every month on the 27th day for the next twenty years.

If there is one show that is undoubtedly Gordon's most memorable and best early radio show, it had to be *Fibber McGee and Molly*. Although the show started in 1935 and ran to 1957, for at least seven years the series had the highest ratings when the show really hit a nerve with audiences. Gordon would appear on it practically every week from 1940 to 1942, and again from 1945 to 1953. When he enlisted in the Coast Guard, he would still visit the show five times during 1943.

The couple, Fibber McGee and Molly, played by Jim and Marian Jordan offered various simple and mundane small-town experiences, which would always turn humorous. The comedy in each show would come as the couple interacted with a number of odd (or eccentric), but nonetheless interesting, neighbors.

Gordon played different roles on *Fibber McGee and Molly* throughout 1940 and 1941 after first playing Molly's ex-boyfriend Otis in 1939.

For 1940, he played the unnamed man who knows the McGees, but they do not know him on the January 16 show ("New License Plates," AKA "Stolen Car") and the January 30 show ("Old Suit"). He appeared as a lawyer named Mr. Corpus on the February 13 show ("Good Luck Egyptian Gold Ring"). He played a wacky Doctor Cyclops on the February 27 show ("Fibber Catches a Cold"), a maître d on the March 12 show ("Fibber Takes Molly to Lunch"), a postman on the March 19 show ("Dog License Problems"), a store owner named Mr. Plummer on the May 21 show ("Fibber Gets a Job in a Hardware Store"); and he played Buster Dawson, co-owner of a circus, and an usher on the May 28 broadcast ("Circus Comes to Town").

Some logs for the fall of 1940 reported that Gordon played the character named Doc Gamble beginning on October 8 ("Fibber Gives up Cigars"). However, Gordon's doctor is just "Doc." The town doctor part would evolve into "Doc Gamble" when Arthur Q. Bryan played it.

For the October 15 show ("Missing Screwdriver"), he played a hardware store clerk, then a motorcycle cop on October 29 ("Driving to the Football Game"), a wacky doctor on November 12 ("Fibber's Black Eye"), a sales clerk at the BonTon on December 24 ("Gildy's Radio Phonograph") and a banker/refinancer named Mr. Wolf on December 31 ("Fibber Finds a Gold Watch").

In 1941, he began the year on the January 7 episode of *Fibber McGee and Molly* show ("Fifty Thousand Dollar Deal") playing the business college manager named Mr. Hamilton Quigley; and he played a clerk in the music store as well as one of the piano movers on January 21 ("Piano Lessons"). On the February 25 show ("Fibber's Bottle Collection"), he appeared as the owner of a grocery store named Mr. Sale. As a doctor on the March 4 show ("The McGees Throw a Dinner Party"), he repeats certain phrases, such as "Ah yes, yes, yes, yes."

On the March 18 show ("Fibber Gets His Draft Notice"), he played a postal worker named Mr. Bagworthy and an army colonel. He was a judge who screams and yells at one point, and denies

McGee's petition to change his name on the March 25 show ("Fibber Changes His Name"). He played Professor Hercules Wittakind of Mount Witney Observatory on April 8 ("Fibber Builds a Telescope"), an oculist on April 15 ("Fibber Needs Glasses"), a morale recreation officer named Captain Gordon on May 6 ("Games and Books for the Army"), and a recording engineer named Aza M. Taint of the Wistful Vista Recording Studios on May 27 ("Gildersleeve's Ladder"). When Molly questions him about his name he explains his name is like Molly's oft-repeated phrase "Taint funny McGee."

Due to a misunderstanding, McGee and Molly mistake Gordon to be a photographer on the June 10 broadcast ("Photo Album"). Gordon is really an electric company employee who takes their $15 and clumsily fumbles around the studio equipment. When the real photographer arrives, he says he charges $7.50 for photos. The receptionist reveals to her boss that Gordon had said, "Never mind," as he took the McGees' $15 to pay an overdue electric bill.

On the June 17 broadcast ("Amusement Park"), he plays a RKO Pictures representative who follows them around the park. McGee thinks he is a con man. They have several run-ins before he gets to explain himself. Apparently, Gordon was observing the McGees for he wants to star them in a film called *Look Who's Laughing*.

Gordon plays Dr. Davenport from the Here Today Gone Tomorrow Insurance Company on the June 24 broadcast ("Leaving for Hollywood"). He greets them saying: "How do you do? How do you do? How do you do?"

Oftentimes the information that circulates is erroneous. For instance, some have credited the October 7, 1941 show ("Fifty Thousand Dollars") as Gordon's first appearance, even though, as we have seen, he had appeared many times in earlier shows. The show sounds like a reworking of the January 7, 1941 show where Gordon plays the business college manager.

However, what is the most important date is the show from October 14, 1941 ("Fire Commissioner") as that is the first broadcast when Gordon is heard in the part that he is best remembered for; that is, as the pompous Mayor LaTrivia. Some have said that this character had been a take-off on New York's Mayor La Guardia. Gordon seemed to indicate otherwise as in an interview with Schaden where he noted Don Quinn wrote the Mayor part with him in mind.

Gordon's portrayal in each episode is brief as the town's Mayor, which would often find him getting completely exhausted and exasperated after talking to the McGees. Gordon would sputter his final line to listeners' delight. However, in the early episodes, we see the calm and controlled Mayor of Wistful Vista.

Some of the other cast members in the celebrated *Fibber McGee and Molly* series included Bill Thompson playing the Old-Timer ("That's not the way I heared it, Johnny, the way I heared it. . ."), the hen-pecked Wallace Wimple, and Horatio K. Boomer (the W.C. Fields' sounding character). Of course, there is also the egotistical Throckmorton P. Gildersleeve, who soon would have his own show, *The Great Gildersleeve.* Audiences never tired of certain predictable aspects, such as Molly's oft-repeated lines, such as "Taint funny, McGee," and "Heavenly days," or the hall closet that would release its contents on McGee whenever he opened it.

Gordon told Mel Simons how his role of Mayor LaTrivia came about. Gordon: "Well, Mayor LaTrivia came about because I did one shot on the McGee show. Many, many years ago there was a character who was supposed to be Marian's—a boyfriend of her early youth, who has gone away from Wistful Vista and made a great deal of money and he was coming back to Wistful Vista for a visit, and his character's name was Otis Tadwalader. . . .

"I waited for laughs, which is the thing Jim (Jordan) was afraid of. Being a dramatic actor, he didn't think I'd wait for laughs, but I did wait for them and got along very well with him, so Don Quinn, the writer, said, 'Well, we've never had a Mayor of Wistful Vista, and he got this wild idea of Mayor LaTrivia, and he wrote it with me in mind, and so I started in a week or two after I finished the Otis Tadwalader sketch as Mayor LaTrivia. . ."

Gordon stands corrected here, as the character in the show is Cadwalader with a "C," not Tadwalader with a "T." In addition, the fact that the shows survived proved that Gordon's memory failed him, as he played so many different parts for nearly two years before the character of Mayor LaTrivia came into the show (not "a week or two later"). Indeed, Gordon clearly showed his versatility and capability in playing a number of different parts, and many shows came after the Otis sketch—which was a long time before the Mayor LaTrivia part came about.

Gordon told Simons: "And so the episode was my coming to town, and it was written ahead of time. Marian and Jim were both trying to make an impression of this rich, city man, so they got Gildersleeve to act as a butler, and they put on the dog for the sake of Otis Tadwalader, and so forth.

"So that was my first introduction to Jim and Marian Jordan and the director. I can't think of his name at the moment, but anyway, he suggested me for this part, and Jim and Marian were a little reluctant, because they thought of me as a dramatic actor.

"People in the audience if they know you're going to say something, they always knew I was going to give McGee a big come down, and—

Mel Simons: "When you would pause and say 'McGee!' that was hysterical. You know, it's the type of thing where you knew just what was coming. And you would say, 'McGee!' and you would laugh just as hard each and every week."

Gordon: "Yeah. Well, you see in the meantime while you're waiting the audience is making up all kinds of things that you might be going to say, and so even if you don't say exactly what they thought you were going to say, it's the idea of waiting that long that makes them more anxious."

Years later, a letter from Bill S., Studio City, in the "We Get Letters" feature in one of Cecil Smith's columns ("Rerun Request Too Logical to Happen") revealed:

"Your recent discussion re network blue pencillers with noses to match brings to mind a Don Quinn saga when he was writing *Fibber McGee and Molly* for radio. He tried on a number of occasions to get the exchanges between Fibber McGee and Gale Gordon (as Mayor LaTrivia) a bit saltier, not with double entendres, but just more heated so Gale's 'M'GEE—' after a pregnant pause would be more effective.

"But the blue pencil lads at NBC kept cutting and censuring the lines. Finally, he let it be known that he was writing a book about his experiences in broadcasting, particularly with NBC censors—and they got off his back almost completely. The book he never wrote was to be called 'Idiots Delete.'"

Schaden asked Gordon about the origin of his Mayor character. Gordon: "Was that because the LaTrivia character was a take-off of

(New York's) Mayor LaGuardia and then when LaGuardia died and they didn't want to use that character?"

Gordon replied, "No. No. (Uh, uh,) I did appear, appeared on the show with Jim and Marian as a one shot. I played her ex-boyfriend who was coming to town and I'd become very successful and Jim and Marian got Gildersleeve to act as a butler. They were trying to put on the dog to impress me because I was a rich man and had been very successful. And I did that as a one-shot and they liked me. And I got along very, very, well with them.

"And Don Quinn came up with an idea of Foggy Williams the weatherman. As a rather quick second show, a third I did with them. And they decided they liked to have me as a regular, and Don said you know Wistful Vista has never had a Mayor. So he created the part of LaTrivia for me. So it's the only part written for me right from scratch, and that's how I became Mayor LaTrivia."

Again, Gordon erred when he said the Foggy character came before the Mayor character. Actually, Foggy did not come into being until 1947, after the character of the Mayor was temporarily retired. After a year of the Foggy character, Mayor LaTrivia returned.

Chapters Ten and Eleven in Part Two of this book will elaborate further on the character of Mayor LaTrivia, which would first fully expose us to Gordon's fine comedic talent, particularly his verbal brawls with the McGees. There I provide excerpts from LaTrivia's exchanges with the McGees for the first two seasons that he played the character, so one can better understand the importance of the development of the Mayor LaTrivia character on many of Gordon's later radio and television characters.

Chapter Four: Busy On the Air!

"I've never been bored in my life working. A lot of people get bored after five minutes. They want to go home and pick up their check. That's never been the case for me. I'm always the first to arrive and the last to leave because I truly enjoy what I'm doing. That's why I have been in show business for so long. I love it!"

—Gale Gordon

Besides doing *Fibber McGee and Molly* in 1940, Gordon played on a radio show called *In His Steps*, based on a best-selling novel concerning a small town clergyman and his church members.

In the January 4 episode of *Good News of 1940*, Gordon played a police dispatcher. He played "Marryin' Sam" on *Li'l Abner* broadcast on March 22. Gordon lent his support on *Lux Radio Theatre* for their production of *Love Affair* on April 1, *Midnight* on May 20, and *Wings of the Navy* on October 7. He was heard on *Little Old Hollywood* on May 6, *The Adventures of Jungle Jim*, *Front Page Drama* and the *George Burns and Gracie Allen Show* (continuing thru 1941).

One of the regular parts Gordon played for the Burns & Allen show is a Texan. He always seemed to come in talking about oil wells, and he took what Gracie said lightly and thought she was joking. Gordon played him with what seemed like an unconvincing and inauthentic accent. He also played other incidental roles on the show.

When Schaden asked Gordon: "You played a Texan didn't you? Gordon responded: "Yes, Tex Judson his name was. His characteristic was every time he stubbed his toe up came another darned oil well. He was just rolling in money (Schaden laughs). What he adored about Gracie was her sense of humor. And she opened her mouth and he'd fall over and just screamed with laughter and it was a delightful character to do and I had a lot of fun doing it. I still see George every once in a while. We have the same barber. We've been going to the same barber for 35 years I guess. So I see George there every once in a while now. We say hello and talk over old times. And they were delightful people to work with. Just wonderful."

He continued in 1941 making several appearances on *Lux Radio Theatre*, including *Wife, Husband, and Friend; Virginia City; The Lady from Cheyenne; Unfinished Business; Blood and Sand*; and doubling for *Kitty Foyle*. Gordon even had appeared on the first *Cavalcade of America* show entitled "Waters of the Wilderness." That show, broadcast on October 13, would be his first of eleven appearances on *Cavalcade*.

He played in the audition show of a proposed summer replacement comedy-detective radio series named *Miss Pinkerton Inc.*, broadcast July 12. In it, an aspiring female lawyer (Joan Blondell) inherits a detective agency. Gordon plays the lawyer connected to the woman detective's deceased uncle. In her first official case, she captures jewel thieves. Gordon doubled here playing a thief.

Gordon voiced the November 3 episode of *Orson Welles Theatre*, entitled "Wild Oranges," about a beautiful woman and a homicidal maniac on a deserted island off the coast of Georgia. He portrayed President Abraham Lincoln for *Your Red Cross Roll Call* broadcast on November 15. The show, sponsored by the Red Cross Fund Appeal, told the story of Florence Nightingale and the founding of the organization. On December 1, 1941, Gordon returned to *Cavalcade of America* in their rendition of *Cimarron*.

In 1942, he did a 15-minute air trailer for the film *Wake Island*, syndicated by Paramount, with dramatized scenes from the film, as well as offering a military recruiting announcement along with Stafford, and Elliott Lewis. He also appeared on *The Pepsodent Show* on March 17, which featured a story about stolen tires with Gordon playing an eerie butler seemingly haunting an old dark house to the dismay and comedic amusement of Bob Hope and Skinnay Ennis.

In the *Cavalcade of America* episode "A Continental Uniform," broadcast on April 13, Gordon doubles again, playing General George Washington and another soldier in this story all about Benedict Arnold's treason. He again doubled on the *Cavalcade* episodes broadcast for April 20 ("In This Crisis"), May 18 ("Remember the Day"), and May 25 ("Young Tom Jefferson").

He often did premiere episodes of shows as with the first broadcast on May 16 of *The Whistler*, entitled "Retribution," in which he narrates.

In *Lux Radio Theatre* broadcasts from July 20 of *The Philadelphia Story* (credited as a war bonds benefit called *The Victory Theatre*) and September 21 of *How Green Was My Valley*, Gordon narrates. In addition, Gordon's mother Gloria doubles in the shows. Gordon played a part in *Love Crazy* on October 5 and *Wake Island* on October 26 broadcasts of the series.

The name of "Gale Gordon" was not unique. As World War II raged on, rationing news became ubiquitous. In a *Chicago Daily Tribune* clipping, entitled "Ration 835 Tires and 462 Tubes on Southwest Side," October 11, 1942, a "Gale Gordon" is among the 156 motorists allowed to buy a designated amount of tires and tubes. The "Gale Gordon" named had a Chicago address of 6312 Wentworth and he received an allotment of 4 tires, 0 tubes. Of course, this is not Gordon the actor, who would be entering the Service for the Coast Guard in a very short time.

When the war ended, one of Gordon's co-starring dramatic roles is the little gem broadcast on October 15, 1945 soon after he returned from the Coast Guard. The show, *Cavalcade of America*, offered an episode for Gordon of art imitating life entitled, "Children, This is Your Father." Gordon does not embellish the character with any of those typical Gordon touches, but he plays the part of Lieutenant Sam Lester in an appropriately straightforward manner. Though he has the same amount of airtime as his co-star Loretta Young, he unfairly is not credited before or after the story. Film star Young who plays his wife Peggy gets all the attention from the announcer.

After some four years in non-combative military service, Sam returned home without any medals to find that his two children, Mickey and Karen, do not know him. He is not even sure if they like him at all. Sam comes to learn that his children are disenchanted as their mother Peg made up stories and built-up his valor and courage, including saying that he wiped out a whole regiment of Germans when he actually was simply a desk sergeant for the supply depot.

Sam asks, "Why didn't she tell them the truth?" He laments that his family thrived without his presence these past years. However, things change when Mickey fiddles with the waffle iron and breaks it. Sam takes strong action by giving his son a whipping. Peg says that Mickey did deserve it, but that Sam should not have done it, as it was as if a stranger was hitting him.

When Mickey seems to have run away, Peg wants Sam to call the police. However, Sam, not one to panic, says he would leave the home if Peg calls the police. Peg thinks Sam is somewhat unfeeling and even calls him "a brute." Fortunately, Mickey really went to the movies.

As it turns out by the finale, the children actually like and respect their father after he stepped in to show he cared about their behavior. When Peg asks Mickey if the whipping hurt, he says to his father, "Gosh, ain't women silly?" Finally, he calls his father "Dad," and acknowledges to his Mom that his Dad hits much harder, but "it don't hurt, naahhh!"

One of the problems revealed here is that the two parents are not coming to an agreement on how to raise the children. The method of physical discipline as being the way to rear children does somehow date the show. Though probably unintended at the time of this broadcast, the show is worthwhile for it suggests that the mother has unresolved issues as regards gender relations. As do most people even today, she seems to have too quickly bought wholesale the stereotypical male/female gender expectations, and then she struggles to let them play out with all of their ramifications. In short, Peg follows gender expectations for Sam to be a statue of heroic strength and stability, and she herself acts as the stereotypical worried and over-anxious mother always dumping her insecurities on others, such as her husband.

The story brings to the surface the issue of whether a man is less of a man because he held a desk job rather than active duty in the Service, and whether the call to duty in serving your country supersedes a man's dreams and life with one having to forgo all else. In addition, the matter of how the returning veteran could be a stranger in his own home certainly makes for an interesting subtext to the story.

"Children, This Is Your Father" concludes with Sam and Peg reciting a wish poem earlier said by Karen and Mickey:

SAM:	"Hey, what comes out of the chimney?"
SAM AND PEG:	"Your wish and my wish will never be broken."
PEG:	"Touch green, my will be seen."
SAM:	"Touch green, my will be seen."
PEG:	"Touch red, my wish will be said."
SAM:	"Touch red, my wish will be said."
PEG:	"Touch blue, my wish will come true."
SAM:	"Touch blue, what the heck, my wish HAS come true!"
PEG:	"Ohhh!"

Gordon played a part in *Mail Call* from October 27, 1942 when Jack Benny and Ann Shirley appear in a dramatization of *George Washington Slept Here*, about a city dweller purchasing a house in Pennsylvania.

Gordon entered the Coast Guard at the end of the year, and did not return permanently until late in 1945. Then he made some appearances on radio shows upon returning from the service, including as Mayor LaTrivia again on *Fibber McGee and Molly*. In 1946, he was heard on *Cavalcade of America* on January 28 ("Commencement in Khaki"); *Hollywood Star Time*, on February 17 (*The Mark of Zorro*); and *The Theatre Guild on the Air* on May 12 (*Payment Deferred*). He followed up on the show the week later with, *They Knew What They Wanted*; *Birds Eye Open House* on May 23 with Betty Lou Gerson, Dinah Shore, and Harry Von Zell; and he did the *Maxwell House Coffee Time* on December 19.

Also in 1946, Gordon continued his appearances on episodes of *Lux Radio Theatre* with *The Valley of Decision* on January 14, *Honky Tonk* on April 8, *Whistle Stop* on April 15 and *Gaslight* on April 29. A caller to Schaden's program asked Gordon if he remembered playing the police officer on the radio version of *Gaslight*. Gordon said he knew he did many episodes of *Lux*, but "I don't recall that at all. *Gaslight* escapes me but then I did so many shows, several a day, at times. It was the way we could exist; make a living. You must forgive [me] but I don't remember that."

Gordon kept busy with *Lux*; for May 6 *Tomorrow Is Forever*, for October 7 *Dragonwyck*, November 18 *O.S.S.*, for December 2 *Meet Me in St. Louis*, and for December 15 *Killer Kates*.

In addition, that same year Gordon promoted a new series on the last Mutual network episode of *The New Adventures of Sherlock Holmes*, with Basil Rathbone and Nigel Bruce entitled "The Singular Affair of The Baconian Cipher," broadcast on May 27. He announced a forthcoming show in which he would play the lead of an importer/amateur detective living in a Nob Hill penthouse in San Francisco. Gordon appeared at the program's conclusion offering information about the character of Gregory Hood in the new series, *The Casebook of Gregory Hood*, which replaced the Sherlock Holmes series.

The exchange of dialogue between announcer Harry Bartell and Nigel Bruce (Dr. Watson) follows:

ANNOUNCER HARRY BARTELL (HB): "Well doctor, that was a fine story, what are you fidgeting for?"

NIGEL BRUCE AS DR. WATSON (DW): "Fidgeting . . . wah, I'm expecting a guest. I thought I heard him just now, oddly the front door."

HB: "A guest? (Laughs) You're being as mysterious as Mr. Holmes."

DW: "Oh no, not quite, you see I, Ah ha, Come in."

GALE GORDON AS GREGORY HOOD (GH): "Doctor Watson, how are you? You old rascal?"

DW:	"Gregory my boy, it's great to see you again. Mr. Bartell, Meet my friend, Mr. Gregory Hood."
HB:	"Not *The* Gregory Hood?"
GH:	"Mr. Bartell, I like the way you say that."
DW:	"Yes Mr. Bartell, this is *The* Gregory Hood."
GH:	"Mr. Bartell, if you listen to Dr. Watson he'll lead you to believe I am much more important than I am. I am quite a simple person, really. I'm kind to dogs. Just love little children, and always help old ladies cross the street. I also know how to make a fire by rubbing two sticks together."
DW:	"Yes, and unlike my old friend Holmes, you pretend to know very little about criminals and crime. And yet you're one of American's outstanding criminologists."
HB:	"So I've heard."
GH:	"A hobby, Mr. Bartell, a hobby. My real business is importing. Headquarters San Francisco. Need any old masters? Perhaps I can sell you a nice piece of jade, or uh, would you rather have a bit of old Balinese sculpture?"
HB:	"No, wait a minute. This is all a little too fast for me."
DW:	(*laughs*) "You'll learn that Mr. Gregory is a little too fast for everybody. Ah but Mr. Bartell, I'm sure you'll get to know Mr. Hood a good deal better. You see as I've told you, I always wanted to take a trip back to England, and now I have a chance to do so."

HB:	"But doctor won't I see you again? What about our stories?"
DW:	"Oh I'll shall be back in the fall but meanwhile I asked Mr. Gregory Hood to get together this time every week and tell you some of his experiences."
GH:	"Which of course makes me feel very important."
DW:	"Mr. Hood as you know has been involved in many famous cases dealing in crime. His importing business and his hobby criminology—and a strange combination, I learned that he keeps a diary of these cases, and it's a fascinating book, *The Casebook of Gregory Hood*."
HB:	"*The Casebook of Gregory Hood*. Sounds intriguing."
DW:	"Intriguing, Huh! It certainly is!"
GH:	"Thank you."
HB:	"Well then I can tell all our friends, be sure to listen next week at this same time and every Monday night through the summer to *The Casebook of Gregory Hood*."

Apparently, the earliest dated episode of *The Casebook of Gregory Hood*, before Gordon offered the plug on the Holmes program (May 27), was the episode on April 24 (broadcast again on June 24), entitled "The Adventure of the Beeswax Candle." However, "The Three Silver Pesos," broadcast on June 3, was the first official show of this new series, which ran for three seasons in total. The show followed the same format as the Sherlock Holmes broadcasts, the latter moved to ABC.

In the June 10 episode entitled "The Black Museum," Gregory Hood imports an Aztec sacrificial knife that has a curse on it.

Gordon manages to be convincing as an amateur detective. He

makes the character enjoyable in various ways including the way he voices his romantic leanings and love of gourmet cooking. In the June 17 show, "The Murder of Gregory Hood," Hood fakes his own death so he can solve a murder. By the finale, he gets close to the gorgeous Sherry. When they move to the sofa lit by the moonlight, the two are close to a hot, sexy moment. Sherry unexpectedly pulls a knife on Hood.

Hood quickly reacts, "Why you little devil!"

Sherry insists, "You got this coming to you!"

HOOD: "Why a knife! There's only one answer to that darling!"

Hood knocks her out cold.

Later, his friend "Sandy" (Sanderson Taylor, here played by Art Gilmore) gives his opinion of Hood's reaction: "That was not a very gentlemanly action, Gregory."

Hood, who often quotes his father, states, "I know Sandy, but my old father said 'Never strike a woman until she pulls a knife on you.'"

SANDY: "Shouldn't that be *unless*?"

HOOD: "My old father said *until*. Maybe that's why I'm still a bachelor."

After explaining how he pieced together the clues, including the fact that Sherry attempted a frame-up, Hood laments his ability to solve the case due to the allure of a knockout.

HOOD: "I almost wish I hadn't pieced it together quite so fast, Sandy."

SANDY: "Why Gregory?"

HOOD: "Oh, the man asked why. Sherry was a very beautiful girl, Sandy. And the moonlight was quite potent. Sometime I must tell you what my old father used to say about that."

In the fifth episode, "Murder in Celluloid," broadcast on July 1, Hood is in Hollywood where he is giving his friend some help for a film called "Passport to Danger." On the set, Hood finds Anne, an eight year old, so enamored by him; she calls him "Robin Hood." Her supposedly "stolen map" makes Hood aware that there might be spies on the set. Then Hood finds an actress strangled, and so he is involved in solving the case.

The murderer turns out to be a movie actor with Fascist leanings who strangled the actress as she was helping the spy, but stupidly confused Anne's map with the real one that is sought.

Hood confronts the murderer. The latter tries to shoot Hood, but Anne on the catwalk drops a paint bucket. That stunned the strangler, and knocked him out cold.

The cute finale in this 1946 episode would raise some eyebrows nowadays and probably be misinterpreted. Of course, Gordon plays it so that he perfectly conveys the intended innocence of the scene:

Hood asks Anne on the catwalk, "Anne darling, how can I ever thank you?"

ANNE: "Take me out to dinner, Mr. Hood. Then we could go dancing together. Is it a date?"

HOOD: "Yes darling, it's a date!"

An instrumental version of "I'm Getting Sentimental Over You" plays in the background.

HOOD: "Anne, you dance beautifully."

ANNE: "So do you, Robin Hood. I'm afraid I'm a little short for you, though."

HOOD: "Not a bit of it Anne. I like my woman petite. By the way young lady . . ."

After Anne explains how she shadowed him and came to save Hood's life. Hood again asks, "How can I ever repay you?"

ANNE:	"Well, there, is one way, Mr. Hood."
HOOD:	"What is it, Anne?"
ANNE:	"You told me at lunch that you never married because you haven't met the right woman."
HOOD:	"That's right, Anne."
ANNE:	"Keep on waiting Mr. Hood! Please keep on waiting!"

More episodes with Gordon's Hood followed; "The Derringer Society" on July 8, "South of the Border" on July 15. In "Death from the Red Capsule" broadcast on July 22, Hood unveils a poisoning that backfired. Other titles included "The Forgetful Murderer" on July 29, "The Double Diamond" on August 5, "Secret Society" on August 12, "Mad Dancer" on August 19, "Ghost Town Mortuary" on August 26, "Murder on the Archery Range" on September 2, Title Unknown on September 9, and "Missing Memoirs" on September 16.

The Casebook of Gregory Hood is Gordon's brief but fascinating foray into the "radio noir" detective genre. One critic called the show "the poor man's Sam Spade," but it seemed to have some potential for Gordon as a regular lead player introducing a new character to a national audience. It is disappointing to know that he left the series after the summer run, known to be only sixteen episodes in total, unless others surface. The show ran thru several replacements, including Elliot Lewis and Jackson Beck.

Another summer replacement series in 1946 in which Gordon played the lead is *Jonathan Trimble, Esquire*. Here he played an elderly newspaper editor in 1905 who sees his simple way of life changing due to the advances of the new century, and does what he can to fight it.

By now, Gordon had proved he could be a great character actor, and he could excel in all kinds of radio genres; including adventure, comedy, light comedy, detective, drama, historical and period productions, juvenile, and even soap operas with his finely honed vocal skills and perfect diction.

Besides appearing in *The Casebook of Gregory Hood* and *Jonathan Trimble, Esquire* in the summer of 1946, Gordon gave character support on *The Fabulous Doctor Tweedy*, featuring Frank Morgan as Dr. Tweedy, Professor of Philosophy and Dean of the College. Gordon played Mr. Alexander Potts, Chairman of the Board of Trustees. A typical episode, such as the July 21, 1946 show, has Gordon's Mr. Potts getting frustrated and flustered. In that show, Mr. Potts wants a winning Basketball team, but Dr. Tweedy manages to get him all riled up over the matter.

Gordon continued playing Mr. Potts into the following year. In the March 12, 1947 episode, "Dr. Tweedy Hires a Secretary," Dr. Tweedy (Morgan) tries to help the boy-crazy and beautiful Southern Miss Culpepper (Shirley Mitchell). The latter assumes the part as Tweedy's secretary. Of course, Dr. Tweedy comes under fire from Mr. Potts (Gordon) when Miss Culpepper sports a mink coat and a new convertible, and it is especially disturbing as a large sum of money goes missing from the office. Mr. Potts confronts Dr. Tweedy, thinking he is making a fool of himself over a woman.

Trouble ensues as the Colonel defends Miss Culpepper's honor, upholding that giving a Southern gentlewoman an expensive mink shows an intention of marriage. The Colonel boldly asks Mr. Potts, "Didn't you tell me you were brushing your toupee on Miss Culpepper's behind?" Wild audience laughter ensued for this risqué remark. The Colonel's remark turns things around by the finale as the Gordon's upright Mr. Potts is stuck in a misunderstanding and Dr. Tweedy is delighted in seeing his boss upstaged.

A week later, on the March 19 episode, "Dr. Tweedy, the Matchmaker," we have an example of how Gordon as Mr. Potts can move back and forth from one mood to another with seemingly no effort even though the flips in character might seem ridiculous at times. Despite an overly complicated plot, we hear Gordon's fine vocal skill evidenced, as his Mr. Potts is happy to announce his wife is going off on a private vacation, to leave behind housekeeper Laura. The latter is a Southern girl who Mr. Potts says will cook for him while his wife is away.

The wife fires Laura when she breaks dishes, and decides to stay home, thereby ruining Mr. Potts' planned break from being with his wife. However, the usual demonstrative and firm-sounding Mr.

Potts now sheds tears, even running away in fear ("run for the hills"), and wanting to save his own life from his wife's wrath.

Tweedy convinces Mrs. Potts to hire Laura back, but he ruins the situation when he reveals to Mrs. Potts that Mr. Potts was happy she was vacationing. Mrs. Potts complains of her husband's flirting and the fact that he went to a blonde manicurist for eight manicures in a week to help her business.

Mr. Potts is saddened and becomes distraught upon learning from Dr. Tweedy that Mrs. Potts is now planning on leaving for good and getting a divorce after twenty years of marriage. He sobs and moans, crying incessantly. Dr. Tweedy manages to restore the union, reuniting the troubled couple. But Tweedy's flattering about her beauty goes a little too far for Mr. Potts' comfort when he soft-soaps Mrs. Potts with his "inspired idea" that the two should go on a vacation to a private spot—a second honeymoon.

A delighted and charmed Mrs. Potts exclaims, "Oh, Dr. Tweedy what an exciting idea. Alexander and I together, alone, nothing to do but make love!" Mr. Potts moans with disgust as only Gordon could do so in order to get the most laughs out of the turn of events. Mr. Potts: "Ohhh!"

Throughout all the changes in his character, ranging from confident to fearful, to beside himself and suicidal, and then to overwhelmed with disgust and desirous of physically punishing Tweedy, we are made to laugh by the brilliant manner Gordon plays all the different moods of his character.

When told by a caller to Schaden that he sounded like Frank Morgan, Gordon remembered: "Oh yes dear Frank. I worked on his show. He did a radio show, *Dr. Tweedy*, and I was on that show with him. I was the head of the college. He was a dear, dear, sweet man and a wonderful man. I loved him very much."

Other 1947 activities for Gordon include making the Decca transcription of *The Freedom Train* episode entitled "The Man without a Country." He also appeared on *The Drene Show* starring Frances Langford and Don Ameche. Gordon apparently played various roles beginning with episode #4 on January 5. The week later, Gordon even played a psychiatrist trying to talk Danny Thomas out of a phone booth.

On the January 9 episode of *Maxwell House Coffee Time*, Gordon played a bank president named Mr. Vanderlip. As the story goes, Gracie is looking for work at that bank so she can get some checks back, but Gordon thinks she wants a loan. The misunderstanding gets seriously out of control thanks to Gracie. Gordon would continue to appear on episodes of that show thru the fall of 1947.

Gordon had appeared on the *Baby Snooks Show* on April 25, *The Life of Riley* show on May 10. He continued appearing on *Lux Radio Theatre* with *Leave Her to Heaven* on March 17, *One More Tomorrow* on June 9, and *The Seventh Veil* on September 15.

Gordon played a landowner named Abner in *The Greatest Story Ever Told*, broadcast on June 1, entitled "The Fruitless Fig Tree." When Abner relents and gives a man a chance to cultivate what he felt was not valuable—a fig tree, he is rewarded with a bounty. The man convinced Abner to give him a chance to show what he could do with patience.

Gordon played the prosecutor in the June 16 episode of the *New Adventures of Sherlock Holmes* entitled "Death in The North Sea." He returned the following week in "The Adventure of the Speckled Band." In the latter show, he played an angry doctor who says he traced his stepdaughter's visit to Holmes. He warns Holmes not to meddle in his affairs, and insists that he is a dangerous man when messed with. Finally, he expresses his frustration by double-bending Holmes' poker into knots.

Gordon's publicist Druxman recalled: "When he heard I was writing a book on Basil Rathbone, Gale asked me why I hadn't asked him for an interview. He then informed me that he had played 'Inspector Lestrade' on the Sherlock Holmes radio show, and then proceeded to relate several amusing Rathbone and Nigel Bruce anecdotes that I wound up using in my book *Basil Rathbone: His Life and His Films* (1975). . . . Later I set him to talk about Rathbone at a dinner meeting of the local Sherlock Holmes Society . . ."

Gordon would have had to play Lestrade between 1939 and before 1946 when Rathbone left the series. The episodes that have credited his appearance are those with Rathbone's replacement, Tom Conway. More importantly, in those with Conway, Gordon does not play Lestrade in them. However, which episodes and how many he did earlier playing Lestrade with Rathbone and Bruce has not been determined.

Gordon told Kulzer: "I also worked in several scenes with Basil Rathbone in the Sherlock Holmes radio series he did with Nigel Bruce. And that was wonderful, because here were two English gentlemen . . . and Basil Rathbone had this wonderful ability as an actor. But they were both like two school kids at play when it came to the radio show. They were getting paid, they thought, to do something that was terribly, terribly amusing—reading off of a piece of paper instead of memorizing lines. But they were both like two naughty boys. It was a complete revelation to me to see Basil Rathbone who was the epitome of dignity, class and charm, acting like a kid! They (Rathbone and Bruce) were unequally delightful!"

The summer of 1947 brought Gordon another recurring role when he played a priest named Father Leahy, on the short-lived waterfront series entitled *Johnny Madero, Pier 23*. The show, broadcast on June 19 with Jack Webb as the title character, resembles the later Webb success, *Dragnet*. Gordon's Fr. Leahy is an unusual character since he is a priest who acts as a private detective in assisting Madero by uncovering information Madero seeks.

Gordon kept busy with a *Cavalcade of America* episode broadcast on August 25, entitled "The Red Stockings" about Albert Spalding, and on September 29 entitled "Big Boy" about Babe Ruth. He also heard in *Here's to Veterans* broadcast in November (regarding *Fibber McGee and Molly*), and the *George Burns and Gracie Allen Show* on December 18.

He first appeared as retired millionaire neighbor Rumson Bullard in *The Great Gildersleeve* on November 12. The character did not appear in every episode of the show, but he appeared often enough to warrant offering excerpts from a selection of over 30 episodes in Chapter Twelve of this book.

Shirley Mitchell got to work with Gordon often, especially when he appeared on *The Great Gildersleeve*. In a phone interview in 2008, she recounted to me those exciting and busy wonderful days as a radio performer. In that show, she regularly played Gildersleeve's on-and-off-again girlfriend, the southern belle Leila Ransom.

She noted at first that she did not know how Gordon came to be on the show as Gildersleeve's neighbor Bullard. Though the show ran from 1941 to 1957, Gordon's acting on the show began in 1947.

However, she did recall how she got her part on the show. Radio performers, such as Gordon and others, shared an enthusiasm that Mitchell expressed for working in the medium back in the Golden Age of Radio.

Mitchell: "Well, they knew that I could do it. I had gone on *Gildersleeve* as doing something else. And I remember a time that I can do a Southern. And they wrote a Southern lady in one week. And then they kept me. It was fun. It was exciting, and I really miss it, even though I still do a few voiceovers. . . . I loved that part. And I'm still doing that at conventions. And when I last did it, all I said was, 'Yoo hoo, Throckmorton?' And they all started to applaud, so I guess they all loved that character. . . . There was nothing like radio then. It was just a ball!"

As regards the typically busy routine of the radio performer in her heyday, Mitchell explained: "I did four or five shows a day. We were in a contract you know, like *The Great Gildersleeve* and *The Old Gold Show*, and you'd go from show to show. The shows coincided, like, for example, you did one at two and you had another at three. You had to run from CBS to NBC. You always had a page at the door where the audience was already in(side). The special page would be waiting to open the door to let you in. You'd run in. The producer would see you, and say, 'Listen can you go onstage?'. . . I mean, you had to be pretty versatile." Shirley laughed.

As far as the scripts, changes in them, and seeing them ahead of time, Mitchell stated, "Well, yes, sometimes I didn't. But most times, I did. You would have a rehearsal. We couldn't rehearse all at the same time. One rehearsal one day, one rehearsal next morning, and then we would go out. But, if you missed a rehearsal and [in] the show there would be cuts, they would have to come out and then show you the cuts, because they have to cut it for you."

The excitement for radio performers working with other actors evolved so naturally. Mitchell: "We were all friends. It was more like a family. We all did the same shows week after week. It was really great! Gale had a fabulous sense of humor. He and his wife had a wonderful marriage. She had been an actress, Virginia Gordon. And she was jolly too and she adored him . . . so they had a great relationship. They were an enhancement to any show. Gale also got along great with his mother, who also was an actress.

"We worked in *Fibber McGee and Molly*. In fact, we worked together on quite a few shows. I really enjoyed when *Fibber* would have a cast party and we would all be together. He would have a little drink and then would tell us stories, and we would all go hysterical. He had great stories. He was a big gas offstage and onstage.

"I mean he never took the actor thing that seriously. He was a typical British man and enjoyed his drink—I mean after a show, or whenever we had a party. And he would tell the most wonderful stories. Unfortunately, I don't remember any of them. He kept us hysterical all the time. He had a fabulous sense of humor. And he played that droll Englishman, you know. And he did it brilliantly. There was never anybody quite like him after he finished."

Of course, Mitchell erred when she said Gordon was "a typical British man."

Mitchell continued: "Then he came on *The Lucy Show*, I guess it was the second Lucy show. I wasn't on that one. The show was great as long as he was on it. I don't know sometimes I think they didn't know how to use him. But by then I think Lucy missed Desi so much and so nothing would have saved that show."

Gordon did not stay in character when his scene was over, unlike those actors that keep being their characters all the time. Mitchell: "No, no, he was not like that. All the characters were quite different from the man. Gale was a darling sweet man. When he got to know you, he had an explosive humor, and everybody adored him. I don't think he had an enemy in the business. I'm sure he didn't."

This might be true but for Mel Blanc. In his autobiography, *That's Not All Folks!* Blanc mentioned an incident that kept him from ever socializing again with Gordon. To be fair to Blanc, the entire reference follows:

Blanc writes, "About the only person in our informal clique that I didn't get along with was Gale Gordon, the 1930s radio voice of *Flash Gordon*, among many others. He also played Lucille Ball's crusty, tormented foil on TV's *The Lucy Show* and *Here's Lucy*. If ever there was an example of typecasting, Gordon as Theodore J. Mooney and Harrison Otis Carter (eventually a reprise of the same role) was it.

"I ran into him a few days after Noel was born and announced proudly, 'Gale, guess what?—I'm a father!'

"His eyes narrowed, his mouth puckered—the same sourpuss expression for which he'd later be paid exorbitantly—and he sneered: 'Big Deal!' Not only didn't I receive his good wishes, Gordon went into a tirade about never wanting children because they 'pester you to death.' I thought to myself, *You schmuck*. Ironically, he and his wife eventually adopted. But from that day on, I steered clear of him."

However, Blanc's claim that Gordon adopted may have been a rumor and it remains unconfirmed. The only adoptions for the Gordons seemed to have been their dogs.

When Mitchell learned of what Blanc said in his book, she responded: "I was surprised that Mel did that, I really am." She explained that such exchanges between people do happen, and things can be taken the wrong way. However, Mitchell added, "I don't think it was that important. It was what one man wanted, and the other man didn't. And you have to respect people for what they want and what they don't want." Even Mitchell did not recall that the Gordons ever adopted a child.

Mitchell: "Oh, everybody adored him and he was a brilliant actor, a brilliant comedian." As regards his perfect comic timing, Mitchell acknowledged, "That's right, it was perfect." Mitchell recalled that Gordon did not need a lot of rehearsal time: "No, I mean we all rehearsed the same amount. His first reading was just as good as when he did it on the air!"

The Gordons got home and put aside their professional life. He would be doing things with his dogs, his swimming pool, and so forth. As far as she knows, they were loners and kept to themselves. They read a lot. Mitchell simply concluded: "They were homebodies. They weren't big social people."

In fact, Mitchell explained that she did not know Gordon outside of the time she spent doing shows with him on radio. Mitchell: "I know he liked me, and he liked my work. That I know. I don't know anything very personal. I never was in their home. We didn't do anything like that. No, we're just very good friends. I always saw him at work . . . . And I saw his wife at work a good deal."

Unfortunately, Mitchell said she did not really see Gordon much after the Golden Age of Radio ended. Mitchell: "No, you got too involved. When you were on T.V., you just went from show to show. It was in radio that I know him well because we had worked together . . . . I [then] saw him at Bob Sweeney's funeral. Yes, he was good friends with him. We just exchanged a big kiss of love and that was the last time I saw him."

In 1948, Gordon began an association with Lucille Ball that would last for many years when he played a part in *My Favorite Husband*. In that radio precursor to television's later *I Love Lucy*, Gordon acted as her husband's boss, the banker named Rudolf Atterbury.

As the typical over-controlling boss, Atterbury expected his worker George and spouse Liz to do things to please his clients. As an example, he wants Liz to teach his client's son how to dance. Liz self-deprecatingly agrees saying, "Gladly, she says, with a cold muzzle of a revolver at each temple."

Of course, the oblivious Atterbury tends not to take his workers' concerns seriously. One time, when Liz tells George he should ask Mr. Atterbury for a raise, the cocky Atterbury thinks George does not have even the nerve to ask him.

Gordon told Schaden: ". . . the idea in those days that anyone that was a boss of a bank had to be a blowhard." It is well-known that Gordon had a fondness for working with Lucy. He declared happily that it was, "Always a joy working with her in no matter what media."

Besides working with Lucy on radio in that comedic role, he continued playing serious parts: case in point, a sinister role in the March 7 episode of *The Shadow* entitled "The Beast of Darrow." The legendary story has a thirty-year-old hound that defends his dead master's mansion and the money hidden therein. Gordon plays the villainous accented Dr. Lyle Travick, a paranormal authority, who pretends to help an ancestor who inherited the house by hiring a dog trainer to spook the woman. Bret Morrison plays the Shadow.

Some news clips at this time gave Gordon attention, in particular the following:

On February 25, 1948, *LAT* reported, "Gale Gordon, identified with the Burns and Allen radio show, will do a featured part in Jack Chertok's *Hill of the Hawk* production." What happened to this production is unknown.

On March 10, 1948, *LAT* reported, "Gale Gordon is seeking to assemble stock company made up of radio actors who are anxious to vary their activities with stage appearances. Martin Ragaway and William Tracy are in on the plan and they hope to build a theater."

On April 11, 1948, *New York Times* noted, "Barbara Whiting stars as Judy Graves and Gale Gordon plays her father in *Junior Miss* comedy show on CBS Saturdays at 11:30 p.m."

On May 21, 1948, *LAT* revealed, "Gale Gordon will portray the father of Eddie Bracken in *.750 Smith*, Bracken's independent feature." However, for some reason, Gordon did not do the film.

One undated press clip from this time noted, "Gale Gordon is proposing a revival of the John Barrymore play, *My Dear Children*, and would like to obtain Elaine Barrymore for a leading part."

Another clip entitled "Gale Gordon to Tour," announced, "Gale Gordon, character actor, will make a personal tour in Texas and Louisiana in late August. Gordon has a large fan following in Texas."

In "Gale Gordon Signs for Laguna Stage," *LAT*, August 1, 1948: "Gale Gordon, who will appear in the Eddie Bracken film, *.750 Smith*, today signed to star in a summer theater engagement of *My Dear Children*, the John Barrymore play of several years back. Gordon will also be cast as the father in a Laguna Beach presentation of *Junior Miss*."

Some may say it may have been simply the publicity machine churning out the article, "Gale Gordon Chalks up 5,000 Radio Appearances," *Chicago Daily Tribune*, December 5, 1948. The clipping noted, "Gale Gordon, who's been on *Fibber McGee and Molly* and several other NBC shows, made his 5,000th broadcast recently. He's been in radio for 20 years and averages 26 shows a month." It does seem very likely that he could have reached that number of appearances given his very busy schedule; although the total number shows that could be confirmed, at this point, is closer to 2,000.

On *The Phil Harris-Alice Faye Show*, Gordon played Mr. Scott, the sponsor's representative, as well as other parts early on. He appeared in *The Charlie McCarthy Show, Cavalcade of America* ("The Enlightened Professor"), and *The Little Immigrant* audition on June 15. He did the *NBC University Theatre's* version of *Gulliver's Travels* on September 24, and *Tell It Again's* version of *Gulliver's Travels* on December 12.

The Little Immigrant happened to be the first show of a new series, which would become the script used on *Life with Luigi* for

September 21. Gordon would join Margaret Whiting and Norma Jean Nilsson in *Meet Me in St. Louis* on May 29. The latter would be an audition for a proposed musical comedy radio show based on the movie of the same title.

Gordon played different parts when he worked on Dennis Day's show. He showed his flair for being a con artist in an episode of *A Day in the Life of Dennis Day*, broadcast January 14, 1948, entitled "Modern Art." Dennis and his girlfriend's father, Mr. Anderson, pretend to be cops to obtain a "stolen" forged painting with the name of modern artist Dunning (Gordon). It turns into a windfall for Dunning when he realizes it is not one of his originals. He makes a trade with them for one of his real "Dunning originals." However, he actually swindled them out of what was really an original Picasso painting worth $10,000.

Gordon continued his characteristic blowhard later that year in another episode of Dennis Day's show, entitled "The Bookie," broadcast June 23. When Dennis does an errand for Mrs. Anderson (his landlady) to pick up a layette for her friend expecting a baby, he mistakenly takes the $50 and bets the money on a horse at a bookie club. Then he tries to stop the bet to retrieve the money. As a result, Dennis manages to drive one of the bookies crazy, none other than a tongue-tied and intensely exasperated Gordon in a funny phone exchange.

In the *Judy Canova Show* broadcast on October 23, Gordon does doubles. He plays a Southern accent-sounding cigar spokesman showing his deadpan humor and adeptness at poking fun at commercials by the way he delivers the copy. Gordon also plays Judy's agent, Mr. Mansfield.

Here Judy dreams of getting an Oscar and acts like a dramatic actress. When Judy tries to impress him with her dramatic acting, Mansfield pretends along with Judy's hammy dramatics to act like her British servant (and her straight man). In response, he tells her: "Oh Judy, be yourself, anyone can make an audience cry, but who can make them laugh?" When a man named Oscar acknowledges her skill, Mansfield says, "Well Judy, you finally won your Oscar!"

In 1949 and 1950, Gordon continued on six to seven shows every week regularly making appearances on *Fibber McGee and Molly, The Great Gildersleeve, My Favorite Husband, Our Miss Brooks, The Phil*

Harris and Alice Faye Show, and *A Day in the Life of Dennis Day.* In addition, he did some episodes of *Blackstone, The Magic Detective.* The February 27, 1949 episode of the latter show has Gordon playing a producer friend named Steven Philips who is part of a baby-kidnapping scheme. He continued doing episodes of *Lux Radio Theater* as with the February 14 broadcast of *Sitting Pretty,* besides returning to *Maxwell House Coffee Time.*

Gordon would do two audition shows (one for private viewing by potential sponsors) playing the lead character Dr. William Todhunter Hall in *The Halls of Ivy,* beginning on June 23. The following year, 1950, the show reached the airwaves with the lead played by Ronald Colman. Gordon would lend support playing Charles Merriweather. Don Quinn wanted to do something else, so he wrote *Halls* after quitting as writer of *Fibber McGee and Molly.*

Also in 1950, Gordon would play Judge Beshomer Grundell on the summer show episodes of *The Penny Singleton Show,* beginning on May 30.

A new entry for Gordon began a few months earlier on March 30 with *Granby's Green Acres,* about a city bank clerk, John Granby (played by Gordon), who quits his job and decides he wants to be a farmer and grow his own food. Granby's farm is replete with all sorts of unexpected problems, as he cannot do anything right. Bea Benaderet played John's wife Martha. Parley Baer played Eb, the hired hand who knows more than Granby. The radio show purportedly inspired the 1960s television series, *Green Acres.*

The audition show focuses on mounting problems when Granby realizes how ill prepared he is to run a farm. One of the problems is that he has no electricity, and he does not want to pay to install it. Gordon's Granby gets tongue-tied alone here, and he does not need the McGees (as in *Fibber McGee and Molly*) to facilitate his confusion.

Only six episodes circulate of the nine shows produced. On the episode broadcast on July 10, entitled "Granby Plants a Crop," the question of whether to plant corn or wheat becomes Granby's obsessive concern. He tries to gauge what will be in most demand at the market. He eventually decides to split his farmland by growing corn, wheat, and soybeans only to be dismayed to learn that red warblers (potatoes) hit a ten-year high. This episode's opening features

John, Martha and Janice singing a line to the tune of "Old MacDonald Had a Farm." Gordon sings the line, "Old John Granby had a farm."

On the July 17 show, "Mr. Granby Discovers Electricity," Granby decides he needs an electric milker, so he sells the cow to raise money to pay to wire the house for electricity.

On the July 24 show, "Mr. Granby Fights the Love Bug," Granby is having a problem with his corn crop, but he will not take advice.

On the July 31 show, "Mr. Granby Lays an Egg," Granby buys two hundred chickens for egg production and wonders why they are not laying. Of course, he realizes too late that they are all roosters!

For the eighth and final show of the summer series, broadcast on August 21, "Mr. Granby Breaks Down," Granby's problem is that the noise on the farm is taking its toll on him. Granby complains that his "nerves are on edge. . . I think I'm gonna have a nervous breakdown!" Even when he tries to sleep, everything affects him; including the ticking clock, birds chirping, and a dripping faucet. He reluctantly goes to Dr. Pearson, a woman doctor who gives him a prescription that makes him feel good right away. He finds out it is simply sugar and water! Unsatisfied, he goes to the city to see a specialist named Dr. Conried.

In order to find out why he cannot sleep, the doctor asks Granby what his occupation has been for the past 20 years. Granby starts to run down the various positions he held at the bank, but then the doctor interrupts him.

DR. CONRIED: "Mr. Granby, you don't have to tell me anything more. I know exactly what is wrong with you."

GRANBY: "What?"

DR. CONRIED: "You need an occupational readjustment."

GRANBY: "An occupational readjustment?"

DR. CONRIED: "Yes, you should get out of the city and buy yourself a farm."

GRANBY: "Doctor?"

DR. CONRIED: "Yes."

GRANBY: "I'm going to kill you!"

The show concludes with the announcer bringing back Gordon's John Granby who asks listeners to send a postcard to tell their local CBS station how much they enjoyed the show's summer run (and they will forward the messages to the show's makers). Apparently, audience response was insufficient, and the show did not return in the fall. Clearly, the show became somewhat tiresome with each successive episode, despite the humor of some silly situations. The show needed something more than just an excited Gordon raising his voice.

Next Gordon appeared on *The Lucky Strike Program Starring Jack Benny* from October 1, 1950 about the time when someone stole Jack's Maxwell. Gordon played in *The Halls of Ivy* for October 11 and November 1. He did the audition recording for the Cary Grant-Betsy Drake series, *Mr. and Mrs. Blandings*, on November 8. The latter show would run weekly beginning in 1951, and Gordon would be a cast regular starting with the first show on January 21.

Gordon's first television appearance came in 1950 (exact broadcast date unknown), when he played a doctor in *The Marionette Mystery*. Regis Toomey presented this murder mystery with various players giving their own impressions of what occurred.

In 1951 and 1952, Gordon continued with his recurring roles on *Fibber McGee and Molly*, *My Favorite Husband*, *Our Miss Brooks*, and *The Phil Harris-Alice Faye Show*.

In 1951, Gordon did an audition for a new situation comedy *All About Anne* on March 30. It told the story of a family in Scarsdale and their lovable teen-age daughter. Though unconfirmed, it sounds similar to *Junior Miss*.

Gordon played in the *Lux Radio Theatre* on November 19 in *Samson and Delilah*, and on December 24 in *Alice in Wonderland*. Gordon played the Caterpillar in the latter Lewis Carroll classic.

In 1952, Gordon was heard on *The Halls of Ivy* (including the January 23, May 14, and June 11 shows), *The Adventures of Ozzie and Harriet* (April 18), and *Junior Miss* (October 2).

In 1953, Gordon continued with *The Phil Harris-Alice Faye Show* for June 14 and *Richard Diamond, Private Detective* on September 6.

When Gordon played the typical stuffy situation-comedy father Harry Graves in *Junior Miss*, he brought laughs to the radio show by acting prissy and his family does not take him seriously. In the January 5 episode, Harry is absorbed in his planned solo with the Glee Club, singing at the breakfast table and in the bathroom. His daughter, the loveable teenager Judy (Barbara Whiting), decides to become an actress even though her father Harry does not approve. The wife goes along with her daughters correcting Harry for tending to change his mind and confuse the children.

When Harry tries to make another point, he upsets his children (Judy and Lois) when he gets literary characters from Dickens mixed up, such as thinking Ebenezer Scrooge is in *Oliver Twist*. He does not know where the different characters belong in Dickens' books.

HARRY: "I don't care where they belong. All I care about is that Judy belongs in school, not out trying to be an actress. Just get the idea of the stage out of your head."

JUDY: "Gee."

HARRY: "We don't need any Gees."

Not happy with his situation, he tries to be patient. We can hear in his voice the levels of restraint as well as tension, indicating what a master Gordon could be when called upon to make it all sound convincing. Gordon knew how to play it so that you could feel sorry for him and his family's predicament.

Eventually he talks so much that he loses his voice by the finale ("Father, do you want us to get the throat spray?") Now we know his frustration will overwhelm him for he will not get to do his solo.

There is a certain pomposity to Gordon's character here in *Junior Miss* just as in other radio shows, such as *Fibber McGee and Molly* and *Our Miss Brooks*. Gordon created the same basic characterization on these and other radio shows. He would continue to use it when he appeared on television. Undoubtedly, Gordon's lesser-known radio career significantly influenced and determined his now better-remembered television career.

The following year in another episode of *Junior Miss*, this one broadcast July 1, 1954 the question is "What to do on a lazy Saturday afternoon at home?" The episode, commonly entitled "The Rainy Day," revolves around how all typical weekend plans are ruined by the weather. Of course, everyone is upset and disappointed. For example, father wanted to go play golf. Judy wanted to go to Jones Beach with her friend. In short, all look out the window lamenting their lost day. Harry's wife Grace also adds to the spoiled day by telling him he is not good at golf.

When accused of doodling on magazines, father denies it. When he finally admits it, the question is, why does he draw earrings on Clark Gable? He explains that he just wanted to see how Gable might look with them.

Gordon brings life to his modulating voice (changing tempos and almost like singing it): "Alright I do doodle, I like to doodle, I like to doodle, I love to doodle, I love to doodle!" With the final line, he brings audience laughter. Gordon's father character here seems to be the sensible one at times, but his family is somewhat mocking and not giving him the deserved respect.

When Judy plays a song multiple times on the piano, it drives father crazy. Gordon's character is getting exasperated, raising his voice. Judy still plays the piano feeling it is a good thing to stop thinking about the rain. Lois and mother file their nails. When long-suffering father tries to distract himself and read a book, he still cannot concentrate. He continues to be irritated. Eventually father starts yelling in frustration. He says he would rather listen to the rain than what he calls "a Spike Jones concert."

Then Judy's friend comes over and suggests playing Lotto; however, father is doubtful that would be a good thing. Of course, a simple game turns into still more opportunities to knock father in some way and his game playing. Nevertheless, their tiredness in playing so many games keeps them from thinking about the weather. Apparently, the housekeeper Hilda saw how occupied they were, and she did not want to interrupt the family togetherness to tell them the rain stopped.

Strangely rejuvenated, the show ends humorously as father decides they will continue now until midnight playing, with him calling the numbers fast, and even forcing Hilda to play. Gordon manages to make it funny by his bossy and curmudgeonly manner.

Moreover, we see the pattern common to so many of his later characters already established firmly by this time. Gordon's character foibles involve him taking things seriously, bossing everyone around, being an uptight asshole, and showing he is not in control of anything. All the while, he made it so funny.

During 1954 through 1957, Gordon continued regularly on *Our Miss Brooks*, and little else. In 1955, Gordon joined radio's *My Little Margie*. In the April 10 episode from that year, Margie's father Verne Albright decides to run for mayor, but he is seemingly threatened by a gambler named Johnny Velvet. The latter said he would push Mr. Albright into concrete. However, his intentions were benign as it turns out what he meant was he really would make a statue of him in tribute. Gordon played the fast-talking Texan named Mr. Peters, the President of the Merchants Association.

The one character that Gordon achieved the greatest height of success, already mentioned in passing, but deserving more attention now, had to be the only character he played on both radio (and television); that is the ill-tempered Osgood T. Conklin on *Our Miss Brooks*.

Chapter Five: "Oh You Do-o-o-o!"

"We were just a family. You can't work with people for six days a week, which is what it was with the radio show and the TV show. Gale treated me as if I were a relative. . . . Gale was a second father to me."
—Gloria McMillan, actress,
Harriet Conklin on *Our Miss Brooks*

If there were one radio show that best exhibits the quintessential comedic talent of Gale Gordon, then it would be his successful stint as high school Principal Osgood Conklin in *Our Miss Brooks*. Some of his expressions, said infrequently, would stay with the listener long after hearing the programs. The utterances, such as "Oh You Do-o-o-o!" and variations of that, such as "Oh You Did-d-d! and "Oh He Does-s-s!," were said in such a way that only Gordon could make such remarks sound so incredibly funny when said at the right moment.

His comedy is one of a careful alternation between loud and exaggerated emotions followed by calm and quiet reacting. His comedy is one of absurd situations and his extreme gestures and outbursts. The trick of making it all so funny is definitely in Gordon's superb and captivating delivery, and mastery of the double take and the slow burn.

Gordon found a plum role as the pompous and overbearing Mr. Conklin, who oftentimes found himself physically hurt or perhaps stuck at the dirty end of situations thanks to the careless and often stupid machinations led by the wisecracking high school English teacher Miss Connie Brooks. Eve Arden played the teacher magnificently tongue-in-cheek, and it is worth detailing how Gordon got the part as it shows that sometimes Gordon's ever-increasing salary demands may have prevented him from getting more work, at least initially.

Gordon explained: "As it happened, I had left in the middle of *Fibber McGee and Molly*, and had come back to that show. They paid me $150 a show, and that was a lot of money in those days. I was grateful that my job was waiting for me when I came back from the service.

"So I went to work for them and got my $150 a week. And then other people would call and offer me $50 or $25 a show, which as a salary was very small in those days. I turned them down. When I'd tell people that I wanted $150, they almost fainted. They thought I was an upstart and an egomaniacal idiot.

"Finally, a man called from CBS. 'We're doing a summer replacement show with Eve Arden, and there's a part we'd like you to do.' I said, 'That's very nice.' And they said, 'How much do you want?' I replied, '$150 a show.' He shouted, '$150 A SHOW!' and almost fainted. I'm sure he had a mild stroke. He said, 'CBS cannot pay that amount of money.' So that was that.

"My wife and I went on a brief vacation at Santa Ysidro Ranch near Santa Barbara, California. While we were there, we heard the radio show of *Our Miss Brooks*. We both looked at each other when the show was over and Virginia said, 'Thank God they didn't pay you the $150 because that's the worst show I've ever heard.'

"They had a high school Principal on there who was barking like a dog, and speaking in improper English, which is one thing that drives me crazy. We're just congratulating ourselves when the producer called the next day and said, 'Alright, we'll pay you the $150. We want you to do the part.' They hadn't liked the man who played the role. And that was how I got the role in *Our Miss Brooks*. The only episode I didn't do was the first one."

Gordon remembered correctly the inferior quality to the episode he heard, particularly that the Mr. Conklin character seemed to bark. What happened is that every time Mr. Conklin got angry his dog would start barking. Of course, his wife and others told Mr. Conklin to stop barking.

One thing Gordon did not mention is that before he played Mr. Conklin, there are at least two shows with the same storyline, each with a different actor playing the principal. Besides, before those shows, there is the surviving pilot episode, recorded on April 9, 1948, but not broadcast, featuring Shirley Booth as Connie Brooks. This is the only time Arden did not play the English teacher.

The second audition of *Our Miss Brooks*, this one broadcast on June 23, 1948, had Joseph Forte as Mr. Conklin. What may be the third recorded episode, broadcast on July 19, 1948, had Will Wright as Mr. Conklin, and this one is considered the show's debut even though it is a re-staging of the June 23 audition. There are possibly two more shows with Wright (July 26, 1948 and August 2, 1948), before Gordon took over the role of Mr. Conklin beginning with the August 9, 1948 episode.

Anyone listening to the *Our Miss Brooks* shows with Forte or Wright will quickly realize that they both admittedly lack the truly inspired delivery and comedic timing offered by the inimitable Gordon.

Gordon told Simons a slightly different account that credits himself, not his wife, who realized, "I said, 'Well, thank God I turned that down, because it's going to be thrown off the air. No town or PTA would be happy to have a principal sounding like an idiot,' and we'd hardly finished talking about it, and the phone rang, and CBS said, 'We'll pay you the $150. That's starting next week,' and then I was furious I hadn't asked for more money."

Gordon told Kulzer: "Very often people would stop me on the street and ask, 'why are you so mean to Miss Brooks?' The audience took it very literally. People still do that today. They expect you to be funny on a moment's notice, or in my case, they get angry. Once I had a woman stop me and say, 'Please, yell at my children!' People forget that it's all put on. We're pretending!"

Kulzer told of how Gordon remembered with tenderness the cast. Gordon: "The whole troupe was like a family. Gloria McMillan, the girl who played my daughter 'Harriet' . . . her father died when she was quite young. When she got married, I stood up for her, and gave her away."

McMillan got married in 1954, and a photo appeared in the papers with the headline, "SURPRISE!—Eve Arden, who plays title role in CBS Radio's *Our Miss Brooks*, and Gale Gordon, who plays principal, display proper surprise at news Gloria McMillan, who plays Principal's daughter, is to wed Gil Allen, SC student. From left, Miss McMillan, Gordon and Miss Arden. Gordon will give radio daughter away."

Gordon remembered: "Also, Eve had a Christmas Party every year just for the cast. To avoid buying presents for everyone, we'd draw names out of a hat, and buy a gift for the person in the cast whose names we had drawn. This made shopping very exciting trying to figure out what to get for Dick Crenna or Janie Morgan. The holidays were very important to Eve. She'd bring a Christmas tree down to the studio during Christmas week. We'd have treats and goodies.

"I had high regard for a great many actors. I started out as a serious actor. I didn't start out as a comic actor at all. That just developed because I happened to be louder than anyone else. If they wanted a blowhard character, they called on me. I've had innumerable people that I've respected and venerated. As a matter of fact, in later life, got to play with some of them which delighted me."

Of course, Arden worked her character superbly and offered wonderful deadpan humor and one-liners. Gordon: "Eve Arden was a dear, dear woman. That part came on radio in 1946. I remember that it was 1946 because it was a year after I had gotten out of the service. My wife, while I was gone, had decided that since I missed out on so much during the years I was in the service that I ought to establish a fee, a salary, and not to do any show for less than that certain fee." Gordon erred here as the *Our Miss Brooks* show began in 1948.

Life imitates art as Gordon acted as a surrogate father to the actress who played Harriet. In a 2008 interview McMillan revealed, "Gale was a second father to me. My father died when I was ten in Los Angeles. I came to Hollywood when I was seven. And my first job [was] with Edward G. Robinson on *Big Town*. And I worked all my life until I got married. And Gale being my surrogate father . . ."

As regards memories of Gordon and the rest of the cast, McMillan stated, "Oh gosh. I have so many memories. Not specific stories, but I would go out on dates or I would come back, or I would bring someone I was dating to the set, and, oh boy, I had a family, I tell ya. They all gave me their opinion, you know, in their own good-natured way. And they'd say, 'no, I think he's too old for you,' or, 'no, I don't know about that. You're too young . . .' They were literally involved in my life. They really were. And when I got married then, of course,

Gale was the only one I would've had to escort me down the aisle. He was a wonderful human being. He later was godfather to my daughter Janet . . . . Four years after I got married I had my first child."

As regards to the show and Gordon, McMillan recalled, "I think the most unique thing about the show I said to you was whenever anybody had problems, anyone had things to celebrate or anything we really were a family. There was no fighting at all. And I say that with total honesty. There were no egos to be fed. Gale was one of the finest human beings I ever known. Dick Crenna and Gale Gordon spent most of the time on the set with Eve. And all of us laughing, telling jokes, making fun. It was not like work. There were no egos, no star. And he and Gale set that tone. There were no stars. We were just family, a company, ensemble.

"[Gale] was hysterical. He would spend the time off camera when they would be resetting a shot or if we took a break or had whatever— Gale and Dick Crenna, and Eve. It was like a comedy show. They were so—we had so much, Eve, just had so much fun. Even the crew said, 'Gosh, we never worked [on] a show like this. It's just so much fun going on. Everybody likes everybody.' And I do think that was due to Eve . . . She didn't think of herself as a star or better than anybody else. She simply was part of us. And that really, that went through everybody—the costumes people, the wardrobe people, the prop people. Everybody was a family to her and she was very kind and gracious. And there was no star attitude whatsoever. Not with any of them.

"Gale would tell stories. He would sit at the desk and one particular set that was his office in the high school as you remember it. And he would put his feet upon the desk, and Dick Crenna (would) go in and sit down and the two of them would proceed to make everybody just laugh. Everybody would just have fun. I'm telling you it was very rare because (on) most of the television sets there always stars and a kind of an edge. You know, as a kid growing up I worked with many film stars and there was always that feeling of 'they were stars, and we were the actors.' And it was never like that on *Brooks*. . . And that was due to Eve, Gale, Dick, and everybody."

Upon examining some of the shows, one gains an appreciation for the seemingly lost art of outrageous and ridiculous comedy. One example of Gordon's superb mastery of the double take is the April 24, 1949 episode, entitled "Dress Code Protest."

When high school student Walter Denton wears Miss Brooks' dress in protest of the new dress code. Mr. Conklin mistakes Walter for a girl.

MR. CONKLIN: "Now, what's your name?"

WALTER: (nervously) "Walter Denton."

MR. CONKLIN: "I see. Well, that's a lovely dress you have on Walter. I wish some of our (pause, and then shouts) THAT'S A LOVELY DRESS YOU HAVE ON WALTER?"

There is the issue of how incredulous Mr. Conklin can be when he emphatically does not believe Miss Brooks claim that her skirt was ripped bending down in her classroom. He does not buy her phony explanation of why she is wearing Harriet's gym bloomers. Miss Brooks is ordered by Mr. Conklin to put something on besides the bloomers (what he calls "those black laundry bags").

Later, Mr. Conklin himself sees how easily this could happen as he is caught, by the school superintendent Mr. Stone, wearing Miss Brooks' torn skirt because his pants were taken to get cleaned after they got damaged.

Mr. Stone demands an explanation similar to the way Mr. Conklin does the same to his staff. It is interesting to see the sheepish subordinate Mr. Conklin get a dressing down now from his superior.

The ever-increasing absurdity of many of the *Our Miss Brooks* episodes becomes quite apparent as the series continued. In order to garner laughs, the show chose to pick ridiculous situations that would require listeners to bring with them a strong suspension of disbelief. For example, in the August 7, 1949 episode entitled "Heat Wave," the plan is to break Mr. Conklin's fan so he cannot stand the heat, and consequently he will cancel classes. Then the faculty and students could go swimming.

A poorly coordinated effort has everyone scheming. This leads Miss Brooks, Mr. Boynton, and a student (Stretch Snodgrass) to be packed into Mr. Conklin's closet, with Miss Brooks turning on his electric heater. Undoubtedly, this causes Mr. Conklin's coats to catch on fire.

Oftentimes, Mr. Conklin is the constantly battered and frustrated victim of mishaps. An example is the episode broadcast on October 16, 1949, entitled "School Safety." Miss Brooks, in an effort to avoid causing any mishaps to Mr. Conklin, finds out how difficult that can really be.

The number of mishaps mount without consideration to probability. First, a careless Miss Brooks damages Mr. Conklin's car. Then she closes the car door on his arm. Next Miss Brooks throws a student's lit firecracker in the supply closet not realizing Mr. Conklin is in there. Then she pushes Mr. Conklin to go in the elevator, not realizing there is no elevator—so he falls in the shaft.

A SURPRISED MR. CONKLIN YELPS: "Ahhhhhh!"

MISS BROOKS: "Are you alright, Mr. Conklin?"

MR. CONKLIN: "I'm splendid. But WHERE'S THE ELEVATOR?"

In addition, Miss Brooks squirts Mr. Conklin with the fire extinguisher. Then she drops it on his foot. The abuse continues as Mr. Conklin falls down the stairs due to a broken handrail. Of course, Miss Brooks failed to warn Mr. Conklin in time. Finally, Mr. Conklin falls down the elevator shaft again because he thought the elevator now worked. That is, a student removed the "Out of Order" sign that was there earlier, and placed it on a broken fire extinguisher.

One of the typical examples of Gordon getting to do his slow burn and blowhard shtick and the persistent comic absurdity of many of the *Our Miss Brooks* shows is the October 8, 1950 episode (some date it as January 22, 1950), entitled "Walter's Radio" or "The Hurricane Warning."

Here, Mr. Conklin discusses his order of brand new custom-built Malacca bamboo furniture. Walter Denton responds with his opinion, "Oh, I don't know. I think bamboo furniture is kind of icky myself."

GORDON: "Oh You Do-o-o-o!"

Simply told, this episode is about the confusion caused by Denton's home-built short-wave radio receiver. The latter is receiving weather alerts warning that listeners should board up all windows and doors with bamboo. The alerts cause Mr. Conklin to follow instructions, which means the destruction of his new furniture.

The confusion becomes apparent when the radio announcer adds, "Disperse all natives to the hills." Soon thereafter, Mr. Conklin realizes something is wrong when the announcer offers the last official warning: "Before you prepare to your storm cellar, be sure to tether your elephants carefully! Tether your elephants carefully."

MR. CONKLIN: "Quick, quick, there's not a minute to lose. Get outside and tether my elephants. (Double take) Elephants? Did that man say elephants?"

BOYNTON: "I thought he did, Mr. Conklin."

MR. CONKLIN: (shocked) "Who keeps elephants?"

Then the radio announcer gives the location of the station as downtown Bombay, India. They all start laughing. Gordon too is laughing, but he is slowly working himself up the anger ladder.

The scene is an example of how Gordon's slow burn builds-up to an angry outburst.

Mr. Conklin reviews the situation, saying, at first calmly, "Imagine closing down an entire high school, wrecking a room full of furniture, because a report on some idiot's home-made radio, (tension builds) telling of a hurricane, (screaming) 5000 MILES AWAY!"

In short, Mr. Conklin has come to realize the folly of his reaction to the radio reports that made him destroy his new furniture.

Although it did not happen too often, there are moments when radio's greatest talents, such as Gordon and Arden, flubbed their lines. One example of this is in the *Our Miss Brooks* episode from May 31, 1953, called by some "The Cosmo Article," in which *Cosmopolitan Magazine* is planning to do a story about Madison High. Interestingly, Eve Arden flubs her first lines. Jeff Chandler messes up his lines, and Gordon misreads a line. The fun in listening to so many of these shows, especially with a pro like Gordon, is searching for the line errors made in these live radio broadcasts.

Art imitates life when Gordon's wife Virginia played Mr. Conklin's wife in *Our Miss Brooks*. Gordon: "She played the role on radio and for the first year of the television series. But we were in an automobile accident, a truck rammed us while we were on vacation. She had a whiplash and had to give up the role. She never went back to it. However, she was the original 'Mrs. Conklin.'" Unfortunately, so little is known about Gordon's wife as she seemed to stay out of the limelight, and Gordon had little to say about her.

Television had beckoned for the cast because of the radio success of *Our Miss Brooks*. CBS broadcasted the television show from October 3, 1952 to September 21, 1956. Produced by Larry Berns for Desilu, the show ran for a reported one hundred and twenty-seven episodes. Audiences finally could see how a radio talent like Gordon acted and the way he looked after hearing his elaborate histrionics for years on radio. Gordon portrayed the character with his perfect facial mannerisms and body language, which would make viewers go wild with laughter.

McMillan: "I started in *Brooks* when I was, let's see, gosh, I was a young teenager, and I did the radio show from day one. . . . For a number of years we did the radio and the television show concurrently, and we also did a film for Warner Brothers, a movie of *Our Miss Brooks*. . . . And I think our show was unusual because they didn't audition for those parts. They didn't audition for the film. They didn't audition for the television show. We were always a unit, and I think that's really unusual. There's always somebody that's cut out, or that doesn't get taken with the company. I know that's very rare, very unusual.

"One day we just came to work to do the radio show and the producer (Larry Berns) said, 'Well, guess what? We're going to television and you're all going with us and that's what happened. . . . Jane Morgan, who played Mrs. Davis our landlady, would say, 'Well Larry, I don't know anything about television.' Many of us did movies and so that wasn't a big change into TV. Of course, Eve had done Broadway, and done everything for years. But he (Berns) said, 'Oh, you're going to be fine. We're all going to be fine. It's going to be magnificent. It's going to be a hit, and don't even think about it.' So that was the producer's attitude and the director's (Al Lewis) — and he directed many of our shows. . . Al did all of the writing. . . It was so rare, so unusual, and as we went on the television show. I was exclusively under contract to CBS as everybody else was. And then in the summer we went on hiatus, and I can do other things."

Of course, the director/writer Al Lewis referred to by McMillan is not the same Al Lewis who acted with Fred Gwynne in television's *The Munsters*.

The *Our Miss Brooks* radio show was taped at CBS on Sunset Blvd. McMillan, as regards the television show: "We were on the same set where Lucille Ball was. We were at another (Los Angeles) facility not at CBS, (as) that was strictly radio. I was living with my mom. We lived in Beverly Hills — my sister and my mom (talent agent/manager Hazel McMillan). And I lived there until I got married."

Gordon told *Hollywood NOW*, December 9, 1969: "The entire cast [from the radio series] went, with the exception of Jeff Chandler. He, of course, had become a picture star. The show had many wonderful characters and an appeal to many different viewers."

Gordon told Schaden regarding Chandler: "Universal wouldn't let him appear in the television show because he was signed to star within at Universal Pictures and that is when they got, oh dear . . . Bob Rockwell . . . dear, dear sweet man."

From that same interview, Gordon would acknowledge the interviewer's comment that *Our Miss Brooks* had plenty of criticism. Gordon: "Well, yes, but the people loved it and it did run for many years."

Of course, audiences were not only treated to seeing Gordon's masterful slow burns heard on radio; but now with television, the impact of seeing Gordon as Mr. Conklin reacting to things happening to him and being oftentimes the suffering victim brought many more laughs.

In a sample television episode, "Home Cooked Meal," broadcast June 3, 1955, we enjoy learning Mr. Conklin is a real cheapskate. Mr. Conklin has been sneakily using the school cafeteria freezer to store his personal home food. As one might expect something must go wrong, and so he is locked into the freezer accidentally for four hours when Miss Brooks closes the door. The sight of Mr. Conklin looking like a snowman is at the same time unbelievably ridiculous and hilarious.

When Miss Brooks and Mr. Boynton release him, Mr. Conklin is slowly defrosted. At least he learned from this experience for he says he will now buy a home freezer unit.

However, to make matters worse, he needs to pass a physical examination, but things keep happening to him, such as Miss Brooks knocking something from his desk onto his leg, spilling water on him, etc. Mr. Conklin manages to get hurt the most when Miss Brooks invites Mr. Boynton over for a real home-cooked dinner prepared sneakily with help from her landlady, Mrs. Davis. Boynton arrives and realizes that her stove is leaking gas with her new automatic-lighting feature. Boynton and Brooks go to call for help. Enter Mr. Conklin, who arrives and he lights a match to see in the darkened kitchen where the tool chest is. Of course, the stove explodes and again we laugh when we see the tattered Mr. Conklin exiting the kitchen.

Five weeks after the TV's *Our Miss Brooks* premiered; Gordon appeared on the CBS Special, *Stars in the Eye*, broadcast on November 11, 1952. This live variety show featured Gordon and Bob Sweeney playing network executives Hubbell Robinson and Harry Ackerman who fear that Jack Benny's meddling will ruin their new TV Special. Many stars appeared; including the casts from TV shows, such as *Amos 'n' Andy, I Love Lucy, Life with Luigi, My Friend Irma,* and *Meet Millie*.

Before it would leave the air for good, the setting for *Our Miss Brooks* changed. That is, Miss Brooks and Mr. Conklin moved from Madison High to a private school. Most of the other characters, including her reluctant suitor Mr. Boynton, disappeared from the series.

Larry Wolters, referring to Arden, reported, "Meanwhile she has acquired a new and more aggressive admirer in Bob Sweeney, a funny fellow, who was featured last season in *My Favorite Husband*." Sweeney played the Vice-Principal.

Some of Gordon's newspaper publicity indicated that he would still return to local stage productions from time to time. *Jane*, a hit show from New York's stage in 1952, played in California the following year with Gordon. On June 8, 1953, *LAT* reported, "Second play of the season is to be S. N. Behrman's comedy, *Jane*, starring Edna Best, Howard St. John, Gale Gordon known to audiences as Mr. Conklin in *Our Miss Brooks*, and Brenda Forbes will be in the cast."

A month later, *LAT*, July 10, 1953 in "Maugham's *Jane* Staged Brilliantly," the Broadway production of *Jane* is being performed at the summer playhouse stage in the local high school in La Jolla. The article noted, "The only principal who did not perform in *Jane* in the East, Gale Gordon (the Osgood Conklin of TV's *Our Miss Brooks*), keeps high the level of sophisticated hilarity as Miss Forbes' divorced husband, a globe-trotting author."

Gordon's foray as an artist became apparent in *Chicago Daily Tribune*, October 18, 1953. Wolters, referring to Arden, stated, "Her collection of primitive American painting is said to be one of the finest in the west. Many of these are paintings of children. One rather unusual one—of a white New England church—hangs in a bedroom. We asked about that one. It was done by Gale Gordon . . . and was a gift to her."

One of the TV listings from *LAT* in the fall of 1954 summed up the reason for Gordon's high point of *Our Miss Brooks* best: "This comedy show, even when not too funny, gets by on the excellent performances of Eve Arden and Gale Gordon."

A 1955 clip announced, "Come Oct. 7 and the *Our Miss Brooks* TV show undergoes a major overhaul. It's all being handled in a subtle way with good old T.V. Madison High School being torn down to make way for a freeway. Eve Arden and Gale Gordon will shift down to become a teacher and principal of a San Fernando Valley grammar school."

On March 24, 1955, Lawrence Laurent, (*Washington Post* and *Times Herald*) named Gordon as among the "Happy Stooges." The others included Art Carney, Carl Reiner, Howard Morris, Vivian Vance, Bill Frawley, Bea Benaderet, Hal March and Rocky Graziano.

A few months before *Brooks* ended its run, Gordon appeared as Dr. Raymond Forrest on an episode of CBS' *Climax!* The episode, entitled "A Trophy for Harry Davenport," starred Dennis O'Keefe, Ruth Hussey and Billy Chapin in this June 28, 1956 broadcast. It tells of an overly sentimental manager of a Babe Ruth league baseball team that turns down a youngster's request to pitch in a big game. As a result, the broken-hearted boy runs away from home.

Besides stage and radio work, Gordon appeared in motion pictures. However, there is not much to his film roles, as the parts he played seemed to be merely an extension of the type of characters that he played so well on radio and television.

By now cast-type, Gordon would continue to play annoying and/or pompous characters in motion pictures. However, his output in this capacity had been limited with him appearing in one film released in the 1930s, one in the 1940s, seven films in the 1950s, six in the 1960s, and one in the 1980s.

Gordon offered minor support as an adequate character actor. He first appeared in films starting as a radio announcer in 1933's *Elmer the Great*. His next appearance did not come until 1942, when he appeared with Fibber McGee and Molly in *Here We Go Again* as Otis Cadwalader, which was his first appearance in the radio series.

In 1950, he played a station clerk in *A Woman of Distinction*; and, in 1952, he was H. J. Bellows in *Here Come the Nelsons*.

Three years later, he played District Attorney Evans in *Francis Covers the Big Town*. In *Chicago Daily Tribune*, July 16, 1953, Mac Tinée wrote, ". . . the characters maintain a surprising freshness, thanks to a lively script which demonstrates imagination as well as deft handling of the idiotic. . . . It's light and nonsensical entertainment which the whole family can enjoy." As usual, Gordon gets no mention except for the listing in the cast box.

Also in 1953, Gordon played Principal Osgood T. Conklin in the film version of *Our Miss Brooks*. The movie produced by Warner Brothers, had the television show cast, including Robert Rockwell as biology teacher Philip Boynton (not Jeff Chandler from the radio series).

Columnist Richard L. Coe in "Miss Brooks in Her Prime," offered, "Of All TV's simple-minded staples, I've most enjoyed Arden's *Our Miss Brooks*. It's slipped pitiably of late, but a super-sized screen version that suggest Connie in her prime is on view at the Metropolitan and Ambassador.

"At first I was rather aghast at this bitter treatment of schoolteachers, but when the teachers themselves nominated Eve as the something or other of the year, I decided I should stop being stuffy and take *Our Miss Brooks* as good clean fun. After all, I can be as healthy a schizo as the next guy.

"So, thus excused, Miss Brooks, Walter Denton, Principal Conklin, Mr. Boynton and Miss Davis are favorites of mine and my only quarrel with the full-sized deal—which takes about as long to see as three TV slots—is that the movie version doesn't have enough of those inane conversations Miss Arden carries on with Richard Crenna, who plays the human microbe, Walter. And far too much time is spent on Connie's pursuit of the shy Mr. Boynton, with Robert Rockwell continuing his TV role, as is the apoplectic Gale Gordon as the snoopy principal.

"By now you should know how you stand on *Our Miss Brooks*. And while her movie isn't very good, it's so much better than this year's TV version you almost feel it's the Good Old Days at the Met."

Looking beyond the movie version of *Our Miss Brooks*, perhaps his best and most prominent movie role ever, Gordon continued showing up in movies as usually some sort of an authoritarian figure, many times a military or high-ranking official. For instance in 1958, he played Brigadier General W. A. Thorwald in *Rally 'Round the Flag*. In 1959, he had two films; playing Congressman Mandeville in *Don't Give Up the Ship*, and Raven Rossiter in Lou Costello's last film, *The 30-Foot Bride of Candy Rock*.

He started the new decade off by playing a somewhat different character when he played Bob Mayberry, an obsessed neighbor trying to prove an alien landed in the Jerry Lewis comedy, *A Visit to a Small Planet*. Mayberry's attempts to capture him fail, including even the attempt to take a picture of him.

In 1961, Gordon did three films; playing Oliver Dunning in *All in a Night's Work*, the Colonel in *Dondi*, and Rear Admiral Bintle in *All Hands on Deck*. In 1965, he had the role of Captain Weiskopf in *Sergeant Deadhead*, and three years later, that of R. W. Hepworth in the Elvis Presley vehicle *Speedway*.

Gordon's final role came 21 years after the Presley film when again he played a neighbor Walter Seznick in *The 'Burbs* (1989).

Of course, Gordon's film career was lack-luster because he had little to do in many of these films. As far as press, he was lucky if he even got a simple mention in the reviews' cast credits. However, it did not really matter to Gordon as he really had enough to do with his television work to keep him occupied to the point of complete satisfaction. Movies did not seem as appealing to him as it would to others. He had succeeded with his acting on stage, radio, and now television.

Chapter Six: Finally, a Television Co-Star?

"Two remarkable character actors—Gale Gordon and Bob Sweeney—have a field day playing two remarkable characters. . . . And Gale and Bob are both hoping The Brothers *will become a permanent part of TV history, too."*
— The Brothers, as described in *TV Radio Annual* 1957

Gordon's next television success after playing Osgood T. Conklin in *Our Miss Brooks* is when he played Harvey Box. Few people, if any, even remember it, though it can be considered a minor achievement for Gordon. However, though some may argue that his participation on Lucy's two series were more significant, playing on *The Brothers* series is still unique. Gordon did not play just a supporting actor here, but instead it is the only television show where he really played as a co-star.

On that series, Gordon told Schaden: "Oh yes. That was a lot of fun to do. Sweeney is a great, great director and a very imaginative fellow. It was a little ahead of its time, but we had much fun doing it. Yes."

Gordon told Kulzer: "In those days, many people thought that all the comic dialogue was said on the spur of the moment. They couldn't believe that people rehearsed this—that writers actually wrote these lines for someone else to say. They thought we just made it all up as we went along."

On September 30, 1956, Walter Ames in "Gale Gordon Happy about Freeways, Even if Fictional," *LAT*, observed, "Gale Gordon is one happy fellow about freeways even though, in his case they happen to be fictional. . . . Gale's thankfulness started a year ago when (the) producers of *Our Miss Brooks* Eve Arden starrer decided she needed a change. They had a fictional freeway run through Madison High School, thus eliminating the locale. Eve and Gale moved into a private school and that's where [Bob] Sweeney made his entrance as a Vice-Principal.

"'Bob was looking for a partner.'

"Gale explained, 'I was looking for an escape from being an ill-tempered school Principal. We got together on things, developed an idea Bob had, sold it to CBS and here we are. Now all we have to do is satisfy the viewing public and everyone will be happy.'"

The show, produced by Edward H. Feldman (formerly VP of Desilu Productions) and directed by announcer/actor Hy Averback, ran for 26 episodes on CBS Tuesday nights (8:30 to 9) from October 2, 1956 through March 26, 1957. Gordon, Sweeney, Feldman, and Averback formed Dallad Productions with 50% ownership; CBS owned the other 50%. The episodes had location shooting in Northern California.

W. A. Sheaffer Pen Company and the Procter & Gamble Company sponsored the Desilu filmed series. By the time of the show's cancellation, one of the sponsors, Lever Brothers Company, was considering replacing the show with Ann Sothern's *Private Secretary.*

A clip from "Tips from Hollywood" reported, "CBS is higher than the proverbial kite about its new tryout film, *The Brothers.*" Before the opening episode, the press reported, "Tonight's opener, concerned with Sweeney's birthday, serves mainly to introduce all the characters. Only mildly amusing but Sweeney's a funny fella', so give this series a little time to get going."

Neither Gordon nor Sweeney reached the heights of TV stardom as Lucille Ball and Jackie Gleason, yet critics were hopeful. On October 2, 1956, Wolters in *Chicago Daily Tribune* explained: "This show, on the basis of a preview, is likely to be a fall sensation, maybe as big a hit as *Sgt. Bilko*, starring Phil Silvers. [Incidentally, *The Brothers* will follow Silvers on the air and would naturally inherit a sizable audience.] The names of Gale Gordon and Bob Sweeney, its co-stars, are not exactly unknown. . . . But Gordon and Sweeney seem destined to become big name TV comedians through this series . . ."

After broadcasting 13 weeks of episodes, the press reported, "Nice to see that the Gale Gordon/Bob Sweeney starrer on KNXT (2) at 8:30 tonight has survived a critical segment and starts on the second 13-week cycle this evening. Some of our eastern cousins were ready with the burial rites after the first show."

The Brothers is about two brothers who are co-owners of a San Francisco photography studio. They experience mishaps as they both try to make it in the business world. The comedy comes as they play opposites. Gordon played Harvey Box, and Sweeney played his brother Gilmore Box. Ann Morris played Dr. Margaret Kleeb. Frank Orth played Captain Sam Box, a role that Howard McNear took over. Nancy Hadley, Oliver Blake and Robin Hughes completed the cast.

Ames, in *LAT*, September 30, 1956, explained the show: "Gale is on the stuffy side and aims to regain the family spot atop Nob Hill in San Francisco. Bob likes to live it up and, as expected, gets into trouble that keeps Gale busy straightening out."

Sweeney later commented to *TV Guide*: "In character, Gale Gordon does something nobody else can do. He just stands there, not saying or doing anything, and all of a sudden he's the balloon that makes you want to reach for the pin. The fun is seeing this marvelous balloon settle down to your own level."

LAT reported in "Lunch to Benefit 1957 Heart Fund," on February 23, that Gordon and Sweeney made presentations for the Fund at a spring fashion show and luncheon held at the Hollywood Epsilon Chapter of Epsilon Sigma Alpha in the Ambassador.

Gordon's next television appearance would be on CBS' *The Ed Sullivan Show* on April 21, 1957. He did a comedy sketch with Sweeney about refinishing the attic of their home.

On November 10, 1957, Cecil Smith's column in *LAT*, pictured Gordon with the caption: "REHEARSAL—Preparing for *Playhouse 90*, Director Burgess Meredith, center, gives pointers to Gale Gordon, left, Donald O'Connor."

On November 14, 1957, Gordon would appear in a live episode of *Playhouse 90* on CBS called "The Jet-Propelled Couch." In this comedy-drama directed by Meredith, Gordon played General Milton Dagby in this tale about an atomic physicist (David Wayne) whose imagination convinces him he lives part of his life on another planet. Donald O'Connor plays a psychiatrist, with Peter Lorre, and Phyllis Avery co-starring.

Probably one of Gordon's last radio appearances occurred on December 29, 1957. In "Radio Roundup" by Jean McMurphy, *LAT* noted, "Gale Gordon plays Sir Francis Drake on C.P. MacGregor's show, KFI, 7:30 p.m."

The following year, Gordon joined an NBC television cast in an attempt to save the series named *Sally*. The Frank Ross-produced show for Paramount TV ran on Sundays (7:30 p.m., KRCA). For 20 weeks, the show took a tour of Paris, Rome, London, Monte Carlo and Algeria.

Gordon did not help to save the show as the networks had already planned to drop a number of television shows before the season ended. On February 13, 1958, *LAT*'s Cecil Smith reported, "One of the major surprises among them is the decision to drop *Sally* on March 30. Most of the departures will be quiet enough but not *Sally*. She's going out alive and kicking!

"For the last seven episodes (from February 14 to March 30, 1958) the show has a new format, set in a Los Angeles department store (where it all began anyway); new permanent additions to the cast, including Gale (Mr. Conklin) Gordon, Johnny Desmond and Arte Johnson—in short, it will be a New *Sally*."

Joan Caulfield starred as Sally Truesdale, a former traveling companion to a wealthy widow named Mrs. Myrtle Banford (Marion Lorne). Sally takes a job at a department store when they return home from their travels. Mrs. Banford needs to take care of some business at the Banford and Bleacher Department Store.

Gordon played the new character named Bascomb Bleacher, the store manager. In short, he is Mrs. Banford's partner. Arte Johnson, Jr. played Bascomb's son, and Johnny Desmond played Jim Kendall.

Smith: "*Sally* came to the air last September with the brightest prospects in the galaxy of new shows. It brought back blond and beautiful Joan Caulfield and wonderfully wacky Marion Lorne. Moreover, it marked the TV producing debut of Miss Caulfield's husband, Frank Ross, one of the most astute and successful producers of motion pictures this town has known (ranging from *The Robe* to the upcoming *Kings Go Forth*).

"I cornered Ross in Lucey's to ask what happened to *Sally*. 'First, I made a mistake,' he said. 'I thought people must be tired of seeing the same cast in the same setting week after week in a situation comedy. So we got this great idea of sending Joan and Marion all over the world, new countries, new people, new situations each week.

"'But that's wrong. The audiences of situation comedies WANT the same people, the same family week after week. They WANT Bilko surrounded by his squad; they WANT to see Bob Cummings' family. They WANT their stars surrounded by recognizable people, not new ones.

"'Second, I failed as a producer. Don't ever believe that a man who is a successful movie producer can be successful at producing television. It's a different form, another medium. It's like a novelist who tries to write a screenplay—he runs into trouble, it's another form.'

"'I BELIEVE one major function of a producer is to take the blame for everything that goes wrong. I don't blame the time as hurting *Sally*, the success of *Maverick* or anything of that sort. A great show doesn't mind competition—and we didn't have a great show. We might have been a mild success in another time slot—but I didn't want that. I wanted a very successful show or none.'

"'Don't get the idea I'm giving up. We overhauled the show, spent some money—and we'll be fighting for a sale next year. Joan pulled me into TV but now I'm in till the finish. And I've learned a great deal about producing TV.'"

The day after the show's changes occurred, the press reacted: "To try and lift its sagging rating, *Sally* switched to a new story idea last night over Channel 4. But despite the efforts of its star, Joan Caulfield, and superior comedy performers such as Marion Lorne and Gale Gordon, the show continues to suffer from script deficiency. Last night's episode, taking place in the executive office of a department store, was thin fun indeed."

Gordon made another appearance on *Playhouse 90* on March 13, 1958. The live production, entitled *The Male Animal*, adapted by Don M. Mankiewicz from the play by James Thurber and Elliot Nugent, and directed by Vincent Donehue, starred Andy Griffith as the bedeviled professor, with Ann Rutherford, Edmond O'Brien, Charlie Ruggles, and Dick Sargent in the cast. The story is about an

English professor (Griffith) who gets into trouble with his wife, the college dean, a trustee, and an old flame of his wife. Gordon played a character named Ed Keller.

Gordon received some criticism at times. Laurent: "MY ADMIRATION for the talents of Andy Griffith has been written many times. However, I cannot recall any time that any performer has been more woefully miscast than was Andy in *The Male Animal* last Thursday night (CBS, WTOP-TV). *Playhouse 90*, in happier days, had great success in breaking actor's type casts. With Professor Tommy Tucker, a superbly written character of introspection, comedy and courage, Andy was lost.

"It didn't help, either, to have Andy supported by the predictable antics of Gale Gordon (who played his role exactly as he plays Osgood Conklin in *Our Miss Brooks*)."

Not all reviews criticized the program or Gordon. On March 13, 1958, *LAT*'s Cecil Smith noted that the comedy, "has provided the brightest hours in the American theater for nearly twenty years now. Twice a Broadway hit, a superb movie—it's a story that has a kind of timeless quality despite the fact that it deals with a theme that was particularly applicable to its time, academic freedom to discuss ideas despite their popular disfavor."

On March 24, 1958, Gordon appeared on CBS' live broadcast of *Studio One in Hollywood*, in an episode entitled *The Award Winner*. Eddie Bracken, Jack Oakie, and Joanna Moore starred. Here Gordon played a character named R. J. Fuller in this tale about a package designer for a toy company named George Short (Bracken). He is in the limelight with complications arising when his cousin Frank uses George's name on a successful screenplay.

In an episode of *The Westinghouse Lucille Ball—Desi Arnaz Show* from December 1, 1958, Gordon plays a domestic court judge in an episode entitled "Lucy Makes Room for Danny." This Desilu Studios crossover episode featured the cast of *The Danny Thomas Show*.

With NBC's *This Is Your Life* with host Ralph Edwards, Gordon appears as a friend of honoree Leo Carrillo broadcast on April 15, 1959. Carrillo is best remembered today as "Pancho" on *The Cisco Kid* television series. However, years earlier Gordon co-starred with Carrillo several times, including in the stage play *Lombardi Limited*.

An episode called "The Screen Test" of ABC's series *The Real McCoys*, broadcast on October 29, 1959, provided Gordon with the part of P. T. Kirkland (a name reminiscent of P. T. Barnum). He tells a character named Hassie (Lydia Reed) that he could arrange a screen test for her. The question arises as to whether or not he is simply a con man with a scheme.

Gordon closed the 1950s in the first of several appearances on CBS' *The Danny Thomas Show*. He played the landlord in the December 21, 1959 episode, called "A Dog's Life," AKA "The Landlord." When Rusty (Rusty Hamer) and Linda (Angela Cartwright) bring a large St. Bernard dog home, the landlord moves to evict the Williams' family from their apartment. Of course, complexities arise when the dog gives birth to a litter.

Perhaps of all of his television appearances in the 1950s, two are most memorable and familiar to most viewers. They came at the time Gordon contracted as a regular cast member of *Our Miss Brooks*. It is then that Gordon appeared twice on *I Love Lucy*.

Of course, we know that Ball wanted Gordon to play the landlord named Fred Mertz in the series. However, Gordon's exclusive commitment to *Brooks* on radio prevented him from doing TV's *I Love Lucy*. William Frawley entered to play the irascible Mr. Mertz. Yet it would have been interesting to see how different Gordon would have played the miserly character.

Bart Andrews said Gordon explained: "It sounds a little egotistical for a performer to say something like this, but Lucy did want Bea [Benaderet] and me in her show. We had played Iris and Rudolph Atterbury on the radio show [*My Favorite Husband*], and she wanted us to be in on the TV venture. I had worked with Lucille way back in the early forties in *Look Who's Laughing*, an RKO movie version of the *Fibber McGee and Molly* series. But when *I Love Lucy* came along, I was under exclusive contract to CBS Radio to do *Our Miss Brooks* with Eve Arden, and Bea had already begun playing Blanche Morton on Burns and Allen's television show, so neither of us could do it."

Schaden asked Gordon, "So you must have been rather versatile to have stayed employed all of those years and . . . You made a wonderful transition to television from radio, didn't you?"

Gordon replied, "But yes. But then I've been in the theater. So very easy. A lot of the people I worked with in radio who were just superb. Radio actors never did make it into television because they couldn't walk and talk at the same time. They were so used to standing in front of the microphone and fading in and out for a few steps that they didn't know how to use their bodies when it came to doing television. Well I did because I've been on stage."

Regarding his memorable appearances on *I Love Lucy*, Gordon told Schaden: "Yes, I did two or three of them, not as any (uh, uh, uh) established character. I played the owner of the nightclub where Ricky worked on one occasion and I don't know I did another appearance on one of them. By that time, I was doing *Our Miss Brooks* and it was rather difficult. Only once in a while can I do her show."

In the first of two appearances on *I Love Lucy*, entitled "Lucy's Schedule," broadcast on May 26, 1952, Gordon played Alvin Littlefield, the new owner of the Tropicana Club, where Ricky Ricardo performs. The plot revolves around Ricky starting on a bad note with Littlefield when Lucy makes him late for Littlefield's dinner invitation. This leads Lucy to plot revenge with the aid of Littlefield's wife Phoebe (Edith Meiser) when the Littlefields arrive for dinner at the Ricardos.

Gordon's second appearance on *I Love Lucy*, "Ricky Asks for a Raise," broadcast on June 9, 1952, Gordon again plays Ricky's boss Mr. Littlefield. This time Lucy gets Ricky fired and replaced by Xavier Valdez when she tells Littlefield that Ricky needs a raise since he has gotten better offers from other nightclubs. Lucy schemes with the help of Fred and Ethel Mertz to make Littlefield take Ricky back again at the Tropicana.

Chapter Seven: A New Way of Life

"'The desert is like the sea, an ever-changing thing that never changes. I guess I come here' and he seemed hesitant saying it, as if uncovering a hidden part of himself, 'to find my soul.'"

—Gale Gordon
quoted by Cecil Smith, *LAT*, April 7, 1969

The readers of local California newspapers; such as the *San Diego Union* and the *Borrego Sun*, at least from 1960 onwards, knew something about Gordon's private life in the desert. Just a sample of some of the headlines says it all: "Lost Acreage Brought Gale Gordon to Desert," "Gordon Finds New Way of Life," "The Successful 'Stuffed Shirt,'" "The Former Mrs. Conklin of TV Stars as Wife of Gale Gordon," "Borrego Group Names Actor," "A Borrego Squire Named Gordon," "Gale Gordon Becomes First Little League Charter Member," "Gale Gordon Loves Borrego, and the Feeling is Mutual," "Gale Gordon Speaks . . . . Tells of Love for Coyote Canyon," "How Gale Gordon Escapes Tensions," "TV Actor Prefers Life in Borrego to Hollywood," and so on.

To understand Gordon more fully means to know what a great value he put on his life in Borrego Springs, California. That location is what one might call simply "Gale's Green Acres."

Many Hollywood stars have seen Borrego Springs as a superb haven to relax and a place to enjoy some privacy sometimes. The current Borrego Springs Performing Arts Center originated from a community theater group started there in 1950 by Lon Chaney, Jr. Other actors made it their home. Leo Carrillo helped create the Anza-Borrego State Park. Burgess Meredith built a get-away home at De Anza

Country Club, and Frank Morgan served as the first Honorary Mayor.

However, Gordon connected the desert locale to himself on another level altogether. He took the place so seriously and just loved it so much, that to him, it did indeed become "a new way of life." In fact, with his intense love of the locale and his previous tenure as Wistful Vista's Mayor, it seemed only natural that he would love to be the Honorary Mayor of Borrego Springs.

Cecil Smith, who was the husband of *Here's Lucy* producer Cleo Smith, offered some fascinating information about Gordon and Borrego. He said Gordon told him and others that his vaudevillian mother, Gloria, had loved land. She never could resist the fast-talking land dealer. As a result, his mother was suckered into buying a ranch somewhere in the desert area. For years after her death, Gordon took annual pilgrimages in search of it. With the help of a surveyor he hired, he finally found Borrego, but it took some time.

Interestingly, Gordon once got a letter from a rancher who asked if he could have an easement across the land owned by Gordon's mother to his place. Gordon wrote back, "I told him I'd give him the easement if he'd show it to me. Now, at last I know where it is."

As a vast State Park surrounds Borrego Springs (population then of 1,000), the town can never expand physically beyond its borders. The location has been used over throughout the last century in a number of movies; including most recently in Sean Penn's 2007 release *Into the Wild*. The silent beauty of that locale, in particular the magnificent view of Borrego Valley, appealed especially to the Gordons, as it did later to Cecil and his wife Cleo.

Today the Chamber of Commerce for Borrego Springs describes the locale as "an unincorporated area of northeast San Diego County. Borrego Springs is a village within a park completely surrounded and protected by the amazing 600,000-acre Anza-Borrego Desert State Park. Here in San Diego's only desert community, the nearest stoplight is fifty miles away. We have no big-box or chain stores. The slower, uncomplicated pace, the scenic beauty and the human scale of the place combine to produce a rustic, authentic desert experience, a special place, in all seasons."

When Schaden asked Gordon, "Where exactly is Borrego Springs, Gale?" Gordon elaborated its location in relation to other places:

"Well, (laughs) ah you know where the Salton Sea is? You know where San Diego is? Well, we're north and east of San Diego. We're between the Ocean and the Salton Sea, which is below sea level and we're low desert. We're near San Bernardino. And we're fairly near Ramona—which a name that most people know because of the story of Ramona. And we're in San Diego County inland from the coast about 80 miles, and that's about it—and there's nothing. Julian is the nearest town. And another town called Brawley, so which nobody has heard of. And nobody's heard, well very few people have heard, of Borrego Springs. That's why we like it. Because, it isn't overcrowded. We haven't grown very much in 35 years that we've been here and that suits us fine. We're just very quiet and away from the rat race."

The exact date when Gordon came to Borrego is uncertain, but it seems likely that it was around 1950. Gordon told Schaden, referring to Los Angeles: "Well we have a house in town so when I'm working up there I have a place to stay and we're very, very comfortable." Gordon added (referring to Borrego): "We have our dogs down here. My wife and I have been married for 52 years, and so we're very content to be here with our dogs and take things easy."

Smith: "We came to Borrego because Gale had talked about it as an ideal getaway from Hollywood and the film industry, unlike Palm Springs." The Smiths would take their kids in their Buick and drive down to Borrego for the weekends. Sometimes they even leant their house to friends. Anne Baxter stayed there to learn her lines for a Broadway play.

In a *LAT* article entitled "On the Scent of Wild Flowers in Borrego Desert," Smith noted, "It was Gordon who first showed me Borrego a decade ago and I have been its perennial guest ever since. I remember asking Gordon's wife Virginia what she found to do in the long desert days when her husband was at work in a film or on the road in a play and she said: 'The year is not long enough for me to count the varieties of birds . . . .'"

Smith concluded, "I love the peace of Borrego, the solitary life, the dense silences. Gale Gordon, the actor whose Tub Farm overlooks the valley, says the desert, like the sea, is man's last uncluttered space. It allows you to breathe."

As has been recounted a number of times, what we know about Gordon's wife Virginia is that she oftentimes sat all day on the front stoop while Gordon was working in Hollywood. There she spent endless hours and days just happily tracking and counting the numerous bird varieties that came into the valley.

As their getaway from the Hollywood surrounds, Gale and Virginia lived at the ranch, called Tub Canyon Farm. When not on the TV stage, the pipe-smoking Gordon would spend three days a week wearing his coveralls and keeping himself physically busy and fit on his 150-acre ranch.

The couple had plans drawn up for the house that they wanted to build. However, they never did get around to building it, even though they were there for some fifty or so years. Smith concluded that it must have been because Gale and Virginia had argued for years about which way the house should face, and thus never broke ground!

Word circulated that Gale had built his own home in Borrego. However, this is contrary to what Smith remembered. Could he have built the cabin he lived in? Smith disputed that saying, "What was there to build? It was a dinky cabin of maybe four rooms. Possibly, he built the huge workshop behind the house. He put the swimming pool in for the dogs, and there was another building, farm tools, and other storage. . . . There was a porch, I think."

Smith in his 1969 column quoted Gordon as saying himself that he lived in "a temporary three-room shack." In addition, Smith described the tiny cabin they lived in was built by the homesteader who first owned the property.

In a circa 1950s documentary about Borrego Springs, it is explained that to make desert living comfortable the buildings in Borrego Springs are designed to take advantage of the sunrays by using the traditional one-story ranch design. That includes adobe walls, which are mud walls made up of sand, clay, water and organic material. In addition, the buildings have broad eaves, slanted windows, breatheways, filtered sunlight, insulation and air conditioning.

Nevertheless, Smith visited the "shack" that the Gordons lived in. He declared that it was truly a dreadful house. Embarrassingly, the small rooms had sagging furniture. If that was not bad enough, what you would call the "kitchen" was basically a room full of electrical appliances all hooked by cords to a socket in a hanging fixture in the center of the room.

Gordon did build the large enclosure and kennel for up to as many as 13 dogs at one point. The dogs' swimming pool had its location in the enclosure.

Smith noted that the childless Gordons had what you might call "friends" whom they wanted to adopt; namely, a nearby young couple. They apparently died before the Gordons could adopt them.

In 2008, the ninety-year old Smith remembered many details about the Gordons' home; however, some things he honestly could not recall. He believed that Gordon parked his Bentley (or maybe Rolls) outside, though there may have been a garage built at some point. They had a Peugeot that only Virginia drove. In addition, Gordon received a small red jeep from Lucille Ball, which she had gotten from Henry Kaiser.

"He was often seen in town in his vehicle. I believe it was a Rolls Royce that he would drive to the Post Office to get his mail," noted Fred Jee from the Borrego Springs' Chamber of Commerce.

Jee added, "Lucille Ball gave him gifts and I think one of them was a car (not the Rolls). She had a house here in Borrego Springs near La Casa del Zorro. Many other celebrities had homes here; including, Burgess Meredith until his death, George Duning—musical director, James Arness and Dennis Weaver for a short time, Lon Chaney, Jr. who started the theater concept here in Borrego, Charles Starrett—old time western star, Harry Oliver—art director at Warners, and more who have not been confirmed. The Hoberg was active from 1948–1954, which is now The Palms at Indianhead. Many stars of the Golden Era came here to rest and relax . . . Gable, Monroe, Laughton, Crosby, Lanchester, and others."

Behind the house, Gordon had erected a massive workshop with all of the latest woodworking tools and gadgets for the hobby. The ranch's amenities included an underground gasoline tank, a gas pump, and all first-rate farming equipment.

Gordon told Kulzer what he liked most about the place: "I don't have to hear anyone's television or radio. It's what I've always wanted. My wife and I loved to read. We're going to have to move out to make room for the books! And we have our dogs . . . we're very happy here!"

Desilu employee Howard Rayfiel noted that he worked with Gale's agent Marc Newman. Gordon is unique as he was Newman's only client not in the music business. Rayfiel's wife Eileen recalled that Gale and Virginia owned a vineyard. Rayfiel: "They apparently knew wines very well. They gave us excellent vintages every year for Christmas. Gale must have been happy with the deal we made."

Some reports paint a picture of the successful actor Gordon proving himself worthy of praise for his farming achievements. However, Smith remembered hearing that whatever Gale planted each year on the ranch ended up a disaster. Smith: "I know nothing about agriculture, just gossip. . . . It was a local joke that whatever Gale farmed, failed; but he did put in some carob trees and this may have been a successful venture."

If the rumors of his failure were correct, then this would be ironic, as it would indicate that life imitates art again, albeit not exactly here, as Gordon's experiences mirrored the farmer he portrayed in the short-lived 1950 radio comedy series, *Granby's Green Acres*. In retrospect, seeing the possible irony of Gordon's life imitating art gives the show a sweet charm that makes it worth hearing again.

In "He Trades His Frown for Smile in Kitchen," *Chicago Tribune*, January 24, 1964, Freida Zylstra revealed: "When Gale Gordon portrays an ill-tempered or miserly character on television or the screen, it's strictly an act, but when he turns on a smile and invites friends in for a dinner which he cooks himself, he's not pretending."

Gordon told Zylstra: "Most of our entertaining is done on week-ends and while I'm on vacation between shows. We have a guest house and frequently have friends spend a weekend with us."

Gordon: "I do a good bit of the cooking around our house and find it a relaxing and satisfying hobby." He offered to readers one of his own recipes, one he called "Eggs a La Tub Canyon," named after his ranch (See Appendix).

Zylstra: "He also spends a lot of time in his workshop at his hobbies of painting and writing."

In "Borrego Fete Opens Today," October 21, 1966, *LAT* reported that at the first Borrego Springs Desert Festival, "television star Gale Gordon, who is Honorary Mayor of this unincorporated desert resort, will preside." The fete included tours of the Anza-Borrego Desert as well as an exhibition of desert paintings and color photography.

In a photo piece called "Mr. Mooney Goes Rustic," by Richard

Arthur, *Washington Post*, January 19, 1969, Gordon received pictorial coverage of his life at his ranch. Arthur: "Two recent chores included sifting sand (to make concrete for a swimming pool he is building) and repairing a weathervane. As you can see, he's never too busy for a short frolic with four of his nine mongrel dogs. Nor is he too occupied to watch as his wife prepares a midday snack."

In the press, few mentions were made of Gordon's pre-Lucy days. Perhaps no one really cared what Gordon did before he became Lucy's dependable and irrepressible foil. In fact, some insist Lucy's second and third series in the 1960s would have not been nearly as successful, or even possible, without Gordon as her foil. They argue that Gordon essentially made Lucy's show the big hit that it was.

However, at least one reporter, in "A Beary Popular Fellow." The *Wall Street Journal*, December 22, 1969, Susan Hauser remembered Gordon's early days on radio, such as his *Cinnamon Bear* show appearances as the stork and the ostrich.

In "A Dog's Best Friend" by Norma Lee Browning, *Chicago Tribune*, December 23, 1973, Gordon explained: "When my wife and I moved to Borrego Springs (a desert community about 175 miles from Hollywood) some years ago, we bought a 150-acre farm which included a small house, a large swimming pool, and a children's wading pool.

"I thought the wading pool would be just perfect for the dogs (all mutts) so I put an aerating system and built some brick steps going down into the water. All the dogs love it [except Eric] and you can hear them splashing for hours."

BROWNING: "All the dogs, that is, except Eric—who hates the water, which is just as well, because Eric doesn't mingle with the other six who have the spacious fenced run with pool. He lives inside with the Gordons."

GORDON: "Eric was dropped in our front yard one night about six years ago. We heard them yipping inside our gate and found a little black dog, along with a bag of food and a blue bowl. And there was a note, in a child's scrawl, attached to his collar.

	"It said, 'Mommy and Daddy say I can't keep Eric. I love him. He eats out of the blue bowl when I come home from school. I love him. Candy.'"
BROWNING:	"Of course, Gale adopted him, despite the fact that the other six, all from the same litter, didn't like the intruder. But since they lived outside anyway, Eric became the house dog."
GORDON:	"You should hear what goes on when Eric ventures out and approaches the run. And when we go away—which isn't often and never too long because we don't like to leave the dogs—we have to take them to the boarding kennels in separate cars. They are a lot of trouble but they're worth every second of it."

Browning noted that although dog-loving Gordon received nominations for an Emmy four times, it does not really matter to him as he has his "seven furry friends."

In a 1950s circa travelogue, one will find confirmation that Borrego Springs is of utmost importance to understand Gordon. Some have dated the short as 1950, such as the Chamber of Commerce of Borrego Springs, which listed it as a Copley Productions/FYI Films from 1950. More likely, the film came out in the mid or late 1950s, since it refers to a country club that opened in 1954. Though the actual date of release of the short is uncertain, the film's end credits simply acknowledge several individuals.*

The documentary is entitled *A New Way of Life*, directed and filmed by John Schaaf, screenplay by Ray Sperry, edited by Walt Jenevein, music edited by Art Pabst, with Howard Matson as production supervisor.

Gordon quite effectively narrates the program. The 20-minute

---

* A YouTube posting claims it is dated 1964; however, the style of the cars indicates late 1950s. Go to:
https://www.youtube.com/watch?v=PNKyNqkWGco.
The Gordon narrated program begins at 25:35 minutes.

development/promotional short film encourages visitors and residents alike to come to Borrego Springs, and it even includes Gordon briefly talking on camera and operating his ranch tractor.

Anyone watching the program will understand that this is not just someone else's publicity for the locale. Though Gordon did not script the short, it appears certain, or very likely, that Gordon himself is in total agreement with the information presented, and that he is sincerely telling of his own love of his private life there in the desert. Herein lay the secret to Gordon's personal and private life that others overlooked as he spent a good portion of his adult life there, perhaps over fifty years.

Gordon narrates: "This land has held an attraction for man since the days of Juan Baptista de Anza. From the early 1770s, man has talked about and returned to this land searching for a personal satisfaction. It is this satisfaction, this searching for individual goals, that has given the desert its multitudinous values.

"Today the desert offers lush havens, surprising sanctuaries, real and optical wonders. Today's desert offers luxuriant earth, a fantastic array of natural colors, unique plant determination. But probably the greatest attraction of the desert for the modern man is its wonderful serenity."

At this point Gordon appears on camera getting out of his tractor and talking directly to the viewer. Gordon: "Of course there are some who just wouldn't accept all of this without a few modern conveniences. Oh yes, yes, I'm one of those spoiled creatures of our modern mania. I expect comfort, serenity, beauty, privacy, modern conveniences, and of course, a sound investment. And that's rather hard to achieve. But I really believe that I have found the answer to all of my desires, here in this valley. I first saw it some thirty years ago. Considered myself a pioneer.

"Today I one of the fortunate ones lucky enough to escape the tensions of big city life and live in peace and comfort—here. It would give me great pleasure to show you what I call 'A New Way of Life.'

"'A New Way of Life' is a rule rather than an exception in Borrego Springs. This is more than a community, it is the center of activity and home life for an area that is surrounded by a 470,000-acre game and wildlife preserve.

"Practically everyone has heard of Borrego, but few other than we natives realize how close it is to being the center of the Great Southwest. When we consider Borrego the center of a 250-mile circle, the neighboring cities of San Diego, Los Angeles, Santa Barbara, Las Vegas, Phoenix, Tucson, and Yuma are easily accessible from the air or by car. The neighbors of old Mexico are also but a short hop away.

"Although air travel is becoming increasingly popular in the desert regions, it is the expanding highway network that enables the people of the Southwest to travel in comfort throughout the immenseness of this region. The more people that visit our area, the more the old misconceptions of desert life disappear, to be replaced with an up-to-date picture of the fun-filled West."

Other facts that Gordon explains using the film's lines is that the recreational area of the Salton Seas is 30 miles from Borrego Springs, and the mountains of Julian are minutes away as well. The surrounding proximity of the Anza-Borrego State Park flora and fauna, with entertainment both active (swimming) and passive (playing cards). The place runs the gamut—exercise for the rum to exploration for the bum.

In addition, the scenery is beyond compare for the geology enthusiast, the photographer, the hiker, or the student of history. The merchants satisfy resident and tourist, a place where the rare elephant tree grows, the roving eye finds a profusion of color. Gordon: "Borrego Springs with its new way of life is an entirely new atmosphere which nature and residents have blended for a wonderful tranquility."

Gordon admitted: "This is the wonderful escape from the pressures of big business that has brought myself and many others to the valley. This is desert living—helpful, comfortable peaceful desert living."

Then most poignant is when the travelogue superbly waxes philosophical with Gordon reflecting: "And in the desert there's a special time of day, as the sun begins to dip behind the mountains, and the cool of dusk takes over. When the ever-changing shadows add an extra grandeur to the desert. It is the time when visitor and native alike realize an inborn appreciation for God's wonders. It is this time of the day that makes every visitor wish that Borrego was his home. The intenseness of the sunset's beauty is always inspiring—even for the natives."

While the film shows Gordon divining for water, he explains the general concern some have expressed about finding water in the desert, noting that the water table is at a safe level. The current reservoir is o.k., and there is little danger of it ever running out. "In Borrego Springs, there's an abundance of water. Here the the rich underground watershed can be compared to an oil-field reservoir with a rich supply available. In fact, Borrego now produces more water daily than is used in nearby San Diego, a city of more than a half a million. The famed DiGiorgio Fruit Corporation alone has drilled 14 wells in the Borrego Valley, which produce 50 million gallons of water daily. This supply would be adequate for more than 80,000 average homes. It is little wonder that the rich soil will grow literally anything under the desert sun.

"Borrego is the home of the earliest grapes to reach the eastern market. Here is the entire county allotment of cotton. The rich soil produces eight crops of alfalfa a year, 160 acres are devoted to the finest asparagus in the nation, and this is the home of the only pink grapefruit outside of Texas. Gladiolus cut in Borrego expect to blossom throughout the United States. . . ."

The film insists that there is fun and leisure there. In addition, although there is growth, it concludes: "expansion, yes; disastrous boom, no."

Gordon's narration mesmerizes the viewer with the abundant and enticing details of the locale. In summarizing the assets of the locale, Gordon offers: "If a person wants wide-open spaces and a guarantee that he will be forever surrounded by the natural beauty of the plant and wildlife preserve, Borrego is the answer. If it is a pleasing blend of suburban and outdoor life that offers an appeal, Borrego still satisfies the desire. If it is the availability of wonders of the great Southwest and room for roaming, Anza-Borrego area is the last great frontier. If your wish is for a year-round escape from the prying pace of big-city life, you will find yourself in agreeable surroundings.

"If you want luxury, comfort, rest or health, you need look no further. If you want to get away from the problems of life for a few days, and surround yourself with pleasure, Borrego offers an easy to reach answer. And when pleasure and business are combined for a gathering of representatives, there is no better gathering place than this healthy, restful atmosphere. The one extraordinary advantage of Borrego Springs is that it offers the businessman everything for work or for play. . ."

After viewing this short and hearing Gordon's sincere and intense love for the place expressed in his narration, one knows why Copley Productions chose him to extol the virtues of Borrego Springs.

When Gordon talks about "the businessman" and explains that there is golf for all, we know this is the commercial aspect of the promotional film slipping through. Of course, the film received financing probably to bring people to the newly built De Anza Country Club.

The film production company was the brainchild of James S. Copley (1917–1973), journalist and publisher of several San Diego, as well as other California and Midwest, newspapers. He also owned the community's paper, *Borrego Sun*, from its inception in 1948. Copley and others, like Robert Di Giorgio and A. A. Burnand, Jr., helped make Borrego become the place that it is.

Although the documentary emphasizes that an expansive protected un-commercialized beauty surrounds the area, and that there is an ever-changing color scheme of the desert in one's own backyard, the production is hoping to attract the visiting or working businessman.

Gordon asks: "Where else is the soil so rich, water so abundant, color so vibrant? Where else is there such a flagrant disregard for tension, strife and big city frustration? For the visitor or for the resident, Borrego Springs offers a more pleasant way of life. The pace is slower, the enjoyment more lasting. Life is casual as a rule, but it can be exciting."

He concludes the film saying, "But somehow there is something familiar about the new faces because we expect to see them again. It invariably happens when people come to Borrego Springs, they take one good look and vow to return. And when they do come back, Borrego is ready to welcome them, because we want to share our 'New Way of Life.'"

If anything reveals anything about Gordon's simple, but quite satisfying personal life in Borrego Springs, it is this production.

In *LAT* from April 7, 1969, "How Gale Gordon Escapes Tensions," Smith observed, "A remarkably disciplined man as well as one of the finest comedic actors of this era, Gale's routine rarely varies. He finishes his week's work on the studio sets, hops in his Porsche and zips through the horse country around Corona over the mountain plateau of the Warner Ranch, down the new Montezuma Highway carved out of the mountainside above Tub Canyon to his book-lined 'shack.'"

Smith explained, "Now that TV seasons grow shorter, Gale spends more and more time on the farm. He turns down offers for movies or TV guest roles in the off-season. Only charitable causes can pull him away, like a recent flight to Louisville to make a speech to spearhead a cancer fund drive. He keeps a small house in Hollywood, but Borrego is home."

"Some people are frightened by the desert. The solitude disturbs them, the vast emptiness. Across the mountains at Palm Springs, there are glitter and clamor and neon dazzle where tourists and movie stars gambol. Though show folk own great tracts of Borrego (among them, Bing Crosby, Jascha Heifetz, Chuck Connors, Eddie Albert and Margo), there is here quiet, muted peace."

"'When I get in my car to come here,' says Gale Gordon, 'I can feel the tensions slacken, the muscles relax. By the time I'm here, I'm a different man and Hollywood seems light years away. The desert is like the sea, an ever-changing thing that never changes. I guess I come here' and he seemed hesitant saying it, as if uncovering a hidden part of himself, 'to find my soul.'"

Ultimately and strangely, life imitates art as Gordon the actor played radio's comedic Mayor LaTrivia of Wistful Vista in *Fibber McGee and Molly* for nearly a dozen years. Later on, Gordon the man held the real-life position as Honorary Mayor Gale Gordon of Borrego Springs, California for a dozen years from 1962 to 1974. Hon. Mayor Gordon did some of the ordinary administrative things that mayors do. For instance, he declared June 24, 1964 a holiday in Borrego Springs after the Montezuma Valley Road into Borrego Springs was completed. The road, carved down the San Ysidro Mountain, reportedly involved using 160,000 tons of dynamite.

Jee concluded: "I know he was very active in Borrego and served as Honorary Mayor with the Chamber of Commerce, he was a big supporter of the Anza-Borrego State Park, and spoke on their behalf many times while he was living here. He was here for the opening of the Montezuma Grade highway project and was a big environmental supporter. He was involved in the controversy over the opening of

Coyote Canyon with a highway he opposed."

Smith's April 7, 1969 column explained Mayor Gale Gordon's jurisdiction: "His constituents are about 1,000 permanent residents whose homes appear suddenly in the cacti or cluster around lush golf courses in this 45,000-acre private island surrounded by the vast, historic wilderness area of the Anza-Borrego State Park. During this year, some 450,000 people visit the park in hopes of seeing the bighorn sheep leap the mountain crags or to look down into the frightening, wind-carved sandstone desolation of the Borrego badlands, or to see dinosaur tracks or search for relics left 200 years ago when De Anza brought first colonists to California through this valley and where the first European child was born."

Undoubtedly, Gordon made Borrego Springs a very important part of his life and his connection to the place is inseparable. McMillan noted, "He and his wife Virginia were lovely people. They had no children. He had a godchild. A friend in New York had a daughter, it was his godchild." Some have said that inextricably his love of Borrego forever changed him. McMillan recalled, "I don't know what happened to him. He became very quiet, kind of stowed away to Borrego."

Some have said that it appeared that Gordon seemed to be less active when he moved to Borrego. McMillan had this impression too when she added, "He just really got out of the business when they moved there. . . . We lost touch when he moved to Borrego and I moved to San Francisco with my husband. And we did lose touch. I was out of the business for a while."

Chapter Eight: Lucy's Foil

"Lucille Ball and Gale Gordon don't do much that's new on Here's Lucy. *But they do what they do better than any comedy team in television. Each is a seasoned professional, disciplined and competent and each can be counted on for a display of skill whenever cameras are rolling."*

—From the photo piece,
"Lucy and Gale, Comedy Experts"

Just before Gordon would work regularly with Ball on her second and third television series, he still made guest appearances on various shows.

On May 9, 1960, Gordon played a famous painter on television's *The Danny Thomas Show*. The episode has him move in with the Williams family for a few days to capture the "real them" on canvas.

A precursor to the 1962 show, Gordon appeared on a pilot episode of CBS' *Pete and Gladys* called "Bowling Brawl," broadcast on November 21, 1960. Harry Morgan, Cara Williams, Verna Felton, Barbara Stuart, and Shirley Mitchell starred in the show. Pete (Morgan) thinks it is time for Gladys (Williams) and Uncle Paul (Gordon) to end their long-standing feud. Yet Gladys is not satisfied to do so at the celebration dinner. She decides she has to prove she is a sport.

Gordon returns to play the landlord, Mr. Heckendorn, in *The Danny Thomas Show*, broadcast on January 2, 1961. This time he spots a potted plant that a fan sent to Danny, and he declares that it is a rare and valuable species requiring special care. Gordon told Schaden: "Yeah, I was a Mr. Heckendorn . . . I was on it for quite a number of shows. That was fun too."

Several weeks later on January 30, Gordon appeared again on *The Danny Thomas Show* in an episode entitled "The Rum Cake." This time it is after 11:00 p.m. as the landlord Heckendorn (Gordon) arrives with an ultimatum that if the noise from the Williams' party does not cease, Danny must go. Then Heckendorn samples some rum cake, and he promptly gets drunk!

In an episode of *Angel*, entitled "The Insurance Policy," broadcast March 30, 1951, Gordon plays John's boss named Mr. Stanley Johnson. John makes Angel (Annie Farge) cut down on her television viewing, but Susie (Doris Singleton) fills her in on programs she misses. Many of the shows she watches deal with people murdered for their insurance money. Mr. Johnson insures John, which causes Angel to panic.

Gordon returned to *Angel* in the episode entitled "Unpopular Mechanics," broadcast April 19, 1961. Gordon again played Mr. Johnson who bought an expensive car as a gift for his wife, and he leaves it in John's garage. Angel and Susie sneak off for a drive and crash right into the garage.

A couple of months after his last appearance, Gordon returned to *The Danny Thomas Show* in "The Scoutmaster," broadcast on April 24, 1961. When Rusty's troop needs a new scoutmaster, Danny decides to compete for the job when he realizes that Heckendorn (Gordon), a man with delusions of military grandeur, is a candidate.

Several weeks later, Gordon as the landlord again appeared in "The Party Wrecker," another episode of *The Danny Thomas Show*, broadcast May 22, 1961. Not invited to a party, Danny is upset. What he does not realize is that the party is a surprise for him.

Pete and Gladys gave Gordon another recurring role for a year from September 18, 1961 to September 10, 1962. He played Uncle Paul in this show produced by Parke Levy and Devery Freeman for El Camino Productions. The show's thirty-five episodes involve the amusing and vexing life of insurance man Pete Porter (Harry Morgan) who must deal with his slightly scatterbrained wife (Cara Williams).

Gordon played the miserly Merril Davis, a long-time client of Harrigan, Sr. (Pat O'Brien) in an episode of the ABC series *Harrigan and Son*, broadcast on September 22, 1961. Surprisingly he shows up at the firms' office sporting a new suit and handing out cigars.

On January 11, 1962, Gordon played Mr. Webley on ABC's *The Donna Reed Show*, in an episode called "Dr. Stone and His Horseless Carriage," about how embarrassment ensues when Dr. Stone receives a 1911 antique car as a payment for a medical bill.

In one of his few interviews, Gordon told Jack Linkletter how he overcame his childhood speech impediment in *Here's Hollywood*, broadcast on February 13, 1962 on NBC.

He returned to *The Donna Reed Show* in "Donna Meets Roberta," the May 3, 1962 episode about how insider information affects the sale of Roberta Summer's house.

On May 16, 1962, Gordon made an appearance on an episode of *The Bob Newhart Show*.

After *Our Miss Brooks*, the next most memorable regular television role for Gordon came unexpectedly when he got the chance to play Mr. Wilson's brother in *Dennis the Menace*. The series, produced by Harry Ackerman for Screen Gems (Columbia TV), based its humor on the Hank Ketcham comic book. Jay North played Dennis Mitchell, Herbert Anderson played Dennis' father Henry, Gloria Henry played Dennis' mother Alice, and Sara Seeger played Eloise Wilson. Character actor Joseph Kearns played the part of Mr. Wilson, opposite Sylvia Field as Martha Wilson.

Gordon told Schaden: ". . . Joe Kearns, who was a very old friend of mine, worked in radio with me in many, many, many shows passed away very suddenly and they called me. And I went in and played his brother and sort of took his place and kept the show going for an extra couple of seasons, yes."

Kearns had died in his sleep from a heart attack towards the end of the third season. Gordon stepped in then to play for the final six episodes of the 1961–1962 season. Then he went on to do thirty-seven more episodes in the fourth and final season of the show. Gordon's appearances ran from May 27, 1962 to September 22, 1963.

Gordon told Kulzer: "I enjoyed working with Jay North. I've always enjoyed working with people. I've worked with very few that I considered unpleasant. *Dennis the Menace* was a joy to work on. Jay, at the time, was 11, playing a 9-year old. He was terribly embarrassed about having to wear that little jumper suit. He fretted a little about that.

"Jay and I got along beautifully. We had fun together. It was great fun and there was a friendly family feeling with that troupe too. And that's terribly important when you see a cast (with) people who are together for a long time or even a short time. If there's friction among the cast members, I think it shows in the final result."

Jeanne Russell played Margaret on the show. Russell in 2008 wrote telling me, "I don't have any specific standout stories, but I can tell you that I liked Gale a lot. He joined our show at a difficult time, after the sudden death of Joe (Kearns). Gale quickly won acceptance. He loved everything about show business, including working with children. While Joe was easy and great to work with, he would disappear into his dressing room when not on.

"Gale Gordon remained visible during down time. He would hang out and tell stories and talk to everyone. He loved the business, loved being around actors—even kid actors—and he brought great energy to the set. I liked working with him and have one huge overall warm memory of him. Roddy McDowall was like that, too. And Gale's work on the show speaks for itself. He was an overall great addition and bridged a difficult time on our show."

After he finished his first six episodes of *Dennis the Menace*, Gordon appeared in the July 10, 1962 pilot episode of *Comedy Spot*. This unsuccessful show's episode entitled "For the Love of Mike" offered Shirley Jones a part portraying former singer Betty Stevens. She decides to resume her career to help ends meet with her intern husband Michael (Burt Metcalf).

Finally, Gordon would reach the pinnacle of his television career with Lucy's second series, *The Lucy Show*. *New York Times* reviewer Frank Rich once spoke of "the cartoon world" of Lucille Ball and Gale Gordon in which we see exhibited "the formulas of the old-time television sitcom."

Well, it really was a cartoon-world like show.

Once again, a delighted Gordon found another regular television role to dig into since *Our Miss Brooks*. With it lasting a number of seasons, we see Gordon savor his hotheaded but charming characterization. The comic relief Gordon offered listeners to radio paid even bigger dividends when he teamed up with Ball on television. He continued to play the same pompous and grouchy personality that he mastered years earlier. Now once again, audiences can see the comedic talent of Gordon.

Finally, he arrived at that role which would keep him on prime-time television in two shows for a dozen years total. With the stubborn and stuffy bank manager named Theodore J. Mooney on *The Lucy Show*, Gordon had that characterization down pat for five years. He pulled audience attention and generated plenty of laughs week after week as the flustered, grumpy, and overbearing comic foil to Lucy with her often-outlandish escapades.

The repetition of the successful Lucy shows on television for years imprinted on millions of people Gordon's perfect timing and well-honed characterization. No matter how predictable the outcomes of the stories were, and that audiences knew what to expect, it never seemed to matter. Viewers would laugh anyway. By the finale of the episodes, with Ball's Lucy scheming and inevitable foibles, we witnessed Gordon's Mr. Mooney unleash one, and often more, temper outbursts.

The Lucy Show depicted the endless troubles of the widow and part-time bank employee named Lucy Carmichael and her two children who share a home with divorceé Vivian Bagley (Vivian Vance) and her son. The Desilu show had producers Elliot Lewis, Jack Donohue, Tommy Thompson, Bob O'Brien, and Gary Morton. Gordon would enter the show with the second season on September 30, 1963, and he would stay five seasons for one hundred and twenty-six episodes, until the series' end.

Rayfiel, who handled negotiations at Desilu, remembered Gordon. Rayfiel: "We were, as you know, 'family' at Desilu and at Lucille Ball Productions, Inc.; Gale was not necessarily a 'father' figure, but he was a formidable 'presence,' on-stage and off. I have dealt with many agents who represented many important clients, but I never enjoyed negotiations as much as I did with Gale's agent."

Rayfiel noted, "My memory of names fails me these days. . . . There was never any pressure, only the desire to achieve what was best for his client and my company. This, I'm sure, reflected Gale's own appreciation of our communal interests. Stars generally complain about all kinds of things, especially things like living quarters, dressing rooms, and the like. The Gordons were, I believe, delighted with the house I rented them when we were on location. No complaint about anything, although it wasn't exactly the Beverly

Wilshire. That's the kind of people they were."

Not one to really complain or have gripes, Gordon spoke kindly of people he worked with. There were those who had problems with Ball and her perfectionism. Nevertheless, Gordon often spoke highly of her.

Again as with *I Love Lucy*, Ball had wanted Gordon in *The Lucy Show* from the start. With *I Love Lucy*, he was committed to TV's *Our Miss Brooks*. Now he had signed to do *Dennis the Menace* in May of 1962 through September of 1963. Therefore, in September of 1962, Ball got Charles Lane to play the banker named Mr. Barnsdahl. With the second season of *The Lucy Show*, beginning in October of 1963, Gordon was free to join the cast as a banker—now called Mr. Theodore J. Mooney.

In an episode of one of the shows with Ball, the floor opened and Lucy fell in, recalled a caller to Schaden. Gordon explained: "Ah yes, yes, that was almost a tragedy too because that trapdoor when we were filming—the cable broke. And we didn't just, we weren't just let down through the floor. We actually fell about ten feet and almost shook our teeth loose. We landed on the ground with a terrible jolt and Lucy's main concern was that there was a man, the special effects man, underneath the stage who was controlling the cable and her first thought was maybe we crushed his leg or his foot.

"And that she was very concerned about him and she knew I was alright. We were both standing there. But while the audience was applauding and laughing at, going through the floor, we were trying to make sure that the man underneath, the special effects man, hadn't had been very badly injured, and nobody knew it. The show ended. The audience left and we were pulled up. So was the man, the special effects man was not hurt at all. Thank God, but it was a very near thing. And those are things that happened that the audience never realizes."

As far as doing their own stunts, Gordon told a Schaden caller: "You did them all alone. So did Lucy. She never had a double do anything for her. Never, never. We couldn't. There was an audience within 30 feet of the set. We knew we planned it. We filmed it in front of an audience. You couldn't have a double walk on because everyone would have seen. No. Anyway, of course no matter what Lucy had to do, she learned how to do it and she did it beautifully.

If she had to walk on stilts, she learned how to do (that) and did it. And if she had to roller skate, she roller skated and was better than most people after years of constantly doing it. She was a perfectionist in every way. She worked harder than anybody in the show and she expected other people to work hard. And that's one of the things I admired about her—loved her for, because she was not satisfied with second best at all. It had to be perfect or don't do it."

Gordon told another caller: "We never did any adlibbing at all. Everything was rehearsed. We knew exactly what lines were going to be because with the system of filming that she and Desi invented, which is three cameras. There were three cameras turning at all times when we were doing a scene. And they moved according to the dialogue that was spoken. 'A' camera would have to move to get a shot of me. 'B' camera would have to get a shot of her, and a 'C' camera would have to move to get a shot of both of us together or three or four other people so there was never any adlibbing. No, we knew exactly where we were going. What we're doing. We rehearsed for two of the four days of rehearsal with the cameras making the moves with us."

Another Schaden caller asked if Gordon would ever change the scenes or make any jokes during the rehearsals. Gordon replied, "In rehearsals, we used to ad-lib and make jokes to break each other up. Yes, yes to relieve tension. But when it came down to filming, we did, we stuck exactly to the script as rehearsed.

"It was like doing a three-act play because we did them scene by scene and in sequence. And there was very little pause between, unless it meant a very big change in costume or makeup for Lucy, for instance. Or for any one of us, if we got or fell in a vat of chocolate or something and you had to get cleaned up and dressed up for the next scene. But the whole play was done from beginning to end in front of an audience, and they waited in the gaps between setups. And somebody would entertain them. Gary Morton, Lucy's husband, would entertain the people to keep them happy. While the changes were being made, makeup was being changed, but the audience there saw the whole show as the people at home saw it finally when it was all put together."

Apparently, Gordon did a complete somersault on an episode of *The Lucy Show*. He revealed to a Schaden caller that he learned that at the age of six.

Gordon told Kulzer: "Lucille would never allow anyone to double for her. If she had to learn to ice skate, she'd ice skate. If she had to go down a staircase in skis then that's what she'd do. She wouldn't allow a double to do it because the cameras were very close. None of us had doubles do stunts for us. If I fell in the mud or got stuck in a hunk of cement or fell down a trap door then that's what I did.

"Lucille didn't care about messing herself up. A lot of stars of her stature wouldn't do physical comedy because they were afraid they'd get their hair messed up or they'd look bad. I remember once she fell into a vat of green dye. She came out with not only her hair green but everything was green. It was tremendously funny to see her come out all green, but it took hours to get her cleaned up and her make-up put on to do the rest of the show. But things like that were important because they looked real. And this is very, very important when you're doing comedy. You've got to believe that it is happening and it has to be real."

"I think anybody who has been in theater, prefers it. Television is a factory. You turn out things on a revolving assembly line. You don't have time to perfect anything in television. If you're doing a weekly series it's very difficult to make each episode of the series as good as it should be because you don't have time to devote to it. This was one reason that Lucy was such a hard worker, and many people didn't like going on her show because they worked from the moment they got there until the show was filmed. And that was four days. And in those four days we had to learn the show and do all the camera rehearsing, because there were three cameras in each scene all going at once.

"Guest actors had to rehearse with us as performers because each word that an actor might have said might be a cue for the camera to move or turn in order to get a different angle. All those technical things that television requires takes away from the concentration that you should be giving the character itself. For that reason, Lucy worked very hard for the four days. The results show. Her work has endured for some 40 years or more because she was never satisfied.

"She would never say, 'Oh, we can get by with this, it won't matter,' because if it mattered to one viewer—that would have ruined it as far as Lucy was concerned. And that's why television is a sausage factory. Radio wasn't so bad because you didn't have to memorize your lines. But you did have to do everything because your own character was in your voice — that took a little doing. Most people thought that if you could speak English or read then you could be a radio actor. Well that wasn't so. You had to put a great deal into your reading to convince somebody who was just listening that a certain character is speaking."

While doing *The Lucy Show*, articles appeared looking back at the career of Gordon. "A Man of Many Faces," *Chicago Tribune*, April 12, 1964, stated: "We sat over lunch with him and his charming wife, Virginia, who has worked with him in both radio and TV. The Gordons had come from southern California to judge a baking contest in Aurora.

"He says today: 'Looking back, I almost killed radio before it was old enough to fight back.' However, he was soon established in soap opera and likes to recall today that in the *Second Mrs. Burton*, a real washboard weeper, he played Mr. Burton. . . .

"Gordon has grown in stature thru the years. He was big and bad in *Gang Busters*; a sly villain in *Stories from the Black Chamber*, he was a loudmouthed Texan on the *Burns and Allen* series, and Mr. Wilson on *Dennis the Menace*. He's done a lot of things on the stage. He sings in musical comedy, too. . . . If you still refuse to be impressed, this fact may do it: He played the original *Flash Gordon*."

Gordon would appear in a CBS Special called *The Lucille Ball Comedy Hour: Mr. And Mrs.*, broadcast on April 19, 1964. The show's story is about Lucille Ball as television studio head Bonnie Barton, who sets out to sign her comedian husband Bill Barton (Bob Hope) for a TV special. Gordon plays Mr. Harvey, a member of the Board, who has suggested that Bonnie resign if she fails. Although the Bartons have kept America rolling with laughter for months, they are in trouble with the sponsor now because the show's ratings have slipped to second place. Jack Weston, Max Showalter and John Dehner are among the cast.

From April 19 through April 23, 1965, Gordon appeared along with Betty White as the celebrity players on *The Match Game*. The NBC show with host Gene Rayburn offered cash to contestants for answering questions and matching as many responses among teammates as they can.

On May 1, 1966, a nostalgic review of the guest stars and favorites of radio and television history utilized Gordon's rehearsals with Ball. Arthur Godfrey hosted this CBS Special called *Magic of Broadcasting*. The other guests included Fred Allen, Milton Berle, Ben Bernie, Fanny Brice, Bing Crosby, Sheldon Leonard, Helen Morgan, Rod Serling, Arthur Tracy, John Scott Trotter, and Rudy Vallee.

Gordon showed his skill at playing game shows when he won $250 during his appearance on the daytime edition of *Password*, hosted by Allen Ludden. In the rare surviving episode broadcast on September 19, 1966, Gordon appeared for a round paired off with Lucy and for a round paired off with her husband Gary Morton. Mary Wickes, Dick Patterson and his wife also appeared on the show.

Lucy humorously introduces Gordon as "The Meeney, Miney, Mooney, Money Man."

Ludden asks Gordon if he's "The Meeney, Miney, Mooney, Money Man?"

Gordon: "Yes I am."

Ludden asks Gordon, "You're gonna be nice to this girl?"

Gordon, not hearing the question, responds, "Pardon?"

Ludden asks again, "You're gonna be nice to her in this game?"

Gordon, in reference to *The Lucy Show* retorts, "She better be nice to me or she won't show up at the bank Tuesday."

Interestingly Gordon, when given the password "Diamond," gives teammate Lucy the clue of "Kohinoor," which is a world famous diamond. At first, she is noticeably bewildered. She looks to Ludden when she does not understand what Gordon said. Ludden tells her, "He's your friend." She then suddenly gets it . . . "Diamond."

When the password is "bawl," it passes from Morton and Wickes. Lucille gives Gordon the clue of "Lucille" and Gordon immediately answers correctly.

When Morton teams with Gordon, the password is "Giraffe." All Morton has to do is give the clue of "animal" with a look of awe, and Gordon guesses correctly.

In a 1966 interview, Gordon unashamedly explained: "I'm not a compulsive actor. To me it's just a job to do. I turn it off as soon as I leave the studio, I couldn't give you a single line of dialogue the next day. I can't stand these actors who are always 'on.'"

Gordon played Fire Chief Warren Packard in another unsuccessful pilot for a CBS series called *Vacation Playhouse*. In "Where There's Smokey," broadcast on August 1, 1966, Smokey (Soupy Sales) is a bungling firefighter who lives with his sister and brother-in-law. The Fire Chief will try anything to get Smokey to move out, and that includes pushing him into matrimony.

He made two talk show appearances in 1967. On August 30, Gordon joined Eve Arden on *The Mike Douglas Show*. He also appeared on *The Woody Woodbury Show* on November 28.

On the December 11, 1967 broadcast of *The Danny Thomas Hour*, called "The Royal Follies of 1933," Thomas plays Bachelor Prince Wolfgang who needs to elude a husband-hunting heiress by taking refuge in a Broadway show menaced by gangsters. Gordon played a character named Baxter. Former co-star Eve Arden, along with Ken Berry, Hans Conried, Bob Hope, Shirley Jones, Jackie Joseph and Kurt Kasznar joined Gordon.

From April 1 through April 5, 1968, Gordon appeared on NBC as a guest panelist for *The Hollywood Squares*. Others in the shows were Jim Backus, Bill Bixby, Jack Cassidy, Barbara Feldon and Shirley Jones. The regular contestants Rose Marie, Wally Cox, and Charley Weaver joined the host Peter Marshall and announcer Kenny Williams. The show involved the contestants determining if celebrity panelists are giving correct answers to questions as they play games of tic-tac-toe for cash and prizes.

The fall of 1968 would bring us Gordon in a new show and character name with Ball. However, it was really the same part. In short, Gordon would bring us the same basic characterization from *The Lucy Show* to Lucy's third series, *Here's Lucy*. Now he played Harrison Otis Carter, the cranky employment agency owner and Lucy's brother-in-law.

The Lucy Show would transition to *Here's Lucy* with the start of the new season on September 23, 1968. The characters' names and setting changed but the zany comedic possibilities continued unchanged.

This would happen one more time when he appeared once again for Lucy in her fourth series a dozen years after *Here's Lucy* went off the air. By the time of that last entry, *Life with Lucy*, audiences though amused were so tired and overly familiar with the whole "Lucy comedy world-view."

In a brief photo piece, "Lucy and Gale, Comedy Experts" their characters are described: "In the television series Lucy is unfailingly scatterbrained, lovable and well intentioned. Gordon's character is just the opposite: vain, pompous, bombastic, threatening and often wrong. The combination is good, the chemistry is just right and Lucille Ball remains the undisputed queen of all television."

The reason for the name change of Ball's series is that after six seasons, Lucy sold the rerun rights to *The Lucy Show*, as well as all of Desilu Productions for $17 million dollars in Gulf & Western stock. Bart Andrews: "One of the conditions of the sale required her to abandon *The Lucy Show* format and come up with a new series."

In stepped Lucy's two real-life children to play her children in the show. Gordon would play her brother-in-law and employer Harrison Otis Carter, known simply as "Uncle Harry." As Lucy Carter, we watch week after week as she endures working for the harsh and blustery Harrison Carter who runs the Unique Employment Agency. In return, Carter has to endure widowed Lucy's misadventures as she tries to raise her two teenage children, Kim (Lucie Arnaz) and Craig (Desi Arnaz, Jr.).

From an episode, here is a typical interaction between the two:
Harry is quietly reading at his desk. In enters Lucy.

LUCY:	"Well, hi Harry, what are you doing here so early?"
HARRY:	(firmly) "I am not here early. You are here late. And this habit you have of not getting to work on time is getting worse."
LUCY:	"No it isn't Harry, it is getting better."
HARRY:	(rises out of his chair)"What do you mean getting better?"
LUCY:	"This is the earliest I've ever been late."
HARRY:	"Well you better get busy, or it will be the earliest you've ever been fired."

LUCY: "You sure know how to make a person feel good."

The one hundred and forty-four episodes of *Here's Lucy* were produced for Lucille Ball Productions by her husband Gary Morton, Tommy Thompson, Cleo Smith and William Maginetti. The show featured many celebrity guest stars; including Jack Benny, Carol Burnett, Richard Burton, and so on. Mary Jane Croft, who played several roles, including a recurring role as Lucy's next-door neighbor Betty Ramsey from the final episodes of *I Love Lucy*, returned as her friend Mary Jane Lewis.

The last episode of *Here's Lucy* aired on March 18, 1974. Although Gordon had received nominations for an Emmy as Outstanding Supporting Actor in a Comedy for *Here's Lucy* for three seasons of the show; 1966–67, 1967–68, and 1970–71, he never won.

Gordon's steady work for a dozen years had ended when Lucy decided to call it quits. Andrews said Ball explained: "I think it was the fact that we were all tired of having to lean on the same formula over and over again. My writers were tired of having to repeat themselves. Gale Gordon had other, fresher things he wanted to do. And, frankly, I couldn't figure out why, at my age [sixty-two], I was still kicking up my heels and hanging from chandeliers. And besides, I wasn't making that much money, being in such a high-income tax bracket."

Wanda Clark, personal secretary to Ball, recalled first meeting Gordon on the set of *The Lucy Show* during the second season when both started working for Lucy. Clark: "He was a sports car enthusiast at the time, and after seeing me in the parking lot driving my little old '56 MG, he decided I was O.K. and we would have something to talk about."

Clark remembered visiting his Hollywood Hills home where he would stay during the weeks of shooting. He commuted to Borrego on weekends. She recalled one time, just a few years before he died, that Gordon visited Clark at her home (also in Hollywood Hills) for a party. She said it was sometime in the early 1990s.

Clark: "He told me the first house he built in the Laurel Canyon area where he took his bride was just down the street on Wonderland Avenue.

"Besides his wonderful talent and incredible and impeccable sense of timing, which just seemed to get better as years went by, Gale Gordon was the nicest gentleman in Hollywood. Lucy loved working with him. She trusted and depended on his support as evidenced by his presence in her shows. I wasn't there at the time, but the story goes they wanted Gale for the part of Fred Mertz, but he was committed to another series at the time. However, he did guest-shots in *I Love Lucy*, and the fact that they did find the wonderful Bill Frawley for the part was most fortunate.

"I remember how Richard Burton was impressed with Gale when he and Elizabeth Taylor appeared on an episode of *Here's Lucy*. They seemed to have long conversations during rehearsals."

On a clip from *The Merv Griffin Show*, October 4, 1973, with Bob Hope, Lucille Ball, and others, Gordon remained silent during the following discussion of his talent, smiling and looking interested at various points. Ball's husband, Gary Morton, remembered Burton's reaction when he did one of the *Here's Lucy* shows—in fact it was one of the highest rated episodes of the series.

Morton: ". . . When Richard and Elizabeth were on our show, and I was sitting next to him in the chair like this (placing his hand to side of his face in a studied manner), while Elizabeth was rehearsing a scene, Richard turned to me and said, 'What's that fellow's name?'

"I said 'That's Gale Gordon, and we're very proud of him.'

"And he said, 'Oh he's absolutely wonderful I can't believe this man's performance. Where is he from?'

"I said, 'Well I think he's from here. He's been working with Lucy for six, seven years.'

"And Gale walked over, and Richard said to him, 'you must be English, you act so well. You couldn't be American.' (Everyone laughs)."

Ball's daughter Lucie is heard saying: "It's true, he's born in England."

This is what most people think, but it is not true.

Then Ball gave her appreciation of Gordon's talent.

Ball: "You know something wonderful about Gale. From the time he goes through the first reading, he does it, not exactly, but he's up, like he is on a full show. From the very first reading at the table, then we're on our feet after the second and we do our show from Monday to Thursday. But Monday morning he sounds like as if he could go on. Not that he necessarily knows his lines—he doesn't have to. That's the way he operates all the time—tops. It's fantastic."

In 2008, Lucie best acknowledged Gordon's impact on her life. Lucie: "As far as anecdotes, most I will be saving for when I finally sit down and write my own book. But what I can tell you is [that I never worked with] a nicer, gentler, more professional man in this business, and I have been in it 42 years now. He was a wonderful teacher to me as far as how to get things done without the drama usually associated with actors' egos. There will never be another Gale Gordon!"

After Burton died, Cecil Smith, in "All the World's His Stage: From interviews to Sitcoms, Burton Was On," remembered how Burton came to appear on *Here's Lucy*:

"'I adorrre your show,' Burton cried, pointing one eloquent finger at Lucille [Ball]. 'I want to do it.'

"La Ball stared, open-mouthed.

"'It's true,' Elizabeth Taylor said. 'He loves the Lucy show. He keeps yelling that he wants to do it. Please let him. It's the only way to shut him up.'

"Six weeks later, Burton and Taylor reported to Stage 20 on what had been the Desilu lot, now Paramount. Madelyn Davis and Bob Carroll, Jr., the original *I Love Lucy* writers, had returned to the fold to write a very funny script for this special appearance. The director was Jerry Paris. I was there because the script called for several newspaper people on the entertainment beat to play themselves in the final scene.

"Though Taylor had a couple of key scenes, most of the action involved Burton and Ball supported by that marvelous old farceur Gale Gordon. . . .

"Rehearsals were an absolute joy. Gale Gordon out of more than a half-century on the boards never gave Burton the same cue twice. He threw in bits of Shakespeare, did elaborate takes, tried breaking Burton up with melodramatic mugging. Burton usually gave as good as he got, but sometimes the old comic would destroy him and he would roar in helpless laughter."

Gordon likewise admired Burton. Gordon told Kulzer: "I remember we did an episode with Richard Burton. Lucy and I were both thrilled to work with someone of his caliber. He was utterly charming and delightful and so was Liz Taylor. I had admired Richard Burton for years and years before I had ever worked with him. He was a great, great actor. It was a joy to get to know him as a person."

Gordon continued to make appearances in other television shows while committed to playing Harrison Carter. He made one appearance in 1968 and then three appearances during 1970 on NBC's *The Dean Martin Show*. For his first appearance with Martin, in a show broadcast on December 19, 1968, Gordon was among a number of others that were uncredited in this Christmas show, including Lucille Ball, Tony Bennett, Jack Benny, Phil Harris, Bob Hope, Paul Lynde, Don Rickles, Red Skelton, etc.

In 1969, his next appearance came on the afternoon talk show, *The Merv Griffin Show*, on January 26 with Arthur Treacher and George Jessel.

In his first of three 1970 appearances with Martin, he played the harried personnel director trying to handle employees' complaints in an episode broadcast on January 8. Two months later on March 5, Gordon returned to the show to play a fussy fisherman plagued by his noisy buddy (Martin). A Christmas episode broadcast on December 17 had Gordon peddling perfect gifts for people you hate ("especially for your enemies?").

In an interview with *Hollywood NOW*, December 9, 1969, Gordon spoke of the differences as far as appearing on Martin's variety shows. Hal Bates asked Gordon, "Is it true that because Dean is so casual, everything on the show follows suit?"

Gordon: "Yes, it seems to be. To me, it's quite terrifying. I'm used to working with Lucy and we know exactly what we're going to do every moment, and we rehearse very, very thoroughly. Here they just wander through a sketch. Half the time Dean isn't here so somebody stands in for him. You finally get to work with him when you're on the air, so to speak."

As far as comparing his experiences with Lucy and Dean Martin, Gordon explained: "I could talk for hours about it [*The Lucy Show*] and about Lucille Ball. She's an extraordinary woman, a superb talent and a great gal. She's a fascinating and brilliant woman in many, many ways. She knows camera angles, comedy lines, everything about this business. She made a point of learning everything. Don't forget, she started out as a Goldwyn girl many years ago, and she's been through the mill.

"I have been in this business 47 years and I still learn while working with Lucy. I find her delightful and intriguing because she is such a perfectionist. There is no shuffling through a rehearsal. She doesn't mumble her lines. She studies her character in order to become that person. She truly works at her profession. In my opinion, this is the mark of a great performer. She's been at the top for nearly 20 years, and there doesn't seem to be an end in sight.

"In truth, Lucy's method for this show would be completely wrong because Dean is a very relaxed man. For one thing, this is a variety show. It is not a situation comedy where the characters are the same week after week. The Martin show employs different elements all the time—guests, music, [and] comedy. To try and drive Dean would kill the character he so successfully presents. He has his own great charm."

Bates asked Gordon, "How do you, as an actor, contend with these types?"

Gordon: "It's very difficult, but one adjusts. On Dean's show we work out a sketch, do it and then wrap it up. With Lucy, we start on a Monday, do scene after scene, rework them until they're right and by Thursday have a finished product. For Lucy, we memorize our lines, and here we have to rely on idiot cards. It's easier to work this way, but it sure is harder on the nerves."

In looking back over his career, Gordon aptly observed how his characterization has changed little from the 1940s thru 1969. Gordon: "I've generally filled the role of blowhard, as you know. That stems back to the days of *Fibber McGee and Molly* on radio. It was the first time in a continuing part where I had to get angry and blow up.

"I had been in radio for years playing heavies and leading men. I did very little comedy, mostly drama. It was on the *McGee* show, as Mayor LaTrivia, that I became a blowhard. Ever since then I've been cast as someone with a big voice. I've never been called on to do anything else. *Our Miss Brooks* on television was the first time people actually got to see my blowing up."

When asked what his feelings about situation comedies were, Gordon explained, "It's a little hard to pinpoint. In general, I like them. I loved the *He and She* series and Dick Van Dyke. They had the ingredients necessary for good shows, excellent writing and performers. It follows that if performers in a series impart a warmth that reaches the public, it's a great asset.

"Naturally you get the finest writers to write a situation comedy, but if people in the show have no rapport with the audience, then they've got nothing. By the same token, a sit-com with very likeable people and no great writing, could also flop. In other words, the combination of the two elements would almost guarantee a successful show."

On December 3, 1970, *LAT* reported in "Yule Parade Set in Pomona," that Gordon was the Grand Marshall at the "Christmas Fantasy" parade sponsored by the Jaycees on the Pomona Mall. The Saturday, December 5, 1970 nine-block long parade started at 6 p.m. with an estimated 128 units; including floats, bands, marching units, equestrian units, antique cars and special displays.

The following year, on April 1, he made an appearance on the daytime talk show, *The Virginia Graham Show.* The next year, on February 23, 1972, Gordon celebrated the life of radio, TV, and film actor Richard Crenna when he appeared on Ralph Edwards' syndicated show *This is Your Life*. Gordon spoke of how Crenna lived with him and his wife for several months back in the 1950s.

On May 26, Gordon made his second appearance on *The Merv Griffin Show*; Gordon shared the talk with Ball, Morton, Douglas Fairbanks, Jr., and comic Richard Dawson. He returned to Merv's show the following year, on October 4, 1973, joining Ball, Morton, Desi Arnaz Jr., Lucie Arnaz, and Bob Hope. Lucy did a musical number from her upcoming film release of *Mame*.

On August 29, 1974, *LAT* reported that Gordon joined the cast of *Sugar* as a replacement for actor-director Sir Cyril Ritchard's understudy, Joe Ross. The latter is temporarily replacing Ritchard, who suffered an apparent heart attack. This Civic Light Opera's production at the Dorothy Chandler Pavilion had Gordon in the role of a millionaire playboy who proposes marriage. *Sugar* is a musical adaptation inspired by the movie *Some Like it Hot.*

Chicago Daily Tribune, September 1, 1974: "Jule Styne flew out when Sir Cyril was replaced by Gale Gordon."

In 1975, NBC offered *A Dean Martin Roast: Lucille Ball*, broadcast on February 7. This Special featured Lucy surrounded by her colleagues. Gordon joined the many comedy luminaries that worked with Lucy to offer her good-natured barbs and put-downs.

Later that year, on October 12, a piece by Marie Mattson in *Chicago Tribune*, noted that the Redwood Room in the Clift Hotel: "You're apt to see celebrities here: Vincent Price comes for eggs Benedict; Gale Gordon and Nanette Fabray like the salmon . . . This restaurant long has been a standby for American food . . ."

Gordon's resemblance to another actor caused a reader to write to the *Chicago Daily Tribune*'s TV Mailbag, "Chicago—My dad says the man who plays Higgins on *Magnum, P.I.* is the same man who played Mr. Mooney on the old *Lucy Show*. I know they are different persons. Please clear this up—K.N." The paper responded showing photos: "John Hillerman portrays the stuffy Higgins on *Magnum P.I.*; Gale Gordon portrayed the tyrannical Mr. Mooney of *Lucy* fame."

On November 30, 1975, James Brown's article in *LAT* reported that Gordon appeared at The Beverly (Dinner Theater) in Baton Rouge, Louisiana. The Los Angeles Pacific Pioneer Broadcasters had a gathering at the Sportsmen's Lounge on November 21 to honor and salute radio's "Second Bananas." Hal Kanter emceed the event. Brown: "Two of the more familiar second bananas—Gale Gordon and Jim Backus—sent along recorded greetings and thanks."

Though Gordon did not attend, the event had assembled many of radio's secondary players; Edgar Bergen, Mel Blanc, Shirley Mitchell, Frank Nelson, Richard Crenna, Mary Jane Croft, Lurene Tuttle, Alan Reed, with a special brief appearance by Bing Crosby to salute Ken Carpenter, and others. Some have said that Gordon's non-appearance at this gathering had to do with his unwillingness to get over Mel Blanc's criticism of him, and so he decided not to be there in Blanc's presence.

In 1976, Gordon appeared on three shows. First, NBC's *The Tomorrow Show* on October 26 saluted radio comedy's second bananas. Tom Snyder hosted the show that had guests Bill Baldwin, Frank Nelson, Edgar Bergen, Jim Backus, and Ernestine Wade.

On November 16, Gordon appeared on Dinah Shore's talk show along with Ball, Morton, Burnett, and Valerie Harper. *Dinah!* offered a program of talk, music, homemaking advice and cooking recipes.

CBS Salutes Lucy—The First 25 Years, broadcast on November 28 offered a selection of clips and introductory segments in tribute to Ball and her TV work. Again, Gordon provided his praise along with other Lucy associates.

In 1977, Gordon made two appearances. On November 21, CBS offered Lucy another Special. The show, *A Lucille Ball Special: Lucy Calls the President* provided an actual script this time. In the story, Lucy Whittaker (Ball) puts in a phone call to then President Jimmy Carter on a matter of local interest and finds herself hosting the Chief Executive when he decides to visit for dinner. Gordon played Omar. The cast included Vivian Vance, Ed McMahon, Mary Wickes, Steve Allen, Mary Jane Croft, and the President's mother, Miss Lillian Carter. Gordon played a part that recalled his work with Lucy, and earlier with Eve Arden.

A week after that Lucy Special on CBS, Gordon made his second appearance for 1977 in the ABC Special, *The Honeymooners Christmas*. When the Raccoon Lodge mounts their production of *A Christmas Carol*, Ralph Kramden (Jackie Gleason) is the director, and Gordon plays Ralph's boss.

An April 27, 1978 piece in *LAT* uses a word nowadays deemed offensive. In "Olympic Games for Retarded Set May 6," the article reported, "Gardena—The Exchange Club and the Southwest Assn. for Retarded Children has rescheduled its Olympic games for retarded youths for 1 to 5 p.m. Saturday, May 6, at the Gardena High School Athletic Field. Other celebrities will include Gale Gordon of *The Lucy Show*. . ."

In 1978, he made three appearances; first, on the popular CBS children's show *Captain Kangaroo* broadcast on September 21. That show provided Gordon a chance to visit the Treasure House. The episode starred Bob Keeshan, Hugh Brannum, Cosmo Allegretti and James Watt.

Two months later, Gordon discussed his long career when he appeared on *The Mike Douglas Show* on November 20.

Later on the same day, he reunited with Arden in a CBS Special, *Bobby Vinton's Rock 'n' Rollers*. The musical look back at the 1950s included Fabian, Stockard Channing, Penny Marshall and others. "TV Review: Vinton's Special: A Salute to Rock" noted: "Gale Gordon and Eve Arden just manage to retain their dignity in a bloated malt shop sketch, then lose it altogether with a duet of 'Sha-boom'. . ."

In 1979, 1980, 1981 and 1982, Gordon made just one known appearance per year on television.

In 1979, he returned to CBS to visit *Captain Kangaroo*.

On October 18, 1979, in "Borrego Daze on tap first weekend in November," *LAT* announced, "Borrego Springs in northeast San Diego County will celebrate the beginning of a new winter season with Borrego Daze, on Nov. 2-4. Two old films about Borrego Springs, which were made by Copley Productions, will be shown continuously Nov. 3 in The Mall area. One of the films is narrated by Gale Gordon of the *I Love Lucy* show, who has lived in Borrego Valley for many years." The latter film is *A New Way of Life*, already discussed here in Chapter Seven.

Lucy had the task of developing a new situation comedy in *A Lucille Ball Special: Lucy Moves to NBC*, broadcast on February 8, 1980. Gordon assists her in lining up talent for the show. The result is "The Music Mart," starring Donald O'Connor and Gloria DeHaven as Wally and Carol Coogan, music-store owners whose son is devoted to rock music. This unsuccessful pilot for a proposed series included among the cast Johnny Carson, Gary Coleman, Bob Hope, Gene Kelly, Jack Klugman and Ruta Lee.

On the same day of the show, *New York Times* columnist John J. O'Connor reviewed the pilot program noting that Gordon: "Offers some of his nifty slow-burn turns. . . . Miss Ball is reduced to the part of a small walk-on. The idea of a series is not bad, but its usurpation of what is supposed to be a comedy variety special is disastrous."

In addition, an unsuccessful attempt by Ball as Executive Producer and Director of another pilot named *Bungle Abbey*, appeared on NBC on May 31, 1981. Gordon played the Abbott who watches over a group of zany monks who wish to help a children's orphanage by selling a painting hanging in their monastery.

On May 31, 1982, Gordon made what may be one of his last appearances on a daytime talk show when he visited *The John Davidson Show*, along with Ball, Morton, and Dean Paul Martin.

Gordon continued to keep busy in his later years with dinner theater productions at various locations, particularly in Canada. Hilliard Harper in "A Look at San Diego Dinner Theaters," mentions

Gordon's name as one of the active performers.

On September 9, 1983, *LAT* reported that Gordon performed at the Lyric Dinner Theatre in La Mesa—a San Diego suburb, the Lawrence Welk Theatre outside Escondido, and the Fiesta Theatre in Spring Valley. It noted that the Lyric dropped musicals for comedies as star vehicles.

Gordon's understanding of comedy explains his own long-time success at playing comedies. As regards how comedy is to be played, Gordon told Kulzer: "The secret of comedy, if I may be so bold as to make a statement like this, is that for comedy to be good it has to be played straight. And again, the greatest example of this is Lucy Ball. No matter how wild the shows were that we did, no matter how bizarre the situations were, they were never played as if they were funny. They were played like serious incidents of everyday life. And that's why they are terribly funny and are still considered classic comedies.

"What's wrong with most of the comedies nowadays is that actors know they're funny or think they are. That takes away from the comedy right away. The ones that play comedy straight are the great ones—the ones people love to watch."

The insecurities that plagued other actors seemed never to affect Gordon. He was content with often playing supporting parts throughout his acting career. The secondary nature of supporting parts never seemed to bother Gordon. Perhaps it is because he understood the responsibilities and the pitfalls connected with being the leading actor. Nor did he get bored quickly as some would. Understandably, he had every reason to be bored, given the repetitious nature of the parts he played over the years.

One thing is certain: he kept himself intensely busy throughout most of his career at work and at home. He truly found contentment with his work and life, and he avoided the problems and wasted energy that would come to the typical actor with an unbridled ego. Undoubtedly, Gordon behaved just as the true professional should, particularly avoiding the prevalent screaming matches or arguments expected between temperamental actors. In short, he was praiseworthy for achieving a balance that few actors ever really achieve.

Chapter Nine: "A Wonderful Person"

"That's right, I take it as it comes along and enjoy it. I loved the radio. I loved television. I loved the stage and I'm very lucky to be working all that time. And I'm very grateful for that. I enjoy it!"
—Gale Gordon radio call-in with Chuck Schaden, May 13, 1990

For one more time, Gordon did get to be on primetime with a new weekly show, reaching millions of television viewers. In *Life with Lucy*, Ball tried in 1986 once more for another hit series. In this, her last one, Gordon appeared as Curtis McGibbon, co-owner of the Californian M & G Hardware Store. Ball played Lucy Barker, heir of her husband's interest in the business after he died. Ball and Gordon are in-laws since their children are married to each other.

Gordon told Schaden: ". . . in the third series so . . . they made me a part of the family because it was much easier for the writers to include someone who was part of the family, like going on vacation. They couldn't if I was a banker."

The show ran from September 20 to November 15, 1986. Lucille Ball Productions/Aaron Spelling Productions had a number of producers; namely, Aaron Spelling, Morton, Bob Carroll, Jr., E. Duke Vincent, Linda Morris and Vic Rauseo. Of the thirteen episodes produced, only eight episodes aired.

A week after the show stopped running; the cancellation of *Life with Lucy* did not adversely affect Gordon. On November 21, 1986, *LAT* reported in "Gordon to Be Cited," that "Veteran actor Gale Gordon will be honored by Pacific Pioneer Broadcasters at a luncheon today at Sportsmen's Lodge. Gordon has played Lucille Ball's comic foil in three series and also portrayed Mr. Wilson on *Dennis the Menace* and pompous Principal Osgood Conklin on *Our Miss Brooks*."

Life with Lucy failed to remain on the air for the entire season for several reasons. At the outset, ABC made a big mistake in allowing Lucy to have complete creative control, without any requirements for a pilot or anything. The 75-year old Lucy did not wish to change the formula that she established in three previously successful shows. However, times were changing. Smart socially conscious comedies like *All in the Family* had already appeared. The old physical comedy formula that worked for Lucy before now was tired, tedious and dated.

Before he even saw a preview of the series, Steve Daley (in "Burstyn Show Not Bursting with Laughs") did not offer any optimism for the success of *Life with Lucy*. Daley: "Taking a look at what happened to Mary Tyler Moore, the Lucy of the 1970s, in her last sitcom attempt, the morning line on *Life with Lucy* isn't promising."

However, Gordon wanted to appear in the show with Lucy no matter what he thought of it. Moreover, he did so by staying true to his familiar blowhard character to the intense pleasure of viewers. Nevertheless, he effectively retired at this point, although he continued with some stage productions in California.

Never did Gordon forget his immense appreciation for the women in his professional life. Indeed, he expressed his deep admiration for Eve Arden and Lucille Ball.

Schaden asked Gordon, "Of all the things that you've done, can you pick out anything specific that you liked the best?"

Gordon responded: "(Uh), no, nothing really especially, except working with Lucy was a joy, but also working with Eve Arden was. I, I, I've been very lucky and the people that I worked with have all been very inspiring people. Very, very capable and talented and very nice people. And I, I consider that one of the greatest glories of this profession is having known so many people who were real people, really good, good people as well as being talented and delightful."

As regards Arden, Gordon said, "I went to her services, of course. It was for me like losing a very close and dear friend, which, of course, she was. I feel very fortunate to have worked with such delightful people like Eve and Lucy. Great talent and great ladies. It's extremely rare to find talent and friends like they were."

As regards Ball, Gordon revealed after her death that she did not see herself as a funny person. Gordon: "But when she told a story or recalled an event that happened, she always illustrated it with her body and her face. . . She never saw it, but she was extremely amusing."

Wanda Clark, Lucy's secretary noted: "It was so important for Lucy to have Gale with her. I think she personally guaranteed something in order to get him cast. That is, because of Gale's age, there was some difficulty with insurance for the filming of *Life with Lucy*."

Stuart Shostak, owner of Shokus Video, had the pleasure of working with Gordon in the series. Shostak: "Gale was one of the nicest, kindest, friendliest people I've ever had the pleasure to meet and work with. He told me some stories about how over the years when people would recognize him, parents would say, 'I want you to yell at my kid so he'll do better in school.' He would always reply that he usually got paid for doing things like that and then smiled back."

In fact, Gordon had this happen to him throughout his career. He seemed to get a kick out of people coming to him and telling him to yell at their child.

Shostak: "I had gotten to know Gale very well during the course of the series, and he really was the opposite of the characters he used to portray.

"When I was lucky enough to get a part in an episode of *Life with Lucy*, there was some business I was supposed to do as I was leaving the hardware store, and I was supposed to turn and yell at Gale. Well, after getting to know him as I had, I said to him during a rehearsal that it was going to be very hard for me to yell at him because he was such a nice man. He looked at me and said, 'Well, you just think of me as that mean, old bastard you were used to watching all those years and you'll do fine.' He was a wonderful person."

Two years after Lucy's series flopped, Gordon appeared on *The 40th Annual Emmy Awards*, broadcast on August 28, 1988. Gordon presented the award for Outstanding Individual Performance in a Variety or Music Program to Robin Williams for *ABC Presents a Royal Gala*.

In a 1989 letter to *LAT*'s TV TalkBack column, a reader L.M.F., Santa Monica asked, "I am writing to ask if Gale Gordon that used to be on Lucille Ball is dead? Some say he is some say not." The columnist answered: "Gale is alive and well. Now that Lucille Ball is off the tube in a weekly series, Gale is enjoying life in his farm near San Diego where he raises dogs."

Gordon told Schaden when asked about his health: "Very good! Very good. I'm 84 and I'm going to do a play that only has two people in it. I've been doing it for the last year, and I'm going to do it again in September in Victoria, Canada in September."

The play Gordon referred to is the two-person play called *Mass Appeal*. As far as being grueling for him, Gordon told Schaden: "Well, it's two hours of two people talking so it keeps me alert, let's say.... I don't dare go to sleep in the middle of an act." When a caller asked to give more details about the production, Gordon responded: "It's a story written by Bill C. Davis. Yes, it was played in New York off-off-Broadway. And it finally went to Broadway, but it's been around quite a while. It's a story about two priests, an elderly priest myself who is very fond of his wine and his comfort. And he has a young seminarian who comes to him really inspired.

"It's a little complicated to explain in a few minutes but the young man makes the older man realize that he, the older man, has not been a very good priest to his parish because he is always kowtowing to them and getting his wine from them. All kinds of sparkling Burgundy, which he loves. And spiritually, he's not really much a priest as this boy who wants to be one. And this is the story of his training him—the boy, and realizing that this young man is what he was, the older man, when he was the young—. And he realizes he has not lived up to all the dreams and all the sincerity and Christ-like qualities that he dreamed about and its, the whole thing is an exercise and is trying to get this young boy into the priesthood and the conflict with the church authorities who set certain rules and regulations and so forth.

"And it's a play, that although they're Catholics, the, it is not sectarian in any way. It doesn't preach Catholicism. It just preaches a relationship of two men who are very sincere in what they do. And the priests, and the cardinals, and the other people who come to see the show just love it. And the nuns love it because they see some of their teachers in these two, in this character that I play and they all see themselves as the young boy who is so really Christ-like in his approach to things. And it makes the older man realize where he is let down. It's a very telling play and it has a lot of humor, but it has a lot of wonderful sentiment and warmth. And I love doing it because it isn't outright slapstick comedy by any means, although there a lot of wonderful laughs in it. I enjoy doing it very much. . . . It's a beautifully written play. It's been very successful. It's been around, and many, many people have done it."

The caller asked Gordon the obvious; namely, what part did he play? Gordon said, "I played the older priest of course. Yes, I'm 84, I wouldn't play the young one." When asked if he was sitting at a table in this play, Gordon noted, "No, I have a desk that I use. But I walk around. I even do a little dance when I am a little bit under the influence of wine—but no. Why did you get that idea?"

When asked if he would do the show in Chicago, Gordon stated, "Well, if somebody asks me, offers me, a chance to do it. Well I'll be there." As far as another live show, film or video production, Gordon added, "Well if a part in TV came along I like, with a show that I liked, I'd be very happy to do it. But I do spend six or seven months a year in Canada doing the dinner theater which I enjoy very much. I love the contact with the audience and but I'm still available for television (laughs).

"A lot of people think that I long since disappeared into limbo I guess because it's been so many years since I [had] done a TV show. I've had several offers of things but they didn't seem very nice or right for me. So thank God I can pick and choose. So I just stuck to the thing that is most entertaining to me which is the dinner theater, and I don't certainly get rich on it. It's the theater, and that is my first love. And so I mean I love working. Enjoy it. That's why I've done it for so long."

In the year before this interview, Gordon had appeared in Canada in three renditions of *Mass Appeal*. From March 17 thru April 30, 1989, Gordon played opposite Kevin Hare at the Mayfair Dinner Theater in Edmonton, Alberta. Then he played again opposite Hare from June 12 thru July 2, 1989 at Stage West, Calgary, Alberta. Then in September, he did the play opposite Adam Furfaro at a re-staging at Stage West.

The review in the *Edmonton Journal*, March 17, 1989 noted, "On the surface, the gravel-voiced Gale Gordon, he of the patented Hollywood eye-roll and roar, will not be everybody's idea of a cleric. But his stage charm, his fierce deadpan, his droll exasperation stand hip in good stead here. He captures to a 'T' Father Tim's explicit contention that the priesthood is a kind of showbiz sub-specialty (the collection plate is a version of the Nielsen ratings, he says—and he's not joking)."

A more succinct review appeared in the *Calgary Herald* on June 12, 1989. The reviewer reflected, "At an age (83) when he might be expected to coast on his reputation, Gale Gordon pulls out all the stops in Stage West's *Mass Appeal*."

Gordon's last two appearances acting on television came two years later. First, he reprised his role of Theodore J. Mooney in an episode of the ABC show *Hi Honey, I'm Home*, broadcast July 19, 1991. The episode entitled "Meet the Nielsens," has the family of the 1950s sitcom secretly relocated to a 1991 New Jersey suburb, where their wholesome ways clash with contemporary lifestyles. The show starred Charlotte Booker, Stephen Bradbury, Julie Benz, Danny Gura, Susan Cella, Pete Benson, and Eric Kushnick.

Then on September 7, 1991, Gordon appeared in the syndicated *The New Lassie*, in an episode entitled "No Pets Allowed." Gordon plays an old man who sadly learns that he may lose his beloved dog when his landlady (Margaret O'Brien) suddenly decides to banish all pets from her building.

In *Lucy and Desi: A Home Movie*, broadcast on February 14, 1993, Lucie Arnaz offered a tribute to the lives and careers of her parents, Lucille Ball and Desi Arnaz, via film clips, stills and interviews with those who knew and worked with them. Gordon was among those seen in the NBC Special.

In 1994, Gordon reportedly narrated "Bah Humbug" for the California Center for the Performing Arts.

Gordon may not have been as interesting off-screen as his characters were onscreen. Also, just because he stayed out of the Hollywood limelight, and remained (along with his wife) what some would call "loners," this does not justify considering him misunderstood or enigmatic.

There is one person that probably knew Gordon as well as anyone, especially in his later years. His name is Michael Druxman: "I was his publicist for most of the run of *Here's Lucy*. I don't recall how many years that was, but during that period Gale would do a lot of summer stock/dinner theatre when he wasn't working."

His assessment of Gordon is telling: "He was so unlike his angry, frustrated, on-screen persona. When fans asked him why he was always so mean to Lucy, his stock reply was, 'I only get mad for money.'

"Gale was an easy client to represent. He expected little from me, just to set an occasional interview and to send out photographs and press materials when he was doing a play in dinner or regional theatre, which he did frequently when *Here's Lucy* was not filming. *Never Too Late* was the stage play that he did most often.

"He was a generous man, always willing to donate his time to a worthy cause. On one occasion, I set him to make an appearance at a fund-raising event for the Santa Ynez Branch of the Chumash Indian Reservation, located in the mountains above Santa Barbara. Gale drove up to Santa Barbara, stayed in a local hotel (on his own dime), then although I told him that he didn't have to do it, he insisted on paying our admission into the event where he sat for two hours autographing photos, and listening to fans ask insensitive questions, such as, 'Why isn't Lucy here?'

"Gale Gordon may have been a kind, gentle and likable man, but he was not a good interview subject. Indeed, his own agent, Marc Newman (brother of Alfred and Lionel Newman), said he was 'boring' to talk to, and by the time he became my client, virtually every newspaperman in town had interviewed him more than once over the years, so they knew they were not going to get any hot copy out of him. At times, I literally had to beg them to sit down with Gale again."

However, anyone listening to the interview he did with Schaden in 1990, along with his responses to the fans calling-in, could lead one to think quite the opposite as regards being "boring."

As regards to remembering the many programs he did, Schaden observed, "You probably can't even recall half of the shows you were on over all those years." Gordon began running off names of some of the shows: "Well, no. I was Irene Rich's leading man for 9 years for Welch's Grape Juice. I was also, most people don't know I was Mary Pickford's leading man for a year in a series that she had on radio, and with Joe E. Brown and Phil Harris—I was on their shows. I was on Burns and Allen for two or three seasons. . . ."

As to the fans with a good memory of specific episodes, Gordon told Schaden: "Well, they remember more than I do about it. Because when we did them . . . we forgot them right away because we were doing one the next week or whatever it was and some of the people I talk to remember scenes and the lines that I long, long forgotten. I think it's wonderful and it's just amazing to me and very gratifying."

Gordon showed his delight to appreciative fans calling in Schaden's show to tell him how much his shows have entertained them. Gordon: "It's always nice to hear. It just warms the cockles of my heart to know my efforts met with such approval."

One of the few things Gordon never did is voicing for animated cartoons. He told Schaden: "I auditioned for Disney years ago, and (what) for I don't know what it was now. I didn't get it—the part. That's probably why I didn't remember it."

Gordon, when he had an opportunity to talk, was not shy in expressing his views. As far as modern comedy, Gordon complained to a Schaden caller: "Well I, I frankly am shocked by it. When I do plays, for which I have been doing for the last thirteen years in Canada, if there are 4-letter words in the play, I will not say them. I just don't think the theater is the place for 4-letter words. I don't think television is the place for it. I don't think radio is the place for it. Of course, there never were any in radio because the strictures were so very, very severe about what you can say. Lucy for years couldn't say, mention the word pregnant when she was out like a balloon with her first child on TV. But she couldn't say I was pregnant. So uh, and now there are all kinds of words being used that I find, are . . . if you happen to have an adjective in your mind to describe something, don't use a dirty one. Just forget it."

As far as the power of the radio medium, Gordon declared, "Well, that of course, is the great, great benefit of radio as opposed to all the other forms of show business. Radio stimulated the imagination. When you had a mystery show on radio and that creaking door opened, the people listening, their hair literally stood on end. And you looked over your shoulder. You really shivered a little bit because each person listening imagined the most horrible thing that they can think of that would show up when the door opened.

"On television you opened the door, some idiot standing there or somebody with wild makeup on and fangs hanging out or sorts of wild-looking eyes, and half the time you wanna laugh because they're so damn ridiculous—if you pardon the word damn."

When Gordon was asked by a caller whether the pompous characters were determined by the tone of his voice, Gordon explained: "Well I think to be quite honest, the parts I did were because I was louder than anybody else in radio. I could scream louder than most people. And it doesn't take a lot of talent to be noisy. But I had a good lung capacity and that could be very loud. And that's what, what they would, the producers would cast me for. We would want someone loud and blowhard and they said we'll get Gale Gordon. He's louder than anybody else, and that gave me being cast as a blowhard, and gave me a great deal of work which isn't artistic. But it least was truthful, and it kept the wolf from the door."

Caller: "Did you ever wish to play any other type of character?"

Gordon: "No, because I did that in radio. I played leading men, heavies, character people, juveniles, old men, foreigners and everything else. I, no, I didn't miss it at all. I got cast as a blowhard, I got more money for doing it than I did the usual other characters. So I was very happy to keep doing it and cast as a blowhard, and didn't hurt me at all, than I did the usual other characters."

Undoubtedly, Schaden's interview proved there was more depth to Gordon than one would think. Of course, it took someone who thoroughly appreciated his fine abilities to bring a part to life.

Eventually after that call-in, Gordon sold his ranch due to age and declining health between the summers of 1990 and 1993, though the actual date is undetermined. Gordon spent his final days at Redwood Terrace in Escondido, California, a Continuing Care Retirement community in San Diego's North County.

Three years after Schaden's interview, Gordon first admitted his wife, listed as Virginia Aldrich, to Redwood Terrace's Skilled Nursing Home on September 23, 1993. As he wished to be close to her, the facility offered him a cottage to live at while she was there.

The following year, Gordon's health deteriorated so he himself had to enter the Jean Weaver Health Center on June 30, 1994. He spent most of his time there remaining very private. In his final days, he had made no known contact with any outsiders or relatives. His Los Angeles attorneys handled all of his remaining personal affairs. When Gordon could no longer care for their last dog, help came from a family friend who owned Paw-Dre's Club House for Pets, a kennel in San Marcos, California.

Gordon's wife for over fifty-seven years, Virginia Curley, died on May 6, 1995.

Then less than two months later, Gale Gordon, the Mayor of fictional Wistful Vista and the real-life Honorary Mayor of Borrego Springs, died on June 30, 1995 at the age of 89. Gale's sister, Judy Wormser, who lived in Santa Cruz, Arizona and Santa Fe, New Mexico, died three years later.

A caller to Schaden's show wished that Gordon should be around for another twenty more years on radio and television. Schaden adds, "Gale Gordon, if you go 20 years, you will be 104. That'll be alright, right?" Gordon thanks the listener, and tells Schaden, "Well I don't know. I don't think—uh, no. I want to rest before then." Five years after that broadcast, Gordon indeed departed to his final rest.

In looking back over his long career, when asked if he preferred comedies or dramatic roles, Gordon said, "I like comedies because I'm a great believer in the therapeutic value of laughter. There's so much sadness in this world today, so much horror, so much of the mean and the cruel. And that I think we need as a nation, we need good healthy, honest laughter and when I hear an audience laugh, I get a great physical sigh of relief in my old soul because it's something I think that is so important and I love to hear it. And when I can get an honest laugh, I think that I'm doing my job at least in my small way. And I think that comedy is the jam and the little bit of sauce that is put on the veins of life that gives it a little bit of aftertaste and a lovely memory." (Gordon pronounced it "ve-ins.")

To another caller, Gordon offered his own assessment of his talent this way: ". . . As a performer I was cast by somebody who'd written a radio show. 'A.' Let me start out by saying I'm not a terribly funny person, but I've had the opportunity to read some very, very funny lines written by some very, very clever comedy writers to do things that were created by people with creative ability who wrote the things for me to do. A lot of people get the idea that an actor goes up in front of a camera and that he makes up everything as he goes along, and those who do that are geniuses in their own way and the standup comics very often do.

"But I'm a character actor and I translate as best I can the meaning of lines that are given to me to read. I cannot take credit for being terribly funny. I must in all honesty say that I'm funny if the material that is written for me to read is funny."

The caller insisted, "But you're a great deliverer of that work."

Gordon acknowledged that, saying: "Well I, I thank you. That's the least I can do to show my appreciation for getting something funny to do is to give an interpretation that helps the thought or the line itself and that's what I try to do."

Indeed, he always gave his audience the correct and best interpretation for whatever part he played.

Schaden observed, "And I think I speak for so many people, you've entertained us so royally!" Gordon accepted the compliment, saying: "Well, that's very nice to hear."

Undoubtedly, Gale Gordon has made us laugh, and he will always make us laugh as long as his programs survive.

PHOTO GALLERY

November 16, 1934 radio rehearsal for *Mary Pickford and Company* episode, "Little Old New York," NBC's Radio City Studios. Gale Gordon, Mary Pickford.
Courtesy from the collection of Stephen Cox.

On radio in *Granby's Green Acres*. Gale Gordon, Bea Benaderet.
Courtesy from the collection of Stephen Cox.

I Love Lucy. **Lucille Ball, Gale Gordon.**
Courtesy from the collection of Stephen Cox.

Our Miss Brooks. **Gale Gordon, Bob Rockwell. Eve Arden.**
Courtesy from the collection of Stephen Cox.

Our Miss Brooks. **Gale Gordon as Santa Claus, Eve Arden.**
Courtesy from the collection of Stephen Cox.

Our Miss Brooks. **Gale Gordon, Eve Arden.**
Courtesy from the collection of Stephen Cox

The Brothers. **Gale Gordon, Bob Sweeney.**
Courtesy from the collection of Stephen Cox.

Sally. **Marion Lorne, Arte Johnson, Gale Gordon (back), Johnny Desmond, Joan Caulfield (front).**
Courtesy from the collection of Stephen Cox.

The Lucy Show **publicity artwork (Screen Gems). Gale Gordon.**
Courtesy from the collection of Stephen Cox.

The Lucy Show. **Jimmy Garrett, Candy Moore, Ralph Hart, Gale Gordon, Lucille Ball.**
Courtesy from the collection of Stephen Cox.

The Lucy Show. **Gale Gordon, Lucille Ball, Carole Cook.**
Courtesy from the collection of Stephen Cox.

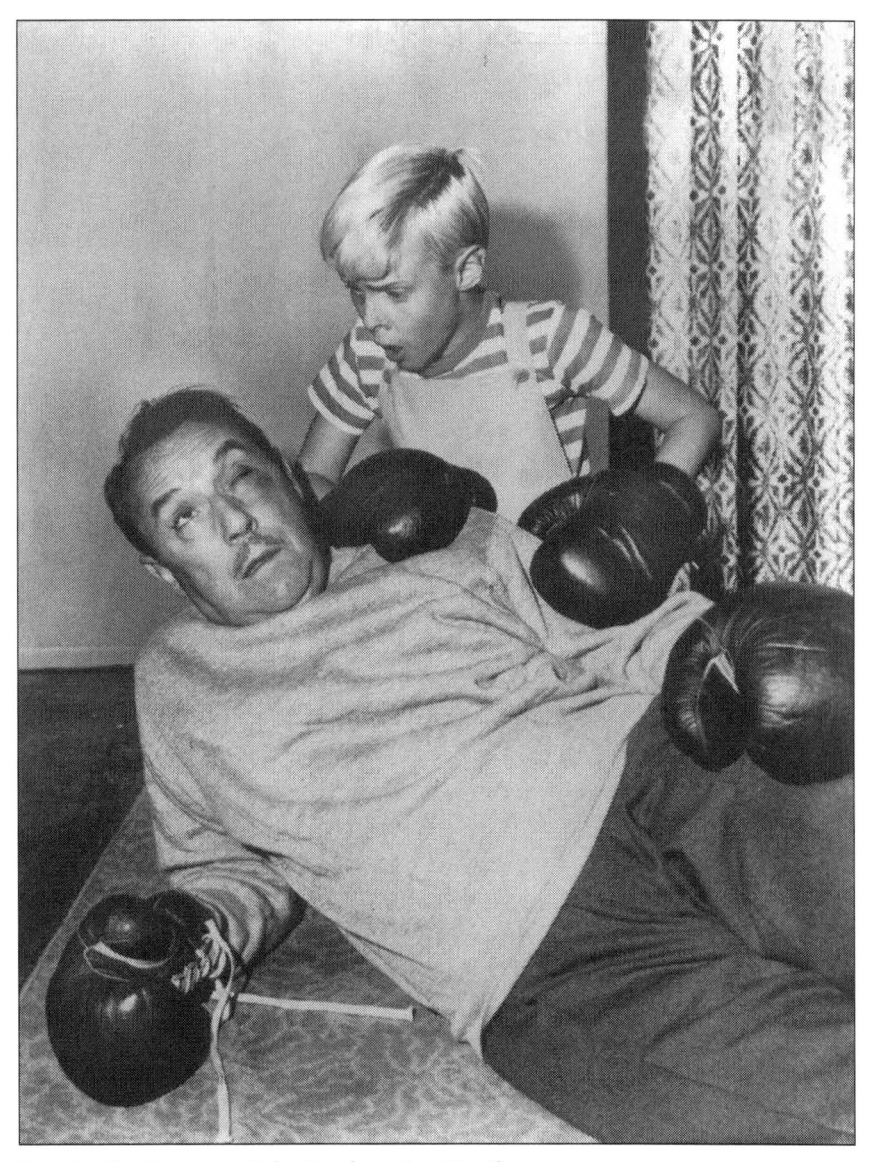

Dennis the Menace. Gale Gordon, Jay North.
Courtesy from the collection of Stephen Cox.

On the cover of *TV Guide: Dennis the Menace.* **Gale Gordon, Jay North.**
Courtesy from the collection of Stephen Cox.

Gale Gordon portrait.
Courtesy from the collection of Stephen Cox.

Gale Gordon portrait.
Courtesy from the collection of Stephen Cox.

Here's Lucy **cast. Back: Gale Gordon. Front: Desi Arnaz, Jr., Lucille Ball, Lucie Arnaz.**
Courtesy from the collection of Stephen Cox.

Here's Lucy **cast. Desi Arnaz, Jr., Lucille Ball, Lucie Arnaz, Gale Gordon.**
Courtesy from the collection of Stephen Cox.

Gale Gordon being stripped in *Here's Lucy*. Lucille Ball, Desi Arnaz, Jr. Gale Gordon, Lucie Arnaz.
Courtesy from the collection of Stephen Cox.

Here's Lucy **with Helen Hayes as a maid. Helen Hayes, Gale Gordon, Lucille Ball, Lucie Arnaz.**
Courtesy from the collection of Stephen Cox.

Gale Gordon as a German field marshal in *Here's Lucy*. Lucille Ball, Gale Gordon.
Courtesy from the collection of Stephen Cox.

Photo Gallery

Gale Gordon in a trashcan dumpster, *Here's Lucy.* **Gale Gordon, Lucille Ball.**
Courtesy from the collection of Stephen Cox.

Here's Lucy. **Lucille Ball, Johnny Carson, Ed McMahon, Gale Gordon.**
Courtesy from the collection of Stephen Cox.

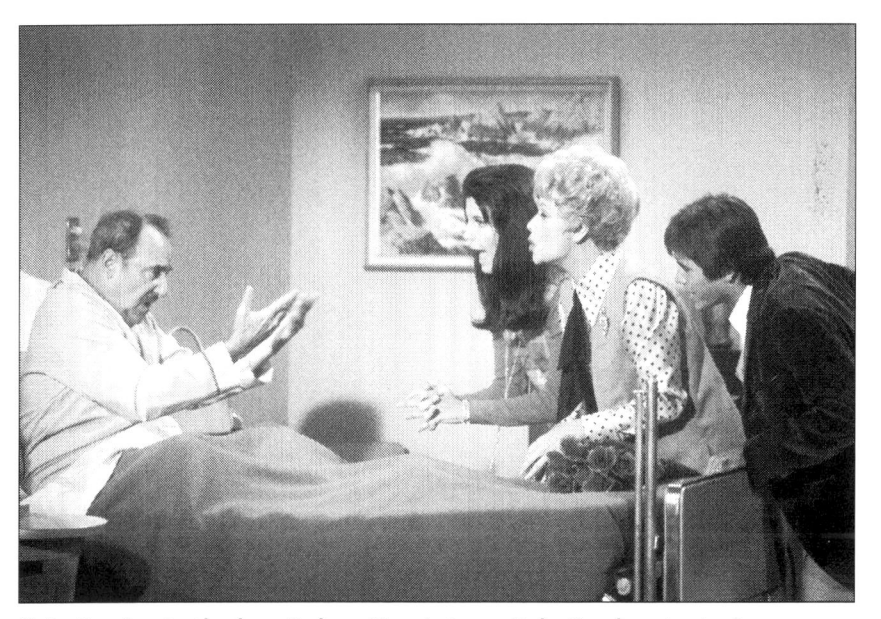

PHOTO GALLERY | 163

Gale Gordon in the hospital on *Here's Lucy*. Gale Gordon, Lucie Arnaz, Lucille Ball, Desi Arnaz, Jr.
Courtesy from the collection of Stephen Cox.

Gale Gordon in Mexican prison on *Here's Lucy*. Gale Gordon, with guest star Vivian Vance, Lucille Ball.
Courtesy from the collection of Stephen Cox.

Here's Lucy. **Gale Gordon at the airport. Gale Gordon, Lucille Ball.**
Courtesy from the collection of Stephen Cox.

Gale Gordon on a mountain top in *Here's Lucy*. Gale Gordon, Lucille Ball.
Courtesy from the collection of Stephen Cox.

PHOTO GALLERY | 167

Ad for Lucille Ball Television Special: "Lucy Calls the President."
Courtesy from the collection of Stephen Cox.

Life With Lucy. **Gale Gordon, Lucille Ball.**
Courtesy from the collection of Stephen Cox.

Gale Gordon portrait in the early 1990s.
Courtesy from the collection of Stephen Cox.

Part Two: Gale Gordon's Comedy Moments on Radio

Chapter Ten: First Season as Mayor LaTrivia (1941–1942)

McGee: "Wohhh, look whose coming? LaTrivia."

Molly: "Oh well, let's not get into one of those silly arguments with him, will you."

McGee: "Oh come on, let's do. Do him good."

—Fibber McGee and Molly, April 7, 1942 ("Scrap Drive")

This chapter and the following two are not a substitute for actually hearing these enjoyable shows from the Golden Age of Radio. Many of the episodes are available online at no cost.

The actual radio show scripts are *not* the source for the following dialogue excerpts, but rather they are transcribed portions developed from listening to the episodes. They capture only the words to some of Gordon's comedy moments from the shows, not Gordon's superb delivery. Please note that there are often gaps between the lines of spoken dialogue transcribed; sometimes those gaps are indicated, and sometimes they are not.

In his first appearance as Mayor LaTrivia on *Fibber McGee and Molly*, broadcast on October 14, 1941 ("Fire Commissioner"), Gordon's character had not developed fully, so the comedic aspect is limited. LaTrivia pompously greets the McGees at their door: "Good day McGee, how do you do Mrs. McGee? I just heard. . . ." He chokes and coughs because McGee had been messing with the fireplace, continuing, "What goes on, fumigating?" In a serious business-like tone, he asks McGee to fill the vacancy pro tem for the Fire Commissioner. McGee accepts.

LaTrivia: "I'll inform the City Council that the office has been filled pro tem." McGee asks what does that mean. LaTrivia: "That's a Latin phrase, meaning try and keep it." He exits to laughter and applause.

After introducing the Mayor character on October 14, Gordon returns to playing a different character the week later on October 21, 1941 ("Finding Old Love Letters"). Here Gordon plays a stranger who passes by and returns Molly's old love letters, which we assume he got since McGee tossed them out the window hitting the stranger's head.

Gordon's character here reveals his pomposity when he explains this situation.

Stranger: "Madam, I assure you I committed no offense against Postal regulations. I'm not a mailbox marauder by nature. I was examining the house next door with a view towards renting it, and passing your home I was suddenly struck on the fedora by an avalanche of Billy dew, and if Billy should do it again, I should be tempted to cram them down his sentimental gullet."

What LaTrivia said in the October 28, 1941 show ("Fibber Meets a Racketeer") is unknown since existing copies are incomplete at 18 minutes, and if Gordon appeared as LaTrivia in the last ten minutes, it has not been determined.

The November 4, 1941 show ("New Furniture") has Gordon again playing a different character. As furniture sales clerk Mr. Twombley, he talks Molly into buying more furniture than the Davenport they were purchasing.

In response to announcer Harlow Wilcox saying he hates football, Gordon says: "I don't understand Mr. Wilcox, why should you have such an aversion to the thrilling spectacle of eleven muscular gentlemen kicking the teeth out of eleven other muscular gentlemen?"

In the November 11, 1941 show ("Premiere of *Look Who's Laughing*"), Gordon doubles playing LaTrivia and a fast-talking usher. LaTrivia briefly comments on the McGees' performance in the movie *Look Who's Laughing.*

LaTrivia tells Molly, "I thought you did a simply splendid piece of work."

McGee asks LaTrivia, "Is it true about me being another Barrymore?"

LaTrivia: "It's possible, if there must be another Barrymore."

In a particularly good episode broadcast on November 18, 1941 ("Mayor LaTrivia Won't Leave"), LaTrivia is heard throughout the episode as he keeps finding excuses not to leave the McGees' home. The problem is the show does not explain why he would not leave, and it does not explain why he came to their home either. He leaves his briefcase behind, asks for water, and continually delays his departure by talking to the usual guests that come and go from the McGees' home.

So far, the Mayor is friendly and not yet condescending or argumentative here as he would be in later episodes. However, as will often happen, LaTrivia begins offering McGee a menial job at City Hall. This time it is to be a dogcatcher.

This episode has the first play on words exchange that later would become the usual humorous exchange between the Mayor and the McGees. LaTrivia says the word "Afghan," but McGee thinks he said "ashcan." Although LaTrivia's words are twisted, the wordplay is limited and not done in an extended manner yet. In future episodes we will see LaTrivia's trademark of getting exasperated with a measure of confused sputtering.

LaTrivia:	"I have an appointment with a Miss Meech, a knitting expert."
McGee:	"You're taking lessons, LaTrivia?"
LaTrivia:	(laughing) "Oh no, no, no, no! She's making an afghan for an aunt of mine for Christmas."
McGee:	(laughing) "Go on, how can anyone knit an ashcan?" (audience laughing).

MOLLY: "No, he said afghan McGee, afghan. It's a kind of a muffler for your hip."

MAYOR: "That's very good Mrs. McGee, very good. . ."

There is a funny exchange offered when the Mayor says, "Well, I simply must be getting downtown, Mrs. McGee (laughing). I'm afraid I overstayed my visit a trifle. I feel like the man who came to dinner."

MCGEE: "Yeah he broke his leg while on the way out, didn't he? Here let me help you down the steps, LaTrivia."

McGee eventually tricks him into leaving by misinterpreting a call from LaTrivia's secretary saying that the City Hall is flooded. LaTrivia rushes down to City Hall, and he is perplexed when he sees nothing amiss, McGee says the Mayor did not let him finish explaining the call. Actually, the Mayor's secretary said his office was flooded with phone calls.

On the November 25, 1941 show ("Beauty Clay Mine"), LaTrivia is at a Better Business Meeting discussing a confidence game thief.
LaTrivia's watchword is, "Before you invest, investigate."
He returns Molly's lost $150 and McGee's lost $500. Molly is surprised to find McGee duped too as he got annoyed at her to learn someone cheated her.

In the December 2, 1941 show ("The Moustache"), McGee asks LaTrivia, "What's cookin'?"
LaTrivia responds, "McGee, if there's anything I deplore it is the idiotic custom of opening a conversation with such senseless questions as, 'What's cookin'?' 'How's everything?' and 'What do you know?' They're meaningless and unanswerable."
A few seconds later, in regards to the aroma coming from the kitchen, LaTrivia asks, "I must say something smells delicious. What's cookin'?" The audience laughs.

MCGEE: "H'mmm! The question is meaningless, but it ain't unanswerable LaTriv. It's a mince pie."

McGee sports a moustache but LaTrivia could not tell what was different about McGee, thinking it is that he had his shoes shined. McGee tells him that it is a moustache.
When he departs, LaTrivia says, "And McGee, tell your moustache that the strange man is leaving and it could come out now."

The December 9, 1941 show ("Forty Percent Off") came two days after the Pearl Harbor attack, and so a jab at the Japanese is expected. LaTrivia comes in saying he was walking around the city and meeting with the citizens, and stopped by. He asks if McGee read "The Arabian Nights" as he refers to a potentate that used to go around mixing with the people.
Molly says, "Of course not, McGee can't read Arabian." McGee adds that he has no energy left after keeping up with *Bringing Up Father, Flash Gordon* and *Smokey Stover.*

LATRIVIA: "That's very amusing, in a pathetic sort of way (laughs). . . . By the way, do you know where can I buy a large globe of the world for my office?"

McGee tells him that he can get one wholesale. . . Molly asks, "You want a globe with Japan on it, Mr. Mayor?"

LATRIVIA: "Well certainly."

MOLLY: "Well, then you better get one quick!"

LATRIVIA: "Splendid, splendid, thank you very much. I'll try to return the favor one day."

McGee asks what happened regarding the City Hall job that the Mayor promised him. McGee tells Molly that LaTrivia was "looking for a smart, level-headed man to look in on the higher ups in the interests of clean government."

| LATRIVIA: | "Oh yes, oh yes, yes, the window washing job. No, that's been filled McGee but I'll keep my eyes open for you." |

McGee is insulted.
LaTrivia comes back complaining about the dirty small 5-inch globe that McGee sent.

| LATRIVIA: | "My globe, it's so old it shows New York as Indian Territory." |

| MOLLY: | "Well it still is. I've seen some scalpers around Times Square." |

In the December 16, 1941 episode ("Fibber Cuts Christmas Tree"), LaTrivia predictably offers McGee a menial job, which insults McGee.

| LATRIVIA: | "I say McGee, about that job that you wanted in the City Hall, I'm still working on it, but I have to have a little information. . . . Well, first can you dominate people? Can you let the ones in that you really want to see and shut the rest out? . . . Another thing McGee, can you stand it physically to be mauled by crowds of people all asking questions? Can you ignore the whispering behind your back? Can you give orders in a loud tone of authority?" |

McGee gives an example of doing so.

| LATRIVIA: | "Oh, eh, this wouldn't be a police job McGee, but one of the elevator operators has just been drafted and I suggested you (audience laughter). I'll let you know later. Good day!" |

In the December 23, 1941 show ("Electric Chime Door Bell"), LaTrivia enters with another insulting job offer.

| LaTrivia: | "Now McGee, you've been hounding me for a job with the City . . . Are we alone? . . . McGee, how are you on disguises?"

McGee tells him about when he did detective work for a railroad. . . . McGee: "I was known as the man with a thousand faces" (audience laughter).

LaTrivia responds, "You had your choice of a thousand faces and went back to your own? . . . Never mind the heroic tales McGee, all I want to know is can you assume a completely different identity and maintain it under trying circumstances for days at a time? . . . You report to City Hall first thing tomorrow . . . . You won't need a gun, the disguise will be enough. You're going to be Wistful Vista's official Santa Claus in City Hall Park. Five dollars a day. I'll see you tomorrow" (laughter and applause).

After the Mayor leaves, McGee complains: "Why that double-crossing political parasite. Who does he think I am?"

Molly responds, "Santa Claus."

In the December 30, 1941 show ("Fix-It McGee"), LaTrivia enters, asking: "Now then McGee, as one of our prominent citizens I wish to ask you . . . we are putting on a drive to sell defense bonds and stamps. . . . The procedure will be something like this, McGee. We will have a large sound truck playing recordings of military music. We stop the truck at prominent corners and well-known citizens make speeches from the back platform and urge the crowds to buy defense bonds and stamps. Your name's been suggested. . . ."

Of course, McGee assumes he is one of those prominent citizens and what a good speechmaker he is.

LaTrivia:	"Excuse me McGee, you don't understand, I'll be making the speeches . . . . You won't make any speeches."
Molly:	"Then what's he doing on the truck?"
LaTrivia:	"Changing the records for the military music.

Meet me at the City Hall tomorrow morning. Uh, good day Mrs. McGee."

For the January 6, 1942 show ("A Night on the Town"), LaTrivia greets the McGees, and then quickly gets down to business.

LaTrivia: "I came to present you with ten dollars' worth of defense stamps."

Molly: "Oh, what for, Mr. Mayor?"

McGee: "LaTrivia, you don't mean . . ."

LaTrivia: "Yes, I mean you . . ."

McGee: "Hold it! Hold it! Hold it! Look LaTrivia when somebody says you don't mean, you gotta take a dramatic pause. Don't you ever listen to the radio?" (audience laughter).

LaTrivia: "Oh (clears throat), I, I'm sorry. Let's do it again. (clears throat again). I came to present you with ten dollars' worth of defense stamps, McGee."

McGee: "You don't mean . . ."

Molly: "One, two, three, four."

LaTrivia: "Yes (audience laughter). The, uh, slogan you sent in is the one we're using in our local campaign."

Molly: "Well, heavenly days! I didn't know you sent them a slogan, McGee. What was it?"

McGee: "Oh it was nothing any red-blooded American boy couldn't of done, but I'm glad you like it though, LaTrivia."

LaTrivia:	"Ah ha, it was the best of the lot McGee by far."
Molly:	"How many did ya get?"
LaTrivia:	(afraid to admit it) "Uh . . . well to be frank, Mrs. McGee, it was the only one sent in (audience laughter). Here McGee, ten dollars' worth of stamps and the gratitude of the Wistful Vista Committee for Defense" (audience laughter and applause).
Molly:	"Well, was the slogan, Mr. Mayor?"
LaTrivia:	(starts to say it, interrupted by McGee) "It was little—"
McGee:	"Let me tell her. I can get more feeling into it. It said if you expect to rate as an American, do it on the back of a defense stamp (audience laughter and applause). 'No lick 'em stick 'em. No lick 'em quick 'em.' Yeah. Ya like it Molly?"
Molly:	"Not much to be frank."
McGee:	'I didn't take enough dramatic pause."
Molly:	"You missed something, but I'm uh glad you won the prize dearie."
LaTrivia:	"Well, at least it shows he's thinking in the right direction, Mrs. McGee. Now I won't keep you any longer. I see you're dressed to go out."
McGee:	"Yeah, we're going to go out to a Jive Dive and trip the light bombastic."

LATRIVIA: "Ha, ha, ha. Splendid, have a good time. You look very charming, Mrs. McGee."

MOLLY: "Awww!"

LATRIVIA: "And you McGee (hesitates). Well that green tuxedo is uh, is that something new?" (audience laughter).

MCGEE: "It ain't green, LaTrivia. It just looks green in a certain light."

LATRIVIA: "Ah, I see, such as daylight and electric light (audience laughter). Enjoy yourselves, Good Night!" (LaTrivia exits to audience laughter).

MCGEE: "What did he mean daylight and electric light? What other kind of light is there?"

MOLLY: "Gaslight."

MCGEE: "Well who uses gaslight?"

MOLLY: "Well I bet the tailor who made that tuxedo did. But don't worry about it dearie, you know it doesn't really look so bad."

MCGEE: "Of course it doesn't, it's the only one in town with seven buttons on each sleeve too!"

On the January 13, 1942 show ("Who Broke Uppy's Window, Part One"), someone threw a rock through Mrs. Uppington's window, and McGee fears he did it while sleepwalking.

MCGEE: "Hey, you used to be a lawyer before you were a Mayor, didn't ya, LaTrivia?"

LATRIVIA: "Oh, yes, yes, yes, yes indeed. I was a junior

	partner in Abernathy, Crownedhight, Massey, Witherspoon, Witherspoon, Smythe, Witherspoon and LaTrivia."
McGee:	"Your clients must have had to kneel down to read your name on the door" (audience laughter).
Molly:	"Say that partner of yours, Mr. Massey, was pretty famous, wasn't he?"
LaTrivia:	"Oh not very, I'm afraid."
Molly:	"Why, of course, he was. Everybody's heard of the laws of Massey" (audience laughter).
LaTrivia:	(put off) "Ah yes. Yes. Ha! Ha!" (laughs and audience laughter). But why did you ask McGee?"
McGee:	"Well I wondered if you'd give me a little legal advice."
LaTrivia:	"Oh, why certainly McGee, certainly. Having trouble with the finance company again?"
McGee:	"No. Yes, but look. About this window. . . smashing thing. What if the guy that did it was walking in his sleep at the time? Could he be held . . . responsible?" (hearty laughter).
Molly:	"What's so funny about that?"
LaTrivia:	(still laughing) "Oh, I was just thinking what a rosy time you'd have convincing a judge that you were asleep (still laughing). Well I've got to meet the D.A. over at Mrs. Uppington's. Good Day! Walking in your sleep, indeed! Ha! Ha! Ha! Ha! Ha! (he exits still laughing).

The January 20, 1942 show ("Who Broke Uppy's Window, Part Two"), continues the story regarding a rock thrown in Mrs. Uppington's window. LaTrivia wants to see Uncle Dennis.

LATRIVIA: "My men are working on a clue. It seems that late that night he went into uh, uh—" (stuttering)

McGEE: "Yeah we know. Yeah he always does."

LATRIVIA: "Exactly. And he asked the proprietor for a rock 'n' rye. They didn't have rock 'n' rye? So he just took a rye. We're checking up to see if he found a rock anywhere, but don't tell him I'm inquiring. Good Night!" (Exits to applause.)

The January 27, 1942 show ("The Blizzard") has Mr. Spellman, a man representing the Governor, stopping by during a snowstorm with a message. However, visitors, including the Mayor, keep interrupting the McGees. We pick up the dialogue when the Mayor explains the reason for his visiting the McGees.

LATRIVIA: "I just stopped in to tell you McGee that a complaint has reached my ears."

McGee misinterprets.

McGEE: "I had the same thing last summer, LaTrivia. It started in my neck and reached my ears in two days. The doctor says it was just a temporary—."

LATRIVIA: "Mr. McGee, please, I was about to say I have received a complaint from the street commissioner that you have been remiss in the matter of snow removal from your front sidewalk."

McGEE: "Oh well, thanks for warning me, LaTrivia. It's a funny thing too. I really enjoy shoveling snow."

LaTrivia:	"You do?"
Molly:	"You do?"
McGee:	"I surely do. I'd rather hear the frosty clang of a snow shovel on a sidewalk than the finest symphony music in the world. To feel the red blood coursing through my veins as I swing that shovel to and fro. That marvelous glow that comes from exercising in the cold winter air. The sharp tang of the wind on my cheeks as my muscles respond to the healthy rhythm. And what an appetite I get. Sleep like a baby. Ah I love the feeling of the—."
Molly:	"Hold it, McGee, where you going Mr. Mayor?"
LaTrivia:	(won over by McGee's story) "I'm going to shovel your walk out for you. I haven't felt like that in YEARS (audience laughter and applause). Where's the snow shovel?"
McGee:	"Snow shovel's right in here, LaTrivia—."
Molly:	"Where McGee?"
McGee:	"Right here in the hall closet."

The expected happens, and McGee utters his usual mantra: "I've got to straighten out that closet one of these days."

On the February 3, 1942 episode ("Lost Diamond Ring"), McGee asks LaTrivia why he was all bundled up?

LaTrivia:	"I regret to say that I neglected my business affairs today and yielded to go out with a small party of friends—we have been boob-sledding."

MOLLY:	"No, no, you mean bobsledding."
LATRIVIA:	"With the frantic little group of sportsmen I was with Mrs. McGee, it is boobsledding (audience laughter). Their imbued with a peculiar idea that to see how close one can steer the sled to a moving streetcar is the height of hilarity."
MCGEE:	"It sounds kind of fun at that, LaTrivia."
LATRIVIA:	"I imagine that would appeal to you McGee. You're the type that rocks rowboats and wears ladies hats at parties" (audience laughter).
MOLLY:	"Why he does not. He always wears a lampshade."
MCGEE:	"Get a much bigger laugh with the lampshade, LaTrivia. That kills 'em."
LATRIVIA:	"Thank you. I shall try to remember that I— uh, but am I intruding, Mrs. McGee, were you cleaning house?"
MOLLY:	"Well yes. . ."

She explains about losing her diamond ring, and LaTrivia asks if he can look around. They oblige him.

LATRIVIA:	"Well I don't see it anywhere" (audience laughter).
MCGEE:	"You couldn't of found a flat car in a phone booth in that length of time."

LaTrivia clears his throat.

LATRIVIA:	"My eyesight is very penetrating, McGee."

McGee:	"Ohh."
LaTrivia:	"In fact, I was quite a student of mesmerism at one time."
Molly:	"What merism?"
LaTrivia:	(correcting Molly) "Mesmerism. Hypnotism (proceeds to show them). Look me in the eye, McGee."
McGee:	"Which one?"
LaTrivia:	"Either one. Now relax. You're slowly coming under my dominance. You have no will of your own."
Molly:	"I've been telling him that for years, and I'm no hypnotist."
LaTrivia:	"Please, Mrs. McGee. Alright McGee, when I snap my fingers you are completely subject to my orders (snaps fingers). There. You see, Mrs. McGee, his mind is a blank. Look at that glassy stare."
Molly:	"That's the way he always looks when he does crossword puzzles. Isn't it McGee? Isn't it McGee? McGee? Well heavenly days, he is hypnotized."
LaTrivia:	(sure of himself) "Of course, he is. Watch this. McGee, you are an Airedale, a big brown Airedale. Speak."

McGee barks, and even tries to wag his tail. He acts like a canine, even jumping up on LaTrivia.

LaTrivia:	"No! No! No! Get Down! Stop jumping up on me! Down doggy, down doggy. Oww! He bit me in the leg! Let me out of here!"
Molly:	"Aren't you gonna unhypnotize him first?"
LaTrivia:	"He'll come out of it shortly. I don't wanna— (Yells): GET AWAY FROM ME YOU BRUTE!" (He goes out the door, and audience applauds).
McGee:	"Boy I sure fooled him, didn't I Molly?"
Molly:	"You fooled me too. I was about to call the drugstore for some flea powder."
McGee:	"Well I had to get rid of that guy someway so I can get back to work. Some act, hah?"
Molly:	"It was wonderful, it was so realistic. McGee pull in your tongue and stop panting!"

On the February 10, 1942 show ("Valentine Candy"), Molly offers LaTrivia candy, and he refuses.

LaTrivia:	"Thank you. No, I'm on a low-carbohydrate diet."
McGee:	"Well you better stock up on them then, LaTriv. They tell me there is going to be a shortage of low carbohydrants."
LaTrivia:	"You don't say. If I might make a suggestion, McGee. It would be to an effect that people that have no clear comprehension of a subject under the discussion would be well advised to maintain a discreet silence."
McGee:	"I don't get it."

Molly interprets for him.

MOLLY: "Well he said Dearie, is that if ignorance is bliss, happy days are here again. Or if you don't know what you're talking about when you pipe up, pipe down."

The misunderstanding keeps building with LaTrivia reacting more to McGee's ignorance. Molly acts as the buffer or mediator. LaTrivia gets in this one.

LATRIVIA: "Alright, but hereafter McGee, please refrain from telling motorcycle policemen that you are a close relation of mine and that they can't do that to you!"

In short, McGee has been asking for special favors by using LaTrivia's name as reference on how to get out of parking violations. The tension increases as they dispute the length of the parking overtime, leading to:

LATRIVIA: "Yes, anyway, McGee, justness of the complaint does not concern me. But what I object to is your assuming that I, as Mayor of Wistful Vista, would use the power of my office to obstruct the due processes of law. Furthermore, you had no business telling the officer that I was your nephew on your mother's side!"

McGee is indignant and complains about how the Mayor is getting personal, dragging family into the argument, etc. LaTrivia reacts and raises his voice. We get an example of LaTrivia for the first time really losing his cool arguing with McGee. He shouts and yells getting so flustered before storming out the door. He resolves angrily screaming what he will do to satisfy McGee.

LATRIVIA: "ALRIGHT! ALRIGHT! I'LL FIX THE TICKET! I'LL FIRE THE POLICEMAN!

I'LL RESIGN! GOOD DAY!" (audience applauds).

McGee laughs as he thinks it is so funny how he got LaTrivia so upset. McGee: "I made him holler Uncle."

As ridiculous as these characters appear to be in *Fibber McGee and Molly*, representing the off-beaten or of anyone being different, still it turns out to be endearing or normal at times. Mayor LaTrivia, just like Mrs. Uppington, may represent the upper class with their manners and speech. They act as if they are more important than they really are. Molly even acknowledges that Mrs. Uppington tries to give the impression that she has more than anybody else has.

On the February 17, 1942 show ("Home Movies"), LaTrivia arrives at the McGees' home with a little girl, eventually named "Teeny" in a later episode. He caught her making red chalk marks on the sidewalk of their house. Both get flustered with her. First McGee tries to find the underlying cause of this.

LaTrivia: "Now listen little girl, defacing community property is a misdemeanor."

Teeny: "Who's she?"

LaTrivia: "Who's who?"

Teeny: "Miss Demeanor?"

LaTrivia: "She isn't anybody, she's. . . Now listen, marking up a sidewalk is very rude and it's unsightly."

Teeny: "I know it."

LaTrivia: "Then why did you do it?"

Teeny: "I was helping my Daddy."

CHAPTER TEN: FIRST SEASON AS MAYOR LATRIVIA (1941–1942) | 191

LATRIVIA: "How were you helping your Daddy by drawing chalk marks on Mr. McGee's sidewalk?"

TEENY: "Yes."

LATRIVIA: "Yes, what?"

TEENY: "Yes I was."

This is reminiscent of the frustrating radio show conversations Daddy would have with Baby Snooks.

LATRIVIA: "I meant . . . (raises his voice and he gives up). Okay McGee, take it."

The reason for Teeny's action is that she heard her father tell her mother regarding party invitations, "No dear we gotta draw the line at the McGees." So she went outside and drew the line.

On the February 24, 1942 show ("The Horse"), LaTrivia simply wishes to purchase their horse.

LATRIVIA: "In view of the rubber shortage McGee, the City Council has decided to supplement our motorized fine equipment with horse drawn vehicles. I'm empowered to offer you any price for your horse." He offers him $100.

On the March 3, 1942 show ("Boomer's Suitcase"), LaTrivia arrives with Mr. Boomer. The McGees assume the Mayor apprehended him for being a thief.

LATRIVIA: "Mrs. McGee, you called the police I believe, and have them arrest Mr. Boomer. . . .I think you better not say anymore until you heard the whole story. We have checked thoroughly on Mr. Boomer. We find that his aunt is moving today. This suitcase and its contents is her property, and Mr. Boomer did leave it with you for safekeeping. There is no case against him whatsoever."

The McGees apologize for the misunderstanding. The Mayor convinced the McGees to give Boomer $100 for the trouble they caused him. Outside they see the Mayor taking $50 from Boomer, and they think he extorted $100 from them and is splitting it. Actually, Mr. Boomer was renting part of the Mayor's home for his aunt. They assumed Boomer was a crook because the contents in the suitcase seemed suspicious to them.

LaTrivia yells that he is going to sue the McGees for defamation of character.

McGEE: "Hey Molly, LaTrivia just called up."

MOLLY: "Well what does he want now?"

McGEE: "He isn't going to sue. He's just scaring us."

MOLLY: "Well, that's nice. . . . Say, how did you happen to have a hundred dollars in your pocket?"

McGEE: "Who me?"

MOLLY: "Yeah, you, where'd you get it?"

McGEE: "Out of that suitcase (laughter). I thought it might be counterfeit. And I was going to check with the bank."

On the March 10, 1942 show ("The Footstool"), McGee apologizes to LaTrivia for thinking the Mayor is a crook from the week before. LaTrivia accepts the apology, but then things turn ugly when Molly invites LaTrivia to dinner.

LaTrivia quickly responds, "Splendid, Mrs. McGee, thank you very much."

Then McGee responds, "Bring your wife."

LaTrivia starts to explain, "Uh No, I don't think that I... I'm sorry Mrs. McGee, but to be frank—."

McGee interrupts him and calls him "stuck-up" and "a snob." Molly says that maybe he has a good reason. McGee does not think so.

LaTrivia: "I have a very good reason, you see—."

McGee will not let him explain why he cannot bring his wife. After McGee calls him "a high-hat," the Mayor interjects.

LaTrivia: "Now just a minute, McGee. If you can restrain your impetuosity for a brief interval."

McGee: "And never mind the big words. I know what you mean. You ain't fooling me with those jawbreakers."

Molly tries to buffer the situation, insisting McGee let LaTrivia finish explaining.

LaTrivia's flustering comes from his attempt to sound self-important by using big words.

LaTrivia: "I merely attempted to interpolate a few words to indicate that you are irretrievably, yes even incongruously, in error. If you think—."

McGee interrupts him, "That's enough! Take off your coat!" The tension escalated and McGee now wants to fight LaTrivia.

Molly: "Now, now stop this . . ."

McGee persists.

Molly: "McGee, let the Mayor talk. Why can't you bring your wife, LaTrivia?"

McGee: "Yeah, why?"

Finally, LaTrivia goes into a tirade when he reveals, "Well if you think I'm going out to get married just so I can bring a wife to your family clambake, McGee, your dripping wet. (blustering) I'LL SEE YOU FOR DINNER THURSDAY!"

McGee wonders, "How did I know he wasn't married. Gee, that was a natural mistake."

It seems likely that listeners had already figured out LaTrivia was not married from LaTrivia's first hesitation here. In addition, you would think listeners by now would have inferred from the many episodes done already that LaTrivia never speaks of a "Mrs. LaTrivia."

In this and several previous episodes, LaTrivia has shown himself to being an argumentative hotheaded character. It seems he resembles the show's Gildersleeve character, almost as if he has become a replacement for him. What is also obvious is that McGee is purposely testing the Mayor, as if he is looking for something to pick a fight with him. In addition, McGee proves he is just as much a hothead as the Mayor.

On the March 24, 1942 show ("Fibber Writes a Song"), LaTrivia is the first drop-in guest at the McGees.

LATRIVIA: "When I was over here for dinner the other evening, McGee, I lost my Phi Beta Kappa key. Did you find it by any chance?"

This simple matter builds into the Mayor losing his temper and storming off when the McGees, especially Fibber, cause him to go into a frustrating tirade. It is as if they are baiting him when they ask him inane questions about the item. This is something that will be a regular aspect to the interactions between the McGees and LaTrivia in many future shows.

LaTrivia tries to explain: "It wasn't a key to anything Mrs. McGee. It was a visible symbol of my membership of the scholastic fraternity, Phi Beta Kappa. . . ."

After McGee interjects, LaTrivia continues: "Apparently McGee you still don't get it. This key has no utilitarian purpose."

He then insults McGee's American Legion button. McGee responds calling LaTrivia names.

LaTrivia: "This key does not unlock any doors. Can't you get that fact through your Neanderthal noggin'!"

Neither McGee nor Molly seem to understand, and they continue to banter with LaTrivia. Of course, this leads to another aspect to the Mayor's character that will be seen often from now on. That is, LaTrivia gets his own words all twisted to the point that he does not know what he is saying. As an example, they offer him a cup of hot tea.

LaTrivia responds, "I don't want a cup of key. I just wanna find my tea, I mean . . . (he goes on getting more angry) . . . "It's just a pin, I just wear it. . ."

This leads to him ranting illogically. Then when he attempts to explain it to the McGees all over again, they seemingly act ignorant just to annoy him.

LaTrivia calmly gives up the explaining when he says, "Never mind. I'm going to turn in my resignation today. I'm going to join the Elks."

McGee: "Boy! Is he dumb?"

On the March 30, 1942 show ("Soap Contest"), the McGees again play their game of confusion with the Mayor.

LaTrivia: "I've just stopped in to have a word with you about your horse. . . . McGee, you're overfeeding that animal. She's much, much, too much overweight. . . . Nevertheless, you're ruining a fine animal. That horse has splendid lines and good blood and I think it comes from racing stock. . . ."

McGee: "What made you an authority on horses, LaTrivia? I know you ran for office on a promise for a stable government but (laughs), I thought it was just a stall . . . Don't you get it?"

Molly: "T'aint funny, McGee."

LaTrivia: "Indeed, it ain't. I mean it isn't . . . I used to own a racehorse myself, McGee, and this horse of yours reminds me a great deal of one of my animals. One of which I entered in the darby at Louisville."

The English word pronounced "darby" is the same thing as "derby." But this is not correctly registering with the McGees as they confuse what LaTrivia is saying to the point where it burns him up even more with this back and forth word confusion.

Finally, exhausted LaTrivia says, "Let It Go! All I came here for was to, to—(Yelling) I DON'T KNOW WHAT I CAME HERE FOR! GOOD DAY!" (audience applauds).

The McGees think this is amusing, and they laugh.

Molly: "You know McGee; we shouldn't really lead him on like that. He'll think we're the two dumbest people in town."

McGee: "I like to see him get exasperated. You know he'd make a swell head of the city government if he didn't have such a swelled head."

Molly: "I think he's nice!"

McGee: "Yeah, he's too nice but stuffy."

Here the McGees reveal their intention. We learn that they like to see the Mayor explode in frustration.

On the April 7, 1942 show ("Scrap Drive"), we see that the arguments with LaTrivia are pre-meditated. McGee sees LaTrivia coming and says, "Wohhh, look whose coming? LaTrivia."

Molly: "Oh well, let's not get into one of those silly arguments with him, will you."

McGee: "Oh come on, let's do. Do him good."

The McGees are putting stuff from the hall closet into a truck. LaTrivia offers to help as he sees Molly up on the truck, and he wonders why McGee is not up on the truck letting Molly hand him things. . . .

McGee: "Now you mind your business, LaTrivia . . ."

LaTrivia: "I just came by to ask if you'd subscribe to *Liberty* magazine."

Molly says 'yes,' but she thinks the Mayor is trying to work his way through college.

LaTrivia: "I'm not working my way through college, Mrs. McGee. I merely wished to tell you that in tomorrow's issue of *Liberty* there'll be a four page article on you and Mrs. McGee."

McGee: "Honest, LaTrivia?"

LaTrivia: "As honest as it could be I suppose considering it's a family magazine."

The Mayor mentions he was in the Glee Club in college, which spurs Molly to say, "Well, here we go again."
They immediately go on to drive LaTrivia to distraction regarding what a Glee Club really is. They certainly know what they are doing to him, but he falls for their teasing every time. Here they seem to torture him in order to knock this pompous peg down to size.
LaTrivia tries to counter, "A Glee Club is for the purpose of group singing."

Molly: "I always sing when I'm happy too, but I don't have to belong to, join a club to do it, Mr. Mayor."

LaTrivia: "I didn't either, Mrs. McGee. I joined the Glee

	Club because I like to sing. But a Glee Club is not necessarily gleeful."
McGee:	"You mean they were unhappy?"
LaTrivia:	"Why, why should they be unhappy?"
Molly:	"Why shouldn't they be?"

He begins to fluster as they are tripping him up with his own words.

| LaTrivia: | "Well, they should be. I mean, no, no. They shouldn't be. WHAT DOES THEIR HAPPINESS GOT TO DO WITH IT?" |

Now the Mayor is boiling mad. The McGees got him, but they keep on prodding. They keep putting more pins in this pompous pincushion.

McGee:	"Now that's a fine attitude, LaTrivia. Not to care whether your own club is happy or not? . . . Why when I went to high school—."
LaTrivia:	"I'm merely trying to explain that the term 'Glee Club' has nothing to do with glee. Is that clear?"
Molly:	"I see what you mean, like if you belong to the Elks, you don't necessarily have to give all your friends one of your front teeth."
LaTrivia:	"That's exactly what uh . . . uh, no, no. What I'm trying to say is that a college Glee Club is formed of people who like to sing."

Nevertheless, the Mayor keeps getting himself into a hole trying to explain. The funny exchange keeps going. Next, the McGees argue over this matter with each other.

Finally, LaTrivia says, "Well, I'll just leave you two good people to argue among yourselves. And don't forget the *Liberty* article. Good Day!"

The McGees got rid of the Mayor, but they forget themselves when they continue to argue again. Then they realize this and laugh.

MOLLY: "Well heavenly days, caught on our own hook."

On the April 14, 1942 show ("Spring Festival Parade"), LaTrivia gets off on the wrong foot when McGee's slang talk is over his head. LaTrivia calls it "modern idiom," which McGee thinks he means "modern idiot." This misunderstanding reduces LaTrivia to a blithering mess once again.

As these *Fibber McGee and Molly* shows appeared at the height of World War II, the characters speak from time to time about the pressing world concerns.

LaTrivia first gives a patriotic speech, which brings audience applause. Then the McGees throw him off by confusing him about the directions when he explains the parade route. The hilarious exchange leads LaTrivia finally to say the following, with the first part calmly and the second part angrily: "Take it any way you want to, AND DON'T BRING IT BACK!"

On the April 21, 1942 show ("Out to the Ballgame"), Molly impresses LaTrivia with her baseball knowledge. The play on words this time is with the word "Lit," short for literature. The McGees pretend they think he is saying, "He was being lit all the time."

Generally, the surviving audio quality of these shows is good, but for part of this episode, it is poor with prominent hissing.

It builds to LaTrivia saying: "CAN'T YOU GET IT THROUGH YOUR HEAD, McGee that (calms himself counting to ten) . . . I promised myself, next time we got into one of these things, I told myself I would not give way to anger, besides I have a mission to perform this afternoon. I wish to present as cheerful a face as public to the possible. I mean I wish to present-."

Molly laughs, asking, "What's the mission, Mr. Mayor?"

LATRIVIA: "... As Mayor I have to throw out the first ball..."

McGee corrects the Mayor's way of tossing, and he volunteers to teach the Mayor how to do it correctly so as not to disgrace himself at the baseball park.

LaTrivia is grateful saying, "This is very decent of you, I'm sure."

Of course, McGee wears LaTrivia's arm out practicing throwing, so he could not lift his arm. He gets blisters from the glove. McGee tells him, "Keep swinging that arm."

As a result, LaTrivia unfortunately cannot do his duty at the game, and so he asks McGee to represent him. In short, McGee found a way to go to the ballgame with Molly, leaving the poor ailing Mayor to recuperate at their home. Afterwards, Molly accuses McGee of setting the Mayor up just to get the free passes to the game.

On the April 28, 1942 show ("Old Straw Hat"), LaTrivia wants McGee to serve on a committee on which he happens to be the Chairman. Its intention is to organize a citizen's letter-writing campaign to friends and family members of those in the Armed Forces.

Then, as usual, it is the McGees time to frustrate the Mayor, which predictably makes him leave after losing his temper. LaTrivia puts his foot in his mouth and is tongue-tied and confused when the McGees talk about his being in the Army, whether he went to Annapolis, being a general in the Navy, and the Army having nothing to do with Annapolis, and so forth.

When LaTrivia calms down, he asks, "McGee, were you in the Army?... Do you still have that old army spirit, McGee?... Fine. I was a Captain and I, due to ATTENTION, LEFT FEET... HUP!"

LaTrivia proceeds to make McGee march right through the bay window.

LATRIVIA: "Yes, well isn't that too bad. Well Good Day, Mrs. McGee!"

On the May 5, 1942 show ("Sugar Substitute"), LaTrivia's intentionally short visit is primarily about government rationing of sugar.

However, his suit is destroyed when he is burned with Nitric Acid, as McGee is experimenting to find a substitute for sugar. LaTrivia leaves screaming in pain.

MOLLY: "McGee, you were very careless. You know the Mayor may have been seriously hurt."

MCGEE: "Well he should have been careful himself. I don't go messing around his office and squawk if I get trampled by a fat alderman, do I?"

As an aside, we finally learned that the little girl, Teeny, threw the rock through Mrs. Uppington's window (January 13, 1942 show).

On the May 12, 1942 show ("Fibber is Being Followed by a Spy"), McGee believes a "spy" is photographing him.

LATRIVIA: "Do I understand you called my office this morning?"

McGee angrily responds, "You were in a Council meeting and couldn't be bothered."
LaTrivia corrects him, "Couldn't be disturbed."
McGee goes into a speech about the how public servants should be there for him for "we're the public."

LATRIVIA: "You seem to be under the delusion that public officials should come running to wipe your little noses every time you sneeze, if Mrs. McGee will excuse my plain speaking."

McGee wanted to report the suspicious looking person carrying a camera under his coat following him around for two days. LaTrivia agrees to help by having him picked up for questioning. However, McGee decides not to sign a complaint when Molly explains how McGee might be in trouble for false arrest, malicious prosecution, and invasion of private rights if the "spy" is innocent.
LaTrivia adds, "You might get out of it for $100,000 in damages."

LaTrivia looks out the window and sees the "spy" too. McGee wants to see if the spy follows LaTrivia when he walks down the street. LaTrivia exits and there is a loud noise as he trips on the rope and falls into the trap that McGee set for the "spy."

It turns out the "spy" is a photographer for a national magazine, and he is getting a picture story on how a small-town busybody spends his time.

The May 19, 1942 show ("Going to be Rich"), has LaTrivia getting confused and exasperated with the McGees with a wordplay on the word "right," "write," and the name "Wright." It is pure Abbott & Costello wordplay fun.

McGee wants to buy a house with his supposed millions, so he asks LaTrivia what kind he likes.

LaTrivia: "Personally, I like a nice Charleston colonial . . . . You know this is an odd coincidence, McGee. I'm going to build a new house myself after priorities are lifted. . . I wrote a letter to Frank Lloyd Wright. . .You think I'd be wrong to engage him?"

Molly: "You're never go wrong to get Wright."

McGee: "What did you write Wright?"

LaTrivia: "What? Ohh! Ohh! . . . I wanted it right so I wrote Wright."

Molly: "Now, now, now. Wait a minute, Mr. Mayor. You're getting me all confused."

McGee: "Me too. I'm in a muddle. You mean you wrote Wright, that if Wright built your house. You knew it would be right because Wright—."

LaTrivia: "WILL YOU, will you let me tell it in my own way?"

MOLLY: "Stop interrupting McGee."

It ends with LaTrivia muddling his explanation saying, "Well, I think I wrote it right. That is, I think I was right in writing Wright because Wright is. Oh good heavens, you got me talking like Abbott and Costello. GOOD DAY!"

MOLLY: (amusingly) "If he could talk like Abbott & Costello, he could afford to build ten houses."

On the May 26, 1942 show ("Uncle Dennis Disappears, Part One"), McGee tells LaTrivia that they lost Uncle Dennis.

LATRIVIA: "Oh, maybe he isn't lost. Perhaps you forgot where you put him."

LaTrivia gives a wacky description of Molly's Uncle to the police. This is the first time we hear him talk to Myrt the Operator.

LATRIVIA: "Hello Operator, please connect me with the Police Department. I beg your pardon. McGee, who is Myrt?"

MOLLY: "Just an off stage character, Mr. Mayor. Don't let her get you down."

LATRIVIA: "Hello Operator, Police Department, please. No, I don't care what happened to your grandmother. I want the Police Department, yes. Hello, Clanahan. This is my Honor, your Honor, Hizzoner. This is the Mayor speaking. Put this on the radio right away: locate and bring in a Mr. Dennis Driscoll, five feet eleven, pink eyes, weight 225, complexion saffron. When last seen was wearing light gray suit and silk lampshade on his head. Yes, keep me informed. Goodbye. Ah, now you don't have to worry Mrs. McGee I'm sure we'll find him."

MOLLY:	"But Mr. Mayor, what was that about the lampshade?"
McGEE:	"Yeah what made you think he was wearing that?"
LaTRIVIA:	"I was wearing it at the party the night before last, and he took it away from me. Don't worry, we'll find him."

On the June 2, 1942 show ("Uncle Disappears, Part Two"), LaTrivia and the McGees argue about famous sayings and who said what in the midst of trying to find the missing Uncle Dennis.

LaTRIVIA:	"As Horace Greeley so well said: 'Don't give up the ship.'"
MOLLY:	"No. I thought John Paul Jones said that."
LaTRIVIA:	"No, no, it was John Paul Jones who said: 'You may fire, when ready, Gridley.'"
McGEE:	"Then who said 'Go West, Young Man?'"
MOLLY:	"Jimmy Doolittle."
LaTRIVIA:	"No, no, that was Patrick Henry, I believe."
McGEE:	"No, it couldn't have been. He couldn't fly an airplane."
LaTRIVIA:	"Who said he could?"
MOLLY:	"Well if he went with Jimmy Doolittle he'd have to."
LaTRIVIA:	"Why that's ridiculous, Patrick Henry was born in 1736."

Chapter Ten: First Season as Mayor LaTrivia (1941–1942)

MCGEE: "Ain't that marvelous? Imagine a guy his age flying an airplane."

MOLLY: "Well maybe one of the younger fellows helped him dear."

LATRIVIA: "But I tell you that was impossible—."

MCGEE: "To guys like Doolittle nothing is impossible . . . ."

The argument continues back and forth, and it becomes heated. The mix-up continues as the McGees think he is talking about the contemporary Patrick Henry who bombed Tokyo, not the Henry connected to the Revolutionary War who said, "Give me liberty, or give me death."

Of course, they confuse LaTrivia's use of the word "contemporary" with "contemptible." LaTrivia becomes hysterical when they purposely misunderstand his remarks by putting words in his mouth, and they criticize him for what they take as snide un-American remarks.

LaTrivia insists: "I made no nasty remarks."

MOLLY: "Aren't you ashamed, Mr. Mayor?"

They threaten to call the FBI. A very exasperated LaTrivia says this is all a misunderstanding and that he is a good American.

MCGEE: "A likely story."

Then LaTrivia shifts into a promotion for nursing students. When he is finished, the McGees admit that they were only fooling; however, they try to pull him into it again.

McGee says, "We knew you wouldn't make any snide remarks about a guy that had gumption enough to fly with Doolittle."

LaTrivia starts to raise his voice, but then stops himself before saying "impossible."

LATRIVIA: "But I tell you McGee that's im—. Never mind, I just hope he enjoyed the trip."

On the June 9, 1942 show ("Pot Roast"), McGee is nervous because he does not want to share his dinner of pot roast. He is worrying about why the Mayor is there. LaTrivia says he wants the McGees' opinion on the new bulletin board on the City Hall's steps, and he does his spiel about how important his job as Mayor is for the citizens.

When LaTrivia refers to "A stitch in time saves nine," the McGees will proceed to aggravate LaTrivia with a literal "ignorant" interpretation, thinking he wants a needle and thread.

In the midst of getting angry, LaTrivia smells the pot roast, which stops him in his tracks.

He manages to wrangle an invitation with subtle hints to stay for dinner. McGee with all his might is determined not to let him do it. Because of all of the interruptions of visitors and McGee faking illness to get rid of the Mayor, Molly burnt the roast.

The McGees go out to a restaurant to have pot roast, and they find it was the specialty of the day. The waitress taking their order tells them she "gave the last one to a gentleman over there." When McGee sees it is LaTrivia, he attacks him. The episode ends with the sounds of physical altercation and LaTrivia yelling in response.

On the June 16, 1942 show ("Mouse in the House"), McGee asks LaTrivia, "How's Trix?"

LATRIVIA: "Oh, Trixie's fine. I took her to a nightclub last night. Oh, oh, you mean everything's fine, everything's fine."

However, what he came over for was McGee's scrap rubber. Referring to the war and a filling station man, LaTrivia says, "As one of them said to me this morning, 'Bring your scrap over here so we can finish that scrap over there.'"

After Molly makes a brilliant speech regarding lines from *Alice in Wonderland*, re cabbages and kings.

LATRIVIA: "We just want rubber, Mrs. McGee, not shoes or cabbages."

McGee defends Molly.

LaTrivia: "I know I just say cabbages are not pertinent to the subject."

Molly asks if he was accusing her of being impertinent.
They play the "ignorant" game and pretend they are insulted.
LaTrivia is tripped up again in trying to explain what he did not say.

LaTrivia: "I didn't say that. I only said . . . (arguing about liking or not liking cabbage)"

McGee calls him a snob.
LaTrivia stops himself. "Never mind, why I don't like it. . . , I don't care. JUST BECAUSE YOU TWIST EVERYTHING I SAY DOESN'T MEAN A THING TO ME, THE SPRING SEASON IS COMING AND I SAY WHAT I PLEASE!"

McGee: "Hey, how would you catch a mouse, LaTrivia?"

LaTrivia: "I'd import a few Russians. They seem pretty good at exterminating rats. Good Day!"

On the June 23, 1942 show ("Packing for Vacation"), first up LaTrivia drops in to wish them 'Bon Voyage,' but then he knocks vacations.

LaTrivia: "You go camping or traveling, you get hot and dusty, can't take so many changes of clothing, can't have a shower whenever you like."

For a brief moment, his speech starts to dissuade Molly. Then she stops herself, "Oh, what I am saying is a vacation is a vacation."

McGee: "Why sure it is, Molly . . . . What's a vacation without a little discomfort?"

LATRIVIA: (laughing, with it heightened by the end of first line) "Well, I'll certainly be thinking of you out in a fishy, smelling rowboat under the broiling sun, fighting off the flies and squirming under your sunburn. Well, enjoy yourself."

Chapter Eleven: Second Season as Mayor LaTrivia (1942–1943)

Mayor LaTrivia on stupid arguments and a new broom sweeps clean: ". . . I'm sick of being baited into these arguous stupements . . . Look when I made the innocent remark that a new clean spoons away, a new spoon brings, a new broom . . ."

—*Fibber McGee and Molly*,
October 12, 1948

On the September 29, 1942 show ("Back from Summer Vacation"), the McGees return from vacation. They meet the Mayor at the station with other friends. LaTrivia explains his job duties while they were away. McGee offers his slogan on the salvage program. LaTrivia wants to hear it.

McGee: "It's a honey. Now just imagine a big sign on the salvage truck that reads, 'we want all kinds of scrap metal so get the lead out.'"

This time they get rid of LaTrivia with their wordplay shtick concerning "incense."

LaTrivia: "So you had a nice vacation, Mrs. McGee?"

Molly tells of how healthy a fishing trip is.

LaTrivia: "Well perhaps I should take a fishing trip myself. A little incident in my office a short time ago made me quite angry. In fact, I'm highly incensed."

McGee: "You are? Come here let me smell."

Molly: "McGee, he means he's furious about something."

McGee: "Oh, maybe you put on too much of that incense, and someone started wisecracking, huh?"

LaTrivia: "McGee, I have not been using incense."

McGee: "Well what if you did, who cares? I kinda go for a good smelling shaving lotion myself. Nothing sissy about that."

Molly: "Why of course not. Besides, the atmosphere in that City Hall is so stuffy that a person almost has to—."

LaTrivia: "I tell you Mrs. McGee, I do not use perfume of any kind."

McGee keeps insisting LaTrivia's using incense.

McGee: "Who said you did? Incense ain't perfume. Incense is great stuff. Keeps the mosquitos away too. And they got some real nice fragrances too. Sandalwood and roses and all stuff like that there. You got mosquitos in the City Hall, LaTriv?"

LaTrivia: "NO we have not!"

Molly: "Then why the incense?"

They almost got him saying that he uses incense. He's fuming because of their misunderstanding.

LaTrivia:	"Because incense is the only, I MEAN I DON'T USE INCENSE. I use the word in the sense of being angry."
McGee:	"What were you sore at, LaTrivia?"
LaTrivia:	"The City Treasurer accused me of being wasteful with public funds, and it's a downright political bluff. I have been the most economical Mayor this city has ever had, I—!"
Molly:	"Oh, maybe he was referring to the incense. Now, uh, did you pay for that out of your own pocket?"
LaTrivia:	"OF COURSE I DID. I MEAN NO I DID NOT. THERE WASN'T ANY INCENSE!"

McGee continues to bug him, saying, "Now, now, now, now. First, you say there was, and then you said there wasn't. We don't care, LaTrivia. You can talk plain to us. Shucks, incense is a trivial item. I can get you all you want for four bits. What fragrance you like?"

Soon LaTrivia has to realize that he better exit quickly to stop this argument. First, his agitation causes him to scream, "I DON'T LIKE ANY! I HATE INCENSE. I DON'T WANT IT AROUND!"

Molly:	"I shouldn't think you would after that incident in your office."
McGee:	"Anyway, if it's just to chase mosquitos, a little pump will do just as well."
LaTrivia:	(he stops ranting in defense and quickly says) "THAT'S FINE. YOU'VE GOT THE JOB! BE IN MY OFFICE IN THE MORNING. A NEWS OFFICE!"

LaTrivia finally storms out.

The October 6, 1942 show ("Otis Cadwalader is Back"), features the supposed return of Molly's ex-boyfriend, Otis Cadwalader. Gordon originally played the character in his first appearance on *Fibber McGee and Molly* in 1939.

LaTrivia enters asking McGee's opinion of something.

LATRIVIA: ". . . . I want to start a citywide, yes a statewide campaign against hoarding. I want to tell our citizens that we've got a hard and bitter war ahead of us and it's got to be 'one for all, and all for one' and not 'everyman for himself.'"

McGee tries to say something, but LaTrivia continues.

LATRIVIA: "I want to tell our people it's not only unpatriotic, but downright stupid to rush out and load up on things every time there's a rumor of a shortage or news of rationing. Hoarding sometimes causes a shortage of things that others might be printable (word indecipherable). If we're going to do our fair share in this fight, we got to take only our fair share of available commodities."

MOLLY: "Well, I think you're perfectly right, Mr. Mayor."

Then LaTrivia acts pompous about his speech and uses a saying that is misconstrued by the McGees. He says he has a knack for the message, "as easy as kicking a little puppy off the sidewalk."

McGee and Molly tease him by taking him literally, and they start to chide him.

The verbal brawl comedy that writer Quinn so brilliantly developed throughout this series is typically a relentless assault of LaTrivia back and forth, alternating from McGee and Molly. In between the McGees' accusations, LaTrivia's response becomes increasingly aggravated. Here is the format without the first series of taunts by McGee and Molly:

McGee taunts.

LaTrivia: (frantic) "I DIDN'T KICK ANY DOG!"

Molly taunts.

LaTrivia: (even more excited, and desperate to be believed) "BUT I DIDN'T KICK ANY PUPPIES! I MERELY USED IT AS AN ILLUSTRATION OF HOW EASY IT WAS TO DO SOMETHING!"

McGee taunts.

LaTrivia: "BUT I DIDN'T KICK ANY PUPPIES! THERE WASN'T ANY PUPPY. IT WAS JUST AN EXPRESSION!"

Molly taunts.

LaTrivia: "BUT I DO LOVE DOGS! I HAVE THREE DOGS OF MY OWN! I WOULDN'T HARM THE HAIR OF A DOG'S HEAD!"

McGee taunts.

LaTrivia: "I TELL YOU I DIDN'T KICK ANY PUPPY! I'M NOT A MAN WHO GOES ABOUT MISTREATING ANIMALS AND I!—"

Molly: "Oh ho, you don't consider kicking a puppy is mistreatment?"

LaTrivia: "OF COURSE IT IS! CERTAINLY!"

McGee: "Ah, then you admit it?"

| LaTrivia: | "I MEAN NO, I DON'T! I MEAN THAT I ADMIT THAT KICKING A PUPPY IS MISTREATMENT, BUT I DON'T ADMIT THAT I EVER DESCENDED TO— (pauses, then calmly says) Never mind, let me out of here." |

Asked where he is going, LaTrivia responds even louder and angrier than before, "I'M GOING OUT AND FIND A PUPPY AND KICK IT OFF THE SIDEWALK!"

LaTrivia departs. The McGees indicate that they were just teasing him.

| Molly: | (laughing) "You really think he really is?" |

| McGee: | "Of course not. LaTrivia's a very tender-hearted guy. He wouldn't do that." |

On the October 13, 1942 show ("Converting the Furnace"), LaTrivia says he is "seriously considering running for Governor. This is confidential incidentally." He then uses a Latin term, "nemine contradicente." He pronounces it "nom-minee contra-dissentay."

| LaTrivia: | "Without a dissenting vote, it's a Latin phrase." |

McGee thinks he had to use Latin at a meeting, which leads to a wacky misunderstanding of this phrase and its meaning. LaTrivia is entangled again, and he raises his voice in order to convey what he really meant.

The McGees typical teasing always leads to Gordon's final angry shouting, followed by his quiet calm reversal. Gordon's vocalizing (from Quinn's scripting) of the shift from a loud outburst to a soft withdrawal guaranteed intense laughter and pleasure to listeners.

| LaTrivia: | "BUT I TELL YOU THERE WEREN'T THREE DIFFERENT LANGUAGES! NOBODY SPOKE ANYTHING BUT ENGLISH! IF I CHOOSE LATIN, IT |

| | WOULD HAVE BEEN GREEK! I MEAN IF ANYTHING BUT ENGLISH!" |

Molly taunts.

| LaTrivia: | "BUT THEY'RE NOT FOREIGNERS! I'M ONE OF THEM MYSELF!" |

McGee taunts.

| LaTrivia: | "YES! I MEAN NO! I MEAN YES! I MEAN NO! I MEAN I'M NOT A FOREIGNER! JUST BECAUSE I USE ONE LATIN PHRASE!" |

Molly taunts.

| LaTrivia: | "OF COURSE! I MEAN NO! WHY DO I EVER TRY TO EXPLAIN THINGS TO YOU PEOPLE? WHY DO I—?" |
| LaTrivia: | (quietly and calmly) "Oh, McGee? What's that on the floor in front of you?" |

Then McGee bends down to look, and LaTrivia kicks him.

McGee:	"What's the idea?"
LaTrivia:	"Oh, nothing, just such a pleasure to see you, STOOP! (audience applause)."
Molly:	"Did he kick you hard, McGee?"
McGee:	"No, but he hadn't any business kicking me at all. We, we're just kidding him. He and his Latin. Can't he take a joke?"
Molly:	"He can take it and he can dish it out too!"

On the October 20, 1942 show ("Family Tree"), LaTrivia turns the tables on McGee as he is tracing his genealogy in this brief account of the interaction.

MOLLY: "Come in, Mayor LaTrivia."

LaTrivia makes fun of McGee's family tree project, and McGee accuses him of sneering.

LATRIVIA: "I was not sneering, McGee."

MCGEE: "Don't kid me. I know when I'm being sneered at. I can take a hint. You know what they say, 'a link's as good as a nod to a blind horse.'"

LATRIVIA: "Oh, I'm sorry. I didn't know. How did it happen?"

MCGEE: "How did what happen?"

LATRIVIA: "About your horse?"

MCGEE: "We haven't got a horse. We sold it."

LATRIVIA: "After it went blind? Was that quite ethical McGee? After all, if you misrepresented—?"

Molly tries to help McGee by agreeing with him that the horse was not blind.

LATRIVIA: "I see then it happened after you sold it. Well the poor animal—"

The accusations by LaTrivia continues.

LATRIVIA: "You deliberately refused to take any responsibility?"

Now McGee is getting his words twisted, and he is upset trying to get the Mayor to understand him. A frantic McGee is struggling to save himself, but LaTrivia is doing to McGee what McGee and Molly have always done to him.

LATRIVIA: "Never mind, let it go. . . . Please, Mrs. McGee. I'd rather not discuss it any further. I came here to offer your husband a position with the City. In spite of his somewhat strange code of morality in the sale of livestock, I still offer him the situation . . . . Commissioner of Streets and it pays six thousand dollars a year."

MCGEE: "Well thanks anyway, LaTrivia. But I can't take it."

LaTrivia says he was only joking about the horse bit.

MCGEE: "Oh I reject it, LaTrivia. I can't take it. It wouldn't be right."

MOLLY: "Why not?"

MCGEE: "Because, I don't want to talk about it. I'm sorry, LaTrivia."

LaTrivia leaves, McGee ridiculously confesses that he had to turn down the job offer because the Peoria's County Clerk called to say that they do not have any records of him, so he was never born.

On the October 27, 1942 show ("The Old Timer on the Lam"), as with earlier shows, topical matters concerning the World War slip in to the stories. Here, the Old Timer is on the lam for hoarding war bonds. LaTrivia enters to ask McGee his opinion of a verse that he wants printed on the back of the City's water bills.

LaTrivia reads, "Remember what happened in 1920 when people starved in the midst of plenty? We oughta be much smarter now. If we want milk, let's feed the cow. Let's all be ready when this is over and start today to plant the clover. Let's all buy bonds and pay our debts for the man what has, is the man what gets."

It impresses Molly who thinks the Mayor wrote it, but LaTrivia reveals that it was Wallace Wimple. When LaTrivia uses the expression "try it on the dog."—meaning testing it on average citizens, McGee gets upset. He thinks LaTrivia insulted Molly, calling her a dog.

McGee quickly gets angry and he wants to fight the Mayor.

At one point, LaTrivia tries to calm him, saying it is just an expression, "Oh, stop waving your paw. Ah, I mean your fist. This is ridiculous."

McGee is just as flustered as LaTrivia is in explaining himself, and he wants to beat LaTrivia to a pulp for these insults.

McGee: "I'm gonna pound you so flat I can mail you home."

Molly: "Oh, my, my, this ought to be very interesting."

Then she points out that the Mayor was an intercollegiate boxing champion.

Upon hearing that, McGee stops himself. Then he backs down and nervously laughs about it.

McGee: "Well glad you dropped in, LaTrivia."

LaTrivia: "Thanks. Good Day Mrs. McGee. And oh, McGee? Let's go out some afternoon and bark at automobiles."

On the November 3, 1942 show ("Duck Hunting with Mayor LaTrivia"), McGee and LaTrivia are sitting in a duck blind at the edge of Mud Lake. Interestingly, McGee is annoying LaTrivia with his bragging. LaTrivia seems to know more than McGee.

LaTrivia: "For goodness sakes, would you keep quiet, McGee?"

CHAPTER ELEVEN: SECOND SEASON AS MAYOR LATRIVIA (1942–1943) | 219

McGEE: "Not so loud, LaTrivia! That's exactly what I'm talking about. You're too gabby."

LaTRIVIA: "I haven't spoke three words since we got here this morning. I'm too cold."

Then McGee ruins LaTrivia's chance to get some ducks overhead when he mistakes them for Army planes.

Then when McGee almost shoots at airplanes, instead of ducks, LaTrivia says, "McGee, Stop it! Don't shoot. Put your gun down. . . . McGee, I'm going home. No. No . . . . I don't want to stay out here with a duck hunter who fires at airplanes and throws kisses to mallards. Who throws the coffee pot overboard and orders me a cold anchor to drink. Who chatters away like a magpie. (Spotting some ducks, LaTrivia starts shooting) LOOK MCGEE, HERE THEY COME! MY FIRST SHOT! KEEP YOUR HEAD DOWN!"

The scene shifts to McGee's home where the humor comes from McGee telling Molly about his bad start earlier hunting ducks with the Mayor.

Referring to LaTrivia, McGee says, "Anything that guy says you can take with a dose of salt."

Then we learn that McGee bought the duck he claims he caught.

On the November 10, 1942 show ("Uppy's Nephew"), the McGees go to see LaTrivia about whether Mrs. Uppington's nephew is working.

LaTRIVIA: "If he's really working, it's a political novelty of no means proportional. What is the youngster's name? . . . How can I give you information about someone whose name you don't know. I'm not a Swami."

McGEE: "So what, I can't swim a stroke myself?"

LaTrivia receives a mysterious phone call. The McGees misinterpret LaTrivia's intentions from hearing his responses to the caller.

LaTrivia, speaking on the phone: "There's only one thing to do. Get a gang of huskies and take an axe to them. You heard me, chop off their heads so nobody will recognize them and hack off their legs and chop up the bodies and haul them away. No, no, no, no, no. I'll meet you there at exactly midnight! Stop worrying. I'll handle the police angle."

The McGees think he is talking about retaliating against people so they wreck his office, and they attack him. Then they try to call the police to report him.

LaTrivia finally explains, "Those aren't people, they're statues. We're chopping up some old iron statues in the park and turning them into, for scrap metal. NOW GET OUT! BOTH OF YOU!"

On the November 17, 1942 show ("Twenty Thousand Dollar Sofa"), LaTrivia arrives when the McGees are in the midst of trying to find $20,000 that McGee's late Uncle Jefferson may have left him in a sofa.

LaTrivia:	"I meant that riches bring obligations to the possessor. You must set an example to those that are not so well off. Help the underdog."

By now, listeners know almost where this is going. The McGees will twist LaTrivia's words and he will blow up. This time they misconstrue his use of the expression "Help the underdog."

Molly:	"Oh, he loves dogs, don't you dear?"
McGee:	"I'll say I do. I gonna get me a nice Irish Setter pup."
LaTrivia:	"I didn't mean real dogs, McGee."
Molly:	"But how can you help a dog if he isn't real, Mr. Mayor?"
LaTrivia:	"I was referring to people, Mrs. McGee."

McGee angrily accuses, "Ohhhh, you think people are dogs, do you LaTrivia? A fine altitude!"

LaTrivia: "I didn't say people were dogs. I merely said that I, as a leader of the people—."

Molly: "Oh, now calm yourself Mr. Mayor; we can't have the leader of the people turning purple."

LaTrivia: "I am not turning people, I mean purple. I started to say that as a pup, a purp, I mean a person, I—."

McGee: "He's not the peep" (indecipherable).

LaTrivia: (very agitated) "I AM NOT! I was trying to say that if a pupson, uh a person wants to be a pup, popular, he'll probably, probably—."

Gordon is clearly a master at delivering these lines, particularly in the way he mangles his words. However, at times he has come to realize where these arguments with the McGees are going. Then he cuts his tongue twisting to a halt by stopping midstream and finding an exit line.

LaTrivia: (he calmly says) "Excuse me if I go out on the porch. I think I have a flea." LaTrivia exits.

McGee: "You know Molly, on second thought I won't buy that Irish Setter LaTrivia was trying to sell me. I'd rather a good Springer, a Springer is a—."

On the November 24, 1942 show ("Fibber Getting in Condition"), LaTrivia insults McGee's bathrobe ("what an atrocious pattern"). Then he learns that Molly bought it for McGee's birthday, and so he tries to recover.

LATRIVIA: "Well uh, I, well what I meant when I said the bathrobe was atrocious was not that the pattern itself was atrocious, I meant it was such attractive material they should have put better tailoring into it. Uh yes, yes. That's what I meant uh . . . did I?"

Then McGee says Molly bought material and made it herself.

LATRIVIA: (continuing to take back his insult) "My dear Mrs. McGee, you did a perfectly amazing job! And those elbow-length sleeves are a very smart act. Very! Personally, I despise full-length sleeves on a bathrobe. Old-fashioned. I might even say corny. Yes, I will say corny. Corny! Now what may I ask—?"

McGee insisting, "These are full length sleeves, LaTrivia. I got 'em rolled up."

MOLLY: "Now maybe they are corny, dearie. I didn't realize."

LATRIVIA: (now trying to get himself out of a corner) "Oh I didn't mean those sleeves, Mrs. McGee. For that bathrobe, those sleeves are perfect. What I meant was if the material, I mean the pattern of the material, that is, the tailoring couldn't, healthy, uh well if the sleeves. Good Heavens, is that clock right? I must be dashing along. Good Day!"

LaTrivia exits, with the McGees quite amused by his remarks.

MOLLY: "Well I never saw a man turn so red in my life, McGee. He must have Indian blood."

MCGEE: "If he ever found out I won this bathrobe for sixty cents at the Elks Carnival throwing balls at milk bottles, he'd tear a ligament. One of my ligaments probably."

As is often the case, we never learn what the Mayor wanted with this visit to the McGees.

As art is made to mirror life, Gordon was just about ready to leave for the Coast Guard as he just enlisted, so Mayor LaTrivia would do the same.

On the December 1, 1942 show ("Gas Rationing"), announcer Harlow Wilcox informs the McGees that Mayor LaTrivia has joined the Coast Guard, and he is leaving tomorrow morning. This show offers us his last regular appearance until October 1945, with the exception of five visits in 1943.

McGee to Wilcox: "LaTrivia in the Coast Guard? Why I didn't think that guy could pass the physical for a crossing watch man. He must have pulled some wires."

McGee is curious to know firsthand how true this is.

LATRIVIA:	"It's quite true, McGee. I leave tomorrow. I just dropped in to say Goodbye."
MCGEE:	"Wasn't joining the Coast Guard kinda sudden for you, LaTrivia?"
LATRIVIA:	"Oh no, I've been trying to wind up my affairs for some time. So I can do it, McGee. I'm very happy I was accepted."

Asked by Molly about his experience with small boats, LaTrivia says, "Oh yes, Mrs. McGee, I've been through the Tunnel of Love at Coney Island" (laughter).

MOLLY:	"Ha, ha. You're just fooling now."
LATRIVIA:	"Yes I am. Seriously. I'm rather an expert on small craft. I once had a little sloop on Long Island Sound."

He explains that he joined as just an ordinary apprentice seaman, and that he did not want a commission until he earns it.

LaTrivia makes an appropriate speech to McGee after he complains about his war gas-rationing card.

LATRIVIA:	"Oh, so you're one of the moaners and groaners. One of those astigmatic individuals who thinks the war is being fought only by soldiers, and sailors, and Marines."
MCGEE:	"Well."
LATRIVIA:	"Let me tell you, it isn't. Everything you do in your daily life has some effect on our war program."
MCGEE:	"Oh yeah, I suppose the way I comb my hair is important too, huh?"
LATRIVIA:	"Yes it is. What's your comb made of? Rubber. It's a piece of rubber that didn't go into a tire. It was made when this country had plenty of rubber. And we haven't got plenty now. We're dangerously short of it. What we have got we need for military purposes and an essential transportation. You belong to a car pool? . . . Are you engaged in any important war work, McGee? . . . Then for heaven's sake, stop your griping! You're lucky you have a car at all. Oh, excuse me McGee. When I get over to Africa or Australia or wherever they send me, I'll be thinking of you McGee and the hardships you're suffering. Well Goodbye, Mrs. McGee, I'll see you when this is over."
MOLLY:	"Goodbye Mr. Mayor and happy landing."
LATRIVIA:	"Goodbye McGee."

MCGEE: "Good luck, LaTrivia. Don't take any wooden anchors."

LATRIVIA: "I won't. And McGee, when you do drive, if you get up to 35 miles an hour, think of somebody who didn't get a rubber lifeboat. Goodbye!" (He exits to applause.)

MOLLY: "Oh my, my, isn't he a nice man, McGee?"

MCGEE: "Yeah, LaTrivia's alright...."

After the episode, Jim Jordan (who plays McGee) speaks saying, "Ladies and gentlemen, Mr. Gale Gordon, our Mayor LaTrivia, was with us for the last time tonight before going into the service. He's only one of many of our little group now in our Armed Forces; musicians, engineers, sound technicians, and others behind the scenes, whose names you probably wouldn't know, but who are valued members of our company just the same. We'd like to take this occasion to wish you Gale, and all the other boys the very best of luck and to assure you all of a warm welcome when you come back."

GORDON: "Thank you, Fibber."

Marian Jordan (who plays Molly): "And if all of you give that big show, everything you gave our little one, your new sponsor, Uncle Sam, will be very happy.

MCGEE: "Goodnight."

MOLLY: "Goodnight all."

A week later, on December 8, 1942, in "Return Boston Symphony to Air after Five Years," *Chicago Daily Tribune* reported, "Gale Gordon, Mayor LaTrivia of the *Fibber McGee* show, has joined the Coast Guard."

With the exception of his war service in 1943, 1944, and most of 1945, Gordon continued on the *Fibber McGee and Molly* show until

1953. He told Simons, he: ". . . did time out and joined the service, and (inaudible) and I was called up much sooner than they thought I would be when I finally signed up, and I got word on a Friday that I had to report for duty down in Long Beach in 14 days, or something like that. So Don Quinn threw out the script he had written on that Sunday, and rewrote the whole script about Mayor LaTrivia going to war, and when I left they had a big party, and the Johnson Wax people gave me a check for $500. . . . Which was a great deal of money in those days."

Gordon returned on leave during 1943 to appear in five episodes (February 16, June 15, June 22, September 28, and October 5) during the nearly three years that he was in the Coast Guard.

On the February 16, 1943 show ("War Worker Shortage"), LaTrivia stops in and says he is now in the Coast Guard. Molly compliments him and says the government took care of him ("you look simply grand").

LaTrivia: "Oh, I feel fine, Mrs. McGee. I'm on leave with a bunch of Coast Guardsmen who just completed a course on Japanese anatomy in Guadalcanal."

McGee: "Took off a little weight didn't you, LaTrivia?"

LaTrivia: "Oh, I've taken it off in some places and added it in other places, McGee. I have two more inches around the chest and three inches less around—."

Molly: "Won't you sit down, Mr. LaTrivia?"

Interestingly, Molly does not let LaTrivia finish saying where he lost three inches. Her quick interruption makes one think he was going to say something risqué. It has been said that Quinn was known to slip into the scripts some off-color bits. Could this be where one of them was planned? What did Molly think LaTrivia would say?

| LaTrivia: | "I hope you and McGee will film me on our base one of these days, Southern Section Training Base in San Clemente, California. We're very proud of it. Our Commending Official, Lt. Howard Shebley, is really turning out sailors there. Uh, think you can pay us a visit?" |

Then, after a little more chatting about the Coast Guard, the McGees get LaTrivia again entangled in the old familiar word play arguments. It starts when Molly asks, "How long will you be in town? How long a furlong have you got?"

McGee:	"You don't mean a furlong, Molly. A furlong is a horse."
LaTrivia:	"A furlong is not a horse, McGee. It's a distance."
Molly:	"Oh, you mean a furlong is quite aways like a fur piece."
McGee:	"I tell you a furlong is a horse! You seen them on racing programs. This race is for seven furlongs. That means there's seven horses in the race."
LaTrivia:	"Oh, don't be ridiculous, McGee. A furlong is two hundred and twenty yards, or one-eighth of a mile."
McGee:	"A likely story. Whoever heard of a horse an eighth of a mile long?"
Molly:	"Stop arguing, dear. You haven't seen all the horses in the world. If Mr. LaTrivia says there are horses that long, I believe him."
LaTrivia:	"But I didn't say that. I merely said . . ."

McGee:	"Oh, trying to back out of it, eh? Now, look here, LaTrivia—."
LaTrivia:	"I'M NOT TRYING TO BACK OUT OF ANYTHING! I JUST SAID THAT A FURLONG WAS AN EIGHTH OF A MILE!"
Molly:	"Well, if that isn't a long horse, I never saw one."
LaTrivia:	"BUT I DIDN'T SAY IT WAS A HORSE! I'M NOT THAT STUPID BY A LONG SHOT!"

McGee goes on taunting him that it is a horse.

LaTrivia:	(continuing to get even angrier and confused) "BUT I TELL YOU, I'M NOT TALKING ABOUT HORSES! I MERELY SAID THAT A FURLOUGH IS AN EIGHTH! I MEAN THAT A FURLONG IS WHEN A SERVICE MAN! HOW CAN A HORSE! A FURLONG! AN EIGHTH!" (indecipherable, as he does not know what he is saying anymore)
LaTrivia:	(shifts to quiet calm voice, but then screams) "McGee, as long as you're a government man, please use your influence to send me to Tunisia or New Guinea or someplace WHERE A MAN CAN SEE WHAT HE'S FIGHTING! GOODBYE!"

On the June 15, 1943 show ("Fibber Fixes Doc's Car"), the McGees mistake LaTrivia for an ordinary sailor. The initial conversations sound like the previous show (February 16, 1943), as when they ask about his weight, and they tell him how good he looks. He is not the Mayor anymore (he says, "I'm a First Class Seaman"), but why is Molly unable to call him "Coast Guardsmen LaTrivia?"

CHAPTER ELEVEN: SECOND SEASON AS MAYOR LATRIVIA (1942–1943) | 229

MOLLY: (regarding the length of LaTrivia's leave) ". . . Just for the day, huh?"

LATRIVIA: "No. I'm on ten days leave, Mrs. McGee. I secured my gear, battened down the fiddler hatches, shut off the scuttle boat, got an O.K. from the C.O.'s, stowed my hammock and came ashore for a land cruise."

The conversation goes awry, but it does not go far enough. It is almost predictable, but funny.

MOLLY: "I just love sailors. You know when I was a girl I adored to read about our first American Admiral John Charles Thomas."

LATRIVIA: "That was John Paul Jones, Mrs. McGee."

The expected word play argument does not happen. Instead, LaTrivia picks on McGee's skill as a mechanic. It seemed he wrecked Doc Gamble's car in trying to repair it. Then, although it is cute scene, it is disappointing that LaTrivia happily leaves with the little girl to have a soda. When LaTrivia returns, he talks to McGee and Wallace Wimple, but the exchanges are not funny in the way we have come to expect from the show. Against our expectations, perhaps this show was written this way to avoid being too predictable.

A week later, on the June 22, 1943 show ("Camping at Dugan's Lake"), LaTrivia's leave is up the next day. However, the McGees make sure he wishes he did not stay to say goodbye.

LATRIVIA: "Yes. Yes, as I was saying to one of our petty officers last week—."

MOLLY: "Now, that isn't a very nice way to talk about your officers, Mr. LaTrivia."

LaTrivia:	"I said nothing derogatory, Mrs. McGee. In the Navy, an officer's rank—."
Molly:	"If an officer's rank, you should keep quiet about. Sure, nobody's perfect Mr. LaTrivia, remember that."
LaTrivia:	"Mrs. McGee, please, I merely made the statement that a superior officer—.

McGee interrupts strongly, "You've got an inferiority complex, LaTrivia. They just seem to be acting superior, because you got no gold braids, see."

LaTrivia:	"I didn't say they acted superior. They're superior officers because the higher the rank—."
McGee:	(shouting) "THEY HIRE THE RANK, WHAT? GO ON AND SAY IT, LaTrivia. But remember, enemy ears are all about us. No disloyalty."
LaTrivia:	"Don't accuse me of disloyalty, McGee. I was only trying to tell you that an ordinary seaman—."

Molly indignantly accuses, "Don't you dare call our sailor boys ordinary seamen, Mr. LaTrivia. Why our sailors are the best seamen there are!"

McGee:	(sharply) "Yeah! Just because you think your officers are petty and act superior, LaTrivia don't you think—."
LaTrivia:	"I DON'T THINK ANYTHING! I MEAN I DIDN'T THINK WHAT I WAS SAYING! YOU'VE, YOU'VE TWISTED EVERYTHING I'VE SAID! Now let's start at the beginning. I said that one of our petty officers—."

| McGee: | (threatening) "Now LaTrivia, I, I warn you, if you persist in that attitude, I'll be forced to report you." |

McGee and Molly continue to act as if they do not get what LaTrivia is saying.

Molly:	"Yes, and you'll be thrown in the grog for ninety days and how would you like that?"
LaTrivia:	"It isn't a grog, it's a brig. A grog is an old Navy term meaning rum."
McGee:	(demanding) "Yeah, well what's so rum about a term in one of our grogs?"
LaTrivia:	"I TELL YOU IT ISN'T A BRIG, A GROG, A BRIG IS A DRINK. NO THAT'S GROG! IN THE NAVY GRIB, A BRIG, DOG, GROC!"
Molly:	"Say, have you been drinking, Mr. LaTrivia?"
LaTrivia:	"I DON'T DRINK AND YOU BOTH KNOW IT! BUT BEFORE I GO I'D LIKE TO STRAIGHTEN YOU OUT!"
McGee:	"DON'T YOU THREATEN MY WIFE, YOU BIG BULLY! YOU'LL HAVE TO STRAIGHTEN ME OUT BEFORE YOU LAY A FINGER ON HER!"
Molly:	"Yes per shame. A man in the United States uniform threatening women with violence. Mr. LaTrivia, I would never talk—."
LaTrivia:	(pleading) "Please, please, please, just listen to me for a moment—."

McGee: "O.K. LaTrivia, but make it snappy before I call the FBI."

LaTrivia is exasperated and sounds like he is crying.

LaTrivia: "Now look, you got me all wrong. I didn't mean to say it, my observations, my officers are the finest—."

Then the McGees burst out laughing as they pulled off their teasing stunt and got LaTrivia all confused again.

LaTrivia: "Say what is this? Have you been pulling my leg?"

McGee: "Yeah and I don't mind telling you, LaTrivia, you've got the stretchenest leg we ever pulled."

Molly: "Oh don't be angry Mr. LaTrivia, but it was just like old times and we just couldn't resist it."

LaTrivia: "Angry? Ah, I'm so relieved I could kiss you. I think I will."

He kisses Molly saying, "Oh, thank you!"
Then McGee thinks he is going to kiss him. McGee resists.

LaTrivia: "Now McGee."

McGee: "Oh, no you don't! You get away from me! I ain't gonna—."

LaTrivia: "Ohh don't be silly I just wanted to shake hands" (shakes McGee's hand).

McGee: "Oh yes."

LaTrivia:	"That's it. Wish you a nice vacation, both of you. Good luck. And I hope when we meet again the box score will be No Hitlers, No ruins, No terrors."
McGee:	"Oh I hope so too, LaTrivia. Happy landings boy."
LaTrivia:	"Goodbye now."

On the September 28, 1943 show ("The McGees Go to the Movies"), LaTrivia came to the theatre to see the manager, Mr. Wellington, as the Coast Guard is putting on a recruiting tour. The exchange in this show is a simple plug for the Coast Guard, and as such, it seems that it is a missed opportunity to do another one of their wordplay brawls.

Molly:	"You need more men?"
LaTrivia:	"We need more women!"
McGee:	"That's the kind of chronic complaint with sailors, ain't it LaTrivia."
LaTrivia:	"This is a recruiting campaign for the SPARS, McGee. That's the women's division of the Coast Guard and a wonderful organization for women between 20 and 36 who really want to do something in this war. I have a selfish interest I'll admit, because every woman who joins relieves a man for frontline duty."
Molly:	"What do the SPARS do in the Coast Guard, Mr. LaTrivia?"
LaTrivia:	"Well they act as chauffeurs, cooks, bookkeepers, teletype and telephone operators and a hundred

other things. Almost everything but actually manning the boats . . ."

Jumping to their closing greetings:

MCGEE:	"Oh, oh, I was thinking."
LATRIVIA:	"About what?"
MCGEE:	"About women being sailors. Must be strange to have a sweetheart with a moustache in every port. Oh well, times do change! Well goodnight, LaTrivia."
LATRIVIA:	"See you soon I hope."

On the October 5, 1943 show ("Renting the Spare Room"), LaTrivia visits Wistful Vista for the last time until two years later when war is over. Fortunately, we are treated to another one of their wordplay brawls.

Molly still does not know what to call LaTrivia.

MOLLY:	"By the way Mr. LaTrivia, look do I call you Mr. or what? What does one call a Coast Guardsman?"
MCGEE:	"Well if it's a good looking Coast Guardsman like LaTrivia, and you're a girl, you don't call him. Just whistle like this (wolf whistles)."
LATRIVIA:	"To answer your very sensible question, Mrs. McGee, which proceeded the witty, if somewhat hackneyed comment of our parlor comic; one addresses a Coast Guardsman by his name unless he's an officer."
MOLLY:	"Well I'll tell ya, you ought to be an officer, a man with your education."

McGee:	"I'll say. It's a shame, a guy that graduated with the highest honors from Barber College."
LaTrivia:	"I didn't graduate from Barber College."
Molly:	"How far did ya get, Mr. LaTrivia?"
LaTrivia:	(getting loud) "I tell you I didn't go to Barber College."
Molly:	"Too expensive?"
LaTrivia:	"Yes. No! I don't know. I tell you I never had the slightest intention of going to Barber College. I went to Yale."
McGee:	"They teach barbering at Yale?"
LaTrivia:	"Of course not!"
Molly:	"Then why'd you go there if you wanted to be a barber?"
LaTrivia:	(irritated) "I tell you I didn't want to be a barber. I had nothing to do with barbers! I shave myself."
McGee:	"With the looks of that haircut, you must cut your own hair too."
LaTrivia:	"I DO NOT! The Coast Guard barber cuts my hair."
Molly:	"Why, of course, McGee. You heard of Coast Guard Cutters."
LaTrivia:	"A Coast Guard Cutter is a ship! A vast seagoing vessel."

MOLLY:	"No wonder your hair is all chopped up. How can anybody get a decent haircut on a speedboat?"
MCGEE:	"He's probably running back and forth—."
LATRIVIA:	"Please, McGee! Mrs. McGee listen: a Coast Guard Cutter has nothing ever to do with my haircut. It is merely a vessel used in various patrol services by the Coast Guard. Is that clear?"
MOLLY:	"Why of course it is. We understand that."
MCGEE:	"Yeah. The part I don't get clear is if you're a graduate from a Barber College, why didn't you get a commission? It seems to me that a college graduate—."
LATRIVIA:	(talking very loudly now) "I TELL YOU I DIDN'T GRADUATE! I DIDN'T GO TO BARBER! I NEVER MENTIONED THE IDEA TO YOU! YOU STARTED THE WHOLE THING! YOU DELIBERATELY INVEIGLED ME INTO THIS—."

LaTrivia shifts to a normal tone: "McGee, I'm sorry I lost my temper."

MOLLY:	"Ah Heavenly days, forget it."
LATRIVIA:	"I'll try not to let it happen again."
MCGEE:	"Ah, don't give it a thought, LaTrivia."

Then LaTrivia explodes in anger with jumbled up nautical terms.

LATRIVIA:	"BUT IF IT DOES HAPPEN AGAIN, YOU

BETTER NOT BE AROUND! BECAUSE I'LL TEAR THE FINNACLE RIGHT OUT OF YOUR BULKHEAD AND BLEMISH YOUR TEALSEND TILL YOU FILLS YOUR FLESH WITH YOUR FIDDLEY! GOOD DAY!"

McGEE: "What did he say?"

MOLLY: "He said uh fiddley diddley."

McGEE: "After the war he oughta open a barber-cue joint. He's always good for a few ribs."

MOLLY: "You know we shouldn't do that McGee (laughing). He's a fine man and a credit to the Coast Guard."

Gordon's visits to Wistful Vista while in the Coast Guard probably occurred while he was in training. After that, Gordon does not have any appearances on radio at all until two years later. Apparently, his service in the Coast Guard took him around the world during his absence from radio acting.

His next known appearance on radio is the *Suspense* episode for September 27, 1945 entitled "The Earth Is Made of Glass," starring Joseph Cotton and Cathy Lewis.

Then his return appearance on *Fibber McGee and Molly* happened a week later on October 2, 1945. That episode has Mayor LaTrivia welcomed home at the railroad station after returning from Coast Guard service.

So after nearly three years from when he first enlisted, Gordon returned from the Coast Guard to make regular weekly appearances again. *Chicago Daily Tribune* on September 27, 1945 reported, "*Fibber McGee and Molly* are making some changes, too, at 79 Wistful Vista, when they open up the place Tuesday, October 2. Their jolly maid, Beulah (Marlin Hurt) will be missing. She [he] has set up business at 8 p.m. Sundays on CBS. Gale Gordon, now in the Coast Guard, will return to play Mayor LaTrivia. Bill Thompson, if and when he gets out of the navy, is expected back to revive Wallace Wimple and the other characters he portrayed. Shirley Mitchell, who played Alice Darling, will not be back. Dr. Gamble, played by Arthur G. Bryan, (misprint, meant Arthur Q. Bryan) will be around again."

Of course, three years earlier they threw Gordon a big going away to war party. Gordon told Simons: ". . . they told me that my job would be there when I got back, and when I did come back after the war and joined them again, the first salary I got to my surprise was all the raises that might have come in each year that I was away."

In 1946, Gordon continued to make his weekly appearances on *Fibber McGee and Molly. Chicago Daily Tribune*, January 3, 1946: "Bill Thompson is out of the navy and will return to the Fibber McGee show as Wallace Wimple on January 15. Thompson will be the third man to return from the military services to the 79 Wistful Vista fold. The others are Gale Gordon as Mayor LaTrivia, and Red Robinson of the King's Men."

For the 1947–1948 season, Gordon's Mayor LaTrivia character quietly and permanently stopped appearing after the September 20, 1947 death of New York City's beloved mayor Fiorello La Guardia. For that season only, Gordon would return as a new character; namely, weatherman Foggy Williams through June 1, 1948. The next season, 1948-49, Gordon would return as Mayor LaTrivia.

The McGees tortuous wordplay game of twisting LaTrivia's words and the Mayor's inevitable tongue-tied blowup continued from 1948 through 1953.

As an example, the same comedic method continued, as with the October 12, 1948 episode in which McGee gives up smoking. However, LaTrivia's scene regards the city treasurer who he says is an example of the adage that a new broom sweeps clean. McGee takes this literally that the treasurer sweeps his own office. Molly joins McGee in this path of argument. Typical is the fact that Gordon always seems to be stuck in an explosive argument with the McGees, eventually trapped by his own words.

LATRIVIA: "I'm sick of being baited into these arguous stupements . . . . Look when I made the innocent remark that a new clean spoons away, a new spoon brings, a new broom. . ."

In an episode from Gordon's last season on *Fibber McGee and Molly*, such as the broadcast of January 20, 1953, McGee is writing an expose called "Inside Wistful Vista." Mayor LaTrivia tells them about how he played the "role" of governor during lunchtime entertainment. McGee and Molly think he means eating a "roll." As usual, the Mayor goes berserk over the confusion. He screams and flubs his words, and quickly gets so frustrated and tongue twisted.

Gordon would regularly appear on the weekly *Fibber McGee and Molly* show offering his typical humor for eight more years beyond the episodes in this chapter. Unfortunately, the comedy moments between LaTrivia and the McGees from over 350 more episodes could not be included here as they would be adequate to fill another book the length of this one.

As a testament to the show's impact and endurance some fifty years after Gordon stopped playing LaTrivia, an appreciative fan in 1990 told Gordon on a radio interview with Schaden: "I think one of the best things I liked is.... when you worked with Mr. McGee. You would start to talk to him, and you guys would get all things turned around, and finally you'd pause and you'd say 'McGee!'"

The fan concluded, "I loved that."

That will always be the thrill of hearing Gordon's Mayor LaTrivia, thanks to Don Quinn's superb comedy writing and, of course, some expert script delivery!

Chapter Twelve: Selected Moments as Rumson Bullard (1947–1952)

Bullard (to Gildersleeve): "You are a nincompoop and a bone-headed jackass, and if I were a Mayor, I'd not only throw you out of the Water Department, I'd run you out of town!"

—*The Great Gildersleeve*,
November 1, 1950: "Election Day"

Another of Gordon's recurring radio characters was that of Gildersleeve's millionaire neighbor Rumson Bullard in *The Great Gildersleeve*.

The Great Gildersleeve is a spinoff show focused on the pompous character of Throckmorton P. Gildersleeve from the *Fibber McGee and Molly* show. Although he remained argumentative, his character changed so that he is no longer a prominent married businessman as in *Fibber McGee and Molly*. Instead, he became the Water Commissioner of Summerfield in an early episode of *The Great Gildersleeve*, and he is the surrogate father to Marjorie and Leroy. Both of them refer to him simply as "Uncle Mort." Gildersleeve had been played first by Hal Peary, and then by Willard Waterman.

Here assembled is a sample of the episodes that show Bullard to be a more limited character in complexity as compared to Mayor LaTrivia. Gordon's Bullard offers enough laughs to reveal his fine comedic skill at making something as banal as name-calling seem so funny. Gordon quite convincingly plays Rumson Bullard as the snobby and nasty neighbor who gets under Gildersleeve's skin constantly. Often referred to as "Mr. Bullard," I refer to him here in this chapter simply as "Bullard." He is a character who seems to like to torture or taunt Gildersleeve. It is a very confrontational relationship between the two men.

The listener quickly comes to dislike a fellow like Bullard who feels he can push people around because of his wealth. Bullard is a conceited blowhard who will walk all over someone like Gildersleeve. The latter plays an apologetic, but loveable schmuck; as such, he is compelled to grovel at Bullard's every whim. Clearly, Bullard does not want to be friends with anyone, especially Gildersleeve. However, Gildersleeve does not see that! In addition, Gildersleeve's passive aggressive approach does not work. He tends to deal with Bullard by sometimes overreacting as a hothead, and at other times, he is overly considerate and bumbling. No matter what he does, he tends to be inept.

In comparing Bullard with LaTrivia, one sees that both tend to use big words, but unlike what the McGees do to LaTrivia, Gildersleeve does not confuse Bullard with word play. In addition, Bullard is more of a fathead and not as likeable as LaTrivia.

For the broadcast on November 12, 1947 ("Gildy Swindled on a Fur Coat"), Gordon did not play Bullard yet. Instead, he plays the dishonest fur and jewelry wholesaler named Mr. Fowler, who laughs and talks in a way to make the listener aware he is a crook. In trying to save money on a coat for Marjorie, Gildersleeve contacts Fowler. He is clueless about Fowler's "hot goods" when he is sold a $500 coat for $30 because he gullibly believes the crook's line that he is giving him a break because he says Gildersleeve has an honest face.

After he comes to realize that he was conned, Gildersleeve confronts Fowler telling him the coat is a fake. Fowler agrees, and then he flatters Gildersleeve, telling him he should be a fur salesman too. Then he cons Gildersleeve into taking the rest of his merchandise, and then skips out the hotel room via the fire escape.

On the January 28, 1948 broadcast ("New License Plates"), again Gordon does not play Bullard yet. The story is about how Gildersleeve procrastinates in getting his license plates. Here Gordon plays a desk sergeant who vents his frustration for just being a desk sergeant and not being the Chief. He complains how everyone just wants to see the Chief to make a confession. He asks as to why someone cannot confess to him sometimes. Of course, he thinks Gildersleeve is a crook who also just wants to make a confession to the Chief.

Chapter Twelve: Selected Moments as Rumson Bullard (1947–1952)

The May 26, 1948 broadcast ("Gildy Drives a Mercedes"), offers an early appearance of Gordon as Rumson Bullard. The character is a snob. Gildersleeve calls him "old Prissy Pants." When Gildersleeve needs his car pushed, Bullard offers a devious laughter. Bullard looks down on Gildersleeve and his old car as if he is afraid to associate with anyone like him.

Then later Bullard is impressed when he thinks Gildersleeve bought a Mercedes, and now he wants to associate with him, including selling him some corporate stock. Gildersleeve keeps up this pretense for Bullard's benefit. In the finale, Bullard is apologetic as he sees Gildersleeve driving his old car. He thinks he hurt Gildersleeve by advising him about buying the railroad stock whose bottom dropped right out the day before.

On the broadcast of October 27, 1948 ("Gildy Proposes to Adeline"), Bullard is using Gildersleeve's driveway as a way of maneuvering his car. Although he is annoyed at Bullard's actions, Gildersleeve pretends to be neighborly. Bullard gets friendly with Gildersleeve's little foundling, and he mentions Mrs. Bullard and her intention of adopting a little girl to grow up alongside their son Craig.

Bullard gets Gildersleeve's goat when he puts down his financial capabilities to raise a child, which causes the bumbling Gildersleeve to feel inferior. He seems to be in competition with Bullard. Gildersleeve dreams about the matter and he comes to think Bullard is considering the adoption of the baby himself. Eventually he asks Adeline to marry him.

Of course, this is at a time when marriage between a man and a woman was the only acceptable way to be able to adopt a child.

Bullard did not plan on adopting the child and double-crossing Gildersleeve. Later Gildersleeve learns that Bullard was at the Courthouse getting a dog license. Gildersleeve exclaims, "I've been double-crossed."

The January 12, 1949 broadcast ("Love Thy Neighbor") is probably one of the best episodes dealing with the problem of Gildersleeve and Bullard getting along.

Although Gildersleeve is determined to be friendlier with Bullard, here that may seem quite challenging because Bullard drove his car into their garbage cans knocking them down.

Bullard says it is Gildersleeve's fault for leaving his can box on the edge of the driveway where it can be knocked over. The same old type of argument ensues between the neighbors.

Later Gildersleeve moves the box over to avoid Bullard backing into it. Interestingly, Gildersleeve gets to release some of his frustration after Craig sneakily throws a snowball at him while Bullard complains that if he had the new can box before, he would not have hit it.

LEROY: "Look out Unc, duck!"

Gildersleeve angrily responds, "Who threw that snowball? Why that little—!"

LEROY: "Craig did—the little sneak."

BULLARD: "Temper, temper, Gildersleeve. Boys will be boys. Ha, ha, ha!"

GILDERSLEEVE: "That does it! Leroy hand me that snowball."

BULLARD: "Gildersleeve, don't you dare throw that snowball at my son!"

GILDERSLEEVE: "I wouldn't think of it. This one's for you!"

With that, Gildersleeve throws a snowball right in Bullard's nose!

BULLARD: "GILDERSLEEVE!"

The scene goes to a commercial break after Gildersleeve tells Leroy, "Leroy keep passing the ammunition."

According to Gildersleeve, though he made an effort at extending the hand of friendship, Bullard bit it. When Bullard rents a sleigh for riding, Leroy feels left out since he did not get invited. To resolve the matter, Gildersleeve decides to make up with Bullard. Gildersleeve apprehensively visits Bullard. Craig answers the door, and calls Gildersleeve an "ignoranimus," and says his father said he is "a big fat ignoranimus."

Then later, the doorbell rings and Bullard surprisingly stops by to pick up Leroy to join the sleigh ride. They were waiting for Gildersleeve, and the latter complains he thought his disagreement with Bullard made Leroy unwelcome.

BULLARD: "Oh, nonsense, I'm not that small, Gildersleeve. Leroy is most welcome to come."

Leroy excitedly runs off.

GILDERSLEEVE: "I don't know how to thank you, Mr. Bullard. We've had our little difficulties. But, well, I just want you to know I think you're a fine fellow."

BULLARD: "You do? Well I still think you're an ignoramus. Good day Gildersleeve (laughs)."

GILDERSLEEVE: (angrily twisting the open bar of the song): "Love Thy Neighbor, step and say—."

On the February 2, 1949 broadcast ("Adeline's Hat Shop"), Gildersleeve wants to start a neighborhood petition against Adeline's upcoming in-house hat shop. Even Bullard gets involved.

BULLARD: "Gildersleeve, I always considered you a boob about business matters, but this time I think you're using your head. You start the petition Gildersleeve, and if you need any help, I'm behind you one hundred percent."

Gildersleeve finds that there is a big profit in the millinery business, and he changes his mind about the petition much to Bullard's chagrin who took over circulating the petition to close the shop.

Now Bullard is upset with Gildersleeve, and he demands, "You started this, now sign it!"

However, Bullard changes his mind too when Craig wants to start a hot dog stand.

On the March 2, 1949 broadcast ("Leroy Meets Brenda"), Leroy likes Rumson Bullard's spoiled niece Brenda. He is borrowing and spending money to impress her, much to Gildersleeve's chagrin, until the latter gets charmed by her mother.

ELLEN: "I don't even have a date for your party at the Country Club tomorrow night. That shouldn't happen to an attractive widow. Surely there must be some dark and handsome eligible bachelor around here?"

BULLARD: "Believe me there's nobody in this neighborhood that fits that description."

ELLEN: "What about Leroy's uncle across the street?"

BULLARD: "Ellen, I hate to sound uncharitable but I will not have a Bullard of Baltimore escorted by that blustering water buffalo" (said snobbishly to laughter).

ELLEN: "Well he looks like he has possibilities to me."

BULLARD: "Oh Ellen! Please."

ELLEN: (giggles) "I do suppose I sound like a desperate woman. I just dare anything resembling a knight in shining armor to glance my way" (then the bell rings).

Rumson introduces Gildersleeve to his sister.

ELLEN: "We were just talking about you."

GILDERSLEEVE: "You were?"

BULLARD: "Yes we were. I was just telling Ellen what (he hesitates) unusual neighbor you are."

He wants to talk to Ellen about Brenda and Leroy. As he excuses himself to leave, Bullard gives a warning to his sister: "Well, if you excuse me I can go now. But Ellen, don't mistake blue serge for shining armor."

GILDERSLEEVE: "What does he mean by that?"

ELLEN: "Oh, um private joke."

Gildersleeve is delighted to get the opportunity to escort Ellen to the Country Club benefit. However, the Water Commissioner learns to his dismay that this fundraiser will be utilizing the money raised for Bullard to drill a well and install his own private water system.

On the April 27, 1949 broadcast ("The Burglar"), Gildersleeve fancies himself a private detective. He tries to catch the thief who broke into the Bullard home and stole his lady friend Ellen's diamond necklace and fur coat. Bullard's opinion of pompous Gildersleeve remains the same.

BULLARD: "Ellen, you knew I'd be back this afternoon. Why didn't you wait and let me handle this?"

ELLEN: "But I was excited, Rumson. I had to call in someone."

BULLARD: "Well, you didn't have to lose your head completely and call Gildersleeve!"

ELLEN: "Now, Rumson, I think you've been wrong about Throckmorton. He's been very calm and level-headed about this."

RUMSON: "That's one of Gildersleeve's biggest problems is he's too level-headed . . . under that poodle dog pompadour. He's a flathead."

ELLEN:	"Oh Rumson, you exaggerate."
BULLARD:	"Not very much."
ELLEN:	"But Rumson, Throckmorton's done quite a study of detective work."
BULLARD:	"I've engaged a private detective from Kansas City. He's coming in this afternoon. Can't you discourage Gildersleeve? He couldn't tell a burglar from a banker."

Gildersleeve plants a false story in the paper to lure the crook. However, he knocks out Bullard's detective. Though he eventually helps catch the crook, he manages to upset Bullard who orders him to, "GET OFF MY PROPERTY!" and "I thought I told you to drop this case."

On the May 25, 1949 broadcast ("Gildy Sues Bullard"), Gildersleeve and his wealthy neighbor are trying to avoid a collision with the other. Each one is offering the other the right of way.

GILDERSLEEVE:	"Go ahead, Mr. Bullard."
BULLARD:	"After you, Gildersleeve."
GILDERSLEEVE:	"Oh no, I stopped first!"
BULLARD:	"Thank you, but go ahead."
GILDERSLEEVE:	"But thank you. But you go first. You pay more taxes than I do (silly giggle)."
BULLARD:	(sounding his horn) "Move on, will you. You're tying up traffic."
GILDERSLEEVE:	"But I'm just trying to be polite."

CHAPTER TWELVE: SELECTED MOMENTS AS RUMSON BULLARD (1947–1952) | 249

BULLARD: "You're being a nincompoop."

GILDERSLEEVE: "Ohp!"

BULLARD: "And you don't have to drive."

GILDERSLEEVE: "Now Bullard!"

BULLARD: "Well if you won't move I will. . . nincompoop!"

GILDERSLEEVE: "Someday I'll cut off his water."

The feud continues with Bullard's son Craig calling him a nincompoop as well. A showdown is inevitable. Gildersleeve threatens to sue him for defamation of character. Bullard tells Gildersleeve that he is afraid to sue him.

GILDERSLEEVE: "That's what you think. Wait till you see the headlines in the paper."

BULLARD: "Oh, what'll they say, 'Prominent Businessman Sued by Nincompoop.'"

Gildersleeve announces it to the newspaper, but then his friend Judge Hooker cannot assist him legally. So then, he realizes he should not sue after all. However, Bullard likes the publicity from the lawsuit, besides the bets he has garnered with his club members. Bullard insists, "If you drop the suit, I'll sue you for every penny you got."

Eventually, the suit is dropped in favor of Bullard as the proof of name-calling is hearsay and so inadmissible. Bullard invites Gildersleeve outside to have a cigar, but the same disagreement of who goes first starts again. Bullard calls him a nincompoop again.

This time Bullard has to pay a fine of fifteen dollars in damages. However, Gildersleeve returns the money so he can call Bullard a nincompoop.

On the September 21, 1949 broadcast, "Gildy, the Songwriter," Gildersleeve thinks about being a songwriter to make extra money after hearing about a housewife turned songwriter who made $2,500 writing a song. There happens to be a music publisher, Henry Krause, staying across the street with the Bullards. When Gildersleeve comes knocking, Bullard insists, "Nobody is going to see Mr. Krause, especially no would-be songwriter."

GILDERSLEEVE: "Would-be? Now see here, Bullard, enough is enough!"

BULLARD: "I agree. Good day Gildersleeve." Bullard shuts the door on him.

GILDERSLEEVE: "Ohp! Bullard what a sneaky way to end a conversation."

Next Gildersleeve attempts to call Mr. Krause so he can sing his song, but Bullard intercepts the call.

GILDERSLEEVE: "How do you like it so far, Mr. Krause?"

BULLARD: "I think it's terrible."

GILDERSLEEVE: "Ohp! Bullard, how did you get on the telephone?"

BULLARD: "Gildersleeve, I owe you an apology."

GILDERSLEEVE: "You do?"

BULLARD: "Yes, there had been times when I thought you were a sorry Water Commissioner. But as a songwriter, I think you're a very good Water Commissioner."

GILDERSLEEVE: "What?"

BULLARD: "Goodnight."

GILDERSLEEVE: (disheartened) "Goodnight."

On the December 28, 1949 broadcast ("Hayride"), everyone is going to Bullard's New Year's Eve Party. However, Gildersleeve believes he was not invited. The love/hate relationship between the two continues.

An angry and jealous Gildersleeve tells Marjorie: "There's some people in this world who just have no business being people . . ."

Marjorie explains it best: "I've seen you go through these things before. One minute you can't stand Mr. Bullard, the next minute, you wanna be friends. You've been going on like this for years, Uncle Mort."

GILDERSLEEVE: "I'm making a New Year's Eve resolution; from now on I'm having absolutely nothing to do with Bullard. I'm all through with him. I'm washed up. I mean he's washed up. . ."

By the finale, they have come to an understanding, except Bullard gets the last laugh.

GILDERSLEEVE: "Things are going to be different in the New Year, eh Bullard?"

BULLARD: "Oh yes, yes indeed. As a matter of fact, Gildersleeve, you're not as big an oaf as I thought you were."

GILDERSLEEVE: "Ohmph! Bullard! I . . ."

Then the clock strikes twelve and the strains of "Auld Land Syne" resound.

On the May 24, 1950 broadcast ("Bronco the Broker"), Gildersleeve is burning the rubbish and the smoke blows across the street in Bullard's open windows. The usual confrontation occurs.

BULLARD:	"Gildersleeve, how in the lottery of life did I draw you for a neighbor?"
GILDERSLEEVE:	"Well, let's see, I came here in 19—. Now see here, Bullard! I might ask you the very same thing."
BULLARD:	"You just waited until the wind was right to burn rubbish."
GILDERSLEEVE:	"No I didn't!"
BULLARD:	"Yes you did!"

Leroy chimes in, "No he didn't!"

GILDERSLEEVE:	"You keep out of this Leroy. No I didn't!"
BULLARD:	"Well, whether you did it on purpose or not, it was a STUPID thing to do!"
GILDERSLEEVE:	"Ohp! Careful who whom you call stupid! I'm a public official. I'm the Water Commissioner."

Bullard threatens, "Gildersleeve, if you fool with me, I'll buy the Water Department and cut off your water!"

GILDERSLEEVE:	"Ohmph!"
BULLARD:	"Good day, nincompoop!"
GILDERSLEEVE:	"Nincompoop? That did it. Leroy, burn the tire!"

On the October 11, 1950 broadcast ("Bullard for Mayor"), Gildersleeve's "son-in-law," Bronco, belongs to the Junior Thinkers Civic Club that wants to support the right candidate for Mayor. It turns out that they believe Mr. Bullard is the finest and most

CHAPTER TWELVE: SELECTED MOMENTS AS RUMSON BULLARD (1947–1952) | 253

civic-minded man in Summerfield. This jeopardizes Gildersleeve's hopes of staying on as Water Commissioner if the incumbent (Mayor Terwilliger) is not elected.

One of the typical Bullard-Gildersleeve confrontations here has Bullard complaining: about his low water pressure, which leads to Bullard saying: "You should be on your way out of office!"

GILDERSLEEVE: "Watch it, Bullard!"

BULLARD: "You'd better watch it, Gildersleeve! Why did the water cut off this morning?"

GILDERSLEEVE: "Well, maybe the men are working on a water main someplace."

BULLARD: "SOMEPLACE? You don't even know. If I were Terwilliger, I'd have you out of there so fast it would make your head swim! GILDERSLEEVE, YOU ARE A NINCOMPOOP!"

In a dream sequence, Gildersleeve appeals to Bullard to keep his job. Bullard tells him: "The only reason you're still my neighbor is I couldn't buy your house. . . .After all you've done to me, how can you presume that I'd ever appoint you Water Commissioner. One, you live across the street. Two, last year you backed into my Cadillac. Three, when I was painting my house white, you burned rubber tires and turned it grey. Four, you ruined my Petunia bed playing detective one night. Five . . . No, I won't appoint a nincompoop. NOW GET OUT, GET OUT!"

Gildersleeve gets the idea he does not stand any chance of reappointment. Then he awakes from the dream to find Bullard visited him with a change of heart. Bullard tells him that when he is elected, he will continue to offer Gildersleeve the Water Commissioner's job. Bullard says he believes Bronco's group is supporting him for Mayor because Gildersleeve had something to do with convincing them to back him.

On the October 25, 1950 broadcast ("Sons of Summerfield"), Gildersleeve wants to be a member of the Sons of Summerfield. He is unnerved when he learns Bullard will be in charge of the initiations. Of course, cowardly Gildersleeve wants to avoid the hazing. He refers to Bullard as "a stuffed shirt."

Gildersleeve decides to go out with Katharine instead. She makes him go to the hospital where a trick is played on him. There he undergoes the initiation inadvertently when he is mistaken for being a doctor, and he has to perform an emergency appendectomy.

On the November 1, 1950 broadcast ("Election Day"), Gildersleeve seems to be supporting Bullard for Mayor who is running against the incumbent Terwilliger. In addition, it seems that Bullard promised him that he would be Water Commissioner under him. After a bad dream, Gildersleeve decides Bullard would not make a good Mayor. Of course, Bullard loses the election to the incumbent.

One of those classic Bullard lines is here. Bullard to Gildersleeve: "You are a nincompoop and a bone-headed jackass, and if I were a Mayor, I'd not only throw you out of the Water Department, I'd run you out of town!"

On the November 8, 1950 broadcast ("Better than Bullard"), Gildersleeve's pride is ruined in front of Leroy when Bullard tackles him after both men brag about their skill in playing football. Then Gildersleeve tries to find something to be better at than Bullard. They decide on hiking up a mountain, but the challenge turns out be shortsighted. As in the past, Bullard calls Gildersleeve a nincompoop.

On the November 29, 1950 broadcast ("Leroy's First Date"), Bullard and Gildersleeve are at it again, this time it is over the dating of Gildersleeve's nephew Leroy and Bullard's niece Brenda.

GILDERSLEEVE: "Well, there's old moneybags Bullard walking home. Look at him marching along with his nose in the air. I hope he catches it in the tree—ooh what a snob that Bullard is . . ."

BULLARD:	"Gildersleeve, I wouldn't let my niece marry into your family if you owned the state of Texas."
GILDERSLEEVE:	"Is that so?"
BULLARD:	"I've said it before and I'll say it again: Gildersleeve, you're a nincompoop!"

On the December 27, 1950 broadcast ("Double Date with Bullard"), Bullard is presented here as someone who can do what he likes just because he has money, except now he is portrayed as widowed or divorced. What happened to his wife we do not know. However, he has two sons that are away from home now. Although he is rich, Bullard is lonely.

For instance, he thinks he can bump other cars so he can park his Cadillac. As regards to his romantic and competitive nature, Bullard the charmer easily makes Gildersleeve worried and jealous about Katharine and Vicki. However, Gildersleeve makes Bullard jealous as well.

On the January 10, 1951 broadcast ("Gildy Needs Sleep"), Bullard is running Gildersleeve ragged, as the latter has not been able to get a good night's sleep keeping up with Bullard. They have been on the go since New Year's Eve. Bullard is really living it up, and the question is, "can Gildersleeve keep up with him?"

Bullard flirts with Gildersleeve's girlfriend Katharine.

KATHARINE:	"Both you boys didn't have to see me to the door."
BULLARD:	"Well I like to be around pretty girls as long as possible (laughs deviously)."

Even after midnight, Bullard wants Gildersleeve to go along with the girls to Joe's Beanery for some chili and beans.

When Bullard's date Vicki cannot go out because of a blister on her heel from dancing too much the night before, Gildersleeve feigns disappointment but he is actually exuberant as he can now stay home for a change. However, Bullard plans to take Gildersleeve's date Katharine out instead, allowing him to get some rest. Of course, Gildersleeve will not stand for this, as he is afraid of losing Katharine.

On the January 31, 1951 broadcast ("A Shower for Marjorie"), Gildersleeve does not want to invite Bullard to Marjorie's shower, even trying to avoid him. Bullard: "Peek-a-boo! I don't know if that was you or Birdie set up a barrel of trash."

Bullard mercilessly teases Gildersleeve for stealing his girlfriend Katharine away from him again. In his rather slow preparations, Gildersleeve inadvertently hands the reins to Leroy, Brenda and Bullard, with the party to be given at his snobby neighbor's house. Gildersleeve now feels left out and uninvited until Bullard asks Gildersleeve to help since Leroy and Brenda ran out to see a movie.

BULLARD: "Gildersleeve, you have to help me. I don't even know who's invited to this party."

Of course, Gildersleeve finds a way to outsmart Bullard again; this time, by taking Katharine home from the party in Bullard's car.

On the April 4, 1951 broadcast ("Sailing, Sailing"), Bullard has bought a sailboat, and he backs it into Gildersleeve's tree. A branch makes a hole in his boat. An argument ensues. Of course, Bullard calls Gildersleeve a nincompoop.

Later when Bullard needs a special license to cross a fenced property owned by the Water Department, he starts being nice to Gildersleeve. He introduces him to his ritzy friends, buys him dinner, etc. Eventually Bullard grovels to Gildersleeve; including, promising to buy him a new tree, and he argues that he wants to let bygones be bygones even trying to charm the whole family, especially Marjorie's twins.

When Gildersleeve realizes that Bullard is being a phony in order to get the easement, Gildersleeve sees it as an opportunity to force Bullard's hand and get Bullard to get him special privileges at the Country Club.

Bullard is ready to call him a nincompoop again before Gildersleeve stops him, and instead Bullard reluctantly calls him "a fine fellow."

Of course, it is apparent that Bullard snookered Gildersleeve when a six-inch tree arrives in the mail to replace the damaged one.

On the April 25, 1951 broadcast ("Leroy's Pony"), Leroy is getting a pony to Bullard's chagrin. Bullard tries to entice Gildersleeve in a shouting match.

GILDERSLEEVE: "Now Bullard, there's no reason for anybody to shout at anybody. The pony's coming and the pony's staying."

BULLARD: "It is not."

GILDERSLEEVE: "It is so."

BULLARD: "This is a residential district, not the stockyards. I'll not tolerate the stockyards. I'll not tolerate a horse. It's enough that I have to live across the street from uh, uh, A WATER BUFFALO!"

GILDERSLEEVE: "He's a hard man to like."

On the May 16, 1951 broadcast ("Boating Date"), Gildersleeve thinks Bullard is up to something because he has been acting too nice lately. Then he admits he has been seeing Gildersleeve's girlfriend Katharine, taking her out on his boat.

BULLARD: "Why shouldn't I be nice to you? You've been nice to me. You haven't once interfered with my seeing Katharine. You thoughtfully withdrew from the competition."

Gildersleeve says he has not withdrawn. He has just been too busy with the family.

BULLARD:	"Well, I've been busy too (devious laugh). Ah. You're taking this beautiful, Gildersleeve. You're a noble loser."
GILDERSLEEVE:	"Noble loser. Even when he's nice, he's a hard man to like."

On the September 12, 1951 broadcast ("Gildy and Bullard Are Fighting Again"), Gildersleeve wants to teach Leroy a lesson about turning the other cheek. So Gildersleeve makes up to Bullard for dumping grass cuttings on his property by giving Bullard two extra tickets to the County Fair. Suddenly Bullard takes back his insulting remarks (such as calling Gildersleeve "a water buffalo"), explaining he just does the name-calling "all in fun."

Everything seems fine until Gildersleeve finds out from Katharine that she is going to go along with Bullard to the Fair with the extra tickets that Gildersleeve gave him. Then his feelings about Bullard turn ugly.

Later when Gildersleeve tries to be friendly once again by telling Bullard he has a flat tire, Bullard's reaction is angry and abusive, screaming at Gildersleeve.

BULLARD:	"Gildersleeve, Gildersleeve, what are you doing to my car?"

Gildersleeve tries to explain, but to no avail.

BULLARD:	(screaming) "GILDERSLEEVE, YOU LET THE AIR OUT OF MY TIRES!"
GILDERSLEEVE:	"I DID NOT!"
BULLARD:	"YES YOU DID! YOU DID IT IN A FIT OF JEALOUSY. HARD LOSER! YOU WATER BUFFALO! YOU, YOU NINCOMPOOP! GILDERSLEEVE, GET DOWN ON YOUR KNEES AND FIX THAT TIRE!"

GILDERSLEEVE: "I'll do no such thing."

BULLARD: "It has to be fixed, Gildersleeve. WHAT DO YOU PROPOSE TO DO ABOUT IT?"

GILDERSLEEVE: (shouts back) "I propose to go home and let you fix it yourself!"

With Leroy's urging, Gildersleeve will change his mind and proceed to help change the tires. As a result, Gildersleeve offers help and Bullard apologizes. The two are friends again.

Katharine gets Gildersleeve to escort her to the Fair as Bullard has another commitment, but then after cancellation of his meeting, he shows up happy to spoil Gildersleeve and Katharine's time together.

On the September 19, 1951 broadcast ("Gildy is Falling for Bullard's Sister!"), Gildersleeve screws up his attempt to be acquainted with Bullard's sister Paula.

BULLARD: "I can read Gildersleeve like a book. A big thick very dull book. The only reason he came over here was to try to meet you."

When Gildersleeve goes to speak to Paula again, Bullard answers the door.

BULLARD: "GILDERSLEEVE, YOU RAIN BARREL ROMEO! GET OFF MY PORCH!"

GILDERSLEEVE: "Rain barrel? Well that does it, Bullard. I'll never speak to you or any member of your family again as long as I live."

BULLARD: "Gildersleeve, I have only one thing to say, HAH!"

GILDERSLEEVE: "Well, HAH to you too!"

On the November 14, 1951 broadcast ("Problems with Oak Tree"), Bullard is all for removing an oak tree on the property where Bronco wants to build a house. At first, Gildersleeve and Bullard go at it over how much it will cost to remove it. Bullard writes a check to remove the tree. Then another confrontation ensues when the children decide to keep the tree. Bullard threatens to sue Gildersleeve if he does not remove it.

GILDERSLEEVE: "Mr. Bullard, you wouldn't sue me. Think of my good name."

BULLARD: "If you don't remove that tree by tomorrow night, you won't have a name. You'll just be a number. HA! HA! (laughs menacingly)."

Bullard decides he will chop it down himself then. That is, until he sees a carving that shows two hearts intertwined with the inscription, "Amy Sue Loves Rumson." Indeed, it seems to have some personal significance for Bullard. Now Bullard wants to preserve the tree after all.

BULLARD: "'Amy Sue Loves Rumson.' Let me look at that again. Hey, this carving looks a little fresh. Wait a minute, aren't these new chips at the bottom of the tree?"

LEROY: (yells from the house) "Hey Unc, have you finished with my jack knife?"

BULLARD: (realizing he has been fooled) "Jack knife? GILDERSLEEVE!"

Gildersleeve runs home.

On the November 21, 1951 broadcast ("Inviting Thanksgiving Dinner Guests"), Gildersleeve tries to invite Bullard for Thanksgiving, but he is getting off on the wrong side of him again.

GILDERSLEEVE: "Even on Thanksgiving, he's a hard man to like."

When asked to join Gildersleeve for dinner, Bullard says, "Me? Well that's very thoughtful of you. (Pridefully) For your information, Gildersleeve, I have countless friends. I'm having dinner today at my Club. Gildersleeve, I don't want anybody feeling sorry for me. You enjoy your dinner and I'll enjoy mine. Good day!"

Bullard insists later that he will be having a fancy dinner he describes and that Thanksgiving is a time, as he says, "to gather your friends around, and although I may not be considered popular by one of my neighbors, I have many friends."

Of course, when Gildersleeve's family decides to go and invite the rest of the children from the orphanage, they find Bullard there alone. A teary Bullard is delighted to learn there is still room for him at Gildersleeve's gathering. An orphan named Mike tells Bullard, "Don't cry Mr. Bullard. You have more friends than you thought you had."

On the December 26, 1951 broadcast ("Opening Christmas Gifts"), Gildersleeve is bothered by Bullard's niece Babs giving Leroy an expensive Christmas gift.

GILDERSLEEVE: "If Bullard doesn't know what's going on, he's a real knucklehead."

Bullard overhears, "Gildersleeve, whom are you calling a knucklehead? Speak up, laughing boy, speak up don't be mealy mouthed, I heard you."

However, Bullard calls Gildersleeve a knucklehead for not knowing Leroy gave Babs a pearl necklace. Both men agree the youngsters have to return their presents, but later they feel bad for them.

On the February 13, 1952 broadcast ("Marjorie's Ring"), Gildersleeve has a few altercations with Bullard. Then Marjorie gives her engagement ring to Gildersleeve for him to take to the jewelers to have the stone tightened. A misunderstanding involving Mr. Peavey has Bullard assuming that Gildersleeve is planning to marry Bullard's sister, Paula. Of course, Bullard tries to do everything he can to prevent what he assumes is a pending engagement.

Gildersleeve continues to let Bullard think this just to teach him a lesson. Eventually Bullard turns the tables on Gildersleeve after Paula informs him she knew about it from Marjorie. Gildersleeve gets the last laugh as Paula offers to take Gildersleeve for a ride in Bullard's car.

On the February 27, 1952 broadcast ("Leroy Gets Independence"), Leroy the teenager is wreaking havoc as usual in the Gildersleeve household. Gildersleeve gives him a lesson in self-reliance for a week. His friend Babs wants the same "independence" too. That causes more friction between Gildersleeve and Bullard.

BULLARD: "If that Neanderthal numbskull represents progress, I'm taking the first rocket to the moon."

This method seems to be working out quite well, but the guardians feel left out.

Bullard sums it up: "Gildersleeve, I just had a horrible thought the children no longer need us. We've lost them. Our little birds have tested their wings and have flown away from what they once considered their sanctuary. . . . Gildersleeve, I like telling people what to do."

When the week is up, everything goes back to normal again.

On the March 5, 1952 broadcast ("Bullard Visits Gildy"), Gildersleeve, who some may want to call "The Great Buttinskey," involves himself in Marjorie and Bronco's financial woes. As he wants a loan for his "niece," Gildersleeve butters up banker Mr. Bullard by letting him stay at his house while Bullard's house is being painted. Neighbor Bullard takes up his offer and becomes the "The Man Who Came to Dinner" with predictable results, as Gildersleeve wants that loan for his niece and her husband.

Bullard expects "five star treatment," including steaks, five-minute eggs, making Gildersleeve sleep in the den so he can take his bed, and he wants to take Birdie as his housekeeper. In short, Bullard becomes the overbearing houseguest.

Chapter Twelve: Selected Moments as Rumson Bullard (1947–1952)

On the March 19, 1952 broadcast ("Gildy Plants a Garden"), Gildersleeve finds himself in competition, as he is envious of Bullard's garden. Some may want to call him "The Great Bumblesleeve," as he tries to plant his own with disastrous results.

GILDERSLEEVE: "You wait until I come back from the nursery, I'll show you what I can do for that yard."

BULLARD: "I have a suggestion that might improve it. Put up a sign, 'No Dumping.'"

Gildersleeve gives up when he realizes how much hard work a garden is. When Bullard comes to gloat with one of his potted prize roses, Gildersleeve is angered and he chases Bullard out of the house, ready to throw the pot at him.

Gildersleeve had planted bare-root rose bushes. To Bullard he says, "Well I surprised you the way I put in this garden . . . What do you think of it?"

BULLARD: "Well Gildersleeve, if the City would build a tunnel under your yard, it will have roses on the ceiling. You planted them upside down!"

Yes, Bullard's response indicates that Gildersleeve is a nincompoop indeed!

Appendix

Selected Bibliography

Author's phone interview with Shirley Mitchell, January 11, 2008.
Author's phone interview with Gloria McMillan, January 16, 2008.
Chuck Schaden's phone interview with Gale Gordon, May 13, 1990, broadcast on WBBM Radio Classics.
Mel Simon's phone interview with Gale Gordon, June 15, 1975 published in *Voices from the Philco*, BearManor Media, 2011.

Correspondence between 2007 and 2015 with Wanda Clark, Michael B. Druxman, Fred Jee, Dina-Marie Kulzer, Lucie Arnaz Luckinbill, Howard Rayfiel, Jeanne Russell, Chuck Schaden, Clair Schulz, Stuart Shostak and Cecil Smith.

The I Love Lucy Book by Bart Andrews, Doubleday, 1976.
That's Not All Folks! by Mel Blanc, Warner Books, 1989.
Life, Liberty & The Pursuit of Hollywood by Michael B. Druxman, BearManor Media, 2013.
Tune in Tomorrow (or How I Found THE RIGHT TO HAPPINESS, with OUR GAL SUNDAY, STELLA DALLAS, JOHN'S OTHER WIFE, and Other Sudsy Radio Serials by Mary Jean Higby, Cowles Education Corporation, 1968, 1966.

Recipe

Gordon offered the following in the article "He Trades His Frown for Smile in Kitchen," published in *Chicago Tribune*, January 24, 1964:

Recipe EGGS A LA TUB CANYON
(Four servings)

1 small onion, diced	6 eggs
1/2 green pepper, diced	1/8-teaspoon sage
3 tablespoons of peanut oil	1/4-teaspoon thyme
1 can (3 1/4 ounces) mushrooms	1/2-teaspoon salt
10 or 12 sliced water chestnuts	1/4-teaspoon pepper
4 or 5 pimento slices	1/2-teaspoon soy sauce

Cook onion and green pepper in peanut oil until tender. Add drained mushrooms, chestnuts, and pimento. Place eggs in a bowl; add seasonings; mix with an eggbeater. Pour egg mixture into a heated frying pan with green pepper and mushroom mixture. Allow eggs to become firm before turning and folding over. Serve when cooked to firmness you like.

[For variety, add 1/2 cup bean sprouts to eggs while cooking.]

Film, Radio and Television Credits

Short Film Appearance

A New Way of Life (circa 1950s) D: John Schaaf.

Gale Gordon.
   Gordon is heard and briefly seen describing modern desert living in the California community of Borrego Springs, emphasizing its healthful, productive, and restful attributes. Written by Ray Sperry. Produced by Howard Matson. Music edited by Art Pabst.
(21 minutes/color)
Copley Productions
   The film may have been a theatrical short or a promotional film syndicated to television stations on perhaps a barter basis, i.e. TV stations could have the film to show without a rental charge in exchange for showing it and having the audience become aware of the product/subject (this case "Come and visit Borrego Springs").

Feature Film Appearances

Elmer the Great (1933) D: Mervyn LeRoy.

Joe E. Brown, Patricia Ellis, Frank McHugh, Claire Dodd, Preston S. Foster, Russell Hopton, Sterling Halloway [Holloway], Emma Dunn, Charles [C.] Wilson, Charles Delaney, Berton Churchill, J. Carrol Naish, Gene Morgan, Douglass Dumbrille, Jessie Ralph, Ruth Clifford, Gale Gordon, George Chandler, Walter Miller, Jane Wyman.

A country boy (Brown) ends up as a homerun-hitting hero for the Chicago Cubs, but his involvement with a gang of crooks almost derails his career. Gordon makes his feature film debut as a radio announcer. Screenplay by Tom Geraghty based on the play by Ring Lardner and George M. Cohan. Produced by Ray Griffith. Portions filmed at the Chicago Cubs Training Grounds, Avalon, Santa Catalina Island, California.
MUSIC BY LEO F. FORBSTEIN.
RELEASED ON APRIL 29.
(74 MINUTES/DVD)
WARNER BROTHERS-FIRST NATIONAL

"Both of radio's favorite comedy couples—together—in their 2nd big screen hit!"

HERE WE GO AGAIN (1942) D: ALLAN DWAN.

EDGAR BERGEN AND 'CHARLIE MCCARTHY,' JIM AND MARIAN JORDAN, HAROLD PEARY, GINNY SIMMS, BILL THOMPSON, GALE GORDON, ISABEL RANDOLPH, 'MORTIMER SNERD,' RAY NOBLE AND HIS BAND, GEORGE CHANDLER, GEORGE CLEVELAND, IRON EYES CODY, STERLING HOLLOWAY, TEALA LORING, MONTE MONTAGUE, CHARLES STEVENS, MARY STUART, JERRY MAREN.

Radio's Fibber *McGee and Molly* (the Jordans) celebrate their twentieth wedding anniversary by taking a road trip across the country. They end up at a resort hotel with fellow audio favorites Bergen and the Great Gildersleeve (Peary). Gordon plays Otis Cadwalader, a sharp operator hoping to sell his shares in a synthetic gasoline concoction. Screenplay by Paul Gerard Smith and Joe Bigelow, from a story by Smith. Additional material by Don Quinn, Zeno Klinker, Dorothy Kingsley, and Royal Foster. Produced by Allan Dwan. Portions filmed at Big Bear Lake and Cedar Lake, San Bernardino National Forest, California.
SONGS:
"Delicious Delirium" (Harry Revel; Mort Greene)
"Until I Live Again" (Revel; Greene)
"Tenting Tonight on the Old Camp Ground" (Walter Kittredge)

Music by Roy Webb.
Released on October 9.
(76 minutes/RCA Sound/DVD)
RKO Radio

A Woman of Distinction (1950) D: Edward Buzzell.

Rosalind Russell, Ray Milland, Edmund Gwenn, Janis Carter, Mary Jane Saunders, Francis Lederer, Jerome Courtland, Alex Gerry, Charles Evans, Charlotte Wynters, Clifton Young, Jean Willes, Gale Gordon, Lucille Ball, Myron Healey, Charles Trowbridge, Harry Strang, Wanda McKay, Harry Cheshire, Gail Bonney, Aline Towne, John Smith, Ted Jordan, Harry Harvey Jr., Walter Sande, Marie Blake [Blossom Rock], Norman Leavitt, Lois Hall, Napoleon Whiting, Lucile Browne, Maxine Gates.

    Scandal threatens a girls' college when a newspaper article alleges an affair between staid dean Russell and British astronomer Milland. Romantic comedy with Gordon as the station clerk. Screenplay by Charles Hoffman, with uncredited contributions from Ray Singer and Dick Chevillat; based on a story by Hugo Butler and Ian McClellan Hunter. Additional dialogue by Frank Tashlin. Produced by Buddy Adler.

Music by Werner R. Heymann.
Released on March 1.
(85 minutes/Western Electric Recording/video/laserdisc)
Columbia

Here Come the Nelsons (1952) D: Frederick de Cordova.

Ozzie Nelson, Harriet Hilliard [Nelson], David Nelson, Ricky Nelson, Rock Hudson, Barbara Lawrence, Sheldon Leonard, Jim Backus, Paul Harvey, Gale Gordon, Ann Doran, Chubby Johnson, Edwin Max, Lillian Bronson, Paul Brinegar, Maynard Holmes, Frank Nelson, Arthur Q. Bryan, Ed Clark, William Haade, Harry Cheshire, Milton Kibbee, Lorin Raker,

Harold Goodwin, Alex Nicol, Stuart Wilson, Irwin Jay Berniker, Edna Smith, Forrest Burns.

It is a busy time for radio and television's Nelson family when Ozzie's houseguest (Lawrence) turns out to be the lovely daughter of an old friend. Harriet retaliates with a guest of her own: handsome Hudson. Meanwhile, two crooks plot to steal the proceeds of a local fair. Gordon plays H.J. Bellows. Story and screenplay by Ozzie Nelson, Donald Nelson, and William Davenport. Produced by Aaron Rosenburg.
Music by Joseph Gershenson, (Herman Stein, Lloyd Akridge, Daniele Amfitheatrof, Milton Rosen, Hans J. Salter, Paul Sawtell, Walter Scharf, Walter Schumann, Frank Skinner, Leith Stevens).
Released on February 23.
(76 minutes/Western Electric Recording/video)
Universal-International

Francis Covers the Big Town (1953) D: Arthur Lubin.

Donald O'Connor, Yvette Duguay, Gene Lockhart, Nancy Guild, William Harrigan, Silvio Minciotti, Lowell Gilmore, Larry Gates, Hanley Stafford, Gale Gordon, Forrest Lewis, Francis (a mule, voiced by Chill Wills), Michael Ross, Louis Mason, Charles J. Flynn, James Flavin, Tim Graham, Eddie Parker, John Qualen, Hal Smith, George Wallace.

Peter Sterling (O'Connor) and his four-legged pal Francis the Talking Mule become reporters for a newspaper, but Peter winds up charged with murder and Francis must testify in his behalf. Gordon is District Attorney Evans. Story and screenplay by Oscar Brodney based on characters created by David Stern (who contributed additional dialogue). Produced by Leonard Goldstein. Portions filmed in Little Italy, Manhattan, New York City.
Songs:
"Funiculi, Funicula" (Luigi Denza; Peppino Turco)
"Missouri Waltz (Way Down in Missouri)" (John Valentine Eppel; J.R. Shannon)

"Snake Charmer" (Sol Bloom)
MUSIC BY JOSEPH GERSHENSON, (FRANK SKINNER, HERMAN STEIN, EDGAR FAIRCHILD, MILTON ROSEN, MIKLOS ROZSA, HANS J. SALTER, WALTER SCHARF).
RELEASED ON JUNE 10.
(86 MINUTES/WESTERN ELECTRIC RECORDING/VIDEO/DVD)
UNIVERSAL-INTERNATIONAL

"She's making passes after classes—and more hilarious than ever!"

OUR MISS BROOKS (1956) D: AL LEWIS.

EVE ARDEN, GALE GORDON, DON PORTER, ROBERT ROCKWELL, JANE MORGAN, RICHARD CRENNA, NICK ADAMS, LEONARD SMITH, GLORIA MACMILLAN, JOE [JOSEPH] KEARNS, WILLIAM NEWELL, PHILIP VAN ZANDT, MARJORIE BENNETT, JUNE BLAIR, JOE FORTE, LEO CURLEY, DAVID ALPERT, HERB VIGRAN, FRANK MITCHELL.

High school teacher Connie Brooks (Arden) romantically pursues bashful biology instructor Mr. Boynton (Rockwell) while guiding a student (Adams) towards a career in journalism. Gordon re-creates his radio and television role as grumpy principal Osgood Conklin. Screenplay by Joseph Quillan and Al Lewis, from an idea by Robert Mann. Produced by David Weisbart. Portions filmed in Stockton, California.
SONG:
"It's Magic" (Jule Styne; Sammy Cahn)
MUSIC BY ROY WEBB.
RELEASED ON APRIL 24.
(85 MINUTES/RCA SOUND/VIDEO/DVD)
LUTE PRODUCTIONS/WARNER BROTHERS

"20th Century-Fox hilariously declares a national laugh holiday...as the cast of the year brings the #1 fun best-seller howlingly alive!"

Rally 'Round the Flag, Boys! (1958) D: Leo McCarey.

Paul Newman, Joanne Woodward, Joan Collins, Jack Carson, Dwayne Hickman, Tuesday Weld, Gale Gordon, Tom Gilson, O.Z. Whitehead, Ralph Osborne III, Stanley Livingston, Jon Lormer, Joseph Holland, Burt Mustin, Percy Helton, Sammy Ogg, Charles Tannen, Nora O' Mahoney, Richard Collier, Murvyn Vye, William 'Billy' Benedict, Tap Canutt, Alan Carney, Bess Flowers, Franklyn Farnum, Jack Ging, Jess Kirkpatrick. Narrated by David Hedison.

When the military plans to install a missile base near a small Connecticut town, the women revolt in opposition to the project. Comedy with Gordon as Brigadier General W.A. Thorwald. Screenplay by Claude Binyon and Leo McCarey, from the novel by Max Shulman. Additional material by George Axelrod. Produced by Leo McCarey.

Song:
  "You're My Boojum" (Charles Henderson; Leo McCarey)
Directors Guild of America Award Nomination:
  (Best Director) Leo McCarey.
Golden Laurel Award Nominations:
  (Top Comedy) Leo McCarey.
  (Top Female Comedy Performance) Joanne Woodward.
Music by Cyril J. Mockridge.
Released on December 23
  (one of the 26 top-grossing films of 1958-59).
(106 minutes/Westrex Recording/DeLuxe Color/CinemaScope/DVD)
20th Century-Fox

"Officer and gentleman by Act of Congress—man, somebody goofed!"

DON'T GIVE UP THE SHIP (1959) D: NORMAN TAUROG.

JERRY LEWIS, DINA MERRILL, DIANA SPENCER, MICKEY SHAUGHNESSY, ROBERT MIDDLETON, GALE GORDON, MABEL ALBERTSON, CLAUDE AKINS, HUGH SANDERS, RICHARD SHANNON, CHUCK WASSIL, MARY BENOIT, HARRY CHESHIRE, PAMELA DUNCAN, BILL EDWARDS, ROBERT ELLIS, FRITZ FELD, MICKEY FINN, DON HAGGERTY, BILL HICKMAN, BERN HOFFMAN, STUART HOLMES, KARL LUKAS, HANK MANN, BURT METCALFE, CHET STRATTON, MARY TREEN.

Bumbling navy ensign Lewis misplaces an entire destroyer escort and then loses his memory. When the heat of Washington, DC, comes down upon him, hapless Jerry sets out to find the vessels. Service comedy with Gordon as Congressman Mandeville.

Screenplay by Herbert Baker, Edmund Beloin, and Henry Garson; from a story by Ellis Kadison. Produced by Hal B. Wallis and Paul Nathan. Portions filmed at the United States Capitol and Union Station, Washington, DC.
MUSIC BY WALTER SCHARF.
RELEASED ON JULY 3.
(89 MINUTES/WESTREX RECORDING/VISTAVISION/VIDEO)
HAL B. WALLIS PRODUCTIONS/PARAMOUNT

"I don't care how BIG she gets! I love every gorgeous yard of her!"

THE 30-FOOT BRIDE OF CANDY ROCK (1959) D: SIDNEY MILLER.

LOU COSTELLO, DOROTHY PROVINE, GALE GORDON, JIMMY CONLIN, CHARLES LANE, ROBERT BURTON, WILL WRIGHT, LENNY KENT, RUTH PERROTT, PETER LEEDS, ROBERT NICHOLS, BOBBY BARBER, JACK STRAW, RUSSELL TRENT, JOE GREENE, JOEY FAYE, DOODLES WEAVER, JACK RICE, VEOLA VONN.

Trash-man and inventor Costello stumbles onto a process that turns his girlfriend (Provine) into a giant lady. Lou then finds himself forced by Provine's father to marry her. Science fiction comedy featuring Gordon as Raven Rossiter. Screenplay by Rowland Barber

and Arthur A. Ross, from a story by Lawrence L. Goldman and an idea by Jack Rabin and Irving Block. Produced by Edward Sherman and Lewis J. Rachmil. Portions filmed at Iverson Ranch, Chatsworth, Los Angeles, California.
MUSIC BY RAOUL KRAUSHAAR, (RUDY SCHRAGER).
RELEASED ON AUGUST 6.
(75 MINUTES/MATTASCOPE, WONDERAMA, AMAZOSCOPE/VIDEO/DVD)
D.R.B. PRODUCTIONS/COLUMBIA

VISIT TO A SMALL PLANET (1960) D: NORMAN TAUROG.

JERRY LEWIS, JOAN BLACKMAN, EARL HOLLIMAN, FRED CLARK, JOHN WILLIAMS, JEROME COWAN, GALE GORDON, LEE PATRICK, MILTON FROME, ELLEN CORBY, BARBARA LAWSON, RICHARD LANE, JOHN DENNIS, MARK RUSSELL, EDWARD G. ROBINSON JR., MICHAEL ROSS, JOSEPH TURKEL, KARL LUKAS, PAUL SMITH, JOHN DIGGS, MAX POWER, CHARLES WARD, PAUL WEXLER, BUDDY RICH, JUNE FORAY (VOICE).

An extraterrestrial visitor (Lewis) comes to Earth to study human behavior and falls in love with the girl next door (Blackman). Comedy with Gordon as Bob Mayberry. Screenplay by Edmund Beloin and Henry Garson, from the play by Gore Vidal. Produced by Hal B. Wallis and Paul Nathan.
SONG:
   "Desdemona's Lament" (composer unknown)
ACADEMY AWARD NOMINATION:
   (ART DIRECTION-SET DECORATION) HAL PEREIRA AND
      WALTER TYLER; SAM COMER AND ARTHUR KRAMS).
MUSIC BY LEIGH HARLINE, (LOU BROWN, GEORGE DUNING, JOHNNY MANDEL, VICTOR YOUNG).
RELEASED ON FEBRUARY 4.
(85 MINUTES/WESTREX RECORDING)
HAL WALLIS PRODUCTIONS/PARAMOUNT

"It's nice work—and you can get it!"

ALL IN A NIGHT'S WORK (1961) D: JOSEPH ANTHONY.

DEAN MARTIN, SHIRLEY MACLAINE, CLIFF ROBERTSON, CHARLIE [CHARLES] RUGGLES, NORMA CRANE, JACK WESTON, JOHN HUDSON, JEROME COWAN, GALE GORDON, RALPH DUMKE, MABEL ALBERTSON, REX EVANS, MARY TREEN, ROY GORDON, IAN WOLFE, CHARLES EVANS, GERTRUDE ASTOR, ROSMARIE BOWE [STACK], KATHRYN CARD, RICHARD DEACON, BESS FLOWERS, GAVIN GORDON, REED HADLEY, WILLIAM LALLY, HARRIET E. MACGIBBON, JOAN STALEY, DICK WESSEL.

When a prominent New York publisher turns up dead in bed at a Palm Beach hotel, his son (Martin) checks out the girl who was seen running away wrapped only in a towel. Romantic comedy with Gale Gordon as Oliver Dunning. Screenplay by Edmund Beloin, Maurice Richlin, and Sidney Sheldon; from the story by Margit Veszi and the play by Owen Elford. Produced by Hal B. Wallis, John H. Hazen, and Paul Nathan.
MUSIC BY ANDRE PREVIN.
RELEASED ON MARCH 22.
(94 MINUTES/WESTREX RECORDING/TECHNICOLOR/VIDEO/DVD)
HAL WALLIS PRODUCTIONS/PARAMOUNT

"The kid who captured an army!"

DONDI (1961) D: ALBERT ZUGSMITH.

DAVID JANSSEN, PATTI PAGE, DAVID KORY, WALTER WINCHELL, MICKEY SHAUGHNESSY, ROBERT STRAUSS, ARNOLD STANG, LOUIS QUINN, GALE GORDON, DICK PATTERSON, SUSAN KELLY, JOHN MELFI, BONNIE SCOTT, WILLIAM WELLMAN JR., NOLA THORP, JOAN STALEY, GUS EDSON, DOROTHY GRANGER, IRWIN HASEN, DEL MOORE.

Young Kory has the title role as a five-year-old Italian orphan who finds himself in America due to his friendship with a group of GIs. Gordon plays the Colonel. Screenplay by Albert Zugsmith and Gus Edson, from the newspaper comic strip by Edson and Irwin

Hasen. Produced by Gus Edson and Albert Zugsmith.
SONGS:
   "Dondi" (Mort Garson; Earl Shuman)
   "Meadow in the Sky" (Garson; Shuman)
MUSIC BY TOMMY MORGAN.
RELEASED ON MARCH 26.
(100 MINUTES)
ALBERT ZUGSMITH PRODUCTIONS/PHOTOPLAY ASSOCIATES/ALLIED ARTISTS

"All hands on deck . . . for the song-and-fun hit of '61!"

ALL HANDS ON DECK (1961) D: NORMAN TAUROG.

PAT BOONE, BUDDY HACKETT, DENNIS O'KEEFE, BARBARA EDEN, WARREN BERLINGER, GALE GORDON, DAVID BRANDON, JOE E. ROSS, BARTLETT ROBINSON, PAUL VON SCHREIBER, ANN B. DAVIS, JODY MCCREA, JOE CONLEY, PAT MCCAFFRIE, LOUISE GLENN, PAUL LONDON, ROBERT CORNTHWAITE, ROBERT FOULK, MILTON FROME, CHUCK HICKS, PAUL LUKATHER, CHET STRATTON, KELLY THORDSEN, OWASSO (A PELICAN, PLAYING ITSELF).

A naval lieutenant (Boone) has all sorts of misadventures when he falls in love with a female reporter and sails to Alaska with an Indian sailor, a turkey, and a pelican aboard ship. Comedy with Gordon as Rear Admiral Bintle. Screenplay by Jay Sommers and Donald R. Morris, from the novel by Morris. Produced by Oscar Brodney. Portions filmed on board the USS St. Clair County.
SONGS:
   "All Hands on Deck" (Ray Evans; Jay Livingston)
   "Somewhere There's a Home" (Evans; Livingston)
   "There's No One Like You" (Evans; Livingston)
   "I Got It Made" (Evans, Livingston)
   "It's a Woman's World" (Cyril J. Mockridge; Sammy Cahn)
   "You Mean Everything to Me" (Evans; Livingston)
MUSIC BY CYRIL J. MOCKRIDGE, (IRVING GERTZ, LEIGH HARLINE, LYN MURRAY).
RELEASED ON MARCH 30.

(98 MINUTES/WESTREX RECORDING/DELUXE
COLOR/CINEMASCOPE)
20TH CENTURY-FOX

*"It's the funniest collection of nuts ever assembled
on a launching pad!"*

SERGEANT DEADHEAD (1965) D: NORMAN TAUROG.

FRANKIE AVALON, DEBORAH WALLEY, CESAR ROMERO, FRED CLARK, GALE GORDON, HARVEY LEMBECK, JOHN ASHLEY, BUSTER KEATON, REGINALD GARDINER, PAT BUTTRAM, EVE ARDEN, ROMO VINCENT, DONNA LOREN, MIKE NADER, ED FAULKNER, NORMAN GRABOWSKI, TOD WINDSOR, PATTI CHANDLER, LUREE HOLMES, MARY HUGHES, SALLI SACHSE, BOBBI SHAW, SUE HAMILTON, ED REIMERS, JOHN HIESTAND, RAY ATKINSON, BOB HARVEY, JERRY BRUTSCHE, ANDY ROMANO, DON EDWARDS, BRUCE BAKER, DWAYNE HICKMAN, JO COLLINS.

An accident-prone sergeant (Avalon) winds up in orbit with a chimp, only to crash back to Earth. When the dust settles, the two impromptu astronauts discover their brains have been switched. Gordon plays Captain Weiskopf. Screenplay by Louis M. Heyward. Choreography by Jack Baker. Produced by James H. Nicholson, Samuel Z. Arkoff, and Anthony Carras.
GUY HEMRIC AND JERRY STYNER SONGS:
    "Sergeant DeadHead"
    "The Difference in Me Is You"
    "Let's Play Love"
    "Two Timin' Angel"
    "How Can You Tell"
    "You Should Have Seen the One That Got Away"
    "Hurry Up and Wait"
MUSIC BY LES BAXTER.
RELEASED ON AUGUST 18.
(89 MINUTES/RYDER SOUND/PATHECOLOR/PANAVISION/DVD)
ALTA VISTA/AMERICAN INTERNATIONAL

"Smooth, fast and in high gear!"

Speedway (1968) D: Norman Taurog.

ELVIS PRESLEY, NANCY SINATRA, BILL BIXBY, GALE GORDON, WILLIAM SCHALLERT, VICTORIA MEYERINK, ROSS HAGEN, CARL BALLANTINE, PONCIE PONCE, HARRY HICKOX, CHRISTOPHER WEST, MISS BEVERLY HILLS [BEVERLY POWERS], RICHARD PETTY, BUDDY BAKER, CALE YARBOROUGH, DICK HUTCHERSON, TINY LUND, G.C. SPENCER, ROY MAYNE, HARPER CARTER, BOB HARRIS, MICHELE NEWMAN, COURTNEY BROWN, DANA BROWN, PATTI JEAN KEITH, CARL REINDEL, GARI HARDY, CHARLOTTE CONSIDINE [STEWART], SANDY REED, GEORGE CISAR, MARILYN JONES, WILLIAM KEENE, BURT MUSTIN, ROBERT STEVENSON, CLAUDE STROUD.

Singing racecar driver Presley gets into financial straits and is pursued by a lovely income tax agent (Sinatra). Gordon is R.W. Hepworth. Screenplay by Phillip Shuken. Produced by Douglas Laurence. Portions filmed at Charlotte Motor Speedway, Concord, North Carolina; and Riverside International Raceway, Riverside, California.

SONGS:
"Speedway" (Mel Glazer; Stephen Schlaks)
"Let Yourself Go" (Glazer; Schlaks)
"Your Groovy Self" (Lee Hazlewood)
"Your Time Hasn't Come Yet, Baby" (Glazer; Schlaks)
"He's Your Uncle, Not Your Dad" (Glazer; Schlaks)
"Who Are You" (Glazer; Schlaks)
"There Ain't Nothing Like a Song" (Glazer; Schlaks)
"Five Sleepy Heads" (Glazer; Schlaks)
"Western Union" (Glazer; Schlaks)
"Mine" (Glazer; Schlaks)
"Goin' Home" (Glazer; Schlaks)
"Suppose" (Glazer; Schlaks)

MUSIC BY JEFF ALEXANDER.
RELEASED ON JUNE 12 (BOX OFFICE: $3,000,000).
(94 MINUTES/METROCOLOR/PANAVISION/VIDEO/LASERDISC/DVD)
METRO-GOLDWYN-MAYER

"He's a man of peace in a savage land . . . Suburbia."

THE 'BURBS (1989) D: JOE DANTE.

TOM HANKS, BRUCE DERN, CARRIE FISHER, RICK DUCOMMUN, COREY FELDMAN, WENDY SCHAAL, HENRY GIBSON, BROTHER THEODORE, COURTNEY GAINS, GALE GORDON, DICK MILLER, ROBERT PICARDO, CORY DANZIGER, FRANKLYN AJAYE, RANCE HOWARD.

Strange new neighbors have a crazy effect on normal Ray Peterson (Hanks), who thinks the odd clan is up to no good. When an old man disappears, Ray and his fellow suburbanites determine to find out their neighbors' secret. Gordon is Walter Seznick. Screenplay by Dana Olsen. Produced by Ron Howard, Larry Brezner, Michael Finnell, Dana Olsen, and Pat Kehoe.

SONGS:
　"Machine" (Alex Mitchell; Gary Sunshine; Ricky Beck Mahler)
　"Bloodstone" (Mickey Finn; Mark Radice; Fernie Rod; Billy Rowe)
　"Locked in a Cage" (Finn; Rowe; Rod; Sami Yaffa)
　"Make Some Noise" (Finn; Rowe; Rod; Yaffa; Ron Tostenson)
　"Questa O Quella" from Rigoletto (Giuseppe Verdi)
　"The Showdown" (Ennio Morricone)
　"Se Sei Qualcuno e Colpa Mia" (Morricone; new arrangement by Jerry Goldsmith)
　"Won't You Be My Neighbor?" (Fred Rogers)

YOUNG ARTIST AWARD NOMINATION:
　(BEST YOUNG ACTOR STARRING IN A MOTION PICTURE)
　　CORY DANZIGER.

MUSIC BY JERRY GOLDSMITH.
RELEASED ON FEBRUARY 17 (BOX OFFICE: $36,602,000).
(103 MINUTES/DOLBY SOUND/DELUXE COLOR/PANAVISON/RATED [PG]/VIDEO/LASERDISC/DVD)
IMAGINE ENTERTAINMENT/UNIVERSAL

RADIO APPEARANCES

(UNNAMED PROGRAM) (KFWB-HOLLYWOOD, CALIFORNIA) 1926.
Gale Gordon strums a ukulele and sings "It Ain't Gonna Rain No More."

THE GOLDBERGS (BLUE/NBC/CBS) (SERIES) CIRCA 1929 TO 1945.

The story of a middle-class Jewish family and its matriarch whose driving ambition is to see her loved ones achieve happiness.
MOLLY GOLDBERG: GERTRUDE BERG
JAKE GOLDBERG: HIMAN BROWN/JAMES R. WATERS
SAMMY GOLDBERG: VAN HEFLIN/EVERETT SLOANE/PAUL STEWART/ALFRED CORN [RYDER]
ROSALIE GOLDBERG: ROSLYN SILBER
UNCLE DAVID: MENASHA SKULNIK
VARIOUS ROLES: JOSEPH COTTEN, ROSEMARY DECAMP, GALE GORDON, JOSEPH JULIAN, BENNETT KILPACK, ALMA KRUGER, KATE MCCOMB, MARJORIE MAIN, JACK MANNING, MINERVA PIOUS, STEPHAN SCHNABEL, GEORGE TOBIAS, KEENAN WYNN
ANNOUNCER: BILL HAY/JEAN PAUL KING/RAY SAUNDERS/ART MILLET/KEN ROBERTS/DON HANCOCK/CARLTON KADELL/JAMES FLEMING/CLAYTON 'BUD' COLLYER
PRODUCED BY GERTRUDE BERG.

MUTINY ON THE HIGH SEAS (SYNDICATED) (SERIES) CIRCA 1930S.

Gale Gordon played various roles (two surviving shows have him as Sir Francis Drake) in this program about ocean-going adventures.
PRODUCED BY C.P. MACGREGOR.

SWEETHEARTS OF THE CIRCUS (SYNDICATED) (SERIES) CIRCA 1930S.

Stories of those who work under the big top. Gale Gordon and Mason Adams play various roles.

Death Valley Days (NBC/Blue/CBS) (Series) 1930 to 1942.

A covered-wagon bugle call fades into stories of the Old West, as told by an elderly frontiersman.
The Old Ranger: Tim Daniel Frawley/Harry Humphrey/ George Rand/Jack MacBryde
Various Roles: Jack Arthur, Richard Barrows, Jackson Beck, Joseph Bell, Rosemarie Broncato, Edwin Bruce, Geoffrey Bryant, Frank Butler, Helen Claire, Virginia Gardiner, Gale Gordon, Harvey Hays, Milton Herman, Irene Hubbard, Jean Paul King, Carl Kroenke, Paul Nugent, Michael Raffetto, William Shelley, James Van Dyk, Charles Webster, Edwin Stanley
The Lonesome Cowboy, vocalist: John White
Announcer: Dresser Dahlstead/George Hicks/Mark Hawley
Orchestra: Joseph Bonime
Produced by Dorothy McCann.

English Coronets (Syndicated-West Coast) (Series) circa 1932 to 1937.

Stories of Great Britain's kings, queens, lords and ladies. Gale Gordon played various roles.
Produced by Kay Van Riper.

Strange Adventures in Strange Lands (Syndicated) "Continental Express," program no. 32, 1932.

A former king in exile has a dramatic train ride in Europe.
Hanley Stafford, Gale Gordon.

TARZAN OF THE APES (SYNDICATED) (SERIES) SEPTEMBER 12, 1932 TO 1936.

A boy whose parents were slain becomes lord of the African wilds after being raised by apes who becomes lord of the jungle. He meets his companion Jane Porter during an expedition and she educates him to the ways of civilization as he continues his role of protector and warrior of his domain.
TARZAN: JAMES PIERCE/CARLTON KADELL
JANE PORTER: JOAN BURROUGHS
CECIL CLAYTON/O'ROURKE: GALE GORDON
CAPTAIN TRACY: CY KENDALL
BILL FRASER: FRED SHIELDS
NIKOLAS ROKOFF: FRANK NELSON
PRINCESS LA OF OPAR: JEANETTE NOLAN
LORD GREYSTROKE: FRED HARRINGTON
LADY GREYSTROKE: EILY MALYON
LT. PAUL D'ARNOT: RALPH SCOTT
VARIOUS ROLES: ART KANE, HANLEY STAFFORD
ANNOUNCER/NARRATOR: JOHN MCINTIRE
PRODUCED BY FREDERICK C. DAHLQUIST, FREDERICK SHIELDS
286 BROADCASTS.

THE LINIT BATH CLUB REVUE (CBS) DECEMBER 25, 1932.

STARS: FRED ALLEN, PORTLAND HOFFA, ROY ATWELL, ALAN REED, JACK [J. SCOTT] SMART.
VOCALIST: CHARLES CARLISLE. ANNOUNCER: KEN ROBERTS.
ORGANIST: ANN LEAF. THE LOU KATZMAN ORCHESTRA.
  A visit to Fred's crazy Mammoth Department Store. Roy does a malapropism routine. Sponsor Linit Bath Salts and Oils offers Christmas greetings to listeners with hopes for a happy holiday.
GALE GORDON.

Calling All Cars (CBS) (Series) 1933 to 1939.

Crime drama stories based on the files of the Los Angeles Police Department. Gale Gordon played various roles. Frederick Lindsley was announcer.

Seal of the Don (Syndicated) (Series) 1933.

A dagger-wielding crusader protects poor Mexicans from the abuses of an evil military despot (Governor Turena).
Don Hancock: True Boardman
Mexican Governor Manuel Mitchell Turena: Gale Gordon
Dolores: Barbara Jean Luddy
Various Roles: Eugene Carman, Charles Carroll, Owen Crump, Cyrus [Cy] Kendall, Mora Martin, Theodore [Ted] Osborne.
Produced by the Charles H. Mayne Company/Conquest Alliance
39 broadcasts.

Mama Bloom's Brood (Syndicated) (Series) 1934.
A Jewish family has humorous escapades. Gale Gordon was included in the cast. Produced by Spot Sales.
78 broadcasts.

Front Page Drama (Syndicated) (Series) 1934-40.
Stories set to appear in Hearst Newspapers' American Weekly are dramatized.
Various Roles: Gale Gordon
Announcer: R.C. Wentworth
Produced by Hearst Syndication.

Mary Pickford and Company (NBC) "The Church Mouse" October 3, 1934.
Star: Mary Pickford.
A shy girl finds work in a bank and romance with its president.

Gale Gordon, Jeanette Nolan, Ted Osborne, James Eagles.

Irene Rich Dramas (Blue) (Series) 1935.

Anthology of various stories.
Star: Irene Rich
Male Lead: Gale Gordon
Announcer: Hal Gibney/Ed Herlihy.

Stories of the Black Chamber (NBC) (Series) January 21 to June 28, 1935.

Bradley Drake oversees a team of code-breakers who aid in capturing America's enemies.
Bradley Drake: Jack Arthur
Betty Andrews: Helen Claire
Paradine, Master Spy: Gale Gordon
Joyce Carraway: Rosaline Greene
Steve: Paul Nugent
Thornton Oliver: Morgan Farley.

Frontier Fighters (Syndicated) (Series) 1935.

Stories centering on individuals and their adventures in the American West. Gale Gordon and Hanley Stafford played various roles.
Produced by Radio Transcription Company of America (Transco).
39 broadcasts.

That Was the Year (Syndicated) (Series) 1935.

The spotlight is on selected annals in history with the parade of noteworthy events that occurred.

NARRATOR: GERALD MOHR
VARIOUS ROLES: GALE GORDON
ANNOUNCER: LINDSAY MACHARRIE
PRODUCED BY TRANSCO.

THE AMAZING INTERPLANETARY ADVENTURES OF FLASH GORDON (SYNDICATED) (SERIES) APRIL 27 TO OCTOBER 26, 1935.

A space-spanning adventurer fights cosmic villains. Based on the newspaper comic strip Flash Gordon by Alex Raymond.
FLASH GORDON: GALE GORDON
DALE ARDEN: FRANC HALE
DOCTOR ZARKOFF: MAURICE FRANKLIN
MING THE MERCILESS: BRUNO WICK
PRODUCED BY HIMAN BROWN.
26 BROADCASTS.

THE MARCH OF TIME (CBS) AUGUST 29, 1935.

NARRATOR: WESTBROOK VAN VOORHIS.
ANNOUNCER: HARRY VON ZELL.
Dramatized news of the week: A prediction from Huey Long that he may be elected President; powerful publisher William Randolph Hearst is leaning towards an old political enemy, Al Smith, to support for President; a vaccine for infantile paralysis has been developed by doctors Brody and Parks in New York City; a Polish newsman has been expelled from the USSR; a car crash has injured King Leopold of Belgium and killed his wife Astrid.
GALE GORDON.

JUNGLE JIM (SYNDICATED) (SERIES) 1935 TO 1954.

Jim Bradley has adventures on the African continent as a safari guide, along with his sidekick Kolu. Based on the newspaper comic strip by Alex Raymond.

Jim Bradley: Matt Crowley/Gerald Mohr
Kolu: Juano Hernandez
Shanghai Lil De Vrille: Franc Hale/Vicki Vola
Various Roles: Kenny Delmar, Gale Gordon, Arthur Hughes, Owen Jordan, Jack Lloyd, Irene Watson
Announcer: Glenn Riggs/Roger Krupp
Produced by Jay Clark.

Johnny Presents (NBC) (Series) December 24, 1935 to June 23, 1936.

The segment "Philip Morris Thrills" offers dramatizations of true-life adventures concerning otherwise ordinary people who have a brush with danger.
Host: Phillips H. Lord
Various Roles: Gale Gordon, Bennett Kilpack, Jerry Lesser, Effie Palmer
Orchestra: Leo Reisman
Produced by Phillips H. Lord
27 broadcasts.

Parties at Pickfair (CBS) (Series) 1936.

Variety, talk, and dramatic sketches centering on Mary Pickford and her guests at a weekly get-together.
Mary Pickford: Herself
Alvin, the butler: Eric Snowden
Various Roles: Gale Gordon, Mary Jane Higby, Lou Merrill, Bret Morrison, Ted Osborne
Vocalists: The Paul Turner Singers
Announcer: Ken Niles
Orchestra: Al Lyons
Produced by Nat Wolfe, Marion Parsonette.

Gang Busters (CBS/Blue) (Series) January 15, 1936 to September 11, 1942.

Hard-hitting tales of true crime and how the mobsters and killers are brought to justice.
Host/Narrator: Phillips H. Lord/Colonel H. Norman Schwarzkopf (later portrayed by) Don McLaughlin
Various Roles: Mason Adams, John Archer, Joan Banks, John Brown, Charles Cantor, Art Carney, Ray Collins, Matt Crowley, Les Damon, Rosemary DeCamp, Ted de Corsia, Kenny Delmar, Elspeth Eric, Betty Furness, Martin Gabel, Will Geer, Gale Gordon, Larry Haines, Florence Halop, Juano Hernandez, Raymond Edward Johnson, Elia Kazan, Nancy Kelly, Frank Lovejoy, Ken Lynch, Mercedes McCambridge, Myron McCormick, John McIntire, Gary Merrill, Agnes Moorehead, Santos Ortega, Edgar Stehli, Paul Stewart, Walter Tetley, Richard Widmark, Lesley Woods
Announcer: Les Griffith/Erik Rolf/Charles Stark
Produced by Phillips H. Lord.

Washington's Birthday Celebration (NBC/Blue) (Special) February 22, 1936.

A program honoring George Washington, first President of the United States. Included are a pageant and remotes from Washington's home in Mount Vernon; McConker's Ferry on the Delaware River (site of Washington's famous crossing); Valley Forge, Pennsylvania; and Independence Hall in Philadelphia. A drama details Washington's career and the early days of this country. Gale Gordon portrays Washington.

Speed Gibson of the International Secret Police (Syndicated) (Series) 1937.

Young Gibson joins a law enforcement agency to battle the criminal organization led by the Octopus.

SPEED GIBSON: ?
BARNEY DUNLAP: JOHN GIBSON
CLINT BARLOW: HOWARD MCNEAR
THE OCTOPUS: GALE GORDON
VARIOUS ROLES: SAM EDWARDS, ED GARDNER, ELLIOTT LEWIS, JACK MATHER, HANLEY STAFFORD.
PRODUCED BY LOU R. WINSTON/RADIO TRANSCRIPTIONS OF HOLLYWOOD
178 BROADCASTS.

CAPTAINS OF INDUSTRY (SYNDICATED) (SERIES) 1937–38.

Stories depicting the lives and careers of American entrepreneurs. Various roles are played by Gale Gordon and Hanley Stafford.
PRODUCED BY ATLAS RADIO CORPORATION.

BIG TOWN (CBS) (SERIES) OCTOBER 19, 1937 TO JUNE 2, 1942.

Crusading editor Steve Wilson of *The Illustrated Press* fights corrupt elements in his sprawling city.
STEVE WILSON: EDWARD G. ROBINSON
LORELEI KILBOURNE: CLAIRE TREVOR/ONA MUNSON
TOMMY HUGHES: ED MACDONALD
DISTRICT ATTORNEY MILLER: GALE GORDON
MISS FOSTER/VARIOUS ROLES: PAULA WINSLOWE, HELEN BROWN
VARIOUS ROLES: JERRY HAUSNER, CY KENDALL, LOU MERRILL, JACK [J. SCOTT] SMART
ANNOUNCER: CARLTON KADELL
ORCHESTRA: LEITH STEVENS
PRODUCED BY CLARK ANDREWS.

GOOD NEWS OF 1938–40 (NBC) (SERIES) NOVEMBER 4, 1937 TO OCTOBER 10, 1940.

Drama and variety with a parade of big-name film stars.

HOST: JAMES STEWART/ROBERT TAYLOR/ROBERT MONTGOMERY/
ROBERT YOUNG/WALTER HUSTON/EDWARD ARNOLD/WILLIAM
GARGAN/DICK POWELL
REGULAR: FRANK MORGAN
BABY SNOOKS: FANNY BRICE
DADDY HIGGINS: HANLEY STAFFORD
VARIOUS ROLES: GALE GORDON
ANNOUNCER: TED PEARSON/WARREN HULL
ORCHESTRA: MEREDITH WILLSON
PRODUCED BY BILL BACHER.

DR. CHRISTIAN (CBS) (SERIES) NOVEMBER 7, 1937 TO MARCH 21, 1939.

A kindly general practitioner administers to the physical and personal troubles of the people living in River's End.
DR. PAUL CHRISTIAN: JEAN HERSHOLT
NURSE JUDY PRICE: ROSEMARY DeCAMP
VARIOUS ROLES: MARGARET BRAYTON, ERIC BURTIS, NOREEN GAMMILL, GALE GORDON, GLORIA HOLDEN, BERRY KROEGER, GERALD MOHR, WILLIAM ROYAL, YNEZ SEABURY, JOAN SHEA, GEORGIA SIMMONS
ANNOUNCER: ART GILMORE
PRODUCED BY DOROTHY McCANN.

THE CINNAMON BEAR (SYNDICATED) (SERIES) NOVEMBER 29–DECEMBER 24, 1937.

Jimmy and Judy Barton go on a magical and sometimes dangerous journey to retrieve the Silver Star ornament that is to be placed on their Christmas tree. The Crazy Quilt Dragon stole the ornament and took it to Maybe Land. Jimmy and Judy follow the adventurous trail with the aid of their newfound friend Paddy O'Cinnamon—a stuffed bear which has come to life.
PADDY O'CINNAMON: BUDDY DUNCAN
JIMMY BARTON: ?
JUDY BARTON: BARBARA JEAN WONG

MOTHER BARTON: VERNA FELTON
CRAZY QUILT DRAGON: JOSEPH KEARNS
SNAPPER SNITCH THE CROCODILE: HANLEY STAFFORD
SAMUEL THE SEAL/SLIM PICKINS THE COWBOY: HOWARD MCNEAR
PENELOPE THE PENGUIN: ELVIA ALLMAN
MR. PRESTO THE MAGICIAN: ELLIOTT LEWIS
SANTA CLAUS: LOU MERRILL
CAPTAIN TIN TOP: FRANK NELSON
CAPTAIN TAFFY THE PIRATE/INDIAN CHIEF: CY KENDALL
WEARY WILLIE THE STORK/THE OSTRICH: GALE GORDON
PROFESSOR WHIZ THE OWL: TED OSBORNE
FE FO THE GIANT: JOE DUVAL
THE WINTERGREEN WITCH: MARTHA WENTWORTH
FRAIDY CAT: DOROTHY SCOTT
ASSISTANT BLOTTO EXECUTIONER: ED MAX
QUEEN MELISSA: ROSA BARCELO
WESLEY THE WHALE/VARIOUS ROLES: LINDSAY MCHARRIE
NARRATOR/VARIOUS ROLES: BUD HIESTAND
VOCALISTS: THE PAUL TAYLOR QUARTET
ORCHESTRA: FELIX MILLS
DIRECTED BY LINDSAY MACHARRIE
26 BROADCASTS.

THE FULLNESS OF TIMES (SYNDICATED) (SERIES) 1938.

The history of the Mormons. Gale Gordon played various roles.
PRODUCED BY GORDON HINCKLEY/CHURCH OF LATTER DAY SAINTS
39 BROADCASTS.

LOG CABIN JAMBOREE (NBC) JANUARY 15, 1938.

STAR: JACK HALEY. ANNOUNCER: WARREN HULL. THE TED FIO RITO ORCHESTRA.

Jack wants to sell his hen Tillie. He tells of his frontiersman uncle who had an encounter with a Jewish Indian. Sponsor Log Cabin

Syrup is offering a copper griddle premium.
WENDY BARRIE, VIRGINIA VERRILL.
GALE GORDON AND HANLEY STAFFORD FOR LOG CABIN SYRUP.

THOSE WE LOVE (BLUE/NBC/CBS) (SERIES) 1938 TO 1942.

Story of the Marshall family, centering on daughter Kathy and her romance with Dr. Leslie Foster.
KATHY MARSHALL: NAN GREY
DR. LESLIE FOSTER: DONALD WOODS
KIT MARSHALL: RICHARD CROMWELL
JOHN MARSHALL: PEDRO DE CORDOBA/HUGH SOTHERN/OSCAR O'SHEA
AUNT EMILY MAYFIELD: ALMA KRUGER
MARTHA NEWBURY: VIRGINIA SALE
ROY MEADOWS/RODNEY KILGORE: GALE GORDON
ANNOUNCER: DICK JOY
ORCHESTRA: EDDIE KAYE
PRODUCED BY TED SHERDEMAN.

LUX RADIO THEATER (CBS) "SEVEN KEYS TO BALDPATE" SEPTEMBER 26, 1938.

HOST: CECIL B. DEMILLE. ANNOUNCERS: FRANK NELSON, MELVILLE RUICK. THE LOU SILVERS ORCHESTRA.
  Cecil promises to cast guest Jack Benny in a movie if Benny can write a play in twenty-four hours. DeMille dispatches Jack to a deserted inn on Baldpate Mountain so he can work in peace—but quiet is the last thing Baldpate offers. Written for radio by George Wells from the novel by Earl Derr Biggers and the play by George M. Cohan. Directed by Frank Woodruff. Intermission guest Efrem Zimbalist [Sr.] plays "The Bee" on violin.
MARY LIVINGSTONE: HERSELF. RITA: MARGARET BRAYTON. HERMIE: TED OSBORNE. BLAND: ROSS FORRESTER. MORGAN/ THIRD MAN: GALE GORDON. KENNEDY: LOU MERRILL. SERGEANT: JOHN FEE. JED/SECOND PRISONER: EDDY WALLER. BELINDA: MARTHA WENTWORTH. A PRISONER: JOE [JOSEPH] KEARNS. BOLLISTER: VICTOR RODMAN.

Telephone Operator/Second Girl: Mary Lansing. Oakley: Frank Nelson. Miss Cole: Dorothy Griwatz. A Girl: Katherine Carlton. Forrest Taylor, Monica Ward, and Gloria Fisher for Lux Soap.

The Joe E. Brown Show (CBS) (Series) October 8, 1938 to September 28, 1939.

Comedy-variety centering on a talent agent and his dealings with the show business world.
Joe E. Brown: Himself
Mr. Bullhammer: Gale Gordon
Jill: Paula Winslowe
Comics: Bill Demling/Frank Gill
Vocalist: Margaret McCrae
Announcer: Don Wilson
Orchestra: Harry Sosnik.

The Wonder Show (CBS) (Series) October 14, 1938 to April 7, 1939.

Musical variety.
Star: Jack Haley
Regulars: Lucille Ball/Artie Auerbach
Vocalist: Virginia Verrill
Announcer: Gale Gordon
Orchestra: Ted Fio Rito.

The Shadow of Fu Manchu (Syndicated) (Series) May 8 to November 1, 1939.

A pair of intrepid adventurers fights against the world-conquering schemes of an insidious Oriental master villain.
Fu Manchu: Ted Osborne
Sir Dennis Nayland Smith: Hanley Stafford

Dr. James Petrie: Gale Gordon
Karameneh: Paula Winslowe
Inspector Weymouth: Edmond O'Brien.

Lux Radio Theater (CBS) "The Awful Truth" September 11, 1939.

Host: Cecil B. DeMille. Announcer: Melville Ruick. The Lou Silvers Orchestra.

A soon-to-be divorced couple living in high society New York City invents witty ways to prevent each other from re-marrying. They soon realize their crazed, madcap efforts are only strengthening their feelings for each other. Written for radio by George Wells from the screenplay by Vina Delmar and the play by Arthur Richman. Directed by Sanford Barnett.
Lucy Warriner: Claudette Colbert. Jerry Warriner: Cary Grant. Barbara Vance: Phyllis Brooks. Dan Leeson: Lou Merrill. Frank/Mr. Vance: Gale Gordon. Aunt Patsy: Ynez Seabury. Armand Luvall: Rolfe Sedan. Judge: John Fee. Mrs. Leeson: Verna Felton. Lawyer/Caretaker: Forrest Taylor. Dixie Belle Lee: Mary McDonald. Joe/Master of Ceremonies: Ted Bliss. Edwards/Mr. Smith: Lee Millar. Gladys: Mollie Jo Duncan. Celeste: Anna Lisa. Hank: Ross Forrester. Mrs. Vance: Gloria Gordon.
The Modernettes Trio [Grace Nielson, Jo Campbell, Vivian Edwards] for Lux Soap.

Lux Radio Theater (CBS) "The Champ" November 13, 1939.

Host: Cecil B. DeMille. Announcer: Melville Ruick. The Lou Silvers Orchestra.

An ex-heavyweight boxing champion with gambling and alcohol problems tries to build a better future for his young son. After failing on multiple attempts, he tries to convince his son to move in with his happily remarried mother. Written for radio by George Wells from the screenplay by Leonard Praskins and story by Frances Marion. Directed by Sanford Barnett.

ANDY PURCELL: WALLACE BEERY. LINDA CARLSON: JOSEPHINE HUTCHINSON. TONY CARLSON: NOAH BEERY. DINK: BOBBY LARSON. SPONGE: LOU MERRILL. JONAH: STYMIE BEARD. LOUIE/ANNOUNCER: GALE GORDON. PHOTOGRAPHER: EDDIE MARR. DOCTOR/FIRST PROMOTER: GRIFF BARNETT. GUARD/REFEREE: WALLY MAHER. DEALER: EARLE ROSS. JOSE: JOHN LAKE. SECOND PROMOTER: WALTER WHITE. BOOKIE: LOU LAURIA. MARY: ETHEL SYKES. STREET VENDOR/MAN (ACT 3): SIDNEY NEWMAN. RACETRACK STEWARD/SECOND MAN (ACT 3): GAUGHAN BURKE. CROWD: SALLY PAYNE. THE MODERNETTES TRIO [GRACE NIELSON, VIVIAN EDWARDS, JO CAMPBELL] FOR LUX SOAP.

LI'L ABNER (NBC) (SERIES) NOVEMBER 20, 1939 TO OCTOBER 4, 1940.

Backwoods family the Yokums have humorous adventures with their country-folk neighbors. Based on the newspaper comic strip by Al Capp.
LI'L ABNER YOKUM: JOHN HODIAK
DAISY MAE SCRAGGS: LAURETTE FILLBRANDT
MAMMY YOKUM: HAZEL DOPHEIDE
PAPPY YOKUM: CLARENCE HARTZELL
MARRYIN' SAM: GALE GORDON
ANNOUNCER: DURWARD KIRBY.

FIBBER MCGEE AND MOLLY (NBC) (SERIES) DECEMBER 26, 1939 TO DECEMBER 1, 1942; (VISITS SHOW WHILE IN COAST GUARD: FEBRUARY 16, 1943; JUNE 15, 1943; JUNE 22, 1943; SEPTEMBER 28, 1943; OCTOBER 5, 1943) AND OCTOBER 2, 1945 TO JUNE 30, 1953.

A tale-spinning town character and his wife get themselves into humorous situations with their friends and neighbors.
FIBBER MCGEE: JIM JORDAN
MOLLY MCGEE: MARIAN JORDAN
VARIOUS ROLES/MAYOR CHARLES LATRIVIA/F. OGDEN 'FOGGY' WILLIAMS: GALE GORDON

OLD TIMER/HORATIO K. BOOMER/NICK DEPOPOLIS/WALLACE WIMPLE: BILL THOMPSON
MRS. ABIGAIL UPPINGTON: ISABEL RANDOLPH
DOCTOR GEORGE GAMBLE: ARTHUR Q. BRYAN
MILLICENT CARSTAIRS: BEA BENADERET
ALICE DARLING: SHIRLEY MITCHELL
LENA: GENE CARROLL
OLE SWENSON: DICK LEGRAND
MILTON SPILK: BUD STEPHAN
VOCALISTS: THE KING'S MEN [KEN DARBY, RAD ROBINSON, BUD LINN, JON DODSON]/MARTHA TILTON
ANNOUNCER: HARLOW WILCOX
ORCHESTRA: BILLY MILLS
PRODUCED BY FRANK PITTMAN.

IN HIS STEPS (SYNDICATED) (SERIES) 1940.

A clergyman (Gale Gordon) in a small town interacts with his parishioners and their problems.

CROSSROADS (NBC) (SERIES) JANUARY 28 TO APRIL 14, 1940.

Ann Cooper sacrifices her happiness to support her family.
ANN COOPER: DORIS KENYON
STEPHEN CRAIG: FRED MACKAYE
MR. PATTERSON, ANN'S EMPLOYER: GALE GORDON
ANN'S GRANDMOTHER: JANE MORGAN
ALSO: ANNE SEYMOUR.

LUX RADIO THEATER (CBS) "LOVE AFFAIR" APRIL 1, 1940.

HOST: CECIL B. DEMILLE. ANNOUNCER: MELVILLE RUICK. THE LOU SILVERS ORCHESTRA.
  Facing a separation after a shipboard romance, Terry MacKay and Michael Marnet make plans to meet six months later. Unfortunately,

an accident occurs which keeps Terry from fulfilling the appointment. Thinking he has been jilted, Michael becomes bitter over the affair. Written for radio by George Wells from the screenplay by Delmer Daves and Donald Ogden Stewart, and the story by Mildred Cram and Leo McCarey. Directed by Sanford Barnett.
TERRY: IRENE DUNNE. MICHAEL: WILLIAM POWELL. KENNETH: GALE GORDON. GRANDMOTHER: BEA BENADERET. COURBE/RADIO ANNOUNCER: LOU MERRILL. SUPERINTENDENT: FRANK MCGLYNN. LOIS: LINDA DOUGLAS. DOCTOR/MANAGER: WARREN ASHE. MISS LANE/WOMAN: SARAH SELBY. PAINTER/ENGLISHMAN: PHILLIPS TEAD. ELEVATOR BOY/PAGE BOY: JAMES EAGLES. PHOTOGRAPHER/SECOND MAN: TONY MARTELLI. GUIDE/FRENCHMAN: ROLFE SEDAN. TAXI DRIVER: EDWARD MARR. PRIEST/STEWARD: GRIFF BARNETT. TRIO/AD LIBS: DORIS BRYAN, GWEN BRYAN, BETTY BRYAN. CHILDREN: BARBARA JEAN WONG, BOBBY LARSON, JOE PENNARIO. SONGS:

Irene (as Terry): "Sing My Heart"

Irene (as Terry), The Bryan Sisters: "Wishing"

KATHLEEN FITZ, JULIE BANNON, LOIS COLLIER, MARGARET MCKAY, YNEZ SEABURY, CAROL BRENNER, NANCY LEACH, JAMES EAGLES, AND CELESTE RUSH FOR LUX SOAP.

LITTLE OLD HOLLYWOOD (BLUE) MAY 6, 1940.

HOST: BEN ALEXANDER. THE GORDON JENKINS ORCHESTRA.

Guest Earl Carroll describes what makes a girl beautiful. Ben narrates an original composition by Gordon Jenkins, "Earl Carroll and Miss America."

VIRGINIA MAPLES, MARGARET BRAYTON, FRED MACKAYE, GALE GORDON, GOGO DELYS.

LUX RADIO THEATER (CBS) "MIDNIGHT" MAY 20, 1940.

HOST: CECIL B. DEMILLE. ANNOUNCER: MELVILLE RUICK. THE LOU SILVERS ORCHESTRA.

Farce of adventurous Eve Peabody (Claudette Colbert), who finds

herself stranded with nothing but a pawn ticket in her purse. She meets happy-go-lucky taxi driver Tibor (Don Ameche) and makes a deal with him: she will double his cab fare if he helps her get a job . . . or nothing if she fails. Written for radio by George Wells from the screenplay by Charles Brackett and Billy Wilder, and the story by Edwin Justus Mayer and Franz Schylz. Directed by Sanford Barnett.
GEORGES FLAMMARION: GALE GORDON. JACQUES PICOT: FRED MACKAYE. HELENE FLAMMARION: ROSEMARY DECAMP. MARCEL: ROLFE SEDAN. JUDGE/GENDARME: LOU MERRILL. LEBON/FIRST TAXI DRIVER: WARREN ASHE. LEON/CLERK OF THE COURT: TED BLISS. BUTLER/SECOND TAXI DRIVER: TONY MARTELLI. DOORMAN/CHAUFFEUR: JOHN LAKE. HOTEL CLERK/FOOTMAN: JAMES EAGLES. PORTER: VICTOR RODMAN.
KATHLEEN FITZ, THOMAS FREEBAIRN-SMITH, AND JO CAMPBELL FOR LUX SOAP.

THE BABY SNOOKS SHOW (NBC/CBS) (SERIES) SEPTEMBER 5, 1940 TO MAY 22, 1951.

A mischievous little girl bedevils her harassed father.
BABY SNOOKS/IRMA POTTS: FANNY BRICE. LANCELOT 'DADDY' HIGGINS: HANLEY STAFFORD. VERA 'MOMMY' HIGGINS: LOIS CORBET/ARLENE HARRIS. ROBESPIERRE HIGGINS: LEONE LEDOUX. JERRY DINGLE: DANNY THOMAS. UNCLE LOUIE: CHARLES CANTOR. MR. WEEMISH: ALAN REED/KEN CHRISTY
VARIOUS ROLES: BEN ALEXANDER, ELVIA ALLMAN, JACK ARTHUR, SARA BERNER, HANS CONRIED, GEORGIA ELLIS, STAN FARR, GALE GORDON, EARL LEE, FRANK NELSON, LILLIAN RANDOLPH, CELESTE RUSH, IRENE TEDROW, MARTHA WENTWORTH
VOCALIST: BOB GRAHAM
ANNOUNCERS: JOHN CONTE/TOBE REED/HARLOW WILCOX/DICK JOY/DON WILSON/KEN ROBERTS
ORCHESTRA: MEREDITH WILLSON/CARMEN DRAGON
PRODUCED BY MANN HOLINER, AL KAYE, TED BLISS, WALTER BUNKER, ARTHUR STANDER.

LUX RADIO THEATER (CBS) "WINGS OF THE NAVY" OCTOBER 7, 1940.

HOST: CECIL B. DEMILLE. ANNOUNCER: MELVILLE RUICK. THE LOU SILVERS ORCHESTRA.

Cass Harrington (George Brent) spends his time designing a new fighter plane demonstrating unheard of performance. While doing so, he falls in love with Irene Dale (Olivia DeHavilland)—a woman also pursued by Cass' brother Jerry (John Payne). Written for radio by George Wells from the screenplay by Michael Fessier. Directed by Sanford Barnett.
HARRY WHITE: TRISTRAM COFFIN. MACK: LOU MERRILL. SPEAKER: GALE GORDON. DR. HARPER: STUART BUCHANAN. CAPTAIN BROWN: EARLE ROSS. CAPTAIN MARCH: STANLEY FARRAR. REPORTER: WALLY MAHER. STEVE: FRANK RICHARDS. ORMSBY: JAMES EAGLES. ROLFE SEDAN, LOIS COLLIER, MARTHA WENTWORTH, DUANE THOMPSON, AND SARAH SELBY FOR LUX SOAP.

SECOND WIFE (CBS-WEST COAST) (SERIES) DECEMBER 16, 1940 TO 1942.

A young businessman prefers his secretary to the girl he married. Sharon Douglas and Gale Gordon were featured in the cast. Lou Crosby was announcer.

THE BURNS AND ALLEN SHOW (NBC/CBS) CIRCA 1941 TO 1950.

Patient George attempts to straighten out the predicaments caused by his nonsensical wife Gracie.
GEORGE BURNS: HIMSELF. GRACIE ALLEN: HERSELF. TOOTSIE SAGWELL: ELVIA ALLMAN. THE HAPPY POSTMAN: MEL BLANC. HERMAN THE DUCK: CLARENCE NASH. TEX JUDSON: GALE GORDON.
VOCALISTS: JIMMY CASH/RICHARD HAYDN
ANNOUNCER: BILL GOODWIN
ORCHESTRA: PAUL WHITEMAN/MEREDITH WILLSON
PRODUCED BY GLENHALL TAYLOR.

Tenth Anniversary Salute to Movie-Radio Guide (Syndicated) (Special) 1941.

Announcer: John Conte. The Meredith Willson Orchestra.
Various NBC stars appear to honor the entertainment industry magazine: Connie Boswell, Frank Morgan, Gale Gordon, Harlow Wilcox, Harold Peary, Jim and Marian Jordan.

Lux Radio Theater (CBS) "Wife, Husband, and Friend" April 28, 1941.

Host: Cecil B. DeMille. Announcer: Melville Ruick. The Lou Silvers Orchestra.
A voice teacher dishonestly convinces his student she has great opera potential and is paid handsomely by her husband. Hubby, feeling a little jealous, tries to gain an advantage over his wife by taking voice lessons from someone else. When he makes his singing debut and promptly bombs, the two teachers exit quickly and love prevails. Written for radio by George Wells from the screenplay by Nunnally Johnson, and the story by James M. Cain. Directed by Sanford Barnett.
Leonard: George Brent. Doris: Priscilla Lane. Cecilia Carver: Gail Patrick. Mrs. Blair: Verna Felton. Hugo: Hans Conried. Craig: Gale Gordon. Operator/Taxi Driver: Edward Marr. Major Blair: Lou Merrill. Jaffe: Abe Reynolds. Fisher: Thomas Mills. Doctor/Stage Manager: Stanley Farrar. Motel Manager: Hal K. Dawson.
For the singing sequences, Lane is dubbed by Mildred Carroll, Brent by Paul Klast, and Patrick by Lynne Davis. Alyn Lockwood [Julie Bannon], Duane Thompson, Fred Shields, Ann Tobin, and Fred MacKaye for Lux Soap.

LUX RADIO THEATER (CBS) "KITTY FOYLE" MAY 5, 1941.

HOST: CECIL B. DEMILLE. ANNOUNCER: MELVILLE RUICK. THE LOU SILVERS ORCHESTRA.
Young department store clerk Kitty (Ginger Rogers) becomes torn between marrying for love or money when she falls for two very different men. After deciding to accept the rich man's proposal, she is chased away by his family's class prejudice against her. Written for radio by George Wells from the screenplay by Dalton Trumbo and the novel by Christopher Morley. Directed by Sanford Barnett.
WYN STAFFORD: DENNIS MORGAN. MARK: JAMES CRAIG. POP: EDDY WALLER. GIONO: LOU MERRILL. WYN'S GRANDMOTHER: VERNA FELTON. DELPHINE: GLORIA HOLDEN. VERONICA: ROSEMARY DECAMP. MRS. STAFFORD: CLAIRE VERDERA. PAT: MARY TREEN. MOLLIE: VIVIAN [VIVI] JANISS. GIRL: ANN TOBIN. WYN JR.: BOBBY LARSON. RADIO/ORCHESTRA LEADER: FRED MACKAYE. WAITER/DOORMAN: GALE GORDON. KANNETT: BRUCE PAYNE. BUTLER: THOMAS MILLS. GRANDMOTHER: GLORIA GORDON. BABY CRY: CELESTE RUSH. JULIE BANNON AND KATHLEEN FITZ FOR LUX SOAP.

LUX RADIO THEATER (CBS) "VIRGINIA CITY" MAY 26, 1941.

HOST: CECIL B. DEMILLE. ANNOUNCER: MELVILLE RUICK. THE LOU SILVERS ORCHESTRA.
During the Civil War, a female rebel operative poses as a saloon girl and meets Terry Bradford (Errol Flynn), a Union agent dispatched to keep gold shipments from falling into the hands of the Confederate army. Written for radio by George Wells from the screenplay by Robert Buckner. Directed by Sanford Barnett.
JULIA: MARTHA SCOTT. HURRELL: WARREN ASHE. ABRAHAM LINCOLN: FRANK MCGLYNN. CAPTAIN VANCE IRVING: GALE GORDON. DR. CAMERON: GRIFF BARNETT. MARBLEHEAD: EDWIN MAX. OLAF: LOU MERRILL. GENERAL: THEODORE VON ELTZ. DREWRY/BARTENDER: FORREST TAYLOR. BLACKSMITH/TAYLOR: CHARLES SEEL. SPIKE/OFFICER: STANLEY FARRAR. DRIVER/SERGEANT: EDWARD ARNOLD JR. SOLDIER: JAMES EAGLES.
SINGER: MILDRED CARROLL.

Julie Bannon, Duane Thompson, and Lois Collier for Lux Soap.

Stars Over Hollywood (CBS) (Series) May 31, 1941 to September 25, 1954.

Anthology of light dramas featuring top film players.
ANNOUNCER: Jim Bannon/Art Gilmore/Frank Goss/Knox Manning/Marvin Miller
VARIOUS ROLES: Tom Collins, Gale Gordon, Pat McGeehan, Lurene Tuttle, Janet Waldo
ORGANIST: Ivan Ditmars
ORCHESTRA: Del Castillo
PRODUCED BY PAUL PIERCE.

Lux Radio Theater (CBS) "The Lady from Cheyenne" June 16, 1941.

HOST: Cecil B. DeMille. ANNOUNCER: Melville Ruick. THE LOU SILVERS ORCHESTRA.
  Schoolteacher Annie Morgan (Loretta Young) settles in Laraville, Wyoming, during the 1860s when the Union Pacific Railroad was auctioning off land to prospective townsfolk. Annie's property is coveted by Jim Cork (Edward Arnold), the town's political boss, who needs it to monopolize the water supply. Written for radio by George Wells from the screenplay by Kathryn Scola and Warren Duff and the story "The First Woman Voter" by Jonathan Finn and Theresa Oaks. Directed by Sanford Barnett.
STEVE LEWIS: Robert Preston. HANK FREEMAN: Forrest Taylor. MRS. McGINNIS: Jane Morgan. ELSIE: Vivian [Vivi] Janiss. BILLY: Lou Merrill. IKE FAIRCHILD: Ferdinand Munier. BARNEY: Warren Ashe. GEORGE: Buck Woods. DUNBAR/MR. LLOYD: Stanley Farrar. THE GOVERNOR/JUDGE: Gale Gordon. EDWARD: Dix Davis. GERTIE: Gloria Blondell. CLAIRE/CONDUCTOR: Bruce Payne. LANDLADY: Celeste Rush. REPORTER/MAN: Tyler McVey. LEO/NOISEY: Dick Ryan. GIRL: Barbara

JEAN WONG. AD LIBS: BETTY JEAN HAINEY, BETTY MORAN, JULIE BANNON (WHO ALSO DO THE COMMERCIAL FOR LUX SOAP).

MISS PINKERTON, INC. (NBC) (AUDITION SHOW) JULY 12, 1941.

A sassy gal inherits a detective agency and decides to become a private eye just to prove women can solve crimes as well as men. She sets out after a trio of jewel thieves. Unsuccessful radio pilot for a proposed series.
MARY VANCE: JOAN BLONDELL. DENNIS MURRAY: DICK POWELL. MR. PARKER: HANLEY STAFFORD. BINGO DOHERTY: EDWIN MAX. ALSO: GALE GORDON, CARL FOREMAN, ELLIOTT LEWIS, FRANK GERMAN, SARA BERNER. ART GILMORE IS THE ANNOUNCER AND LENNY CONN CONDUCTS THE ORCHESTRA. PRODUCED BY J. DONALD WILSON.

ORSON WELLES THEATER (CBS) (SERIES) SEPTEMBER 15, 1941 TO FEBRUARY 2, 1942.

Variety including drama, music, readings, and commentary.
HOST/STAR: ORSON WELLES
JIMINY CRICKET: CLIFF EDWARDS
VARIOUS ROLES: RAY COLLINS, DOROTHY COMINGORE, HANS CONRIED, JOSEPH COTTEN, NANCY GATES, GALE GORDON, RUTH GORDON, ELLIOTT LEWIS, AGNES MOOREHEAD, ERSKINE SANFORD, PAUL STEWART
ORCHESTRA: BERNARD HERRMANN.

BLONDIE (CBS) (SERIES) 1941 TO 1942.

The domestic misadventures of Blondie and Dagwood Bumstead, and their family, friends and neighbors.
BLONDIE BUMSTEAD: PENNY SINGLETON. DAGWOOD BUMSTEAD: ARTHUR LAKE. ALEXANDER/COOKIE: LEONE LEDOUX. J.C. DITHERS: HANLEY STAFFORD. CORA DITHERS: ELVIA ALLMAN. HERB WOODLEY: FRANK NELSON. VARIOUS ROLES: GALE GORDON

PRODUCED BY ASHMEAD SCOTT.

LUX RADIO THEATER (CBS) "UNFINISHED BUSINESS" OCTOBER 6, 1941.

HOST: CECIL B. DEMILLE. ANNOUNCER: MELVILLE RUICK. THE LOU SILVERS ORCHESTRA.

Nancy (Irene Dunne) is a naïve girl from a typical small town who is intent upon acquiring urban sophistication. As such, she flirts with a fellow train passenger and ends up marrying his brother. Written for radio by George Wells from the screenplay by Eugene Thackeray. Directed by Sanford Barnett.
TOMMY: DON AMECHE. STEVE: GALE GORDON. ELMER: DICK ELLIOTT. SHEILA/SARAH: BEA BENADERET. NELL: VIRGINIA GORDON. MRS. HATCH: VERNA FELTON. RICHARD: FRED MACKAYE. ROSS: ARTHUR Q. BRYAN. HELEN: JANE RHEA. CONDUCTOR/WALT: JACK GEORGE. GIRL: BETTY VENTURA. MAN: MUNRO BROWN. BABY: LEONE LEDOUX. JULIE BANNON, NANCY BICKELL, JAMES EAGLES, JO CAMPBELL, AND SALLY MUELLER FOR LUX SOAP.

CAVALCADE OF AMERICA (NBC) "WATERS OF THE WILDERNESS" OCTOBER 13, 1941.

ANNOUNCER: JOHN [BUD] HIESTAND. THE ROBERT ARMBRUSTER ORCHESTRA.

Romance blossoms in the Mississippi Valley of the American Revolution when soldier George Rogers Clark (Gale Gordon) meets the beautiful Spanish Miss Teresa de Leyba (Kay Francis). Written for radio by William Johnstone and Robert Richards from the novel by Shirley Siefert. Directed by Homer Fickett.
LIARD: GERALD MOHR. SUZETTE/FEMALE HOMESTEADER/VOICE 3: AGNES MOOREHEAD. FERNANDO/FIRST SETTLER/VOICE 1: LOU MERRILL. MARIA/INDIAN WOMAN/VOICE 5: BEA BENADERET. TOM PACE/SECOND SETTLER/SECOND HOMESTEADER/VOICE 2: JACK MATHER. SERVANT: GAYNE WHITMAN. FIRST HOMESTEADER/THIRD SETTLER/VOICE 4: PAT MCGEEHAN. SUPERNUMERARIES: CATHERINE CRAGEN, GRACE LEONARD, JERRY GALE, EARLE ROSS.

Gayne Whitman for DuPont Chemical Company.

Lux Radio Theater (CBS) "Blood and Sand" October 20, 1941.

Host: Cecil B. DeMille. Announcer: Melville Ruick. The Lou Silvers Orchestra.

Juan (Tyrone Power), the son of a bullfighter who died in the ring, vows to win fame for himself—and does, even earning praise from the critic who vilified his father. However, Juan's inflated ego soon costs him his wife and career . . . setting the stage for a dramatic comeback. Written for radio by George Wells from the screenplay by Jo Swerling and the novel by Vicente Blasco Ibanez. Directed by Sanford Barnett.

Carmen: Annabella. Dona Sol: Kathleen Fitz. Juan's Mother: Bea Benaderet. Pablo: Gale Gordon. Garabato: Jeff Corey. Curro: Lou Merrill. Captain Martinez: Howard McNear. Padre/El Milquetoast: Bruce Payne. Juan as a Boy: Walter Tetley. Encarnacion: Anne Stone. Manolo: Eric Rolf. Antonio: Paul Dubov. Woman: Elsa Brand. Pulga/Second Man: Nick Toms. Man/Waiter: Lester Sharpe.

Ben Alexander, Julie Bannon, Nancy Bickell, and Lois Collier for Lux Soap.

Your Red Cross Roll Call (MBS) (Special) November 15, 1941.

The story of Florence Nightingale and the establishment of the Red Cross. A fund appeal for the organization.
Abraham Lincoln: Gale Gordon.

Cavalcade of America (NBC) "Cimarron" December 1, 1941.

Announcer: John [Bud] Hiestand. The Robert Armbruster Orchestra.

Sabra Cravat (Irene Dunne), a gentle-bred woman, faces the hardships of the Oklahoma prairie as her husband—part dreamer and

part frontiersman—becomes a great criminal lawyer and newspaper publisher. Written for radio by Paul Franklin and Robert Tallman from the novel by Edna Ferber. Directed by Homer Fickett.
YANCY CRAVAT: GALE GORDON. MRS. VENABLE/MISS WINSLOW: PAULA WINSLOWE. CIM: JERRY HAUSNER. GRAT NOLAN: JACK MATHER. LON YOUNTIS/COPY DESK: HOWARD MCNEAR. MRS. WYATT: DOROTHY SCOTT. MR. OAKES: LOU MERRILL. BOY: BARBARA JEAN WONG.
GAYNE WHITMAN FOR DUPONT CHEMICAL COMPANY.

AIR TRAILER (SYNDICATED) "WAKE ISLAND" 1942.

Scenes from the film are dramatized as a promotion to see the movie. Includes a military recruiting appeal.
HANLEY STAFFORD, GALE GORDON, ELLIOTT LEWIS.

THE PEPSODENT SHOW (NBC) MARCH 17, 1942.

STARS: BOB HOPE, JERRY COLONNA.
VOCALISTS: SIX HITS AND A MISS.
ANNOUNCERS: JOHN LALLY, LARRY KEATING. THE SKINNAY ENNIS ORCHESTRA.
Bob sets out to retrieve a tire stolen from his car. The trail leads to a haunted house, so Bob and Skinnay brave the ghostly abode.
GALE GORDON.

TREASURY STAR PARADE (SYNDICATED) (SERIES) APRIL, 1942 TO 1944.

Drama and music with patriotic themes, featuring name guest stars.
HOST: HENRY HULL/PAUL DOUGLAS
VARIOUS ROLES: PETER DONALD, PARKER FENNELLY, GALE GORDON, LOU MERRILL, DWIGHT WEIST, PAULA WINSLOWE, LESLEY WOODS.
ANNOUNCER: LARRY ELLIOTT.
ORCHESTRA: DAVID BROEKMAN/AL GOODMAN

Produced by Brent Gunts.

Cavalcade of America (NBC) "A Continental Uniform" April 13, 1942.

Announcer: John [Bud] Hiestand. The Robert Armbruster Orchestra.
   The story of Benedict Arnold (Basil Rathbone), which begins at Westminster Abbey, London, and moves to the evening he sold the plans of West Point to the British during the American Revolution. It is the young country's most infamous betrayal by a man ridden with debt and in love with a dubious woman. Written by Robert Tallman. Directed by Homer Fickett.
Peggy Shippen: Rosemary DeCamp. The Aide/The Major: Eric Rolfe. The Surgeon/The Servant: Lou Merrill. George Washington/Hamilton: Gale Gordon. Storyteller/Punch: Elliott Lewis. Tallyrand/Captain Pell: Gerald Mohr. York/Andre: Hans Conried.
Gayne Whitman for DuPont Chemical Company.

Cavalcade of America (NBC) "In This Crisis" April 20, 1942.

Announcer: John [Bud] Hiestand. The Robert Armbruster Orchestra.
Journalist Thomas Paine (Claude Rains) writes Common Sense, putting into words the embodiment of freedom—which spurs the events resulting in America's Declaration of Independence. Written by Robert L. Richards. Directed by Homer Fickett.
The Voice/The Third Minister/The Sergeant: Elliott Lewis. Madame Bonneville: Agnes Moorehead. The Stranger: Ray Collins. Smythe: Don Costello. Hughes/The Printer: John Mather. Attendant/Aitken: Eric Rolfe. First Minister/Marsden: Hans Conried. Second Minister: Gavin Gordon. Fourth Minister/Washington: Gale Gordon. Greene: John Lake.
Gayne Whitman for DuPont Chemical Company.

The Whistler (CBS-West Coast) (Series) May 16, 1942.

Premiere episode of the series entitled "Retribution." Gale Gordon may be in other episodes of the series.
A mysterious lurker in the night tells tales of persons trapped in the toils of their own misdeeds.
The Whistler: Gale Gordon
Orchestra: Wilbur Hatch
Produced by J. Donald Wilson.

Cavalcade of America (NBC) "Remember the Day" May 18, 1942.

Announcer: John [Bud] Hiestand. The Robert Armbruster Orchestra.
As an elderly schoolteacher awaits a meeting with a Presidential nominee, she looks back on her life and the love she shared with a young man. Written for radio by George Barraud from the screenplay by Tess Slesinger, Frank Davis, Alan Scott, and Henry King (stage play by Philo Higley and Philip Dunning). Directed by Homer Fickett.
Nora Trinnell: Claudette Colbert. Dewey, as a man: Gale Gordon. Mr. Steele: Eric Rolfe. Dan Hopkins: Elliott Lewis. Mrs. Roberts: Janet Beecher. Girl: Louise Erickson. Boy: Conrad Binyon. Bellboy: Herb Vigran. Stokes/The Porter: Jack Mather. Dewey, as a boy: Tommy Cook.
Gayne Whitman for DuPont Chemical Company.

Cavalcade of America (NBC) "Young Tom Jefferson" May 25, 1942.

Announcer: John [Bud] Hiestand. The Robert Armbruster Orchestra.
Tom begins his life on his father's Virginia plantation and proceeds to become one of the major framers of America's Declaration of Independence. Narrated by Elliott Lewis.
Written by Robert L. Richards. Directed by Homer Fickett.

Tom Jefferson: Tyrone Power. Dr. Franklin: William Farnum. John Adams/Sergeant-at-Arms: Jack Mather. Peter/The Doctor: Gale Gordon. Jed: Clarence Muse. Farmer: Joe Latham. Hostess/Martha: Georgia Backus. Governor/Chaplain: Hans Conried. Judge/The Chair: Eric Rolfe. Clerk/ Captain: Don Costello. The Host: Norman Field. Henry: Ray Collins. Soldier: Bob Mauch.
Gayne Whitman for DuPont Chemical Company.

Lux Radio Theatre (as a war bonds benefit it is called *The Victory Theatre*) (CBS) "The Philadelphia Story" July 20, 1942.

Host: Cecil B. DeMille. Announcer: John Milton Kennedy. The Lou Silvers Orchestra.

An heiress' charming ex-husband arrives on the day before her wedding with an equally charming gossip magazine reporter. Soon, the woman feels romantically torn between her fiancé, her ex, and the reporter. Written for radio by George Wells from the screenplay by Donald Ogden Stewart and the play by Philip Barry.
C.K. Dexter Haven: Cary Grant. Tracy Lord: Katharine Hepburn. Mike Connor: Lieutenant James Stewart. Elizabeth Embrie: Ruth Hussey. Dinah Lord: Virginia Weidler. Seth: Nicholas Joy. Margaret: Janet Beecher. George: Gale Gordon. Librarian: Verna Felton. Mother: Sandra Coles. Also: Leo Cleary, Charles Seel, Norman Field, and Bruce Payne.
Verna Felton makes an appeal for the purchase of War Bonds.

Lux Radio Theater (CBS) "How Green Was My Valley" September 21, 1942.

Host: Cecil B. DeMille. Announcer: John Milton Kennedy. The Lou Silvers Orchestra.

A close-knit Welsh coal-mining family sees romance, conflict, and tragedy in the sometimes-harsh conditions of life in their labor town. Narrated by Gale Gordon. Written for radio by George Wells

from the screenplay by Philip Dunne and the novel by Richard Llewellyn. Directed by Sanford Barnett.
MR. GRUFFYDD: WALTER PIDGEON. MR. MORGAN: DONALD CRISP. ANGHARAD: MAUREEN O'HARA. HUW: RODDY MCDOWALL. BETH MORGAN: SARA ALLGOOD. DAI BANDO: STEWART ROBERTSON. CYFARTHA: JOSEPH KEARNS. IANTO: PAUL LANGTON. MR. JONAS/GWILYM: KEMBALL COOPER. MRS. NICHOLAS/SECOND WOMAN: GLORIA GORDON. MR. EVANS: FREDERIC WORLOCK. ENID/WOMAN: ESTA MASON. PETERSON: HERBERT EVANS. MAN: FRED MACKAYE. WOMAN: CLAIRE VERDERA. MAN: NORMAN FIELD. AD LIBS: STEPHEN MULLER, JOE PENNARIO, BARBARA JEAN WONG, ANTONIO ORLAND, BILLY ROY. MAN/AD LIBS: TUDOR WILLIAMS. BETTY JEAN HAINEY, JANET WALDO, SANDRA COLES, AND ART GILMORE FOR LUX SOAP.

LUX RADIO THEATER (CBS) "LOVE CRAZY" OCTOBER 5, 1942.

HOST: CECIL B. DEMILLE. ANNOUNCER: JOHN MILTON KENNEDY. THE LOU SILVERS ORCHESTRA.

Steve and Susan Ireland's fourth anniversary finds them still as happy as on their wedding day, but their bliss is not destined to last. Susan's mother arrives unexpectedly, thereby spoiling what was originally planned as a quiet celebration of the occasion. Then, an ex-flame of Steve's and a lunacy commission interfere and almost succeed in parting the Irelands. Written for radio by George Wells from the screenplay by William Ludwig, Charles Lederer, and David Hertz. Directed by Sanford Barnett.
SUSAN: HEDY LAMARR. STEVE: WILLIAM POWELL. WARD: GALE GORDON. ISOBEL: DOROTHY LOVETT. MRS. COOPER: VERNA FELTON. DR. KLUGLE: JOSEPH KEARNS. GRAYSON: FRED MACKAYE. LEO: ARTHUR Q. BRYAN. ATTENDANT/MAN NO. 2: WALLY MAHER. JOE/COP: EDDIE MARR. JUDGE/JANITOR: GRIFF BARNETT. MAN/DR. WUTHERING: FERDINAND MUNIER. TAXI/MIKE: JAMES BUSH. WOMAN/SECRETARY: BESSIE SMILEY. BUTLER: HORACE WILLARD. GIRL/OPERATOR: BETTY HILL. DENTIST: BOYD DAVIS. MAN: NORMAN FIELD.
SANDRA COLES AND JANET WALDO FOR LUX SOAP.

Lux Radio Theater (CBS) "Wake Island" October 26, 1942.

Host: Cecil B. DeMille. Announcer: John Milton Kennedy. The Lou Silvers Orchestra.

A handful of US Marines bravely attempt the impossible—hold a remote outpost during the Japanese attack on Pearl Harbor. Written for radio by George Wells from the screenplay by W.R. Burnett and Frank Butler. Directed by Sanford Barnett.
Major Caton: Brian Donlevy. Joe: Robert Preston. Smacksie: Broderick Crawford. Commander Roberts: Gale Gordon. Doctor/Parkman: Griff Barnett. Lt. Bruce Cameron: Howard McNear. Cynthia: Mary Lou Harrington. Sergeant: Edwin Max. Dog/Probenzki: Pinto Colvig. McCloskie: Wally Maher. Announcer/Talker: Fred MacKaye. Runner: Paul Langton. Tommy/Man: Tyler McVey. Warren: Hal Gerard. Mrs. Cameron: Lillian Bond. Frank: Jeff Corey. Patric: Charles Seel. Johnson/Lewis: Warren Ashe. Kurusu/Orderly: Leo Cleary. Native Girl: Janet Russell. Sparks: Eddie Marr. Hogan: Jack Mather.
Duane Thompson and Betty Jane Hainey for Lux Soap.

Mail Call (AFRS) Program no. 3, October 27, 1942.

Announcer: Bill Goodwin. Vocalists: The King's Men.

Guests Jack Benny and Ann Sheridan appear in "George Washington Slept Here," all about a city couple who buy a run-down house in the country.
Rosemary Lane, Gale Gordon.
Song:
   "The Army Air Corps March."

Suspense (CBS) "The Earth Is Made of Glass" September 27, 1945.

Announcer: Joseph Kearns. The Lud Gluskin Orchestra.
A scientist believes murder can be committed in the 'abstract,' so he sets out to kill a random victim and pull off the perfect crime.

Written by Sylvia Richards. Directed by William Spier.
JOSEPH COTTEN, CATHY LEWIS, GALE GORDON, WILLIAM JOHNSTONE.
TRUMAN BRADLEY FOR ROMA WINES.

CAVALCADE OF AMERICA (NBC) "CHILDREN, THIS IS YOUR FATHER" OCTOBER 15, 1945.

ANNOUNCER: TOM COLLINS. THE ROBERT ARMBRUSTER ORCHESTRA.
    Lieutenant Sam Lester (Gale Gordon) returns home from duty in World War II to find things are not quite the same as when he left; his wife exaggerated his importance in the war to that of a heroic figure. Written by Priscilla Kent. Directed by Jack Zoller.
MRS. LESTER: LORETTA YOUNG. KAREN: MARLENE AMES. MICKEY: TOMMY BERNARD.
GAYNE WHITMAN FOR DUPONT CHEMICAL COMPANY.

LUX RADIO THEATER (CBS) "THE VALLEY OF DECISION" JANUARY 14, 1946.

HOST: WILLIAM KEIGHLEY. ANNOUNCERS: JOHN MILTON KENNEDY, THOMAS HANLON. THE LOUIS SILVERS ORCHESTRA.
    Steel separates 1873 Pittsburgh into rich and poor, master and worker, powerful and powerless. Paul Scott (Gregory Peck), the son of a wealthy mill owner, crosses social barriers when he falls for his family's beautiful maid. Written for radio by S. H. Barnett from the screenplay by John Meehan and Sonya Levien, and the novel by Marcia Davenport. Directed by Fredric MacKaye.
MARY RAFFERTY: GREER GARSON. JIM: GALE GORDON. CALLAHAN/VOICE: CHARLES SEEL. MCCREADY/MAN: NORMAN FIELD. SCOTT: FRANCIS X. BUSHMAN. MRS. SCOTT: JANET SCOTT. WILLIE: GEORGE NEISE. LOUISE: LURENE TUTTLE. CONNIE: TRUDA MARSEN. TED: SAM EDWARDS. DELIA: GWEN DELANO. JULIE: DOROTHY SCOTT. GILES: GUY KINGSFORD. GAYLORD: BOYD DAVIS. PAT: LEO CLEARY. AD LIBS: TED ALBRIGHT, JAMES FLOTO, CLARK KUNEY, EDWIN MILLS, JOSEPH WORTHY.
THE INTERMISSION GUEST IS HELEN O'HARA.

Louis B. Mayer, executive vice president of Metro-Goldwyn-Mayer, guests during the curtain call.
Doris Singleton and Ann Tobin for Lux Soap.

Cavalcade of America (NBC) "Commencement in Khaki" January 28, 1946.

Announcer: Tom Collins. The Robert Armbruster Orchestra.
  Corporal Pete Johnson (Dana Andrews) finds himself being installed as an instructor at an army camp college—and meeting a beautiful WAC—all because of the machinations of his 'king-sized moron' buddy. Written by Harry Granick. Directed by Jack Zoller.
The Lovely WAC: Nancy Kelly. Sime: Eddie Marr. Captain Waters: Gale Gordon.
Gayne Whitman for DuPont Chemical Company.

Hollywood Star Time (CBS) "The Mark of Zorro" February 16, 1946.

Announcer: Wendell Niles. The Alfred Newman Orchestra.
  A Spanish nobleman (Cornel Wilde) dons the mask of a mysterious swordsman to avenge the dishonor brought to his dead father's name.
Joseph Kearns, Lurene Tuttle, Gale Gordon, Cy Kendall, Fred Howard, Ben Alexander.

The Judy Canova Show (NBC) (Series) circa 1946 to 1950.

  A country gal from Cactus Junction, California, never tires in her efforts to land a man of her own and find professional success in Hollywood.
Judy Canova: Herself. Aunt Aggie: Verna Felton/Ruth Perrott. Geranium: Ruby Dandridge. Pedro: Mel Blanc. Benchley Botsford: Joseph Kearns. Gordon Mansfield: Gale Gordon. Mr. Simpson: Gale Gordon/Joseph Kearns.

VARIOUS ROLES: ELVIA ALLMAN, HANS CONRIED, GEORGE NEISE.
VOCALISTS: THE SPORTSMEN
ANNOUNCER: VERNE SMITH/HOWARD PETRIE
ORCHESTRA: OPIE CATES/CHARLES 'BUD' DANT/GORDON JENKINS
PRODUCED BY JOE RINES.

THE SECOND MRS. BURTON (CBS) (SERIES) CIRCA 1946 TO LATE 1940S.

Terry Burton strives to find happiness as the wife of divorced Stan Burton.
TERRY BURTON: SHARON DOUGLAS. STAN BURTON: DWIGHT WEIST. LEW ARCHER: LARRY HAINES. VARIOUS ROLES: JOAN ALEXANDER, BEN COOPER, STAATS COTSWORTH, ELSPETH ERIC, GALE GORDON, JANE MORGAN, ALEXANDER SCOURBY, LES TREMAYNE.
ANNOUNCER: HUGH JAMES
ORGAN: CHET KINGSBURY/RICHARD LEIBERT
PRODUCED BY LINDSAY MACHARRIE, IRA ASHLEY.

LUX RADIO THEATER (CBS) "HONKY TONK" APRIL 8, 1946.

HOST: WILLIAM KEIGHLEY. ANNOUNCERS: JOHN MILTON KENNEDY, THOMAS HANLON. THE LOUIS SILVERS ORCHESTRA.
Candy Johnson (John Hodiak), a con artist run out of one town after another, finally gets wise. He goes out and gets a town of his own by marrying the judge's daughter as part of his scheme. Written for radio by S. H. Barnett from the screenplay by Marguerite Roberts and John Sanford. Directed by Fredric MacKaye.
ELIZABETH: LANA TURNER. BRAZOS: GALE GORDON. JUDGE: LEO CLEARY. GOLD DUST: PAULA WINSLOWE. SNIPER: TYLER MCVEY. MRS. VARNER: NOREEN GAMMILL. BLACKIE: EDWIN MAX. ADAMS: JAY NOVELLO. WELLS: BROOKE TEMPLE. KENDALL/BARTENDER: CLIFF CLARK. MRS. MORGAN: DOROTHY SCOTT. BLAKE/DOCTOR: ALEXANDER GERRY. MAN/CONDUCTOR: STANLEY FARRAR. DESK CLERK: CHARLES SEEL. INTERMISSION GUEST IS NINA FOCH.
DORIS SINGLETON, DUANE THOMPSON, AND FRANKLIN PARKER FOR LUX SOAP.

LUX RADIO THEATER (CBS) "WHISTLE STOP" APRIL 15, 1946.

HOST: WILLIAM KEIGHLEY. ANNOUNCERS: JOHN MILTON KENNEDY, THOMAS HANLON. THE LOUIS SILVERS ORCHESTRA.

A woman with expensive tastes gives up the small-town beau whom she loves to string along with a handsome gambler. Then, murder occurs. Written for radio by S. H. Barnett from the screenplay by Philip Yordan and the novel by Maritta M. Wolff. Directed by Fredric MacKaye.
KENNY DIETZ: ALAN LADD. MARY: EVELYN KEYES. LEW LENTZ: GALE GORDON. GILLO: EDWIN MAX. FRAN: SAMMIE HILL. MOLLY: JANE MORGAN. SAM: LEO CLEARY. JESSIE/OPERATOR: TRUDA MARSON. ERNIE: GEORGE NEISE. BARKER: ED EMERSON. STELLA: ANNE STONE. AL: CHARLES SEEL. INTERMISSION GUEST IS VIRGINIA THORNE. DORIS SINGLETON AND BETTY MORAN FOR LUX SOAP.

LUX RADIO THEATER (CBS) "GASLIGHT" APRIL 29, 1946.

HOST: WILLIAM KEIGHLEY. ANNOUNCERS: JOHN MILTON KENNEDY, THOMAS HANLON. THE LOUIS SILVERS ORCHESTRA.

Paula (Ingrid Bergman), an English singer, marries a handsome man hiding his dubious past. They move into the home Paula inherited from her murdered aunt—but Paula begins to think the old house is haunted when she hears strange noises and witnesses odd events. Written for radio by S. H. Barnett from the screenplay by John Van Druten, Walter Reisch, and John L. Balderston; and the play by Patrick Hamilton. Directed by Fredric MacKaye.
GREGORY: CHARLES BOYER. CAMERON: GALE GORDON. ELIZABETH: JANET SCOTT. NANCY: TRUDA MARSON. WILLIAMS: ERIC SNOWDEN. LADY DALROY: CLAIRE VERDERA. MUFFLIN: RAYMOND LAWRENCE. MRS. THWAITTES/WOMAN: GLORIA GORDON. VOICE/SUPERINTENDENT: CHARLES SEEL. INTERMISSION GUEST IS JANET THOMAS.
DORIS SINGLETON, JUNE WHITFIELD, AND FRANCIS WHITFIELD FOR LUX SOAP.

Lux Radio Theater (CBS) "Tomorrow Is Forever" May 6, 1946.

Host: William Keighley. Announcers: John Milton Kennedy, Thomas Hanlon. The Louis Silvers Orchestra.
  A World War I soldier, previously thought killed in action, returns home twenty years later to find his wife has remarried. Written for radio by S. H. Barnett from the screenplay by Lenore Coffee and the novel by Gwen Bristow. Directed by Fredric MacKaye.
Elizabeth Hamilton: Claudette Colbert. Erich Kessler a.k.a. John MacDonald: Van Heflin. Drew: Richard Long. Margaret: Natalie Wood. Larry: Gale Gordon. Bryan: Tommy Cook. Baby: Leone Ledoux.
Intermission guest is Elsie Sullivan, fan mail department secretary at Metro-Goldwyn-Mayer.
Doris Singleton for Lux Soap.

The Theatre Guild on the Air (ABC) "Payment Deferred" May 12, 1946.

Host: Lawrence Langner. Announcer: Norman Brokenshire. The Harold Levey Orchestra.
  A bank clerk (Charles Laughton), fearing his creditors, murders his wealthy nephew and nets himself a considerable fortune. His own fears and fancies concerning his crime being discovered results in a phobic complex that traps him.
Elsa Lanchester, Edward Marr, Franklyn Parker, Gale Gordon, Gayne Whitman, Herbert Rawlinson, Joseph Kearns, Maria Mamon, Susan Douglas, William Johnstone.
George Hicks for United States Steel.

The Theatre Guild on the Air (ABC) "They Knew What They Wanted" May 19, 1946.

Host: Lawrence Langner. Announcer: Norman Brokenshire. The Harold Levey Orchestra.
  Broadcast from the War Memorial Opera House in San Francisco,

California. A Golden State winemaker (Leo Carrillo) hopes to acquire a mail-order bride, but sends a picture of his handsome foreman (John Garfield) instead of himself. Written for radio by Kenyon Nicholson from the play by Sidney Howard.
JUNE HAVOC, EDWARD MARR, ELLIOTT REID, GALE GORDON, HAL K. DAWSON, HERBERT RAWLINSON.
GEORGE HICKS FOR UNITED STATES STEEL.

BIRDS-EYE OPEN HOUSE (NBC) MAY 23, 1946.

STAR: DINAH SHORE. VOCALISTS: THE KEN LANE CHORUS. ANNOUNCER: HARRY VON ZELL. THE ROBERT EMMETT DOLAN ORCHESTRA.
 Dinah sings, "Coax Me a Little Bit." Her guest is movie-leading man Richard Greene.
BETTY LOU GERSON, GALE GORDON.

THE NEW ADVENTURES OF SHERLOCK HOLMES (MBS) "THE SINGULAR AFFAIR OF THE BACONIAN CIPHER" MAY 27, 1946.

STARS: BASIL RATHBONE, NIGEL BRUCE. ANNOUNCER: HARRY BARTELL. THE DEAN FOSLER ORCHESTRA.
 A newspaper column leads Holmes to a murder case involving a physically disabled Shakespearean actor. Written by Denis Green and Anthony Boucher. Gale Gordon appears after the story to announce his new detective series, *The Casebook of Gregory Hood*, will replace Sherlock Holmes next week.

THE CASEBOOK OF GREGORY HOOD (MBS) (SERIES) JUNE 3 TO SEPTEMBER 16, 1946.

 A world traveler and importer gets involved with various mysteries.
GREGORY HOOD: GALE GORDON
SANDY SANDERSON: WILLIAM BAKEWELL, ART GILMORE, CARL HARBORD, AND HOWARD MCNEAR, ETC.
ANNOUNCER: HARRY BARTELL

Orchestra: Dean Fosler.

Jonathan Trimble, Esquire (MBS) (Series) Summer 1946.

An elderly newspaper editor in 1905 sees his simple way of life changing due to the advances of the new century, and does what he can to fight it.
Jonathan Trimble: Gale Gordon. Mildred: Jean Gillespie. Alice Trimble: Irene Tedrow. Mayor Turner: Earle Ross. Also: Jack Mather, Victor Rodman, Roderick Thomas.
Announcer: Tony LaFrano/Art Gilmore.

Drene Time (NBC) (Series) September 8, 1946 to June 1, 1947.

A married couple, the Bickersons, conduct a non-stop array of humorous arguments. Danny Thomas provides comedy skits and routines.
John Bickerson: Don Ameche. Blanche Bickerson: Frances Langford. Co-Star/Brother Amos: Danny Thomas. Various Roles: Gale Gordon.
Announcer: Tobe Reed. Orchestra: Carmen Dragon. Produced by Carlton Alsop.

The Fabulous Dr. Tweedy (NBC) (Series) October 2, 1946 to March 26, 1947.

A slightly scatterbrained professor is always eager to aid faculty and students at Potts College, but his advice is often not helpful.
Dr. Thaddeus Q. Tweedy: Frank Morgan. Miss Tilsey: Nana Bryant. Sidney Tweedy: Harlan Stone Jr. Mary Potts: Janet Waldo. Timothy Welby: Harry Von Zell. Alexander Potts: Gale Gordon. Beauregard Jackson: Will Wright. Kitty Bell Jackson: Sara Berner. Student: Barbara Eiler. Announcer: John [Bud] Hiestand. Orchestra: Eliot Daniel.

Lux Radio Theater (CBS) "Dragonwyck" October 7, 1946.

Host: William Keighley. Announcers: John Milton Kennedy, Thomas Hanlon. The Louis Silvers Orchestra.
   A menacing estate owner on the 1800s Hudson River acts like a feudal lord, as his young wife discovers the deadly secret he holds. Written for radio by S. H. Barnett from the screenplay by Joseph L. Mankiewicz and the novel by Anya Seton. Directed by Fredric MacKaye.
Miranda: Gene Tierney. Nicholas Van Ryn: Vincent Price. Dr. Jeff Turner: Gale Gordon. Johanna: Margaret M. Meredith. Katrine: Gloria McMillan. Wells: Norman Field. Magda: Janet Scott. Peggy: Truda Marsen. Otto/Dr. Williams: Griff Barnett. DeGrenier/Clergyman: Jay Novello. Bleecker/Man: Jeff Corey. Mother: Sondra Rodgers. Driver/Tomkins: Herbert Lytton. Dirck/Mayor: Charles Seel.
Intermission guest is Mara Carpenter, script supervisor at Warner Brothers.
Doris Singleton, Julie Bannon, and Janet Russell for Lux Soap.

Lux Radio Theater (CBS) "O.S.S." November 18, 1946.

Host: William Keighley. Announcers: John Milton Kennedy, Thomas Hanlon. The Louis Silvers Orchestra.
   The members of American spy unit Team Applejack risk exposure and death in Nazi-occupied France as they work undercover to blow up a vital bridge. Written for radio by S. H. Barnett from the screenplay by Richard Maibaum. Directed by Fredric MacKaye.
Martin: Alan Ladd. Ellen: Veronica Lake. Commander Brady: Gale Gordon. Meister: Joseph Kearns. Bouchet: Richard Benedict. Colonel Field: Charles Seel. Albert/Scientist: Norman Field. Brink: Jay Novello. Gates/Engineer: Rolfe Sedan. Madame Prideaux/Woman: Noreen Gammill. Pilot/Corporal: Ed Emerson. Farmer/First German: George Neise. Gerard: Howard Jeffrey. Second German: Harry Roland. Archibald/Fireman: George Sorel. Girl/Woman: Truda Marsen.

LeFevre: Robert Coote.
Paramount Pictures starlet Lucille Barkley guests during intermission.
Doris Singleton for Lux Soap.

Lux Radio Theater (CBS) "Meet Me in St. Louis" December 2, 1946.

Host: William Keighley. Announcers: John Milton Kennedy, Thomas Hanlon. The Louis Silvers Orchestra.

A close-knit Midwestern family, with four beautiful daughters, copes with the alarming news that they will be moving to New York—at the same time the older girls are dealing with love, heartbreak, and small town life. Judy Garland, who plays Esther, sings "The Boy Next Door," "The Trolley Song," and "Have Yourself a Merry Little Christmas."

Written for radio by S. H. Barnett from the screenplay by Irving Brecher and Fred S. Finklehoffe; and the novel by Sally Benson (along with her *New Yorker* magazine stories). Directed by Fredric MacKaye. Tootsie: Margaret O'Brien. John Truett: Tom Drake. Alonzo: Gale Gordon. Rose: Coleen Gray. Mrs. Smith: Regina Wallace. Grandpa: Norman Field. Lon: Billy Roy. Katie: Noreen Gammill. Costello: Dick Ryan. Warren: Clarke Gordon. Braukoff: Charles Seel. Girl, Act 1: Truda Marsen. Glennie: Johnny McGovern. Johnny: Joel Davis. Tommy: Jerry Farber. Boy: Howard Jeffrey. Girl, Act 2: Lois Kennison.
Metro-Goldwyn-Mayer starlet Lola Dean guests during intermission.
Doris Singleton, Helen Andrews, and Alyn Lockwood for Lux Soap.

Lux Radio Theater (CBS) "Killer Kates" December 16, 1946.

Host: William Keighley. Announcers: John Milton Kennedy, Thomas Hanlon. The Louis Silvers Orchestra.

Jeff Morley (Jack Benny) is a Broadway actor who has played the role of a gangster so often; he comes actually to believe he is Killer Kates, hard-bitten racketeer. Written for radio by S. H. Barnett from the unproduced Warner Brothers movie story "The Man They Couldn't Kill." Directed by Fredric MacKaye.

HELEN: GAIL PATRICK. AL BRADY: ALAN REED. DR. ALBERON: GALE GORDON. NORTON: GERALD MOHR. FRANCES: GEGE PEARSON. MAYOR: NORMAN FIELD. WALTERS: ERIC SNOWDEN. STEVE: HERBERT VIGRAN. McCALL/HOPPY: EDDIE MARR. STANLEY/COP: ED EMERSON. BLINKY/MARIO: JAY NOVELLO. PATCH/FIRST STAGEHAND: DICK RYAN. CHIEF/FIRST COP: KEN CHRISTY. DOORMAN/SECOND STAGEHAND: FRANKLYN PARKER. WAITER/SECOND COP: CHARLES SEEL. SINGER: DORIS SINGLETON.

WARNER BROTHERS STARLET JOAN WINFIELD GUESTS DURING INTERMISSION.

DORIS SINGLETON AND JANET RUSSELL FOR LUX SOAP.

THE FREEDOM TRAIN (SYNDICATED) "THE MAN WITHOUT A COUNTRY" 1947.

COMMENTATOR: GEORGE HICKS. THE VIC SCHOEN ORCHESTRA.

A dramatization of the story of Philip Nolan, who becomes expatriated from America. Bing Crosby recites stanzas from "The Star Spangled Banner" that are not usually heard. Music composed by Victor Young.

THE ANDREWS SISTERS [PATTY, MAXENE, LAVERNE], FRANK LOVEJOY, GALE GORDON.

LUX RADIO THEATER (CBS) "THE GREEN YEARS" JANUARY 13, 1947.

HOST: WILLIAM KEIGHLEY. ANNOUNCERS: JOHN MILTON KENNEDY, THOMAS HANLON. THE LOUIS SILVERS ORCHESTRA.

A young Irish orphan, Robert Shannon, comes to live with the family of his aunt and uncle in Scotland. The lad's search for an understanding friend in the strange country ends when he meets Grandfather Gow (Charles Coburn), who helps him in his many trials as a boy trying to comprehend an alien environment. Written

for radio by S. H. Barnett from the screenplay by Robert Ardrey and Sonya Levien, and the novel by A.J. Cronin. Directed by Fredric MacKaye.
ROBERT: TOM DRAKE. ALISON: BEVERLY TYLER. MR. LECKIE: HUME CRONYN. ROBERT AS A BOY: DEAN STOCKWELL. JASON REID: GALE GORDON. MRS. LECKIE: REGINA WALLACE. GRANDMA: MARY GORDON. MCKELLAR: FREDERIC WORLOCK. MURDOCK: GUY KINGSFORD. KATE: JUNE WHITLEY. PRIEST: ERIC SNOWDEN. BLAKELY: COLIN CAMPBELL. DOCTOR: NORMAN FIELD.
METRO-GOLDWYN-MAYER STARLET LEE WILDE GUESTS DURING INTERMISSION.
DORIS SINGLETON FOR LUX SOAP.

LUX RADIO THEATER (CBS) "CLUNY BROWN" JANUARY 27, 1947.

HOST: WILLIAM KEIGHLEY. ANNOUNCERS: JOHN MILTON KENNEDY, THOMAS HANLON. THE LOUIS SILVERS ORCHESTRA.

An orphaned English girl's uncle sends her to work on a country estate as a servant. She becomes friends with a poor Czech professor, who falls in love with her and tries to keep her from marrying a dull shopkeeper. Written for radio by S. H. Barnett from the screenplay by Samuel Hoffenstein and Elizabeth Reinhardt, and the novel by Marjorie Sharp. Directed by Fredric MacKaye.
ADAM BOLINSKI: CHARLES BOYER. CLUNY BROWN: OLIVIA DE HAVILLAND. SIR HENRY: ALAN REED. MR. WILSON: GALE GORDON. MOTHER: BETTY FAIRFAX. ANDREW: JACK EDWARDS JR. BETTY: CONSTANCE CAVENDISH. SERETT: ERIC SNOWDEN. AMES: EARL HUBBARD. MRS. WILSON/MRS. BAILEY: NOREEN GAMMILL. FORRITY: CHARLES SEEL.
ACTRESS BARBARA LAWRENCE GUESTS DURING INTERMISSION.

LUX RADIO THEATER (CBS) "LEAVE HER TO HEAVEN" MARCH 17, 1947.

HOST: WILLIAM KEIGHLEY. ANNOUNCER: JOHN MILTON KENNEDY. THE LOUIS SILVERS ORCHESTRA.

A woman kills everyone her husband loves to keep him all to herself.

Written for radio by S. H. Barnett from the screenplay by Jo Swerling, and the novel by Ben Ames Williams. Directed by Fredric MacKaye.

ELLEN BARRETT: GENE TIERNEY. GEORGE HARLAND: CORNEL WILDE. RUTH: KAY CHRISTOPHER. GLEN ROBIE: ALAN REED. RUSSELL QUINTON: GALE GORDON. DANNY: TOMMY COOK. LUKE: TIM GRAHAM. MRS. BARRETT: LOUISE LORIMER. DR. MASON/JUDGE: NORMAN FIELD. DR. SAUNDERS/METCALF: BILL [WILLIAM] JOHNSTONE. CONDUCTOR/CARLSON: ALEX GERRY. GUTHRIDGE: CHARLES SEEL.

ACTRESS MARTHA HYER GUESTS DURING INTERMISSION.

DORIS SINGLETON FOR LUX SOAP.

LUX RADIO THEATER (CBS) "HOW GREEN WAS MY VALLEY" MARCH 31, 1947.

HOST: WILLIAM KEIGHLEY. ANNOUNCER: JOHN MILTON KENNEDY. THE LOUIS SILVERS ORCHESTRA.

A close-knit Welsh coal-mining family sees romance, conflict, and tragedy in the sometimes-harsh conditions of life in their labor town. Narrated by Gale Gordon. Written for radio by S. H. Barnett from the screenplay by Philip Dunne, and the novel by Richard Llewellyn. Directed by Fredric MacKaye.

MR. GRUFFYDD: DAVID NIVEN. ANGHARAD: MAUREEN O'SULLIVAN. MR. MORGAN: DONALD CRISP. BETH MORGAN: SARA ALLGOOD. HUW AS A BOY: JOHNNY MCGOVERN. IANTO: TONY BARRETT. DAVY: CLARKE GORDON. DAI: IRA GROSSEL [JEFF CHANDLER]. YOUNG SPOILER: BILL [WILLIAM] JOHNSTONE. DR. RICHARDS: FREDERIC WORLOCK. MAN: RAMSEY HILL. MRS. NICHOLS: CLAIRE VERDERA. BOY: HOWARD JEFFREY. ENID/WOMAN: JUNE WHITLEY. IVOR/MAN: CHARLES SEEL. AD LIBS: CAROLE SUE LEEDS, BETTY GRANNIS. ALSO: NORMAN FIELD.

ACTRESS RANDY STUART GUESTS DURING INTERMISSION.

DORIS SINGLETON AND JANET RUSSELL FOR LUX SOAP.

Johnny Madero, Pier 23 (MBS) (Series) April 24 to September 4, 1947.

A waterfront private detective tracks down murderers, staying one-step ahead of the police.
Johnny Madero: Jack Webb. Father Leahy: Gale Gordon. Officer Warcheck: William Conrad. Announcer: Tony LaFrano. Orchestra: Harry Zimmerman.
Produced by Richard Breen.

The Life of Riley (NBC) May 10, 1947.

Stars: William Bendix, Paula Winslowe, John Brown, Tommy Cook, Barbara Eiler. Announcer: Ken Carpenter. The Lou Kosloff Orchestra.
It can only happen to Riley: a batch of his mother's doughnuts gets him into trouble with the local Mother's Day Committee. Written by Alan Lipscott and Reuben Shipp.
Gale Gordon, Jane Morgan.

The Greatest Story Ever Told (ABC) "The Fruitless Fig Tree" June 1, 1947.

Star: Warren Parker. Announcer: Norman Rose.
A gardener stakes his job on the eventual success of a struggling tree.
Gale Gordon, Mercedes McCambridge.

Lux Radio Theater (CBS) "One More Tomorrow" June 9, 1947.

Host: William Keighley. Announcer: John Milton Kennedy. The Louis Silvers Orchestra.
Wealthy playboy Tom meets an ambitious young photographer named Christie and becomes interested in her, as well as in the publishing business. With their new magazine a success, Tom proposes

to Christie—but her preoccupation with her career leads Christie to reject him. Along comes scheming beauty Cecilia attracted by Tom's wealth and social prestige. Cecilia's machinations prompt Christie to begin seeing Tom in a new perspective. Written for radio by S. H. Barnett from the screenplay by Charles Hoffman and Catherine Turney, and the play *The Animal Kingdom* by Philip Barry. Directed by Fredric MacKaye.
TOM: DENNIS MORGAN. CHRISTIE: JANE WYMAN. CECILIA: ALEXIS SMITH. JIM: GALE GORDON. PAT: IRA GROSSEL [JEFF CHANDLER]. FRAN: FRANCES ROBINSON. RUFUS: WILLIAM JOHNSTONE. OWEN/MAN IN ACT 2: STANLEY WAXMAN. WAITER/MAN IN ACT 3: CHARLES SEEL. AD LIBS: EDWIN MILLS, GORDON GRAY, FLORIDA EDWARDS, AND DOROTHY GARNER.
ACTRESS MARIA PALMER GUESTS DURING INTERMISSION.
DORIS SINGLETON AND TRUDA MARSEN FOR LUX SOAP.

THE NEW ADVENTURES OF SHERLOCK HOLMES (ABC) "DEATH IN THE NORTH SEA" JUNE 16, 1947.

STARS: TOM CONWAY, NIGEL BRUCE. ANNOUNCER: JOSEPH BELL. THE ALEX STEINERT ORCHESTRA.
  Aboard an ocean liner, Holmes comes to the aid of an innocent man suspected of murder. Sherlock recruits a French woman to help in his defense, which hinges on an odd clue: a scratch on a porthole. Written by Anthony Boucher and Denis Green.
GALE GORDON.
MODEL AGENCY HEAD JOHN POWERS AND ONE OF HIS MODELS, ELLEN ALLARDICE, DO A COMMERCIAL FOR KREML SHAMPOO.

THE NEW ADVENTURES OF SHERLOCK HOLMES (ABC) "THE ADVENTURE OF THE SPECKLED BAND" JUNE 23, 1947.

STARS: TOM CONWAY, NIGEL BRUCE. ANNOUNCER: JOSEPH BELL. THE ALEX STEINERT ORCHESTRA.
  A woman fears for her life after her sister is killed. Holmes and Watson offer their protection as they search for the murderer. Written

for radio by Anthony Boucher and Denis Green, from the story by Sir Arthur Conan Doyle.
GALE GORDON.

CAVALCADE OF AMERICA (NBC) "THE RED STOCKINGS" AUGUST 25, 1947.

ANNOUNCER: FRANK BINGMAN.
THE ROBERT ARMBRUSTER ORCHESTRA.
　A baseball story about Albert Spalding (John Hodiak), one-time captain and pitcher for the Boston Red Stockings, who devotes his career to producing sturdy sporting equipment and opposing crooks who take advantage of amateur players. Written for radio by Lucy Kennedy from the book *America's National Game* by Albert Spalding.
SARAH: MARY JANE CROFT. JONES: FRED HOWARD. THE JUDGE: GALE GORDON. MOTHER: JANE MORGAN. GROWLEY: GERALD MOHR. GAYNE WHITMAN FOR DUPONT CHEMICAL COMPANY.

LUX RADIO THEATER (CBS) "THE SEVENTH VEIL" SEPTEMBER 15, 1947.

HOST: WILLIAM KEIGHLEY. ANNOUNCER: JOHN MILTON KENNEDY. THE LOUIS SILVERS ORCHESTRA.
　A psychiatrist attempts to resolve the romantic dilemmas of a young feminine concert pianist, who has fallen into a complex and bewildering emotional condition at the hands of her disturbed cousin. Narcosis, hypnosis, and musical therapy are needed to snatch the last veil of reserve from her tortured mind and restore the girl's sanity. Written for radio by S. H. Barnett from the screenplay by Muriel and Sydney Box. Directed by Fredric MacKaye.
NICHOLAS BRANDT: JOSEPH COTTEN. FRANCESCA CUNNINGHAM: IDA LUPINO. DR. LARSON: JOE [JOSEPH] KEARNS. MALLIAM JOHNSTONE. SUSAN: FRANCES ROBINSON. PARKER: NORMAN FIELD. ALSO: GALE GORDON, JANET SCOTT, JUNE WHITLEY. PIANO PASSAGES PLAYED BY IGNACE HILSBERG.
UNIVERSAL-INTERNATIONAL STARLET PATRICIA ALPHIN GUESTS DURING INTERMISSION.

Dorothy Lovett for Lux Soap.

Cavalcade of America (NBC) "Big Boy" September 29, 1947.

Announcer: Frank Bingman. The Robert Armbruster Orchestra.
   Due to the influence of his orphanage coach, baseball great Babe Ruth (Brian Donlevy) holds close the lessons he learned early in life and becomes the most beloved figure in American baseball . . . especially as a hero to the country's youngsters. Written by Brice Disque Jr. Directed by Jack Zoller.
Peanuts and Popcorn/Sports Announcer: Sidney Miller. Cold Drinks/The Italian: Milton Herman. Man/Umpire: Alan Reed. Boy/Kid One: Jimmy Ogg. Babe Ruth as a Boy/Kid Two: Tommy Bernard. Friend/Johnny: Henry Blair. Mathias/Huggins: Howard McNear. Dunn/The Catcher: Gale Gordon. Barrow/Doctor: Fred Howard. Father/Voice: Joseph Bell. Nurse: Ann Tobin.
Gayne Whitman for DuPont Chemical Company.

The Great Gildersleeve (NBC) November 12, 1947.

Stars: Harold Peary, Walter Tetley, Louise Erickson, Lillian Randolph, Earle Ross, Richard LeGrand, Arthur Q. Bryan, Ken Christy. Announcer: John Wald. The Jack Meakin Orchestra.
   A crook is selling coats and rings in Summerfield and Gildy (Peary) becomes his best customer. Written by John Elliotte and Andy White.
W.R. Fowler: Gale Gordon. Officer: Stanley Farrar.
Song:
   Louise Erickson (as Marjorie): "Civilization"

A Day in the Life of Dennis Day (NBC) January 14, 1948.

Stars: Dennis Day, Barbara Eiler, Francis 'Dink' Trout, Bea Benaderet, John Brown. Announcer: Verne Smith. The Charles

'Bud' Dant Orchestra.

Mr. Anderson (Trout) recruits Dennis to help him steal a painting from Mrs. Anderson (Benaderet) to keep her from learning a certain uncomfortable truth about the artwork. Dennis sings "With a Hey and a Hi and a Ho, Ho, Ho." Written by Frank Galen.
Gale Gordon.
Ken Carson (vocalist) for Lustre Crème Shampoo.

The Great Gildersleeve (NBC) January 28, 1948.

Stars: Harold Peary, Walter Tetley, Louise Erickson, Lillian Randolph, Richard LeGrand, Earle Ross, Arthur Q. Bryan, Ken Christy. Announcer: John Wald. The Jack Meakin Orchestra.

While Gildersleeve lobbies Chief Gates to be accepted into a traveling barbershop quartet, Gildy neglects to obtain his 1948 license plates for his car. Written by John Elliotte and Andy White.
Desk Sergeant: Gale Gordon.

A Day in the Life of Dennis Day (NBC) March 24, 1948.

Stars: Dennis Day, Barbara Eiler, Francis 'Dink' Trout, Bea Benaderet, John Brown. Announcer: Verne Smith. The Charles 'Bud' Dant Orchestra.

Dennis purchases a taxicab hoping to earn more money, but he also buys trouble when he overhears a passenger's plans to take over Weaverville in a land-grab scheme. Dennis sings "Zippity-Doo-Dah." Written by Frank Galen.
Gale Gordon, Frank Nelson.
Ken Carson (vocalist) for Lustre Crème Shampoo.

Junior Miss (CBS) (Series) April 3, 1948 to July 1, 1954.

Situation comedy concerning the misadventures of teenager Judy Graves, an often-unpredictable fifteen-year-old.
Judy Graves: Barbara Whiting. Harry Graves, her father:

GALE GORDON. GRACE GRAVES: SARAH SELBY. LOIS GRAVES: PEGGY KNUDSEN. FUFFY ADAMS: BEVERLY WILLS. HILDA: MYRA MARSH.
ANNOUNCER: JOHNNY JACOBS
PRODUCED BY FRAN VAN HARTESVELDT.

OLD GOLD TIME (CBS) APRIL 16, 1948.

STARS: DON AMECHE, FRANCES LANGFORD, FRANK MORGAN. ANNOUNCER: MARVIN MILLER. THE CARMEN DRAGON ORCHESTRA.
   Frank has some misadventures as a lawyer. The Bickersons (Ameche, Langford) attempt to go on vacation in a trailer. Written by Phil Rapp.
GALE GORDON.

CAVALCADE OF AMERICA (NBC) "THE ENLIGHTENED PROFESSOR" MAY 24, 1948.

ANNOUNCER: TED PEARSON. THE DONALD BRYAN ORCHESTRA.
   Benjamin Silliman (Franchot Tone) introduces the study of chemistry at Yale University in 1802. He overcomes vigorous resistance from staid scholars and uses his ill-equipped basement laboratory as a stepping-stone to establish a legitimate field of education in America. Written by Robert Anderson and Bernard Victor Dryer from the biography Benjamin Silliman: Pathfinder in American Science by John F. Fulton and Elizabeth Thomson. Directed by Jack Zoller.
GALE GORDON.
BILL HAMILTON FOR DUPONT CHEMICAL COMPANY.

THE GREAT GILDERSLEEVE (NBC) (SERIES) MAY 26, 1948 TO MARCH 19, 1952.

   Throckmorton P. Gildersleeve, Water Commissioner of Summerfield, raises his orphaned niece and nephew while getting into comedic predicaments.
THROCKMORTON P. GILDERSLEEVE: HAROLD PEARY/WILLARD

Waterman. Rumson Bullard: Gale Gordon. LeRoy Forrester: Walter Tetley. Marjorie Forrester Thompson: Louise Erickson/Marylee Robb. Birdie Lee Coggins: Lillian Randolph. Leila Ransom: Shirley Mitchell. Judge Horace Hooker: Earle Ross. Mr. Peavey: Richard LeGrand. Floyd Munson: Arthur Q. Bryan. Police Chief Gates: Ken Christy. Adelaine Fairchild: Una Merkel. Eve Goodwin: Bea Benaderet. Kathryn Milford: Cathy Lewis. Bronco Thompson: Richard Crenna. Craig Bullard: Tommy Bernard. Bessie: Gloria Holliday.
Announcer: John Wald/Jay Stewart/Jim Doyle/John 'Bud' Hiestand
Orchestra: Jack Meakin/Robert Armbruster
Produced by Frank Pittman.

Old Gold Time (CBS) May 28, 1948.

Stars: Don Ameche, Frances Langford, Frank Morgan. Announcer: Marvin Miller. The Carmen Dragon Orchestra.

The Bickersons have some sumptuous digs in which to stage their latest brouhaha—the Presidential suite of a San Francisco Hotel.
Gale Gordon.

Meet Me in St. Louis (ABC) (Audition Show) May 29, 1948.

A family at the turn of the 20th century has humorous adventures. A big dance and a batch of fudge figure in this radio pilot for a proposed series.
The cast includes Margaret Whiting, Norma Jean Nilsson, Gale Gordon, Lois Moran, Betsy Blair, Rosa Williams, Edwin Mills, William Johnstone, Henrietta Tedrow, and Eric Lord. Ken Peters is announcer and Walter Schumann conducts the orchestra.

The Little Immigrant (CBS) (Audition Show) June 15, 1948.

Luigi Basco (J. Carrol Naish), a new arrival on American shores, sets up an antique business in Chicago. His initial experience in his new homeland is an upsetting one—he may be forced to part with his prized statue of George Washington. Written by Cy Howard and Hy Kraft. Radio pilot for the CBS series *Life with Luigi*, which ran from 1948 to 1954. Producer-director-writer Cy Howard serves as host for this presentation.
Also in the cast: Alan Reed, Mary Jane Croft, Gale Gordon, Bobby Ellis. Wilbur Hatch conducts the orchestra.

A Day in the Life of Dennis Day (NBC) June 23, 1948.

Stars: Dennis Day, Barbara Eiler, Francis 'Dink' Trout, Bea Benaderet, John Brown. Announcer: Verne Smith. The Charles 'Bud' Dant Orchestra.
Dennis bets on a horse by mistake and is desperate to keep the bookie from telephoning the wager in to gambling boss Big Sam. Dennis sings "When the Red, Red Robin Comes Bob-Bob-Bobbing Along." Written by Frank Galen.
Gale Gordon.
Ken Carson (vocalist) for Lustre Crème Shampoo.

Our Miss Brooks (CBS) (Series) August 9, 1948 to July 7, 1957.

Connie Brooks is a high school teacher who hopes to find romance with shy biology instructor Philip Boynton and relief from grumpy principal Osgood T. Conklin.
Connie Brooks: Eve Arden. Osgood T. Conklin: Gale Gordon. Philip Boynton: Jeff Chandler/Robert Rockwell. Walter Denton: Richard Crenna. Mrs. Margaret Davis: Jane Morgan. Harriet Conklin: Gloria McMillan. Announcer: Bob Lemond. Orchestra: Wilbur Hatch.
Produced by Larry Berns.

My Favorite Husband (CBS) (Series) July 23, 1948 to March 31, 1951.

Banker George Cooper may have a zany wife, but they are a married couple who "live together and like it."
Liz Cooper: Lucille Ball. George Cooper: Richard Denning. Rudolph Atterbury, George's boss: Gale Gordon. Iris Atterbury: Bea Benaderet. Katie the maid: Ruth Perrott. Announcer: Bob Lemond. Orchestra: Wilbur Hatch.
Produced by Jess Oppenheimer.

Life with Luigi (CBS) September 21, 1948.

Stars: J. Carrol Naish, Alan Reed, Gil Stratton. Announcer: Bob Lemond. The Wilbur Hatch Orchestra.
First show of the series. A new arrival to America's shores, Luigi Basco (Naish) may be forced to part with his prized statue of George Washington. A re-staging of the 6/15/48 audition show.
Gale Gordon.

Blackstone the Magic Detective (MBS-Syndicated) (Series) 1948 to 1949.

A professional magician also solves mysteries and crime cases.
Harry Blackstone: Ed Jerome. John: Ted Osborne. Rhoda: Fran Carlon. Various Roles: Gale Gordon. Announcer: Don Hancock/Alan Kent. Organist: Bill Meeder.

The NBC University Theater (NBC) "Gulliver's Travels" September 24, 1948.

Announcer: Don Stanley. The Henry Russell Orchestra.
Following a shipwreck, sailor Gulliver washes up on the shores of the kingdom called Lilliput—inhabited by people much smaller than the now gigantic Gulliver. Written for radio by Frank Wells,

from the book by Jonathan Swift.
ANTHONY BORIS, CLIFF CLARK, GALE GORDON, HENRY HULL, JACK CARROLL, JACK KRUSCHEN, KEN CHRISTY, SI STEVENS, STANLEY FARRAR.

THE PHIL HARRIS-ALICE FAYE SHOW (NBC) (SERIES) OCTOBER 3, 1948 TO JUNE 18, 1954.

A brash and vain bandleader—and family man—falls into comedic predicaments despite the levelheaded advice of his wife, a one-time movie star.
PHIL HARRIS: HIMSELF. ALICE FAYE: HERSELF. FRANKIE REMLEY/ELLIOTT LEWIS: ELLIOTT LEWIS. JULIUS ABBRUZIO: WALTER TETLEY. LITTLE ALICE FAYE (JR.): JEANINE ROOS. PHYLLIS FAYE: ANNE WHITFIELD. WILLIE FAYE: ROBERT NORTH/JOHN HUBBARD. MR. SCOTT, SPONSOR'S REPRESENTATIVE/VARIOUS CHARACTERS: GALE GORDON. ANNOUNCER: BILL FORMAN. ORCHESTRA: WALTER SCHARF. PRODUCED BY PAUL PHILLIPS.

THE CHARLIE MCCARTHY SHOW (NBC) (SERIES) OCTOBER 3 TO DECEMBER 25, 1948.

Comedy-variety centering on a mild-mannered ventriloquist mentor and his monocle-wearing dummy.
STAR/CHARLIE MCCARTHY/MORTIMER SNERD/EFFIE KLINKER: EDGAR BERGEN. REGULAR/JOHN BICKERSON: DON AMECHE. BLANCHE BICKERSON: MARSHA HUNT. REGULAR: GALE GORDON. VOCALIST: ANITA GORDON. ANNOUNCER: KEN CARPENTER. ORCHESTRA: RAY NOBLE.
COMMERCIAL SPOKESMEN (VOCALISTS: THURL RAVENSCROFT/THE JAVA JIVERS
PRODUCED BY EARL EBI.
13 BROADCASTS.

Tell It Again (CBS) "Gulliver's Travels" December 12, 1948.

Narrator: Marvin Miller. Announcer: Murray Wagner. Organist: Del Castillo.

After a shipwreck, sailor Gulliver washes up on the shores of the kingdom called Lilliput—inhabited by people much smaller than the now gigantic Gulliver. Written for radio by Ralph Rose, from the book by Jonathan Swift.
Henry Hull, Ken Christy, Gale Gordon.

A Day in the Life of Dennis Day (NBC) January 29, 1949.

Stars: Dennis Day, Barbara Eiler, Francis 'Dink' Trout, Bea Benaderet, John Brown. Announcer: Verne Smith. The Charles 'Bud' Dant Orchestra.

Dennis goes to Weaverville University to help Mrs. Anderson (Benaderet) remove a black mark from her college record. Through a mix-up, he is declared a genius when he takes an exam and his absent-minded professor gives him 100%. Dennis sings "Gal in Galveston." Written by Frank Galen.
Gale Gordon, Frank Nelson.
Ken Carson (vocalist) for Lustre Crème Shampoo.

Lux Radio Theater (CBS) "Sitting Pretty" February 14, 1949.

Host: William Keighley. Announcer: John Milton Kennedy. The Louis Silvers Orchestra.

Mr. Lynn Belvedere (Clifton Webb), a stodgy intellectual, accepts a job looking after a family's three deplorably behaved children. Written for radio by S. H. Barnett from the screenplay by F. Hugh Herbert, and the novel *Belvedere* by Gwen Davenport. Directed by Fredric MacKaye.
Tacey: Maureen O'Hara. Harry: Robert Young. Appleton: Gale Gordon. Hammond: Ed Begley. Edna: Frances Robinson. Bill King: Eddie Marr. Radio Announcer: Bill [William] Johnstone. Radio Announcer/Mr. Taylor: Ken Christy.

CHIEF OF POLICE: CLIFF CLARK. RODDY: LEONE LEDOUX. ALSO: DONALD RANDOLPH, JOHNNY MCGOVERN, JEFFREY SILVER, BOB GRIFFIN, GEORGE NEISE, DAVID LIGHT.
ACTRESS HELEN WESTCOTT GUESTS DURING INTERMISSION.
DOROTHY LOVETT FOR LUX SOAP.

SWEET ADELINE (AUDITION SHOW) APRIL 30, 1949.

Adeline (Una Merkel), who lives with her brother, is wary of his girlfriend—a woman named Peaches Parker. Adeline goes to extremes to keep the pair separated. Unsuccessful radio pilot for a proposed series.
LILLIAN RANDOLPH, GALE GORDON.

MY FRIEND IRMA (CBS) MAY 30, 1949.

STARS: MARIE WILSON, JOAN BANKS, JOHN BROWN, LEIF ERICKSON, GLORIA GORDON, HANS CONRIED. ANNOUNCER: FRANK BINGMAN. THE LUD GLUSKIN ORCHESTRA.
Irma and Al (Wilson, Brown) foul up a surprise birthday party for Mrs. Rhinelander by telling her Mr. Rhinelander is seeing another woman, 'Helen Two' (the name of the cabin cruiser that Mrs. Rhinelander is receiving as a gift).
MRS. RHINELANDER: MYRA MARSH. MR. RHINELANDER: GALE GORDON.

THE HALLS OF IVY (NBC) (AUDITION SHOW 1) "DR. HALL'S REAPPOINTMENT" JUNE 22, 1949.

Dr. William Todhunter Hall (Gale Gordon) awaits word of his reappointment as president of Ivy College. Written by Don Quinn. Directed by Nat Wolff.
VICTORIA HALL: EDNA BEST. ALSO: HERBERT RAWLINSON, GLORIA GORDON, HERB BUTTERFIELD, WILLARD WATERMAN, LEE MILLAR, NORMAN FIELD, LEO CLEARY.

Don Stanley is announcer. Henry Russell conducts the orchestra.

The Halls of Ivy (NBC) (Audition Show 2) "Dr. Hall's Reappointment" June 23, 1949.

A re-staging of Audition Show 1, built around the framework of a man trying to convince a father (Don Quinn) which college his son should attend. (Same cast as Audition Show 1, plus Peter Leeds as Pushy Morgan).

Note: This audition was a private presentation for potential sponsors. The show passed the grade, but the roles of Dr. and Mrs. Hall were ultimately assumed by real-life husband/wife actors Ronald Colman and Benita Hume for both the radio and later television versions of the show.

Guest Star (Syndicated) September 25, 1949.

Announcers: Charles Woods, Harlow Wilcox. Harry Sosnik and the Savings Bond Orchestra.

Fibber McGee (Jim Jordan) hatches another plan to make some quick money. Song: "I'm in Love with a Wonderful Guy."
Molly: Marian Jordan. Mayor LaTrivia: Gale Gordon.

The Jimmy Durante Show (NBC) October 21, 1949.

Stars: Jimmy Durante, Don Ameche, Barbara Jo Allen, Candy Candido, Elvia Allman, Florence Halop, Sara Berner. Vocalists: The Crew Chiefs. Announcer: Howard Petrie. The Roy Bargy Orchestra.

Jimmy and Don have hopes for a television deal with Frank Collins (Gale Gordon) of NBC. Collins is a football devotee of the University of Southern California, but Jimmy gets tickets for a UCLA game. Unable to replace the tickets, Jimmy brings over a TV set he bought from two sharpsters. Jimmy sings "P.S. 33."

RONALD FRISBY: FRANK NELSON. REPORTER/MR. BAILEY: HERB VIGRAN. BAGGAGE MAN/JOE: JERRY HAUSNER.
GEORGE BARCLAY FOR CAMEL CIGARETTES AND ED CHANDLER FOR PRINCE ALBERT PIPE TOBACCO.

THE HALLS OF IVY (NBC) (SERIES) MAY 10, 1950 TO JUNE 25, 1952.

A cultured college president and his wife deal with students and faculty as they take on the various situations that befall the school.
DR. WILLIAM TODHUNTER HALL: RONALD COLMAN. VICTORIA CROMWELL HALL: BENITA HUME. CLARENCE WELLMAN: HERB BUTTERFIELD. JOHN MERRIWEATHER: WILLARD WATERMAN. CHARLES MERRIWEATHER: GALE GORDON. MALE CHORUS: LES BAXTER, GIL MERSHON, BERNIE PARKS, THURL RAVENSCROFT. ANNOUNCER: KEN CARPENTER. ORCHESTRA: HENRY RUSSELL
PRODUCED BY DON QUINN, NAT WOLFF.

THE PENNY SINGLETON SHOW (NBC) (SERIES) MAY 30 TO SEPTEMBER 26, 1950.

Penny Williamson and her daughters make their way in a world where the men are less than perfect.
PENNY WILLIAMSON: PENNY SINGLETON. SUE WILLIAMSON: SHEILAH JAMES. DOROTHY 'D.G.' WILLIAMSON: MARYLEE ROBB. HORACE WIGGINS: JIM BACKUS. JUDGE BESHOMER GRUNDELL: GALE GORDON. MARGARET THE COOK: BEA BENADERET. ANNOUNCER: FRANK MARTIN. ORCHESTRA: VON DEXTER.
PRODUCED BY ROBERT SOTOBERG.

GRANBY'S GREEN ACRES (NBC) (SERIES) JULY 3 TO AUGUST 21, 1950.

John Granby, a city bank clerk, takes his wife to the country—where they set up living as farmers . . . and discover a whole series of comedic problems.
JOHN GRANBY: GALE GORDON. MARTHA GRANBY: BEA BENADERET.

Janice Granby: Louise Erickson, Shirley Mitchell (audition show). Eb: Parley Baer. Announcer: Bob Lemond. Orchestra: Opie Cates.
Produced by Jay Sommers.

The Lucky Strike Program Starring Jack Benny (CBS) October 1, 1950.

Stars: Jack Benny, Mary Livingstone, Dennis Day, Phil Harris, Eddie 'Rochester' Anderson. Vocalists: The Sportsmen Quartet. Announcer: Don Wilson. The Mahlon Merrick Orchestra.

After a lunch stop at the corner drugstore, Jack finds out that his beloved old Maxwell auto has been stolen. He and Rochester go to the police station to report the theft. Written by Milt Josefsberg, Sam Perrin, George Balzer, and John Tackaberry. Mr. Kitzel: Artie Auerbach. Gertrude: Bea Benaderet. Sergeant Vandermeer: Gale Gordon. Mabel: Sara Berner. Drugstore Clerk: Joseph Kearns. Sergeant Carey: Elliott Lewis. Mr. Cassidy: Marty Sperzel. Police Woman: Blanche Stewart. Mervyn/Page/Mad Man Muntz/Woody Woodpecker/Car 28/Maxwell: Mel Blanc.
L.A. 'Speed' Riggs and Del Sharbutt for Lucky Strike Cigarettes.

Mr. and Mrs. Blandings (NBC) (Series) January 21 to June 17, 1951.

A suburban couple attempt to live their ideal existence by building a dream house in the country . . . but run into unexpected complications.
Jim Blandings: Cary Grant. Muriel Blandings: Betsy Drake. Bill Cole, their friend: Gale Gordon. Susan Blandings: Anne Whitfield. Joan Blandings: Patricia Ianola. Janette/Maude: Gail Bonney. Margaret: Jeanne Bates. Announcer: Wendell Niles/Don Stanley. Orchestra: Bernard Katz.

Produced by Nat Wolff.

A Day in the Life of Dennis Day (NBC) February 17, 1951.

Stars: Dennis Day, Barbara Eiler, Bea Benaderet. Announcer: Verne Smith. The Charles 'Bud' Dant Orchestra.
  Gloria (Eiler) is tired of waiting for Dennis to propose, so she makes plans to marry British writer Basil Featherstone. To compete, Dennis becomes an English gentleman—accent, spats, cane and all. Dennis sings "Be-Gilly, Be-Golly, Begorrah." Written by Keith Fowler, Lester White, and Bill Manhoff.
Gale Gordon, Veola Vonn, Paul Frees.
Ken Carson (vocalist) for Lustre Crème Shampoo.

All About Anne (CBS) (Audition Show) March 30, 1951.

  Unsuccessful radio pilot for a proposed series about a Scarsdale family and their teenage daughter.
Gale Gordon, Gil Stratton, Margaret Whiting.

Lux Radio Theater (CBS) "Samson and Delilah" November 19, 1951.

Host: William Keighley. Announcer: John Milton Kennedy. The Rudy Schrager Orchestra.
  The Biblical story of strongman, Samson (Victor Mature), who falls madly in love with a beautiful Philistine woman, Delilah (Hedy Lamarr). Narrated by Gale Gordon. Written for radio by S. H. Barnett from the screenplay by Jesse L. Lasky Jr. and Fredric M. Frank (treatment by Harold Lamb), based on the novel *Judge and Fool* by Vladimir Jabotinsky and the Biblical passages Judges 13-16.
Saran: Edgar Barrier. Ahtur: Leif Erickson. Minoah: Herbert Rawlinson. Hisham: Hope Sansbury. Hazel: Norma Varden.
Also: Kay Stewart, Lynn Allen, Herb Butterfield, Jeffrey Silver, Bill [Willis] Bouchey, Jonathan Hole, Theodore von

Eltz, Robert Griffin, Bill [William] Johnstone, Eddie Marr. Paramount starlet Nancy Hale guests during intermission. Dorothy Lovett for Lux Soap.

Lux Radio Theater (CBS) "Alice in Wonderland" December 24, 1951.

Host: William Keighley. Announcer: John Milton Kennedy. The Rudy Schrager Orchestra.

A young girl falls down a rabbit hole and experiences a parade of surreal happenings with a host of greatly eccentric characters. Written for radio by S. H. Barnett from the screenplay by Winston Hibler, Bill Peete, Joe Rinaldi, Bill Cottrell, Joe Grant, Dell Connell, Ted Sears, Erdman Penner, Milt Banta, Dick Kelsie, Dick Huemer, Ted Orab, and John Walbridge; and the novel by Lewis Carroll. Directed by Earl Ebi.

Mad Hatter: Ed Wynn. Alice: Kathy Beaumont. March Hare: Jerry Colonna. Cheshire Cat: Sterling Holloway. White Rabbit: Bill Thompson. Caterpillar: Gale Gordon. Queen of Hearts: Verna Felton. The Doorknob: Joe [Joseph] Kearns. Tweedle Dee: Gil Stratton Jr. Also: Jack Kruschen, Doris Lloyd, Norma Varden, Jonathan Hole, Margie Liszt, Marian Richmond, Leone Ledoux, Eddie Marr, David Light.

Songs:
  Alice: "In a World of My Own"
  Tweedle Dum, Tweedle Dee: "Very Good Advice"
  Tweedle Dum, Tweedle Dee, Walrus: "The Walrus and the Carpenter"
  Tweedle Dum, Tweedle Dee, Walrus, Carpenter: "Father William"
  Mad Hatter, Queen of Hearts, March Hare: "The Unbirthday Song"

Walt Disney actress Adriana Caselotti guests during intermission. Dorothy Lovett for Lux Soap.

The Adventures of Ozzie and Harriet (ABC) "April 18, 1952.

Stars: Ozzie Nelson, Harriet Hilliard [Nelson], David Nelson, Ricky Nelson, John Brown. Announcer: Verne Smith. The Billy May Orchestra.

Ozzie finds nothing but disinterest when he puts his efforts toward keeping a baseball team in town.
Gale Gordon.

Richard Diamond, Private Detective (CBS) "The Steak Knife Case" September 6, 1953.

Stars: Dick Powell, Frances Robinson, Arthur Q. Bryan, Wilms Herbert. Announcer: Bill Forman. The Frank Worth Orchestra.

Diamond (Powell) aids a young woman when she is found holding a smoking gun over a man who has already been stabbed to death. Written by Blake Edwards.
Gale Gordon.

My Little Margie (CBS) April 10, 1955.

Stars: Gale Storm, Charles Farrell, Verna Felton, Gil Stratton Jr., Will Wright. Announcer: Roy Rowan. The Lud Gluskin Orchestra.

Margie has a unique way to get the apartment redecorated: tell everyone a fortune in stolen pearls is hidden there. Directed by Gordon T. Hughes.
Gale Gordon.

Same Time, Same Station (KRLA-Pasadena, California) "Jimmy Durante Remembers Radio" November 12 and 19, 1972.

Announcer: Bill Browning.

A recording of a Durante show from 1933 highlights Jimmy's

look back at his days on radio.
ROY BARGY, GALE GORDON, PHIL COHAN, GARRY MOORE.

FIBBER MCGEE AND THE GOOD OLD DAYS OF RADIO (SYNDICATED) (SPECIAL) JUNE 9, 1974.

ANNOUNCER: LARRY THOR.
The seventh installment in a seven-part special series. Jim Jordan reprises his role as Fibber McGee, who is fiddling around with an antique radio when Chuck Schaden drops by. They discover the radio tunes in shows from the past. Tonight, the spotlight falls on programs that originally aired on Saturdays: *Let's Pretend, The Judy Canova Show, Grand Central Station, The Life of Riley,* and *Truth or Consequences.* Gale Gordon makes a guest appearance as Mayor LaTrivia.

TELEVISION APPEARANCES

THE MARIONETTE MYSTERY (NETWORK UNKNOWN) 1950.

Regis Toomey presents a murder mystery with the various players giving their own impressions of what occurred.
DOCTOR: GALE GORDON. ALSO: GLORIA HOLDEN, JOHN HOYT, JANET SCOTT.

I LOVE LUCY (CBS) "LUCY'S SCHEDULE" MAY 26, 1952.

STARS: LUCILLE BALL, DESI ARNAZ, VIVIAN VANCE, WILLIAM FRAWLEY.
ANNOUNCER: JAY JACKSON.
WILBUR HATCH CONDUCTS THE DESI ARNAZ ORCHESTRA.
Ricky and Lucy (Arnaz, Ball) get off on the wrong foot with the Tropicana Club's new owner, Mr. Alvin Littlefield, when they are late for his dinner invitation. Ricky then puts Lucy on a tight schedule, which does not sit well with Ethel (Vance) and the club-owner's wife, Phoebe Littlefield. When the two women tell Lucy her

'buckling-under' is spoiling things for females everywhere, the trio plot a proper revenge.
ALVIN LITTLEFIELD: GALE GORDON. PHOEBE LITTLEFIELD: EDITH MEISER.

I LOVE LUCY (CBS) "RICKY ASKS FOR A RAISE" JUNE 9, 1952.

STARS: LUCILLE BALL, DESI ARNAZ, VIVIAN VANCE, WILLIAM FRAWLEY. ANNOUNCER: ROY ROWAN.
WILBUR HATCH CONDUCTS THE DESI ARNAZ ORCHESTRA.

Lucy's impatience with Ricky asking for a raise prompts her to a scheme to convince Mr. Alvin Littlefield (Gale Gordon) that Ricky has had some great offers extended by other clubs. The ploy backfires when Littlefield—not wanting to stand in Ricky's way—replaces him with Xavier Valdez. To save Ricky's job, Lucy schemes with Fred and Ethel (Frawley, Vance) to make Valdez look bad.
MAURICE THE HEADWAITER: MAURICE MARSAC. PHOEBE LITTLEFIELD: EDITH MEISER.

OUR MISS BROOKS (CBS) (SERIES) OCTOBER 3, 1952 TO SEPTEMBER 21, 1956.

A loveable, lovesick, wisecracking English teacher interacts with her madcap friends at Madison High School.
CONNIE BROOKS: EVE ARDEN. OSGOOD P. CONKLIN, SCHOOL PRINCIPAL: GALE GORDON. PHILIP BOYNTON: ROBERT ROCKWELL. WALTER DENTON: RICHARD CRENNA (1952-55). MRS. MARGARET DAVIS: JANE MORGAN. HARRIET CONKLIN: GLORIA McMILLAN (1952-55). STRETCH SNODGRASS: LEONARD SMITH (1952-55). MISS DAISY ENRIGHT: MARY JANE CROFT (1952-54). MRS. MARTHA CONKLIN: VIRGINIA GORDON (1952-53)/PAULA WINSLOWE (1953-56). SUPERINTENDENT STONE: JOSEPH KEARNS (1953-55). ANGELA: JESSLYN FAX (1954-56). RICKY VELASCO: RICKY VERA (1954-55). MR. OLIVER MUNSEY: BOB SWEENEY (1955-56). MRS. NESTOR: NANA BRYANT (1955)/ISABEL RANDOLPH (1955-56). GENE TALBOT: GENE BARRY (1955-56). CLINT ALBRIGHT: WILLIAM CHING (1955-56).

BENNY ROMERO: RICKY VERA (1955-56). MR. ROMERO: HY AVERBACK (1956). ANNOUNCER: BOB LEMOND. ORCHESTRA: WILBUR HATCH. PRODUCED BY LARRY BERNS (DESILU) 127 EPISODES.

Stars in the Eye (CBS) (SPECIAL) NOVEMBER 11, 1952.

THE LUD GLUSKIN ORCHESTRA.

Live variety special to dedicate the new CBS Television City production facility in Hollywood. Network executives Hubbell Robinson and Harry Ackerman (played respectively by Gale Gordon and Bob Sweeney) fear their new TV special will be ruined by Jack Benny and his constant behind-the-scenes meddling. Desi Arnaz threatens to sue because Jack sabotaged *I Love Lucy* on three occasions: by playing a waiter, stealing a kiss from Lucy and hiding in their shower.

LUCILLE BALL, GEORGE BURNS AND GRACIE ALLEN, EDDIE 'ROCHESTER' ANDERSON, EVE ARDEN, MEL BLANC, LOS ANGELES MAYOR FLETCHER BOWRIN, BOB CROSBY, CASS DALEY, WILLIAM FRAWLEY, ART LINKLETTER, GISELE MCKENZIE, THE SPORTSMEN QUARTET, VIVIAN VANCE, CALIFORNIA GOVERNOR EARL WARREN, MARGARET WHITING, ALAN YOUNG, THE CASTS OF TV'S *Amos 'n' Andy* (ALVIN CHILDRESS, SPENCER WILLIAMS, TIM MOORE), *Life with Luigi* (J. CARROL NAISH, ALAN REED, JODY GILBERT), *My Friend Irma* (MARIE WILSON, CATHY LEWIS), AND *Meet Millie* (ELENA VERDUGO, FLORENCE HALOP, MARVIN KAPLAN).

Climax! (CBS) "A TROPHY FOR HOWARD DAVENPORT" JUNE 28, 1956.

HOST: WILLIAM LUNDIGAN. ANNOUNCER: ART GILMORE.

Because he is softhearted and picks youngsters none of the other teams wants, the manager of a Babe Ruth League baseball team usually finds his team last in the standings. Now, for the first time, it looks as if they might have a chance to play in the finals—so he turns down a youngster's request to pitch in a big game. The broken-hearted boy runs away from home.

Howard Davenport: Dennis O'Keefe. Martha: Ruth Hussey. Billy: Billy Chapin. Dr. Raymond Forrest: Gale Gordon.

The Brothers (CBS) (Series) October 2, 1956 to March 26, 1957.

Siblings Harvey and Gilmore Box, co-owners of a San Francisco photography studio, experience mishaps as they try to make a go of it in the business world.
Harvey Box: Gale Gordon. Gilmore Box: Bob Sweeney. Dr. Margaret Kleeb: Ann Morriss. Captain Sam Box: Frank Orth (1956)/Howard McNear (1956-57). Marilee Dorf: Nancy Hadley. Carl Dorf: Oliver Blake. Barrington Steel: Robin Hughes.
Produced by Edward H. Feldman (Desilu) 26 episodes.

The Ed Sullivan Show (CBS) April 21, 1957.

Host: Ed Sullivan. The June Taylor Dancers. Announcer: Ralph Paul. The Ray Bloch Orchestra.
Hoofer Donald O'Connor and comedian Buster Keaton (O'Connor is portraying Keaton in a movie biography). Actor Don Murray does a dance number. The European balancing act the Fredianis. Gale Gordon and Bob Sweeney do a comedy sketch about refinishing the attic of their home. Mitzi Green shows film clips highlighting her movie career as a youngster. Charlotte Rae plays the Grand Duchess in a satire on "Anastasia." An appearance by Chester Gould, creator of the comic strip *Dick Tracy*.
Songs:
  Roberta Sherwood: "Easter Parade"
  Marion Marlowe: "Ave Maria"
  Mitzi: Medley of her early song hits.

Playhouse 90 (CBS) "The Jet-Propelled Couch" November 14, 1957.

Kirk Allen, atomic physicist, is competent in every way except one: he believes that he lives part of his life on another planet. For years, he has kept the secret to himself, but now his strange behavior has become apparent to his colleagues. He is 'away' more than he is at work. Pentagon officials desperately call in a renowned psychoanalyst to try to mend Allen's split personality. The analyst finds that as a boy Allen retreated into a world of fantasy about space travel, and through the years Allen's imagination has made these trips through space seem real. Now Allen is so convinced of their reality that he has worked out intricate maps and star charts for his interstellar journeys. Based on an actual case history. Broadcast live from Hollywood.
Robert Harrison: Donald O'Connor. Kirk Allen: David Wayne. Dr. Ostrow: Peter Lorre. General Milton Dagby: Gale Gordon. Eleanor Harrison: Phyllis Avery.

Sally (NBC) (Series) February 16 to March 30, 1958.

Sally Truesdale, former traveling companion to a wealthy widow, takes a job at a department store when they return home.
Sally Truesdale: Joan Caulfield. Mrs. Myrtle Banford: Marion Lorne. Bascomb Bleacher, store manager: Gale Gordon. Jim Kendall: Johnny Desmond. Bascomb Bleacher Jr: Arte Johnson. Produced by Frank Ross (Paramount TV)
7 episodes.

Playhouse 90 (CBS) "The Male Animal" March 13, 1958.

It's a bad day for Tommy Turner, English professor. Joe Ferguson is in town for the big game, and not only is he the football hero of Tommy's own college days; he is also an old flame of Tommy's wife Ellen. Secondly, an editorial in the student newspaper has just hailed Turner for defying the trustees' attacks on academic freedom. The bewildered Turner, who had never intended to start any controversy,

at once finds himself in trouble with his wife, the college dean, a trustee and Ferguson. Adapted from the play by James Thurber and Elliott Nugent. Broadcast live from Hollywood.
TOMMY TURNER: ANDY GRIFFITH. ELLEN TURNER: ANN RUTHERFORD. JOE FERGUSON: EDMOND O'BRIEN. DEAN DAMON: CHARLES RUGGLES. ED KELLER: GALE GORDON.

STUDIO ONE IN HOLLYWOOD (CBS) "THE AWARD WINNER" MARCH 24, 1958.

ANNOUNCERS: JOHN CANNON, ART HANNES.
  Quiet, meek George Short, a package designer for a toy company, finds himself unexpectedly thrust into the limelight. His cousin Frank, an author's agent, has used George's name on a successful screenplay in order to hide the identity of the real author. Complications set in when George's boss wants him to invest money in the toy firm, and his girlfriend decides to become an actress. Broadcast live.
GEORGE: EDDIE BRACKEN. FRANK REY: JACK OAKIE. R. J. FULLER: GALE GORDON. JUNE: JOANNA MOORE.
BETTY FURNESS FOR WESTINGHOUSE ELECTRIC.

THE WESTINGHOUSE LUCILLE BALL-DESI ARNAZ SHOW (CBS) "LUCY MAKES ROOM FOR DANNY" DECEMBER 1, 1958.

STARS: LUCILLE BALL, DESI ARNAZ, VIVIAN VANCE, WILLIAM FRAWLEY, RICHARD KEITH.
ANNOUNCER: ROY ROWAN. WILBUR HATCH CONDUCTS THE DESI ARNAZ ORCHESTRA.
  Hoping to give his children two months of healthy country air, Danny Williams (Danny Thomas) rents the Ricardos' rural home while Lucy and Ricky are in Hollywood making a picture. On their arrival in Connecticut, the Williams family discovers that the Ricardos' film commitment has been cancelled and they want to return to their home. The strain of two families living in the same household leads to a six-way snowball fight and a date in domestic court.

Kathy Williams: Marjorie Lord. Rusty Williams: Rusty Hamer. Linda Williams: Angela Cartwright. Judge: Gale Gordon. Also: Jess Kirkpatrick.
Lucille Ball, Desi Arnaz, and Betty Furness for Westinghouse Electric.

This Is Your Life (NBC) "Leo Carrillo" April 15, 1959.

Host: Ralph Edwards.

The stage, film and television star, best known for his role of 'Pancho' on TV's *The Cisco Kid*, is honored. Ralph and Maurice Hartnett, General Manager of the Calgary Stampede and President of the International Association of Fairs and Expositions, surprise Leo on a Hollywood backlot. Daughter Antoinette 'Toni' Carrillo tells of their home Rancho Los Alisos in Santa Monica Canyon. Guests Gale Gordon and Helen Ferguson co-starred with Carrillo in the play *Lombardi Limited.*

Other guests: E. J. 'Jack' Carrillo—older brother who built the World's Fair and Idlewild Airport in New York City. Ottie Carrillo—younger brother, a realtor in Santa Monica, CA. Stu Erwin—friend and actor, he and Leo co-starred in the 1934 film *Viva Villa*. William Gaxton—cousin and Broadway performer, they shared the same vaudeville bill many times.

Duncan Renaldo (in western costume)—friend, actor and TV's *Cisco Kid*. Will Rogers Jr.—friend and actor.

The Real McCoys (ABC) "The Screen Test" October 29, 1959.

Stars: Walter Brennan, Richard Crenna, Kathy [Kathleen] Nolan, Lydia Reed, Michael Winkelman, Tony Martinez.

A man named P. T. Kirkland (Gale Gordon) tells Hassie (Reed) that he is interested in arranging a movie test for her—but is he a con man with a scheme?

The Danny Thomas Show (CBS) "A Dog's Life" a.k.a. "The Landlord" December 21, 1959.

Stars: Danny Thomas, Marjorie Lord, Rusty Hamer, Penney Parker, Angela Cartwright, Amanda Randolph.

Rusty and Linda (Hamer, Cartwright) have brought a large St. Bernard dog into the Williams' apartment, violating their lease. When the landlord (Gale Gordon) moves to evict the family, the dog decides to give birth.

The Danny Thomas Show (CBS) "Family Portrait" May 9, 1960.

Stars: Danny Thomas, Marjorie Lord, Rusty Hamer, Penney Parker, Angela Cartwright, Amanda Randolph.

A famous painter (Gale Gordon as Godfrey Gaylord) moves in on the Williams—bag and baggage. He wants to live with the family for a few days in order to capture the 'real them' on canvas.

Pete and Gladys (CBS) "Bowling Brawl." November 21, 1960.

Stars: Harry Morgan, Cara Williams, Verna Felton, Barbara Stuart. The Wilbur Hatch Orchestra.

Pete (Morgan) thinks it is time Gladys (Williams) and her Uncle Paul (Gale Gordon) ended their long-standing feud. However, Gladys is not satisfied just to 'make up' at the celebration dinner—she decides she has to prove she is a good sport.
Janet Colton: Shirley Mitchell.

The Danny Thomas Show (CBS) "The Plant" January 2, 1961.

Stars: Danny Thomas, Marjorie Lord, Rusty Hamer, Angela Cartwright, Amanda Randolph.

A fan sends Danny a potted plant. Mr. Heckendorn (Gale Gordon), the landlord, spots it and declares it is a rare and valuable species that needs special care.

The Danny Thomas Show (CBS) "The Rum Cake" January 30, 1961.

Stars: Danny Thomas, Marjorie Lord, Rusty Hamer, Angela Cartwright, Amanda Randolph.

It is after 11:00pm, but the party still goes on at the Williams' apartment. The landlord Mr. Heckendorn (Gale Gordon) arrives with an ultimatum—if the noise does not cease, out Danny goes. And if Danny isn't in enough trouble, Heckendorn samples some rum cake . . . and promptly gets drunk. In character, Gale Gordon sings "Mademoiselle from Armentieres (Hinky Dinky Parlez-Vous)."

Angel (CBS) "The Insurance Policy" March 30, 1961.

Stars: Annie Farge, Marshall Thompson, Doris Singleton, Don Keefer. Announcer: Roy Rowan.

John makes Angel cut down on her television viewing, but Susie fills her in on programs she misses. Many of the shows deal with people murdered for their insurance money. When John's boss insures him, Angel panics.
Stanley Johnson: Gale Gordon. Mr. Corwin: Hanley Stafford. Mrs. Corwin: Louise Arthur.

Angel (CBS) "Unpopular Mechanics" April 19, 1961.

Stars: Annie Farge, Marshall Thompson, Doris Singleton, Don Keefer. Announcer: Roy Rowan.

Mr. Johnson (Gale Gordon), John's boss, buys an expensive car as a present for his wife and leaves it in John's garage. Angel and Susie (Farge, Singleton) plan to sneak off for a drive—and crash right into the garage.

The Danny Thomas Show (CBS) "The Scoutmaster" April 24, 1961.

Stars: Danny Thomas, Marjorie Lord, Rusty Hamer, Angela Cartwright, Amanda Randolph.

Rusty's troop needs a new scoutmaster and one candidate is Mr. Heckendorn (Gale Gordon), a man with delusions of military grandeur. Danny shudders when he thinks of Heckendorn commanding the boys—so he decides to compete for the job.
Mr. Wills: Robert Carson.

The Danny Thomas Show (CBS) "The Party Wrecker" May 22, 1961.

Stars: Danny Thomas, Marjorie Lord, Rusty Hamer, Angela Cartwright, Amanda Randolph.

There is going to be a surprise party for Danny, and he gets wind that something is going on. He begins to rant and rave because he has not been invited.
Heckendorn: Gale Gordon. Musicians: Jess Kirkpatrick, Johnny Silver. Guest: Harry Ruby.

Pete and Gladys (CBS) (Series) September 18, 1961 to September 10, 1962.

Insurance man Pete Porter finds life more than a little amusing and sometimes quite vexing because of his slightly scatterbrained wife, Gladys.
Pete Porter: Harry Morgan. Gladys Porter: Cara Williams. George Colton: Peter Leeds. Janet Colton: Shirley Mitchell. Peggy Briggs: Mina Kolb. Ernie Briggs: Joe Mantell. Uncle Paul: Gale Gordon. Nancy: Frances Rafferty. Bruce Carter: Bill Hinnant. Orchestra: Wilbur Hatch. Produced by Parke Levy, Devery Freeman (El Camino Productions) 35 episodes (Gale Gordon appeared in eight installments).

Harrigan and Son (ABC) "On Broadway" September 22, 1961.

Stars: Pat O'Brien, Roger Perry, Georgine Darcy, Helen Kleeb.
  Merril Davis (Gale Gordon), a long-time client of Harrigan Sr. (O'Brien), is known for his miserly ways. However, he shows up at the firm's office sporting a new suit and handing out cigars. Harrigan wonders what brought about the sudden change.
Fifi Marlow: Sue Ane Langdon. Ben: Wally Brown.

The Donna Reed Show (ABC) "Dr. Stone and His Horseless Carriage," January 11, 1962.

Stars: Donna Reed, Carl Betz, Shelley Fabares, Paul Petersen.
  Alex (Betz) does not really get upset when he receives a 1911 antique car as payment for a medical bill. In fact, Alex fondly names 'her' Eloise. However, having the auto causes the family to be laughed at all over town.
Dr. Thorgesen: Oliver McGowan. Mr. Webley: Gale Gordon.

Here's Hollywood (NBC) February 13, 1962.

Hosts: Jack Linkletter, Helen O'Connell.
  Actor Gale Gordon tells Jack how he overcame a childhood speech impediment. Actress Madlyn Rhue describes the auto accident which almost ended her career.

The Donna Reed Show (ABC) "Donna Meets Roberta" May 3, 1962.

Stars: Donna Reed, Carl Betz, Shelley Fabares, Paul Petersen.
  The Stones learn that Roberta Summers' house, which is up for sale, is going to increase in value. Problem: Should they take advantage of their inside information—or tell Roberta about it?
Roberta Summers: Roberta Sherwood. Jerry: Jerry Lanning. Don: Don Lanning. Dudley: Gale Gordon.

The Bob Newhart Show (NBC) May 16, 1962.

Stars: Bob Newhart, Joe Flynn, Jackie Joseph, Andy Albin, Dan Sorkin, Ken Berry. Paul Weston and His Orchestra.

Australian musical-comedy star Elaine McKenna makes a return appearance. In a comedy sketch, Bob plays an American tourist in Europe.
Gale Gordon.

Dennis the Menace (CBS) (Series) May 27, 1962 to September 22, 1963.

Mischievous young Dennis Mitchell has humorous scrapes and shenanigans, trying the patience of his long-suffering parents and exasperating his elderly next-door neighbor. Based on the comic strip by Hank Ketcham.
Dennis Mitchell: Jay North. Henry Mitchell: Herbert Anderson. Alice Mitchell: Gloria Henry. John Wilson, next-door neighbor: Gale Gordon. Eloise Wilson: Sara Seeger. Margaret Wade: Jeannie Russell. Mrs. Lucy Elkins: Irene Tedrow. Tommy Anderson: Billy Booth. Mr. Quigley: Willard Waterman. Sgt. Theodore Mooney: George Cisar. Seymour: Robert John Pittman.
Produced by Harry Ackerman (Screen Gems [Columbia TV]) 44 episodes.

Comedy Spot (CBS) "For the Love of Mike" July 10, 1962.

Former singer Betty Stevens and her intern husband Michael are having a tough time making ends meet on Mike's meager income. Betty decides to resume her singing career to help out. Unsuccessful pilot for a proposed series.
Betty Stevens: Shirley Jones. Michael Stevens: Burt Metcalfe. Ed Broxton: Jack Weston. Fran Broxton: Faye DeWitt. Emil Sinclair: Gale Gordon.

The Lucy Show (CBS) (Series) September 30, 1963 to September 16, 1968.

Widow Lucy Carmichael and her two children share a home with divorceé Vivian Bagley and her son.
Lucy Carmichael: Lucille Ball. Vivian Bagley: Vivian Vance (1963-65). Theodore J. Mooney, Lucy's boss: Gale Gordon. Chris Carmichael: Candy Moore (1963-65). Jerry Carmichael: Jimmy Garrett (1963-66). Sherman Bagley: Ralph Hart (1963-65). Eddie Collins: Don Briggs (1963-64), Harrison Cheever: Roy Roberts (1967-68). Mary Jane Lewis: Mary Jane Croft (1965-68). Announcer: Roy Rowan. Orchestra: Wilbur Hatch. Produced by Elliott Lewis, Jack Donohue, Tommy Thompson, Bob O'Brien, Gary Morton (Desilu) 126 episodes.

The Lucille Ball Comedy Hour: Mr. and Mrs. (CBS) (Special) April 19, 1964.

Television studio head Bonnie Barton (Lucille Ball) sets out to sign a funny comedian, Bill Barton—who also happens to be her husband—for a TV special. However, a member of the board (Gale Gordon, as Mr. Harvey) has suggested that she resign if she fails. The Bartons have kept America rolling with laughter for months, but are in sponsor trouble now because the show's ratings have slipped to second place.
Bill: Bob Hope. Cash: Jack Weston. Walter: Max Showalter. Henderson: John Dehner. Potter: Bill [William] Lanteau. Also: John Banner, Rudy Dolan, Stanley Farrar, Sid Gould, Danny Klega, Joseph Mell, Sally Mills, Eddie Ryder.

The Match Game (NBC) April 19 through 23, 1965.

Host: Gene Rayburn.
Contestants win cash for answering questions and matching as many responses among their teammates as they can. This week the celebrity players are Gale Gordon and Betty White.

MAGIC OF BROADCASTING (CBS) (SPECIAL) MAY 1, 1966.

HOST: ARTHUR GODFREY.
A nostalgic review of the great stars and favorite programs of radio and television history. Bing Crosby uses an ancient Atwater Kent radio to acquaint two youngsters with musical stars of the past: Al Jolson, Ben Bernie, Helen Morgan and Arthur Tracy. Lucille Ball is seen at rehearsals for *The Lucy Show* with series co-star Gale Gordon (radio's first 'Flash Gordon'). Sheldon Leonard, producer of TV series *I Spy* and *The Dick Van Dyke Show*. Writer Rod Serling discusses the live dramas of television's 'Golden Age.' Bandleader John Scott Trotter reviews the big bands of yesteryear. Rockers We Five represent the current talent in broadcasting by singing "Beyond the Sea." Films, stills and transcripts include: Freeman Gosden & Charles Correll of radio's *Amos 'n' Andy*; Fanny Brice ('Baby Snooks'); Rudy Vallee; Milton Berle; *Fibber McGee and Molly* (Jim & Marian Jordan) and Fred Allen. In addition, radio show openings, such as *Superman*, *Gang Busters* and *Suspense*.

VACATION PLAYHOUSE (CBS) "WHERE THERE'S SMOKEY" AUGUST 1, 1966.

Smokey is a bungling fireman who lives with his sister and brother-in-law, Fire Chief Warren Packard (Gale Gordon). Warren will try anything to get Smokey to move out . . . and that includes pushing him into matrimony. Unsuccessful pilot for a proposed series.
SMOKEY: SOUPY SALES. BLOSSOM PACKARD: HOLLIS IRVING. MAGGIE DENNISON: LOUISE GLENN. RICHIE PACKARD: RICKEY ALLEN. HOGAN: JACK WESTON. BENSON: CHARLES TANNEN. CHARLIE: ROBERT NICHOLS.

PASSWORD (CBS) SEPTEMBER 19, 1966.

HOST: ALLEN LUDDEN
Two teams of players compete to win cash by providing a one-word clue to help their partner guess the "password" given to one player of each team, the studio audience, and home viewers.

Gale Gordon joined Lucille Ball, her husband Gary Morton, Mary Wickes, Dick Patterson and his wife Gita.

The Mike Douglas Show (Syndicated) August 30, 1967.

Host: Mike Douglas. The Ellie Frankel Sextet.
   Mike's guest co-host is Totie Fields. Mike welcomes actress Eve Arden; actor Gale Gordon; singers the Rhodes Brothers; songstress Kaye Hart; and dog psychologist Dare Miller.

The Woody Woodbury Show (Syndicated) November 28, 1967.

Host: Woody Woodbury. Announcer: Robert Ridgely. The Michael Melvin Combo.
   Folksy nightclub comic Woody helms a talk show with his guests singer-actress Polly Bergen; actor Michael Ansara; songstress Della Reese; Gale Gordon of television's *The Lucy Show*; and musical group Them.

The Danny Thomas Hour (NBC) "The Royal Follies of 1933" December 11, 1967.

Star: Danny Thomas. Narrator: Johnny Carson.
   To elude a husband-hunting heiress, bachelor Prince Wolfgang (Thomas) takes refuge in a Broadway show menaced by gangsters. Von Plinkle: Hans Conried. Thelda: Eve Arden. Hansie: Kurt Kasznar. Peggy: Shirley Jones. Anthony Baxter: Gale Gordon. Skip: Ken Berry. Suzie: Jackie Joseph. Also: Bob Hope.
Songs:
   Danny: "All The World's A Stage," "I'm Cyrano of Hackensack"
   Danny, Shirley, Ken, Jackie: "The Cream in My Coffee," "My Lucky Star"
   Shirley: "I'll Take Romance"
   Ken, Jackie: "Million-Dollar Baby"

THE HOLLYWOOD SQUARES (NBC) APRIL 1 THROUGH 5, 1968.

HOST: PETER MARSHALL. REGULARS: ROSE MARIE, WALLY COX, CHARLEY WEAVER [CLIFF ARQUETTE]. ANNOUNCER: KENNY WILLIAMS.
  Contestants determine if celebrity panelists are giving correct answers to questions as they play games of tic-tac-toe for cash and prizes.
GUEST PANELISTS THIS WEEK ARE JIM BACKUS, BILL BIXBY, JACK CASSIDY, BARBARA FELDON, GALE GORDON AND SHIRLEY JONES.

HERE'S LUCY (CBS) (SERIES) SEPTEMBER 23, 1968 TO SEPTEMBER 2, 1974.

  Lucy Carter, a California widow with two teen children, weathers a multitude of misadventures and misunderstandings while working for the Unique Employment Agency.
LUCY CARTER: LUCILLE BALL. HARRISON OTIS 'UNCLE HARRY' CARTER, LUCY'S BROTHER-IN-LAW AND BOSS: GALE GORDON. MARY JANE LEWIS: MARY JANE CROFT. KIM CARTER: LUCIE ARNAZ. CRAIG CARTER: DESI ARNAZ JR. (1968-71). ANNOUNCER: ROY ROWAN. ORCHESTRA: WILBUR HATCH (1968-69)/MARL YOUNG (1969-74). PRODUCED BY GARY MORTON, TOMMY THOMPSON, CLEO SMITH, WILLIAM MAGINETTI
(LUCILLE BALL PRODUCTIONS) 144 EPISODES.

THE DEAN MARTIN SHOW (NBC) DECEMBER 19, 1968.

STARS: DEAN MARTIN, THE GOLDDIGGERS. PIANIST: KEN LANE. ANNOUNCER: FRANK BARTON. LES BROWN AND HIS BAND.
  Dean presents his Christmas show, with guests Dennis Weaver of television's *Gentle Ben*, comedian Bob Newhart, and comic actor Dom DeLuise. Dean sings "Marshmallow World" and "I'll Be Home for Christmas." Also, uncredited appearances by Lucille Ball, Tony Bennett, Jack Benny, Joey Bishop, Dan Blocker, George Burns, Raymond Burr, Glen Campbell, Diahann Carroll, Johnny Carson, Al Casey, Petula Clark, Vince Edwards, Barbara Feldon, Glenn Ford,

Tennessee Ernie Ford, Melissa Gilbert, Gale Gordon, Peter Graves, Lorne Greene, Andy Griffith, Phil Harris, William Holden, Bob Hope, Michael Landon, Paul Lynde, Dick Martin, Ethel Merman, Greg Morris, Jim Nabors, Charles Nelson Reilly, Don Rickles, Roy Rogers, Dan Rowan, Frank Sinatra Jr., Nancy Sinatra, Red Skelton, and James Stewart.

ADDITIONAL SONGS:
Dennis: "The Marvelous Toy"
Cast: "Hey Li Ley, Li Lay Lo," "Oh Little Town of Bethlehem," "Deck the Halls," "Joy to the World," "Silent Night"
Dean, Golddiggers: "Daddy," "True Love," "We Wish You the Merriest"

THE DEAN MARTIN SHOW (NBC) JANUARY 8, 1970.

STARS: DEAN MARTIN, THE GOLDDIGGERS, KEN LANE. ANNOUNCER: FRANK BARTON. LES BROWN AND HIS BAND.

Guests: actor Peter Graves, singer Petula Clark, Gale Gordon and comic Don Rice III. Dean sings "The Birds and the Bees" and "The Green, Green Grass of Home." Peter does a song-and-dance turn. Gale is a harried personnel director trying to handle employees' beefs.

OTHER SONGS:
Dean, Petula: (medley) "You Are My Sunshine," "We'll Sing In The Sunshine," "Sunny Side Up," "Look For the Silver Lining"
Petula: "Don't Sleep In the Subway," "You And I"
Peter: "Life Is Just a Bowl of Cherries"

THE MERV GRIFFIN SHOW (SYNDICATED) JANUARY 26, 1969.

HOST: MERV GRIFFIN. REGULAR: ARTHUR TREACHER. THE MORT LINDSEY ORCHESTRA.

Guests: comedian and toastmaster George Jessel; singer-actor Ronnie Dyson; comedy writer Jack Douglas and Reiko; Gale Gordon of television's *Here's Lucy*; musical duo Sandler and Young; and politician Adam Clayton Powell.

The Dean Martin Show (NBC) March 5, 1970.

Stars: Dean Martin, The Golddiggers, Ken Lane. Announcer: Frank Barton. Les Brown and His Band.

Guests are pioneer TV comedian Sid Caesar; Barbara Anderson of TV's *Ironside*; country singer Marty Robbins; Gale Gordon of TV's *Here's Lucy*; and comedienne Alice Ghostley. Dean sings "I'm Sitting on Top of the World," "By the Time I Get to Phoenix," and "Young At Heart." Sid plays the flustered husband of Alice, who thinks every man is gawking at her. Gale is a fussy fisherman plagued by noisy buddy Dean. Dean participates in two medleys: one with Barbara, the other with Marty.

Other songs:
  Barbara: "Hello, I Love You, Goodbye"
  Marty: "Camelia"

The Dean Martin Show (NBC) December 17, 1970.

Stars: Dean Martin, The Golddiggers, Ken Lane, The Ding-A-Ling Sisters [Lynn Lathem, Tara Leigh, Helen Funai, Jayne Kennedy], Kay Medford. Announcer: Frank Barton. Les Brown and His Band.

Guests are country singer Glen Campbell; Gale Gordon of TV's *Here's Lucy*; and comic actor Dom DeLuise. Dean sings "She's A Little Bit Country" and "Raindrops Keep Fallin' on My Head." Gale peddles perfect gifts for people you hate and performs "Everybody's Got a Little Song." Dom is a dog psychiatrist and a clumsy waiter. Dean is a western doctor who would rather drink than work.

Additional songs:
  Dean, Glen: 'Sunshine' medley
  Glen: "Gotta Travel On"
  Golddiggers: "Knowing When to Leave"
  Dean, Golddiggers: (Concert Spot) "You're My Everything," "The Best Things in Life Are Free"

The Virginia Graham Show (Syndicated) April 1, 1971.

Host: Virginia Graham.
Daytime talk with guest Gale Gordon.

This Is Your Life (Syndicated) "Richard Crenna" February 23, 1972.

Host: Ralph Edwards.
The radio, TV and film actor is honored. Guest Gale Gordon, Crenna's co-star in both the radio and television versions of *Our Miss Brooks*, tells of how Crenna lived with him and his wife for several months.

Other guests Eve Arden—Actress and co-star in *Our Miss Brooks* on radio and TV. Walter Brennan (via videotape)—Actor and co-star in *The Real McCoys* on TV. Edith Crenna—Mother, owner/manager of Stephens Hotel in Los Angeles, CA. Maria Crenna—Daughter, age 6. Penni Crenna—Wife. Seana Crenna—Daughter and Iowa college student. Richard Crenna Jr.—Son, age 12. Clem Glass—Host of Crenna's first radio show *Boy Scout Jamboree* on KFI in Los Angeles (Ralph was once a guest star). Jo Ann Pflug—Actress and co-star in film *Catlow*. Richard Pollette—Uncle. Robert Wise—Director, worked with Crenna in film *The Sand Pebbles*.

The Merv Griffin Show (Syndicated) May 26, 1972.

Host: Merv Griffin. Regular: Arthur Treacher. The Mort Lindsey Orchestra.
Talk program with guests Lucille Ball and her husband Gary Morton; actor Douglas Fairbanks Jr; *Here's Lucy* co-star Gale Gordon; and comic Richard Dawson.

THE MERV GRIFFIN SHOW (SYNDICATED) OCTOBER 4, 1973.

HOST: MERV GRIFFIN. REGULAR: ARTHUR TREACHER. THE MORT LINDSEY ORCHESTRA.
Lucille Ball in a musical number from her film *Mame* (1974). Other guests include Bob Hope, Gale Gordon, Desi Arnaz Jr., Lucie Arnaz, Gary Morton, and Vivian Vance.

A DEAN MARTIN ROAST: LUCILLE BALL (NBC) (SPECIAL) FEBRUARY 7, 1975.

HOST: DEAN MARTIN.
Lucy is the recipient of good-natured barbs and put-downs by her colleagues.
JACK BENNY, MILTON BERLE, FOSTER BROOKS, RUTH BUZZI, PHYLLIS DILLER, TOTIE FIELDS, HENRY FONDA, GALE GORDON, BOB HOPE, RICH LITTLE, GARY MORTON, DON RICKLES, GINGER ROGERS, DAN ROWAN & DICK MARTIN, NIPSEY RUSSELL, VIVIAN VANCE.

THE TOMORROW SHOW (NBC) OCTOBER 26, 1976.

HOST: TOM SNYDER.
Tom's guests are a group of 'second bananas' from radio's golden age.
BILL BALDWIN, FRANK NELSON, EDGAR BERGEN, JIM BACKUS, ERNESTINE WADE, GALE GORDON.

DINAH! (SYNDICATED) NOVEMBER 16, 1976.

HOST: DINAH SHORE. THE JOHN RODBY ORCHESTRA.
Dinah serves up a program of talk, music, homemaking advice, and cooking recipes. Guests: comedienne Lucille Ball and her husband, producer Garry Morton; actor Gale Gordon; funny lady Carol Burnett; actress Valerie Harper, and circus producer Kenneth Feld. Dinah, Lucy, and Valerie sing "Hey, Look Me Over."

CBS Salutes Lucy—The First 25 Years (CBS) (Special) November 28, 1976.

A selection of clips rounds out this tribute to Lucille Ball and her TV work. Appearing in new introductory segments are Desi Arnaz, Carol Burnett, Richard Burton, Johnny Carson, Sammy Davis Jr., Gale Gordon, Bob Hope, Danny Kaye, Dean Martin, James Stewart, Danny Thomas, Vivian Vance, Dick Van Dyke, John Wayne.

A Lucille Ball Special: Lucy Calls the President (CBS) (Special) November 21, 1977.

Lucy Whittaker (Lucille Ball) puts in a phone call to President Jimmy Carter on a matter of local interest and finds herself hosting the Chief Executive when he decides to visit her for dinner.
Viv: Vivian Vance. Whittaker: Ed McMahon. Aunt Mary: Mary Wickes. Omar: Gale Gordon.
Also: Steve Allen, James E. Brodhead, Miss Lillian Carter, Mary Jane Croft, Joey Forman, Stack Pierce, John William Young.

The Honeymooners Christmas (ABC) (Special) November 28, 1977.

Announcer: Johnny Olsen.
The Raccoon Lodge is putting on a play, "A Christmas Carol," and guess who's slated to direct the effort—everyone's favorite bus-driver, Ralph Kramden (Jackie Gleason).
Ed Norton: Art Carney. Alice Kramden: Audrey Meadows. Trixie Norton: Jane Kean. Mr. Marshall, Ralph's Boss: Gale Gordon.

CAPTAIN KANGAROO (CBS) SEPTEMBER 21, 1978.

STARS: BOB KEESHAN, HUGH BRANNUM, COSMO ALLEGRETTI, JAMES WALL.
Gale Gordon drops by the Treasure House for a visit.

THE MIKE DOUGLAS SHOW (SYNDICATED) NOVEMBER 1, 1978.

HOST: MIKE DOUGLAS. THE JOE MASSIMINO BAND.
Daytime talk with guest Gale Gordon.

BOBBY VINTON'S ROCK 'N' ROLLERS (CBS) (SPECIAL) NOVEMBER 20, 1978.

STAR: BOBBY VINTON.
A musical look back at the 1950s. Bobby sings: "You're the One That I Want," "There I've Said It Again" and "Oh Boy." Guests are Eve Arden, Gale Gordon, Fabian, Stockard Channing, Penny Marshall, Erik Estrada and Susan Buckner. Eve and Gale team to sing "Sh-Boom" and "Hot Diggity." Fabian causes a bobbysoxer riot in a malt shop. Penny tries her luck on skates at a roller rink. A comedy sketch takes place in a fall-out shelter. The entire cast spoofs 'beach party' movies.
OTHER SONGS:
  Fabian: "Turn Me Loose," "Land of a Thousand Dances"
  Stockard: "Something I Can Dance To," "Wheel of Fortune"

CAPTAIN KANGAROO (CBS) 1979.

STARS: BOB KEESHAN, HUGH BRANNUM, COSMO ALLEGRETTI, JAMES WALL.
Gale Gordon makes a return trip to visit the Captain (Keeshan).

A LUCILLE BALL SPECIAL: LUCY MOVES TO NBC (NBC) (SPECIAL) FEBRUARY 8, 1980.

The peacock network assigns Lucille Ball to come up with a new situation comedy. She enlists Gale Gordon's aid in lining up talent. The result is The Music Mart, starring Donald O'Connor and Gloria DeHaven as Wally and Carol Coogan, music-store owners whose son is devoted to rock music. An unsuccessful pilot for a proposed series.
SCOTTY COOGAN: SCOTTY PLUMMER. LOLA: MICKI MCKENZIE. AL COODY: SIDNEY MILLER. WANDA CLARK: DORIS SINGLETON. MICKEY LUDIN: ROBERT ALDA. ALSO: JOHNNY CARSON, GARY COLEMAN, TAKAYO DORAN, BOB HOPE, GARY IMHOFF, GENE KELLY, JACK KLUGMAN, RUTA LEE, TY NUTT, IVERY WHEELER.

BUNGLE ABBEY (NBC) (PILOT) MAY 31, 1981.

STARS: GALE GORDON, CHARLIE CALLAS, GUY MARKS, GRAHAM JARVIS, GINO CONFORTI, PETER PALMER, ANTONY ALDA.
 The Abbott (Gordon) watches over a group of zany monks who wish to help a children's orphanage by selling a painting hanging in their monastery. Unsuccessful, this pilot was executive-produced and directed by Lucille Ball.
EDGAR FORSYTH: WILLIAM LANTEAU.

THE JOHN DAVIDSON SHOW (SYNDICATED) MAY 24, 1982.

HOST: JOHN DAVIDSON. THE JOHN TORBEN BAND.
 Daytime talk with guests Lucille Ball, her husband Gary Morton, Gale Gordon, and Dean Paul Martin.

LIFE WITH LUCY (ABC) (SERIES) SEPTEMBER 20 TO NOVEMBER 15, 1986.

Widowed grandmother Lucy Barker moves in with her daughter's

family and takes over half-interest in a hardware store run by its crusty co-owner.
Lucy Barker: Lucille Ball. Curtis McGibbon, Lucy's partner: Gale Gordon. Margo Barker McGibbon: Ann Dusenberry. Ted McGibbon: Larry Anderson. Becky McGibbon: Jenny Lewis. Kevin McGibbon: Philip J. Amelio II. Leonard Stoner: Donovan Scott.
Produced by Aaron Spelling, Gary Morton, Douglas S. Kramer, Madelyn [Pugh] Davis, Bob Carroll Jr., E. Duke Vincent, Linda Morris, Vic Rauseo (Lucille Ball Productions/Aaron Spelling Productions) 8 episodes + 5 unaired.

The 40th Annual Emmy Awards (FOX) (Special) August 28, 1988.

Outstanding achievement in television during the 1987–1988 season is honored. Gale Gordon presents the award for Outstanding Individual Performance in a Variety or Music Program to Robin Williams for "ABC Presents a Royal Gala."
Bea Arthur, William Hanna & Joseph Barbera, Tony Danza, Danny DeVito, Sam Donaldson, Nora Dunn, Peter Falk, John Forsythe, ALF (voice of Paul Fusco), Sherman Hemsley, Jan Hooks, Penn & Teller, John Lithgow, Penny Marshall, William Shatner, Leonard Nimoy, George Will.

Hi Honey, I'm Home! (ABC) "Meet the Nielsens" July 19, 1991.

Stars: Charlotte Booker, Stephen Bradbury, Julie Benz, Danny Gura, Susan Cella, Pete Benson, Eric Kushnick.
The family of a 1950s sitcom is secretly relocated to a 1991 New Jersey suburb, where their wholesome ways clash with contemporary lifestyles.
Theodore J. Mooney: Gale Gordon.

THE NEW LASSIE (SYNDICATED) "NO PETS ALLOWED" SEPTEMBER 7, 1991.

STARS: LASSIE (A DOG), WILL NIPPER [ESTES], CHRISTOPHER STONE, DEE WALLACE-STONE, WENDY COX.

An old gentleman (Gale Gordon as Horace Peterson) sadly learns that he may lose his beloved dog when his landlady (Margaret O'Brien) suddenly decides to banish all pets from her building.

LUCY AND DESI: A HOME MOVIE (NBC) (SPECIAL) FEBRUARY 14, 1993.

HOST: LUCIE ARNAZ.

The lives and careers of Lucille Ball and Desi Arnaz are recalled via film clips, stills and interviews with those who knew and worked with them.

JAMES BACON, FRED BALL, BOB CARROLL JR., WANDA CLARK, CAROLE COOK, JACKIE COOPER, MADELYN [PUGH] DAVIS, GALE GORDON, VAN JOHNSON, ANN MILLER, CLEO SMITH, BOB SCHILLER, BOB WEISKOPF.

Emmy Award Nominations

1954 Best Supporting Actor in a Regular Series for *Our Miss Brooks*.

1966-67 Outstanding Supporting Actor in a Comedy for *The Lucy Show*.

1967-68 Outstanding Supporting Actor in a Comedy for *The Lucy Show*.

1970-71 Outstanding Supporting Actor in a Comedy for *Here's Lucy*.

Radio Hall of Fame: Gale Gordon was inducted in 1999.

AUTHORSHIP

Two books (circa 1930s) attributed to Gordon:

Nursery Rhymes for Hollywood Babes by Gloria Gordon and Gale Gordon, 38 unnumbered pages.

Leaves from Story Trees by Gale Gordon. 2 One-Act Plays.

INDEX

Numbers in **bold** indicate photographs

Ackerman, Harry 79, 109, 347, 356
Adams, Jr., George M. 27-28
Adventures in Strange Lands 22, 285
Adventures of Jungle Jim, The 29, 33, 41, 289-290
Adventures of Ozzie and Harriet, The 64, 344
Aldrich, Sr., Charles Thomas 12, 15
All About Anne 64, 342
All Hands on Deck 82, 280-281
All in a Night's Work 82, 279
Allman, Elvia 31, 294, 301, 302, 306, 317, 339
Amazing Interplanetary Adventures of Flash Gordon and Dale Arden, The 28-29, 57, 115, 177, 289
Ameche, Don 53, 301, 307, 321, 332, 333, 336, 339
American Weekly, The 28, 287
Ames, Walter 85-86, 87
Andrews, Bart 91, 118, 119
Angel 108, 353
Arden, Eve 69, 70, 71-72, 73, 76, 77, 79, 80, 81, 82, 86, 91, 117, 126, 130, **144, 145, 146,** 275, 281, 334, 346, 347, 359, 359, 363, 366

Arnaz, Desi 57, 113, 134, 345, 346, 347, 350, 351, 365, 369
Arnaz Jr., Desi 118, 124, **156, 157, 158, 163,** 360, 364
Arnaz, Lucie 118, 120, 121, 124, 134, **156, 157, 158, 159, 163,** 360, 364, 369
Arthur, Richard 98-99
Averback, Hy 86, 347

Baby Snooks Show, The 54, 301
Bad Man, The 19, 21
Ball, Lucille 3, 11, 57, 59, 78, 85, 86, 90, 91, 92, 97, 99, 107, 110-112, 113, 114, 115, 116, 117, 118-123, 124-126, 127, 128, 129-131, 134, 135, 136, **143, 150, 151, 156, 157, 158, 159, 160, 161, 162, 163, 164, 165, 166, 167, 168,** 273, 296, 335, 345, 346-347, 350, 351, 357, 358, 359, 360, 363, 364, 365, 367-368, 369
Basil Rathbone: His Life and His Films 54
Bates, Hal 122, 123
Baxter, Anne 95

"Beast of Darrow, The" 59
Beck, Jackson 51, 285
Benaderet, Bea 62, 80, 91, **142**, 299, 300, 307, 308, 330, 331, 333, 334, 335, 337, 340, 341, 342
Bennett, Richard 11-12
Benny, Jack 33, 45, 64, 79, 119, 122, 295, 314, 323, 341, 347, 360, 364
Berns, Larry 77, 334, 347
Big Town 32, 72, 81, 292
Birds Eye Open House 45, 320
Blackstone, The Magic Detective 62, 335
Blanc, Mel 57-58, 125, 302, 316, 341, 347
Blondell, Gloria 305
Blondell, Joan 42, 306
Boardman, True 18, 22, 23, 287
Bob Newhart Show, The 109, 356
Bobby Vinton's Rock 'n' Rollers 126-127, 366
Booth, Shirley 71
Borrego Sun 93, 104
Bracken, Eddie 60, 90, 350
Brice, Fanny 32, 116, 293, 301, 358
Brothers, The 85-87, **147**, 348
Brown, Joe E. 33, 135, 271, 296
Brown, Himan 28, 284, 289
Browning, Norma Lee 99-100
Bruce, Nigel 46-48, 54-55, 320, 328
Bungle Abbey 127, 367
'Burbs, The 82, 283
Burns and Allen (as team and show): 41-42, 55, 59, 91, 115, 135, 302, 347
Burton, Richard 119, 120, 121-122, 365

Calgary Herald 134
Calling All Cars 23, 32, 287
Captain Kangaroo 126, 127, 366
Captains of Industry 30, 32, 292
Carney, Art 80, 291, 365
Carrillo, Leo 19, 21-22, 26, 90, 93, 320, 351
Carroll, Charles 24, 30, 287
Carroll, Jr., Bob 121, 129, 368, 369
Casebook of Gregory Hood, The 46-51, 52, 320
Cassandra 30
Caulfield, Joan 88-89, **148**, 349
Cavalcade of America 42-45, 55, 60, 307, 308-309, 310, 311-312, 315, 316, 329, 330, 332
CBS Salutes Lucy—The First 25 Years 126, 365
Chandler, Jeff 76, 78, 81, 326, 328, 334
Charlie McCarthy Show, The 60, 336
Chicago Tribune 1, 34, 43, 60, 80, 81, 86, 98, 99, 115, 124, 125, 225, 237, 238, 269
"Children, This is Your Father" 43-45, 315
"Church Mouse, The" 24-26, 287
Cinnamon Bear, The 31, 99, 293-294
"City Beautiful, The" 31-32
Clark, Wanda 119-120, 131, 367, 369
Climax, The 18, 19
Climax! 80, 347-348
Coe, Richard L. 81-82
Colman, Ronald 62, 339, 340
Comedy Spot 110, 356
Conway, Tom 54, 328

Crenna, Richard 72, 73, 82, 124, 125, 275, 333, 334, 346, 351, 363
Curley, Virginia B. (wife) 6, 35, 56-57, 70, 77, 95-96, 97, 98, 106, 115, 124, 134, 137, 138, 307, 346, 363

Daley, Steve 130
Dallad Productions 86
Dancers, The 11-12, 13, 29
Danny Thomas Show, The 90, 91, 107-108, 352, 353, 354
Daughters of Atreus 29
Davis, Madelyn Pugh 121, 368, 369
Day in the Life of Dennis Day, A 61, 62, 330-331, 334, 337, 342
Day, Dennis 61, 62, 330-331, 334, 337, 341, 342
Dean Martin Roast: Lucille Ball, A 124-125, 364
Dean Martin Show, The 122, 360-361, 362
Death Valley Days 23, 35, 285
Dennis the Menace 109-110, 112, 115, 129, **152, 153,** 356
Desmond, Johnny 88, **148,** 349
Dinah! 125, 364
Doctor Christian 31, 33, 293
Don't Give Up the Ship 82, 277
Dondi 82, 279-280
Donna Reed Show, The 109, 355
Drake, Betsy 64, 341
"Dr. Tweedy, the Matchmaker" 52-53
Druxman, Michael B. 6, 54, 134-135

Ed Sullivan Show, The 87, 348
Edmonton Journal 133-134
Edwards, Ralph 90, 124, 351, 363
Elmer the Great 81, 271-272
English Coronets 20, 27, 30, 285

Fabulous Doctor Tweedy, The 52-53, 321
Feldman, Edward H. 86, 348
Felton, Verna 107, 294, 297, 303, 304, 307, 312, 313, 316, 343, 344, 352
Fibber McGee and Molly 4, 7, 11, 34, 35-40, 41, 45, 55, 57, 60, 61, 62, 64, 65, 70, 81, 91, 105, 123, 173-239, 241, 242, 272, 298-299, 339, 345, 358
Forte, Joseph 71, 275
40th Annual Emmy Awards, The 131, 368
Francis Covers the Big Town 81, 274-275
Frawley, William 80, 91, 120, 345, 346, 347, 350
Freedom Train, The 53, 324
Front Page Drama 28, 32, 41, 287
Fullness of Times, The 31-32, 294

Gang Busters 115, 291, 358
Gilmore, Art 49, 293, 305, 306, 313, 320, 321, 347
Gleason, Jackie 86, 126, 365
Godfrey, Arthur 116, 358
Goldbergs, The 23, 284
Good News of 1938 32, 292-293
Good News of 1939 33, 292-293
Good News of 1940 41, 292-293
Gordon, Gavin 29, 279, 310

Gordon, Gloria 11, 12, 13-14, 15, 17, 30, 31, 33, 43, 56, 94, 297, 304, 313, 318, 338
Gordon, Virginia see Curley, Virginia B.
Granby's Green Acres 62-64, 98, **142**, 340-341
Grant, Cary 64, 297, 312, 341
Great Gildersleeve, The 7, 38, 55-56, 61, 241-263, 330, 331, 332-333
Green Acres 62
Griffith, Andy 89-90, 350, 361
Gypsy Jim 21, 29

Halls of Ivy, The 62, 64, 338-339, 340
Harrigan and Son 108, 355
Hauser, Susan 99
Henry Duffy Players 18, 19, 26
Her Unborn Child 17-18
Here Come the Nelsons 81, 273-274
Here We Go Again 81, 272-273
Here's Hollywood 109, 355
Here's Lucy 3, 4, 57, 94, 107, 117, 119, 120, 121-122, 134, 135, **156, 157, 158, 159, 160, 161, 162, 163, 164, 165, 166**, 360, 361, 362, 363, 371
Hersholt, Jean 31, 293
Hi Honey, I'm Home 134, 368
Higby, Mary Jean 23, 26-27, 30, 290
Hillerman, John 125
Hollywood NOW 78, 122
Hollywood Squares, The 117, 360
"Home Cooked Meal" 78-79
Honeymooners Christmas, The 126, 365

Hope, Bob 42, 115, 117, 120, 122, 124, 127, 309, 357, 359, 361, 364, 365, 367

I Love Lucy 59, 79, 91-92, 112, 119, 120, 121, 127, **143**, 345-346, 347
"It Ain't Gonna Rain No More" 13, 284

Jane 79-80
Jee, Fred 1, 97, 105
Joe E. Brown Show, The 33, 296
John Davidson Show, The 127, 367
Johnny Madero 55, 327
Jonathan Trimble, Esquire 51, 52, 321
Jones, Shirley 110, 117, 356, 359, 360
Jordan, Jim and Marian 35, 38, 39, 40, 225, 272, 298, 303, 339, 345, 358
Judy Canova Show, The 61, 316-317, 345
Junior Miss (radio) 60, 64, 65-67, 331-332

Kearns, Joseph 31, 109, 110, 275, 294, 295, 313, 314, 316, 319, 322, 329, 341, 343, 346
Kulzer, Dina-Marie 1, 6, 13-14, 55, 71, 85, 97, 109-110, 114, 121-122, 128

Lane, Charles 112, 277
Laurent, Lawrence 80, 90
Leger, Bertha S. see Gordon, Gloria
Lewis, Elliott 31, 42, 51, 111, 292, 294, 306, 309, 310, 311, 336, 341, 357

Lewis, Jerry 82, 277, 278
Life with Lucy 117, 129-131, **168,** 367-368
Life with Luigi 60, 79, 334, 335, 347
Linkletter, Jack 109, 355
Little Clay Cart, The 17
Little Immigrant, The 60, 334
Log Cabin Jamboree 32, 294-295
Lombardi Limited 21, 90, 351
Look Who's Laughing 37, 91, 174-175
Lorne, Marion 88, 89, **148,** 349
Los Angeles Times (LAT) 1, 17, 18, 19, 22, 23, 24, 26, 27, 29-30, 59-60, 79-80, 85-86, 87, 88, 90, 93, 95, 98, 104-105, 124, 125, 126, 127, 128, 129, 131
Love Chiselers 23
Lucille Ball Comedy Hour: Mr. and Mrs., The 115, 357
Lucille Ball Special: Lucy Calls the President, A 126, **167,** 365
Lucille Ball Special: Lucy Moves to NBC, A 127, 367
Lucky Strike Program Starring Jack Benny, The 64, 341
Lucy and Desi: A Home Movie 134, 369
Lucy Show, The 57, 110-112, 113-115, 116, 117, 118, 119, 120, 122-123, 125, 126, **149, 150, 151,** 357, 358, 359, 371
Luddy, Barbara 23, 26-27, 30, 287
Lux Radio Theatre 32-33, 41, 42, 43, 45-46, 54, 62, 64, 295-296, 297-298, 299-301, 302, 303, 304-306, 307, 308, 312-313, 314, 315-316, 317, 318, 319, 322-326, 327-328, 329-330, 337-338, 342-343

Magic of Broadcasting 116, 358
Marionette Mystery, The 64, 345
Martin, Dean 122, 123, 124, 279, 360-361, 362, 364, 365
Mary Pickford and Company 20, 24-26, 27, 135, **141,** 287-288
Mass Appeal 132-134
Match Game, The 115, 357-358
Mattson, Marie 125
Maxwell House Coffee Time 45, 53-54, 62
McMillan, Gloria 1, 69, 71-73, 77-78, 106, 322, 334, 346
McNear, Howard 31, 87, 292, 294, 308, 309, 314, 320, 330, 348
Meet Me in St. Louis 46, 61, 323, 333
Meredith, Burgess 87, 93, 97
Merv Griffin Show, The 120-121, 122, 124, 361, 363, 364
Mike Douglas Show, The 117, 126, 359, 366
Miss Pinkerton Inc. 42, 306
Mitchell, Shirley 52, 55-57, 58-59, 107, 125, 238, 299, 333, 341, 352, 354
Morgan, Frank 52, 53, 94, 293, 303, 321, 332, 333
Morgan, Harry 107, 108, 352, 354
Morton, Gary 111, 113, 116, 119, 120, 124, 125, 127, 129, 357, 359, 360, 363, 364, 367, 368
Mr. and Mrs. Blandings 64, 341
"Mr. Granby Breaks Down" 63-64

My Dear Children 60
My Favorite Husband 59, 61, 64, 79, 91, 335
My Little Margie 67, 344

Never Too Late 135
New Adventures of Sherlock Holmes, The 46-48, 54-55, 320, 328-329
New Lassie, The 134, 369
New Way of Life, A 1, 100-104, 127, 271
New York Times, The 1, 3, 29, 60, 110, 127
Newman, Marc 97, 135
North, Jay 109-110, **152, 153,** 356
Nye, Carroll 24

O'Connor, Donald 87, 88, 127, 274, 348, 349, 367
O'Connor, John J. 127
Our Miss Brooks 4, 11, 61, 64, 66, 67, 69-80, 81-82, 85, 86, 90, 91, 92, 109, 110, 112, 123, 129, **144, 145, 146,** 275, 334, 346-347, 363, 371

Password 116, 358-359
Peary, Hal 34, 241, 272, 303, 330, 331, 332
Pepsodent Show, The 42, 309
Pete and Gladys 107, 108, 352, 354
Phil Harris-Alice Faye Show, The 60, 64, 65, 336
Pickford, Mary 20, 24-26, 27, 135, **141,** 287-288, 290
Playhouse 90 87-88, 89-90, 349-350
Post, Guy Bates 18, 19
Presley, Elvis 82, 282

Quinn, Don 7, 34, 37, 38, 39, 40, 62, 212, 214, 226, 239, 272, 338, 339, 340

Rally 'Round the Flag 82, 276
Rathbone, Basil 46, 54, 55, 310, 320
Rayfiel, Eileen 97-98
Rayfiel, Howard 1, 97-98, 111-112
Real McCoys, The 91, 351, 363
Rich, Irene 34, 135, 288
Ritchard, Sir Cyril 124
Robinson, Edward G. 32, 72, 278, 292
Rockwell, Robert 78, 81, 82, **144,** 275, 334, 346
Ross, Frank 88-89, 349
Ross, Joe 124
Russell, Jeanne 1, 110, 356

Sally 88-89, **148,** 349
San Diego Union 93
Schaden, Chuck 1, 3, 11-12, 14, 21, 28, 37, 39-40, 41-42, 45-46, 53, 59, 78, 85, 91-92, 94-95, 107, 109, 112-114, 129, 130-131, 132-133, 135-136, 137, 138, 139, 239, 345
Seal of the Don, The 22-23, 287
Sergeant Deadhead 82, 281
.750 Smith 60
Shadow of Fu Manchu, The 33, 296-297
Shadow, The 59
Shore, Dinah 45, 125, 320, 364
Shostak, Stuart 131
Simons, Mel 1, 19-20, 34, 35, 38-39, 71, 226, 238

Skidding 18
Smith, Cecil 1, 39, 87, 88, 88-89, 90, 93, 94, 95-97, 98, 104-105, 106, 121
Smith, Cleo 94, 119, 360, 369
Speed Gibson of the International Secret Police 31, 291-292
Speedway 82, 282
Stafford, Hanley 22, 23, 27, 31, 32, 33, 42, 274, 285, 286, 288, 292, 293, 294, 295, 296, 301, 306, 309, 353
Stars in the Eye 79, 347
"Story of John Wanamaker, The" 32
Studio One 90, 350
Sugar 124
Suspense 237, 314-315, 358
Sweeney, Bob 59, 79, 85, 86, 87, **147,** 346, 347, 348

Tarzan of the Apes 22, 29, 286
Taylor, Elizabeth 120, 121-122
Television Series Regulars of the Fifties and Sixties in Interview 6
That Was the Year 28, 288-289
That's Not All Folks! 57-58
30-Foot Bride of Candy Rock, The 82, 277-278
This Is Your Life 90, 124, 351, 363
Thompson, Bill 38, 237-238, 272, 299, 343
Tinée, Mac 81
Tomorrow Show, The 125, 364
Toomey, Regis 64, 345
Treacher, Arthur 6, 122, 361, 363, 364

Vacation Playhouse 117, 358
Van Riper, Kay 19, 20, 22, 24, 27-28, 30, 285
Vance, Vivian 80, 111, 126, **164,** 345, 346, 347, 350, 357, 364, 365
Visit to a Small Planet, A 82, 278
Von Zell, Harry 28, 45, 289, 320, 321

Wake Island 42, 43, 309, 314
Wall Street Journal, The 99
Washington Post, The 27, 80, 99
Waterman, Willard 241, 333, 338, 340, 356
Webb, Jack 55, 327
Westinghouse Lucille Ball—Desi Arnaz Show, The 90, 350-351
Whistler, The 43, 311
Whiting, Barbara 60, 65, 331
Whiting, Margaret 61, 333, 342, 347
Wilcox, Harlow 174, 223, 299, 301, 303, 339
Wolters, Larry 79, 80, 86
Woman of Distinction, A 81, 273
Wonder Show, The 33, 296
Wormser, Judy (sister) 12-13, 138

Young, Loretta 43, 305, 315
Your Red Cross Roll Call 42, 308

Zylstra, Freida 98

Made in the USA
Columbia, SC
23 November 2017